The Pandemic of Inhumanity

a plea for a truly humanitarian society

a chronicle of my growing awareness
during the year 2020

Franz Ruppert

Translated from the German by Simon Lys

'How Healthy is Your Normal' drawing courtesy of Lydia Bauer
Cover design by Simon Lys
Author photograph by Dirk Wächter

Translated from the seventh revised and expanded German edition of 20th
October 2020 along with a new final chapter from 28th December 2020

First English Edition published January 2021

For the latest information on the subject of this book please visit
www.franz-ruppert.de

ISBN 978-3-9822115-2-7

How healthy IS YOUR NORMAL?

The microbe is nothing, the terrain is everything.
Louis Pasteur (1822 - 1895)

There are two things that can make the doctor lose his bread and butter - Health and death. So the doctor, in order to keep his livelihood going, must keep us in a state of limbo between the two.
Eugen Roth (1895 - 1976)

The plague, whilst on its way through the desert, met a caravan. Asked by the leader of the caravan what it wanted in Damascus, the plague answered: '1000 people'.
As chance would have it, they met again in a few weeks time.
'You lied,' the caravan leader told the plague. 'You took 5000!'
'No, no, no,' answered the plague. 'I honestly only took 1000. The rest were taken by fear.'
Abū Battūta Muhammad Ibn Abū (1304 - 1368)

It is easier to fool people than to convince them that they have been fooled.
Mark Twain (1835 - 1910)

War is peace, freedom is slavery and ignorance is strength.
From *1984* by George Orwell (1903 - 1950)

All we need is the right major crisis and the nations will accept the New World Order.

David Rockefeller (1915 - 2017)

The ideas of the ruling class are in every epoch the ruling ideas, i.e. the class which is the ruling material force of society, is at the same time its ruling intellectual force

Karl Marx (1818 - 1883)

Whose bread I eat their song I sing

Friedrich Maximilian von Klinger (1752 - 1831)

Hurt people they hurt people
Is it ever gonna stop?

From the song *Hurt People, Hurt People* by The Script (2019)

Words come easy
When they're true
From the song *Shame* by Robbie Williams & Gary Barlow (2010)

There are two mice. One of them asks, 'So, are you going to get vaccinated?'
'No,' says the other. 'I'm waiting to see how the human trials go first.'

This is not a joke.

Contents

Translator's Note

This book is a collection of over thirty articles that Franz Ruppert wrote and published on his website and elsewhere between February and December 2020. It is supplemented by diary entries, notes, thoughts and other material that Franz wrote during this time as he tried to get a handle on what was going on in the world in terms of the Corona Pandemic, using his unique Identity-oriented Psychotrauma Therapy perspective. He then collated all this into a downloadable PDF of the German text and made it available for a donation via his website.

It has been a great privilege to prepare the text for an English readership. On a personal level it has provided me with an anchor of sanity during these disorientating and traumatising times.

In his original text Franz provides many footnotes and references substantiating what he says. Where possible, unless he is quoting directly in the main body of the text, I have tried to find suitable English language equivalents pointing to the same information. All links were correct at the time of going to press, but even whilst preparing the book some of the links, particularly those on Youtube etc. had been taken down in line with Youtube's policy of stifling any dissent that goes against the official Corona narrative and is deemed as potentially 'dangerous'.

I'd like to thank Andrew Richard Rigby for feedback on the early sections and Lucy Jameson for studiously proof-reading through the whole text over Christmas & New Year to help get it ready for publication.

Simon Lys
Sussex, January 2021

Forward to the English Edition

I am very happy that this book is now available in English. For me, the Corona pandemic is a war against the entire world population. So people of all walks of life across the globe need to wake up and understand what is going on.

I have found an excellent translator in Simon Lys, who has translated the German text with great care and attention. He has also checked the many links and looked for suitable English equivalents where possible. He also found the way to realise this book in print format and as an e-book edition.

Many thanks for this, Simon!

Franz Ruppert
Munich, January 2021

Forward

People are getting coughs, colds, fevers, sore throats and shortness of breath. Some of them are suffering very little from these symptoms, but for others it is more severe and they are forced to go to bed or take a break from their daily routine. In most cases, they are generally well again in a few days or sometimes it takes a week or so. But it is also possible that these symptoms get worse and, in combination with additional stresses in life, unresolved conflicts or other physical problems, the symptoms can become so severe that the situation becomes life-threatening. Incorrect treatments, such as trying to suppress and lower the fever or prescribing the wrong medication can also prevent the healing process and possibly even lead to death.

There is, as far as I can see, no scientific proof that Coronavirus disease 19 (Covid 19), which is associated with the symptoms I've just mentioned, actually exists. I have certainly yet to see satisfactory evidence that there is a causative relationship between the 'SARS-CoV-2' virus and the symptoms of disease listed above. No one has yet been able to adequately clarify the differential in diagnosis between Covid-19 and flu/influenza either. These two categories of disease are suspiciously similar and have not been defined with sufficient precision with regard to the variety of physical symptoms.[1]

So what has happened instead to prove the existence of this apparently virulent disease of 'Covid 19' is detection by a PCR[2] test. But this kind of test is not fit for purpose because it can only detect the presence of a specific RNA sequence of a suspected virus called 'SARS-CoV-2'[3]. It does not matter the level of the virus or whether the virus has actually infected the host or whether it has been dealt with by the host organism or is actually still infectious or if the

---

[1] https://www.bundesgesundheitsministerium.de/themen/praevention/gesundheitsgefahren/influenza.html (retrieved 09/11/20) - The NHS England list of flu symptoms are here: https://www.nhs.uk/conditions/flu/ (retrieved 20/11/20)

[2] Polymerase-Chain-Reaction

[3] Severe Acute Respiratory Syndrome Corona-Virus 2 – already in the name of the virus itself there is no clear distinction made between the virus and the possible consequences that may result from it.
To clarify the name ascribed to the virus (by the WHO) is SARS-CoV-2 and the disease it is claimed to cause is labelled as Covid 19.

presence of the virus is causing any symptoms. So how can any causative relationship between particles of the RNA viral strand and the actual disease or potential infection be proved in this way? However, in the current situation we find ourselves in, a positive test result immediately leads to the conclusion that this person is infected and therefore potentially infectious for others without taking into account any symptoms of disease. If you were considered healthy before, you may now be 'asymptomatically ill'.

Based on the PCR test results in a particular population group, projections are then made as to how quickly this alleged Covid-19 could potentially spread throughout the population and potentially lead to many sick people ending up in hospital intensive care units and potentially dying in their millions. It is all 'potentials' based on something that is faulty in the first place. In order to avoid becoming potentially infected, everyone has to keep their distance (1-2 metres), hardly touch each other, wear masks and hope to be protected and saved from Covid-19 through a miracle vaccination. The idea of a potential disease, although basically only a mental construct of our human psyche, therefore has enormous practical consequences to the extent that whole societies simply close their doors and we all go into lock-down! How is it possible that all this has so suddenly happened in 2020, especially in a world where science claims to be so highly advanced?

I didn't actually want to write and publish another full-length book again so soon after my last one. The theory of Identity-Oriented Psychotrauma Therapy (IoPT) has been developing considerably over the course of my last three books *My Body, My Trauma, My I'*, *'Who am I in a Traumatised and Traumatising Society'* and *'Love, Lust & Trauma'*. The practice of IoPT is currently blossoming and thriving as it continues to find new people all over the world who are interested in exploring it.

So, before 'Corona' I had decided to create a new section on my website, at www.franz-ruppert.de, called 'Comments on Current Affairs'. In this section, I was gradually collating my contributions on topics such as Brexit and the war in Syria, alongside discussions on films such as the controversial 2019 German film 'System Crasher'. I took a look at subjects like terrorist attacks and the motivation behind them, developments in medicine around birth and much more. In my opinion, IoPT has something fundamental and enlightening to contribute to all these discussions.

It was the same for me, as it was, I'm sure, for many of us, that viruses and bacteria were just a side-issue in the grand scheme of life - things of no importance that only had to be dealt with when there happened to be a serious infection. Yes, there was Ebola in Africa, dengue fever in South America, malaria in the tropics - but these were just names for dangers that felt many miles away from our safe European centre. Even when I saw people in Munich, the city where I live, sometimes wearing masks when they were out shopping, they were mostly Asian and I had in the back of my mind the Hong Kong flu epidemic of 1968/69.

Actually, back at the beginning of the year 2020, the global focus was on 'climate change' – that was *the* number one issue. The younger generation had taken to the streets, out of a fear for what was to come, with the slogan 'Fridays for Future!' And with Greta Thunberg, this movement had found a figurehead and icon.

And then, as if out of nowhere, a virus appeared called SARS-CoV-2 or Severe Acute Respiratory Syndrome Coronavirus 2. Very few of us had any way of mentally processing this before suddenly this allegedly 'novel' virus was affecting our lives in such an all-encompassing way that none of us could possibly have imagined: our babies and toddlers were no longer allowed to be taken to the crèche or kindergarten, pupils were forbidden from entering their school buildings, students were locked out of campuses. Chefs and landlords had to close their restaurants and pubs, and everyone else who was not defined as 'key workers' had to shut up shop. Only the supermarkets and grocery stores remained open - for our essential daily needs. Freedom of travel was comprehensively restricted. Demonstrations were virtually forbidden overnight because of travel restrictions.

And even those small and medium-sized companies, which were actually still allowed to work, sent their workers and employees home on reduced hours because all orders fell away within days. Hotels had to shut their doors and in the end even the automobile industry, which in Germany is the heart of the economy, closed many of its plants. Freelancers were left hanging in the air and were now suddenly unemployed because they had no contracts.

Within a few weeks, all social life had been reduced to almost zero. The extensive prevention of social contacts, on the grounds of protection against infection, suddenly prevented any form of human coexistence at every level.

This 'shutdown' or 'lockdown' of society came from individual political leaderships. Starting in China, it spread in rapid succession through the various countries of the world. Some countries, such as Sweden, and initially England, which did not follow this global trend, were severely criticised. Suddenly, countries were governed by decrees drawing from laws that were hardly known about until that point, for example in Germany it fell under the Infection Protection Act. National and regional bans were imposed to varying degrees. Anyone who did not comply with the urgent appeals to 'stay at home' and to keep at least 1.5 metres (2 metres in the UK) distance from each other was now committing an offence and was subject to hefty fines; some 'law breakers' even ended up in prison.

What was it that had suddenly got into all these rulers who otherwise always gave priority to the economy and championed economic growth over everything else such as ecology, social affairs, education and health? Had 'health' and the imperative that 'no one should have to die prematurely' really become the number one priority of political thinking and of all social life overnight?

It was the case too, that from the middle of March, I found my professional practice both as a university lecturer and as a psychotherapist completely thrown into question. I wasn't going to be able to start my lectures and seminars for the 2020 summer semester as usual on the university campus. And cancelling this summer term, in particular, seemed especially galling, when the new university building had just been completed and which the university management has been committedly working towards for so many years! My therapeutic practice, which is essentially based on group seminars and further training in larger groups, was now considered a high-risk case. More than two people in one room was suddenly considered a *dangerous infection scenario*. And anyone who exposed themselves to such a scenario was branded a threat to the common good.

I, like everyone else around me, was soon in the midst of a society-wide situation of coercive measures, which bordered on dictatorship and which annulled democratic rights as laid down in the Basic Law of the land, such as prohibiting by decree the right to resist. I, in Germany, was still able to perceive a situation that was comparatively moderate in contrast to countries such as Italy, Spain, Hungary, Serbia or even China, where the Corona pandemic was abused in the twinkling of an eye for dictatorial arbitrary measures and further presidential self-empowerment.

In India, for example, 'Corona' was immediately seized upon by the nationalist Hindu government to take even more restrictive action against the Muslim population in the country. It was claimed that through their very meetings the Muslims were spreading the virus throughout the country. The novelist Arundhati Roy spoke of her fears that "the situation is approaching something genocidal." She accused Hindu nationalist organisations of having already in the past "likened the Muslims of India to the Jews of Germany. And if you look at the way in which they are using COVID, it was very much like typhus was used against the Jews to ghettoize them, to stigmatize them."[4]

Therefore, out of my own personal interest, I felt compelled to take a closer look at the phenomenon of 'Corona' or Covid-19 (Corona virus disease 2019). When I don't understand something, the way I help myself is to write about it. The Corona pandemic is such a situation, in which I can only keep an inner clarity if I inform myself from as many different sources as I can find and write down what I experience and what goes through my mind from day to day.

So this book is a chronicle of the events since February 14th 2020, which reflect my personal learning and process of realisation and growing awareness. I hope that 'Corona' will soon be history and that mankind will learn its lessons from it. But unfortunately it does not look like that at the moment. The reasons why this pandemic continues, even if the immediate threat is no longer present, will become increasingly clear by the end of this book.

I have used my theoretical and practical knowledge of Identity-oriented Psychotrauma Therapy (IoPT) in my effort to understand the Corona pandemic. Over this period since February, the writings that make up this book became a point of reference for people 'out there' reflecting their own insecurities, their indignation and their search for truth and clarity. When I post on my homepage, articles generally get an average of 700 clicks on each post. But some of these articles, which were then published as a 'daily dose' on KenFM or on the website rubikon.news (two leading German alternative-media organisations) were suddenly getting up to 110,000 hits.

At the beginning, I also offered my articles on the Corona pandemic to major German newspapers like the Süddeutsche

---

[4] https://www.dw.com/en/arundhati-roy-claims-coronavirus-exposes-indias-crisis-of-hatred-against-muslims/a-53167812 (retrieved 24/08/20)

Zeitung, the Zeit, the Spiegel and the Focus, but I received no response from them. Gradually, I came to realise why. The mainstream media have become the propagandists for this pandemic, who not only spread fear and terror about this alleged killer virus with their reports, but also fight off any resistance to the drastic measures that are being imposed with malice and aggressive polemics. Therefore I am grateful that KenFM and Rubikon have become internet-based media platforms on which I could bring my findings and opinions to the public.

If all these measures were really about a common interest like health, safety, protection and healing, then I would be the first person to support them. However, when there is a well-founded suspicion that particular interests are trying to exploit the common interest for their own purposes, then I want to use my emotional, intellectual and communicative abilities to press for clarification and encourage resistance. This book has therefore also become an emotional book in many places, because I have gone through many emotional ups and downs over the last year.

In a war (many leaders, such as Emmanuel Macron and Boris Johnson, have frequently referred to this as a war against a virus), truth is the first casualty. This is an old dictum from 1914 attributed to the US Senator Hiram Johnson[5]. For me it becomes very clear that this has major implications to our health: where the truth isn't allowed, people become physically and mentally ill. Therefore, for me, looking into the Corona crisis was also a way to preserve my own physical and mental health. And if I can also help others with these writings, then it was certainly worth the effort.

There were many ups and downs for me during this period. Today though it is clear to me: a world community, that is traumatised in so many myriad ways already, must be so damaged that dealing with a single virus is enough to bring it to the brink of collapse. Only traumatised people are collectively capable of transforming a natural threat such as a periodically occurring infection into a process of mutual self-destruction and of wearing each other down in perpetrator-victim dynamics. Through the Corona pandemic, already traumatised societies are now donning a crown of thorns, on top of all the festering wounds they already carry within them.

---

[5] https://www.theguardian.com/notesandqueries/query/0,5753,-21510,00.html (retrieved 24/08/20)

Here, we can see, my model of trauma rings true. Even if 100% of all people were traumatised, 100% would still have healthy parts within them. This has been demonstrated in this Corona delusion ('Coronoia'). More and more people, from all aspects of society have spoken out and, little by little, have uncovered the gigantic hoax, which is being deliberately set in motion worldwide through scaremongering and shameless exploitation of our innate willingness to show solidarity with the sick and the weak.

In the long term, we can but hope that we will all, the world over, learn something profound about our existence and our ways of social interaction from all this. That we will confront with compassion the heartlessness and strictly bureaucratic manner with which the Corona virus rules are being implemented - for example, when children's playgrounds turn into restricted zones overnight, when children are forced to wear masks in schools or old people are cut off from their relatives in their nursing homes. That we understand with our hearts that in this way health is not technically possible and is not a commodity that is only about the profits of a health cartel. To stay healthy, we human beings want physical contact, we need good relationships, we need to be physically close to each other in our interpersonal relationships. It is not viruses or bacteria in themselves that make us ill, but fear, isolation, lies and deception and poor interpersonal relationships!

This book has many footnotes with internet references. It was immensely helpful for me during the writing process to have all these sources immediately at hand.

Thanks

My sincere thanks go to all those who have shared their research with me their over the past six months. People who, with their persistent hard work and effort, are helping to create an alternative press to challenge the ruling Corona narrative. Alongside them, I'd like to thank the many individuals, who through their own initiative have set up free internet sites where I could inform myself about the corona pandemic beyond what the mainstream media were reporting, which to my eyes was only fear coupled with testing and vaccination propaganda.

I would like to thank all those who have given me great encouragement during this time of great uncertainty, though often highly unsettled and searching for orientation themselves. My thanks also go to all those who have engaged in hard but fair discussions with me over the past days, weeks and months. With what I have found out and am writing down here, it is not my intention to be right. There are many other points of view that are also justified. As far as I'm concerned, I don't want to fuel the flame in this already traumatised world with a new perpetrator-victim argument and deepen already existing social divisions. In this time of confusion, first of all I want to come back to myself and invite others to hear my thoughts and feelings. I cannot and do not want to save anyone and certainly not 'the world'. Nobody needs to save me either. It is my own autonomous responsibility to do that for myself.

I would like to thank Ms. Tanja Steinlechner for her thorough editing of the original German print edition and Lydia Bauer for the drawing 'How Healthy Is Your Normal?'

Munich, January 2021

For My Safety And The Safety Of All Of Us.

I wrote this book as a private individual – it is not coming from my professional position as a professor of psychology at the Foundation of Applied Sciences (Katholische Stiftungshochschule) in Munich.

At this point in time, as we can see, people are very easily manipulated and seduced into both self-damaging and socially damaging behaviour by all those money-greedy profiteers, pseudo-scientists, false prophets, fame-hungry doctors, pseudo-experts and fake journalists who shout louder than anybody else. Therefore, I say to all those who are still convinced that there is an unpredictable killer virus out there and believe in the measures that are being put in place, to continue to strictly observe the safety rules that are specific to your own country or local area. It is up to everyone to decide for him or herself.

How It All Began
14th February 2020 until …

When China Was Still A Long Way Away

The Coronavirus pandemic crept up on me, like it did for many people. First there were the horrifying pictures coming out of Wuhan: residential areas with their entry and exit roads being cordoned off, people sheathed in all-over plastic body suits pressing thermometers against other people's foreheads. Images of people fainting in the open street and simply left lying there, overcrowded hospitals and a Chinese government quickly building a hospital with an intensive care unit seemingly out of thin air.

Only Healing Helps

In order to get a little more clarity about how seriously to actually take this thing called 'Corona', I suggested, on February 14th 2020, at the end of a five-day international seminar at my Munich practice, that I took a closer look at the issue by using an IoPT self-encounter process[6]. I wrote the following words up on the board as my Intention: 'I, Coronavirus, Causes, Consequences, Healing.'

What happened was interesting. The person resonating with the word 'Consequences' rushed through the large practice room, pursued by 'Coronavirus'. She had great difficulty breathing and was struggling to get air. I didn't know at that point that one of the most feared consequences of a Coronavirus infection was respiratory problems. The 'I' stood up on a chair and tried in vain to keep track of what was going on and keep order. 'Healing' kept getting in the way of 'Coronavirus' in order to protect 'Consequences'. 'Coronavirus' was very voracious and would grab at anything that came his way.

We then brought in 'China' as the state power. Bringing in this element made a big impression on the people resonating with the other elements of the Intention, but 'Coronavirus' was not impressed. It entrenched itself more and more in playing out this perpetrator-victim dynamic with 'Consequences'. While this was

---

[6] For people new to Identity-oriented Psychotrauma Therapy, its methodology and the thinking behind it, I would recommended reading the chapter in this book on 'The Theory of Identity-oriented Psychotrauma Theory (IoPT)' to get some background (p.64) (SL)

going on, only 'Healing' was in anyway able to block 'Coronavirus' in what it was doing. A look at 'Causes' only revealed that viruses have always existed and will continue to exist. They cannot be fought and the resonator for 'Causes' said that humans are probably the greatest enemies of life on earth, not viruses.

When I now look back on this IoPT work in retrospect, the solution was already quite plain to see. Only healing, and for me that means our inner healing, and therefore our immune system, can stop the virus. Then those who have fallen ill can recover from the consequences and get the fresh air they need to breathe again. For this purpose we opened the windows in the practice room and the atmosphere in the room calmed and became clearer.

This piece of Intention work then became the basis for my first article, which I published on my 'Comments on Current Affairs' section of my website. It was clear to me that power and demonstrations of power would not be able to stop a virus.

Just after this I was able to offer a Russian-language training in my Munich practice, but a participant from Kazakhstan didn't travel to join us, because otherwise she would not have been able to travel back from Germany without risking a 14-day quarantine period. Since many virus tests had already been carried out in Germany by then, it became clear that there were many cases of infection and so Germany was quickly considered an area of risk. Where testing had not been done, it follows 'logically' that that area was not a risk area.

Fighting Viruses With Force
First Article - 15th February 2020

What Are Viruses?

A virus is an RNA gene sequence that requires a host body for its self-preservation and reproduction. Viruses take what they can get. This means that any organism that cannot sufficiently protect itself from the virus is gradually devoured by it and may even die as a result of it. Sometimes it is possible to establish a kind of symbiosis between the virus and the host body, so that the virus only has temporary access to the host body, for example when the host body is weakened in its immune defence. The self-protection programs of the host body and the mutations of the virus are in a constant race to see who can stay ahead[7].

This coronavirus appears to be a very 'voracious' virus that not only colonises animal bodies, as was previously the case, but now also human bodies. It can cause them to die relatively quickly by soon robbing them of vital heart and respiratory functions.

Viruses do not care about nationalities and state borders. They migrate with their human host bodies. In a globally networked world, they are quickly found everywhere. Therefore, universal protective measures are required which leave the usual intergovernmental competition as far as possible out of the equation. The coronavirus currently appears to require especially severe protective measures to prevent it from spreading unchecked.

---

[7] This section shows my initial ignorance of what viruses really are. In a typical anthropocentric view, I regarded viruses only as enemies of humans. Yet they are necessary for the evolution of life and they come about as a by-product of the reproduction of already existing cells. They form the blueprints for the attempt to create new cells, which sometimes succeeds and often does not. (FR)

Is That A Helpful Response?

What is happening in China at the moment has very little to do with just the containment of a virus. People are being taken to overcrowded hospitals or forced into mass accommodation, where the risk of mutual infection is increased further and where poor hygiene conditions create the danger of additional infectious diseases. Instead of compassionately offering these infected and already weakened people peace and clean air for their recovery, they are put under pressure, their fears are escalated, so that their immune systems are weakened further. Forced temperature readings on the forehead, with devices that resemble pistols, do not exactly help to reduce stress either. As a result, even those who are not yet infected are increasingly panicking and undermining their own self-healing powers. And instead of relying on their own powers of self-healing, they are looking to the state power to fix it all. Their fears are then coupled with their anger when they feel abandoned, which, as is well known, further escalates the stress reactions in the body.

The Chinese state power, which under normal circumstances claims complete jurisdiction over its population anyway, now thinks that it has to assert its role as leader with demonstrations of power and political show fights. That alone puts tens and hundreds of thousands of people in the country under existential stress and makes them ill. Such weakened people are easy prey for viruses of all kinds.

Corona – A Test Of Strength

The fight against viruses cannot be won by state, police or military force. The more psychological stress something causes us, the weaker our powers of self-healing are. What we need instead in such a situation is a loving attitude towards ourselves and empathic compassion for our fellow human beings who are ill. Whether or not those powerseekers, whose special ability lies precisely in shutting off their feelings as completely as possible, succeed in this is unfortunately more than questionable. For their political survival they often step over corpses without a moment's hesitation. Basically, however, instead of becoming even 'stronger', they too need compassion for themselves and their psychological wounds.

Addendum April 3rd 2020: The Virus Is Now A Foreigner

Since I originally wrote this article, China has called off the pandemic in its country and stopped counting (and therefore generating) cases of infection. Wuhan nevertheless remains a special zone and a ghost town. Anyone who now enters China from Germany, for example, must undergo a detailed interview and then be in quarantine for 14 days. SARS-CoV-2 is now, according to that official interpretation, essentially a virus that is coming in from abroad and against which China must defend itself with all its might.

'Corona!'

As February turned into March, suddenly almost everyone in Germany was now talking about 'Corona' and how dangerous this 'new' virus was. A triumvirate consisting of the Health Minister Jens Spahn, the head of the Robert Koch Institute (RKI) Mr Wieler and a 'chief virologist' from the Berlin Charité Professor Christian Drosten were announcing infection figures and predicting horror scenarios of people suffering from the virus who could no longer be helped in hospitals because there would be too few intensive care beds with respirators.

The RKI and Mr Drosten had already appeased the situation back in 2015 when the WHO wanted to call a pandemic because of these coronaviruses. At that time they were known as MERS: Middle East Respiratory Syndrome. With the irresistible argument that this coronavirus could only be transmitted from camels to humans, the all-clear was given for the rest of the world, where there are not as many camels as in the Middle East. In an interview with Christian Drosten back in May 2013, RTL-aktuell wrote:

> 'In the face of more than 20 fatalities, the World Health Organization (WHO) has issued an urgent warning about the new Corona virus. In Germany, too, a man has died from the pathogen, which occurs mainly in the Middle East. According to the head of the Institute of Virology in Bonn, Christian Drosten, "Germany is nevertheless only indirectly affected by the epidemic. ... For people in Germany Corona is not really important, there is no increased risk," says Drosten. To date, more than 40 infections and 24 deaths have been registered worldwide. According to the Robert Koch Institute (RKI), however, all previous cases were "through direct contact or through another patient associated with the Arabian Peninsula".[8]

So why should this Sars-CoV-2 of 2020 be so much more dangerous, not only for Germany, but for the whole world? Is it because this strain is said to have jumped from bats to humans and bats exist the world over?

---

[8] https://www.rtl.de/cms/toedliches-corona-virus-gefahr-fuer-menschen-in-deutschland-extrem-gering-1520554.html (retrieved 12/04/20) - in German.

The Corona Pandemic Delusion: Who Am I In A Traumatised Society?

Second Article - 19th March 2020, Published As A 'Daily Dose' At KenFM On 18th March 2020

What Is Going On Here?

It is unbelievable to me that in a time when we all have the Internet, when in principle everyone can access a wealth of information on any particular subject, a handful of virologists with their one-sided conventional medical viewpoint still dominate the thinking of most people and also now the actions of our politicians. They say that a new kind of virus has emerged that spreads rapidly through interpersonal contact and that it will, as statistics predict, wipe out a swathe of the population in the not too distant future. However, at the moment only one of these many viruses has been given a name that laypeople can even pronounce and that's 'Corona'. Coronaviruses, which must constantly mutate in order to gain access to human cells, have long been known to virologists. There is no evidence, and certainly no proof, that the newly mutated virus is more dangerous to human health than other influenza or rhinoviruses. Even Hendrik Streeck, an acknowledged coronavirus specialist[9] from Germany, sees no evidence that this current virus type (SARS-Covid-19) is particularly dangerous. So what is going on here? Why are politicians all over the world, and not just in Germany, sending their whole society to the wall?

---

[9]https://m.faz.net/aktuell/gesellschaft/gesundheit/coronavirus/virologe-hendrik-streeck-ueber-corona-neue-symptome-entdeckt-16681450.html#click=https://t.co/yJo6MH2Tgm (retrieved 27/08/20) - Here's an English article detailing Hendrik Streeck's findings:
https://unherd.com/thepost/german-virologist-finds-covid-fatality-rate-of-0-24-0-36/ (retrieved 27/08/20)

The Virus As A Serial Killer

If it were really true that there was a serial killer who could transform every other person they met into a serial killer simply by shaking their hand or breathing in their face then that would truly be an emergency and the killer would have to be stopped as quickly as possible. But in reality what we are currently dealing with are micro-organisms, so called viruses, that are not capable of surviving on their own, but are reliant on a macro-organism in which to find somewhere to shelter. It is not the purpose of viruses to kill these large creatures, but to keep themselves alive in them. As a rule, these large creatures do not like this, which is why they try with their immune police to throw these uninvited guests back out of their house. Sometimes the viruses manage to hide in some corner of the house and come out of hiding when the immune police are overloaded with other tasks. Something like this happens with the herpes viruses, which have carved out a little corner for their existence in many people.

Since it is very costly to make the presence of such miniature creatures visible, no tests are normally developed for them, especially since these viruses constantly mutate in order to camouflage themselves from the immune police.

A Single Test Has Made The Pandemic Seem Real

In the current virus crisis, a non-validated test produced at the Berlin Charité (one of Europe's largest university hospitals and one of Germany's most research-intensive medical institutions) has now transformed a particular strain of virus into a psychologically apparent tangible reality. By giving this special virus a simple and melodious name – 'Corona' - it has been given a reality status that many people feel they can now understand. But 'Corona' is nothing more than an idea in the human psyche and depends on how someone continues to deal with it in his imagination and in his thinking. You can say, OK this is one of many viruses that exist and which, as usual, the immune system will learn to deal with. Or you can get into the horror scenario that everyone who carries the virus within them is now a serial killer and it is only a matter of time before they kill other people.

The Logic Of Trauma

As we look for explanations, as well as employing conventional psychology, it is also worth looking at matters from a perspective of psychotraumatology: there were experiences from my own life story, especially those from my early childhood, which were traumatic for me. These experiences were associated with a fear of death and a loss of control, and they are locked away as enduring memories unconsciously somewhere in my body. These experiences can now be connected with something apparently tangible in my external reality. I can attach my fears to the outside world instead of in my psyche. I now have the hope that I can finally make my mortal fears and inner distress disappear or at least bring them under control by fighting a tangible enemy in my environment. This kind of psychodynamic does not only happen with the 'Corona' virus. Instead of 'Corona' you could substitute 'terrorists', 'Jews', 'Islamists', 'foreigners', 'Russians', 'the left', 'the right', 'eco-alternative lifestyle crusties' and so on as a template for your imagination, in order in the here and now to go into an active fight against the enemy.

Where's The Evidence?

Despite all the warning being proclaimed loudly by a handful of opinion-shaping virologists, there is currently no evidence that this virus is a serial killer that would cause any more suffering than any other known corona and influenza viruses. Even in Italy, which is frequently cited as an example of how murderous this virus is, the current case numbers do not provide any proof. Approximately 90% of the virus carriers tested have absolutely no symptoms, a few have the usual fever, cough and headache symptoms and a small number die of pneumonia, but this is because their bodies are already weak from chronic diseases and bacterial infections and they cannot handle the additional strain. This is normal in every so-called flu epidemic and is also visible now in those who die. These are predominantly very elderly people who are severely compromised by other diseases. Even in China, the rate of deaths attributed to the new Corona virus as a result of the tests has not risen dramatically. In any case, a hospital is a very dangerous place when it comes to pneumonia. There, 20-30% of patients die from hospital germs that are resistant to antibiotics. And if a test proves that the corona virus is present in a dead person that does not mean that 'corona' was automatically the cause of death. Determining the actual cause of death would require autopsies in each individual case.

Question After Question

The idea that the rate of infections must be delayed because otherwise the health care system would be overwhelmed by the sheer numbers of sick people raises the question why are hospitals not already prepared for it, when, as expected, there has been a wave of flu for years with up to 25,000 seriously ill people dying? And should mortality rates now be lowered or should the number of deaths simply be stretched over two years? What about those who are not infected with the 'new form' SARS2-Covid-19 at this time and therefore don't develop an immunity to it, will they then be infected with another new strain of the virus next year? Will the hospitals then have to deal with two different viruses at the same time?

Or is it the case that the healthcare system is currently overburdened because so many people are now rushing into hospitals and GP surgeries because of corona anxiety, even if they are suffering relatively mild symptoms?

In Germany, approximately 954,874 people died in 2018. That is 2,616 people per day. If one assumes that about 50 people have died of 'Corona' in the last 10 days, although no one can conclusively prove this, then this is 0.0019% of the current death rate per day in Germany. This statistic could easily be calculated for other countries as well.[10]

Is it the point of the comprehensive 'corona' infection prevention measures that the overall mortality rate is now reduced in every country?

The WHO's Redefinition Of Pandemic

The virologists, who are now majorly influencing political events, are using a new definition of 'pandemic' by the World Health Organization (WHO) for their form of panic-mongering. Whereas beforehand a pandemic was only declared when a virus caused significant disease rates worldwide, since 2017 the mere spread of viruses has been a reason to initiate a phased plan of monitoring and virus control. However, since all forms of viruses spread rapidly throughout the world because of globalisation, the state of a pandemic is basically then always a given. And every year there are new viruses that spread rapidly through the world population. So it is either down to having a special interest in it or it is just arbitrary whether any one particular virus is declared a pandemic.

At the same time, there would be, in global terms, quite different and actually relevant pandemic issues on

---

[10] In the UK in 2018 - 541,589 people died. That would be 1484 a day. As of today (21/03/20) there have been 177 deaths in the UK, attributed to 'Corona', spread over 15 days since the first death in the UK. That would mean 0.0079 of the daily UK deaths have had the corona virus.

which it would be worth mobilising and concentrating social forces, for example on the issue of sexual trauma.

The division of the globe into risk and non-risk areas is ridiculous anyway. Viruses do not care about nationalities or state borders. They travel with people wherever they go. We have now become a global human family. A high-risk area is always created in a country when enough virus tests for corona are carried out. Where no tests are done, there are no 'corona' cases and therefore no increased risk – regardless of what the actual infection rates are. However, since politicians are responsible for their own national territory, they do not miss the opportunity to close the border in order to demonstrate their special responsibility and leadership for their respective countries by 'head down, charge forward, whatever it takes' action.

My Personal Experience

A year ago I had a bad flu infection. For four weeks I had this dry chesty cough, fever, aching limbs and I was itchy all over. When I was on the point of putting zinc ointment on my skin, I suddenly had a moment of realisation: What am I actually doing? I am battling with the symptoms but I'm not looking at the cause - my lack of immune defence. The next day I went to my practice to do my own IoPT self-encounter process. In my psyche, I discovered a child, about one year old, who was desperate and close to dying of thirst, due to neglect and loneliness. As I sat opposite the person resonating with this part of myself, a great pain and grief slowly came over me. I took this child part in my arms and cried bitterly. Two days later my flu symptoms had disappeared. Since then I have not had any more serious throat or chest infections.

It is clear to me now that part of the reason my immune system had not been very robust during my life was because my mother only breastfed me for a few weeks. I then almost died from the substitute food she subsequently gave me.

I now know from accompanying thousands of self-encounters for other people in my therapeutic work that physical symptoms of illness are very often the result of early trauma and the traumatising mother-child and father-child relationships. This leads to the child psychologically identifying with people who are perpetrators. As a result, he can no longer distinguish between I and you, mine and yours, friend and foe. He is unable to sufficiently protect himself from danger and harm. Early psychotrauma is associated with unbearable feelings of loneliness, being abandoned and panicky fears. It is also linked to feelings of shame and guilt and anger, which must be suppressed and repressed.

The confrontation with the corona virus or the ideas about it in people's minds can now evoke these old feelings of trauma. While looking into it I discovered that the subject of quarantine is connected for me with the experience of my father once grounding me for two weeks during the school holidays because I had accidentally injured a neighbour's boy whilst we were playing. I found this extremely shameful and humiliating. I had to suppress my feelings of rage because I could not cope with my father's violence at that time.

In a one-to-one therapy session with a woman on the 17th March this year, I saw that she was in a complete panic in regards to the current situation. Prior to the session she was even wishing to be quarantined, because at that moment people were far too much for her. During her piece of work, it was revealed that already when she was in her mother's womb (her mother had become pregnant with her unintentionally at the age of 17) she was completely stressed by her mother's voice and the other voices that were probably arguing about why her mother had not been more careful not to get pregnant. She left my practice after the therapy session with much more joy and hope.

A Serious Misalliance

It's my opinion that politics and orthodox medicine are currently entering into a momentous misalliance: in the case of the coronavirus they see only the chain of infection, which must be interrupted or reduced by any means necessary. They are afraid that they have not wielded their political and opinion-forming power sufficiently well and so will be held responsible for deaths. Here, too, psychotraumatology comes into play alongside ordinary psychology. Death often has a traumatic component. When people die, they experience themselves as impotent and helpless. But this is also true for their relatives and friends. The pain and mortal fears of the dying remain after a person has died, especially with their blood relatives or friends. As well as this, those who are still living feel shame and guilt, and, on top of the grief, they may also feel anger towards the possible causes of death. Unbearable feelings can particularly arise when we experience another person dying in agony, for example by suffocation, burning or drowning. It is then these concrete images that burn themselves into people's minds, as is happening in the current Corona reporting in the official media. We are told how people are dying in agony, lonely and abandoned in crowded hospitals.

Death As A Trauma And A Survival Strategy

Traumatic feelings are feelings that are unbearable and which a person's psyche cannot process. When these occur, there are different forms of trauma survival strategies:

- We ignore death as if it did not exist (e.g. as is usually the case with the annual flu epidemic)
- We look away (e.g. when refugees drown in the Mediterranean)

- We are in denial (e.g. the cancer victims as a result of nuclear weapons used in the wars in Iraq and Yugoslavia),
- We repress all of it from our consciousness (e.g. women murdered by their partners),
- We cloud our own consciousness (e.g. by smoking and drinking beer)
- We distract ourselves through work and leisure activities
- We intellectualise and debate (e.g. denying that global warming is dangerous because there are so many other factors that determine the world climate),
- We don't want to worry at all ('We all die some day')
- We indulge in illusions of eternal life (e.g. ideas of paradise or rebirth)
- We control ourselves and others.

The Control-Mania Strategy

Controlling everything to the max is currently the main strategy of politics and orthodox medicine when it comes to the corona virus, even though it is particularly difficult to control viruses, especially when it hasn't been possible to locate and narrow down their point of origin right at the beginning. To help achieve this control, a mono-causal way of thinking is employed – namely virus equals deadly danger – this simplicity of thinking would never be tolerated in other fields of debate.

In reality, the only means of keeping viruses at bay is a healthy immune system and having a great variation between the different bodies that the viruses choose as hosts. Incidentally, this seems to be one of the main reasons for sexual reproduction, so that viruses and other micro-organisms with the ability to adapt do not have it easy when they try to infect a whole population of larger organisms who are all similar.

If we apply this to our consciousness, we can also say that a monoculture of thought, a synchronisation of opinions and the resulting stubborn behaviour is highly risky for a population. Everyone is then in danger of making the same mistakes and all rushing into the abyss together. Germans in particular should know this from their painful history. A diversity of thought, a co-consciousness to which everyone contributes with his or her own insights and life experiences, protects a population far better against all possible dangers.

According to the opinion of the officially spread monocausal control delusion, anyone who now coughs or has a fever is already a suspected case. Indeed, anyone who has been with someone who coughs or has a fever is also already a risk factor. I have noticed myself suppressing a sneeze or trying not to cough in public over the last few days in order not to arouse suspicion of being a corona virus carrier.

Of course there are sensible precautionary measures to protect yourself from being overloaded by viruses or other germs: no close contact with someone who is obviously ill, hygiene behaviour appropriate to the circumstances, clean drinking water, healthy food etc. Experience has shown that epidemics only occur in situations of war and famine, when people have to live together in a very confined space without clean water and healthy food. For example as is currently the case in the refugee camps worldwide.

What is now being implemented as a control strategy in many countries goes, in my opinion, far beyond a reasonable level: with the obsessional idea of stopping all social contacts for the foreseeable future, our entire public, professional, private and now even economic coexistence is paralysed and even possibly permanently crippled for the future. Basically even breathing is now considered a risk factor and is made considerably more difficult by facemasks. For the panic-makers caught up in their control mania the ideal situation at the moment would be if no one went anywhere at all.

Banning all social contact with other people and in effect their whole society is like telling a fish to temporarily go ashore for the foreseeable future because the water is polluted.

People With Obsessive-Compulsive Disorders

This behaviour and way of thinking is very similar to what we observe in people with obsessive-compulsive disorders: Someone with a washing obsession is fixated that viruses and bacteria are always lurking everywhere. Therefore, after washing and showering, they've got to straight away wash and shower all over again because they may have come into contact with viruses and bacteria when they were drying off or getting out of the shower. In the end, because of their delusions and their washing-obsession survival strategy, the person ends up ruining their own life. They also actively destroy their skin's protective system that guards against bacteria, fungi and viruses. They live in constant stress and in the end are totally occupied with what is playing out in their head. They no longer have any confidence in themselves, their body and their defences. In my experience, this is always due to early childhood trauma experiences that have been split off into the unconscious.

At the moment, compulsive thinking in the public media is similarly trapped; its actions determined by the films playing in people's heads, with projections of the numbers of the possibly infected, of which it is statistically predictable that an enormous number will die. The public will then also be infected by this thinking. In the rampant corona virus hysteria, the importance of the immune system as the actual remedy against the viruses is completely ignored. This is why people tend to buy toilet roll rather than vitamin tablets, which would actually make sense in a situation like this where we are allegedly surrounded by viruses.

As If We Were At War

We imagine ourselves to be in a state of war and in a heroic fight against the enemy 'corona'. In fact, President Macron of France said as much publicly a few days ago. Ordinary nurses and doctors are now appointed as the fighters on the front line. And once this war has been officially declared, no one should question the reasons for the war, but only about what they personally can do to help win it. In a state of war no one is allowed to question the personal benefit or harm and cost to the general public – you, the individual, are nothing, the people are everything!

The higher then that the needless costs rise the less obvious the truth becomes: that this is a self-created, man-made catastrophe! Because it seems unbelievable to many that their governments and their medical experts can steer them into such a disaster with their eyes wide open, facts and opinions that prove this are simply not taken note of or are fended off.

It is like the fairy tale of the emperor's new clothes: only one small child dares to proclaim that the emperor is naked.

The worse the crisis scenario becomes and is exacerbated from above, the happier we are to be treated like objects, even though we are adults and often also academically well educated. In France, only those who can present the police with a certificate of entitlement are allowed to go out on the street. For many people it is now like it was in their childhood: my parents punish me but say, 'this is me showing you that I care, because it makes you tough enough for a life that is no bed of roses'. Instead of protecting us, the state decree puts us in protective custody in our own home. Outside the door the police and now even the military are waiting for you if you don't follow the rules.

What Would Actually Be Useful?

So what would it be sensible to do instead, if there is the threat of virus infection? Strengthen your own self-healing powers, build on them and trust them, maintain good relationships with other people, exercise in fresh air, get enough sunlight, eat raw vegetables, reduce stress, work through your own traumas, have hot baths to sweat out any fever and much more.

Anyone who still has to go to a hospital should be seen there as a whole person and not just treated as a symptom carrier and as an object. Actually, hospitals should be called health houses anyway in order not to cause nocebo effects. Nocebo (I shall harm) is the opposite of placebo (I shall please) - the scientifically well-documented knowledge that drugs have healing effects even without any active ingredient, because a doctor promises it. Conversely, in the case of 'nocebo', a doctor's diagnosis such as "You have cancer and will probably only live for six months" can actually cause a person to die out of hopelessness before the predicted period.

Measures That Are Prescribed From Above That Are Actually Health Hazards

The political measures in place are now shaped by monocausal orthodox medical thinking and clearly have nocebo effects:

- The fears about a scary virus are being increasingly stoked.
- Images of deaths in total agony in overcrowded hospitals with absolutely overwhelmed doctors and nurses are disseminated by all media channels.
- People who make a living from their work get into massive financial and professional existential fears overnight.
- Going out into the fresh air and the sun is prevented.

- People locked up in their apartments soon only eat canned food.
- They are increasingly cut off from all their relationships and fall into total social isolation.
- Physical contact of any kind is completely prohibited.
- Millions of people fall into a state of powerlessness and helplessness as a result of the increasingly radical state regulations, and therefore into a traumatic situation from which the only way out for them is to dissociate.

All this considerably weakens people's confidence in themselves and their immune systems. The risk therefore increases that their already existing infections, of whatever kind they are, can grow into a serious illness. As a result all these society-destroying measures do have a foreseeable effect in terms of a self-fulfilling prophecy.

Many still take it with calmness, they hold out in a dissociated mode of survival for a while and think that they show special social responsibility if they follow the increasingly totalitarian restrictions on their way of life. A population placed under such stress will probably soon be so frustrated in their basic needs that this will be discharged into aggression and violence - against their own children, against their partner, against neighbours and all those who do not follow the rules. The need for images of the new enemy will increase. The images of imprisoned Italians singing on their balconies, so popular in the social media, remind me of the prisoners' choir from Verdi's opera Nabucco. In Germany it will probably sound more like Beethoven's Fidelio.

Does It All End In Horror Or Is It A Horror Without End?

If, in spite of all these delusional measures, the great cataclysm of death does not happen and the number of deaths remains within the range of what a normal flu epidemic brings with it every year, the orthodox doctors and the politicians will then pat themselves on the back and say: we got it under control. China, as a repressive surveillance state, has just demonstrated this. And there is even the view that China, in cooperation with the WHO, has deliberately started this pandemic.[11]

I'm reminded of this joke: There is a man sitting on a park bench, clapping his hands at regular intervals. When a passerby asks him what he is doing, he says, "I'm scaring elephants away". The passerby says, "But there aren't any elephants here." And the man says: "Exactly."

So Who's The Crazy One Here?

The 'corona' phenomenon can at the moment provide us with a good opportunity to use our own minds and trust our own intuition instead of letting ourselves be drawn into a mass psychosis and the ruin of the whole of society by traumatised people who are completely cut off from themselves and their own feelings.

Because next year there could well be another pandemic with another 'new strain' of pathogen. Should everything be shut down again then, if indeed there is anything left that can be brought into lock-down?

Hence my urgent appeal to the politicians of this world: show courage and determination to end this control-mania immediately, before it is too late.

---

[11] https://www.youtube.com/watch?v=t-NA4Tb-V3w&feature=youtu.be (retrieved 02/08/20) – In German

Italy Brings It All A Lot Closer

Then the reports came that there were more and more 'corona' cases in Italy, allegedly because many Chinese were entering and leaving northern Italy. Northern Italy becomes the embodiment of the horror that the virus could cause. The bodies of the dead could no longer be transported away from the hospitals fast enough and regular funerals could no longer take place. But even here the question of truth and fake news was already rearing its head:

Figure 1: Coffins with corpses of alleged corona deaths in Italy as circulated on social media

'On March 18, a Facebook user posted a picture of coffins with flowers on them. He wrote: 'Germany too will have to get used to this picture. Especially if all resolutions continue to be trampled underfoot. PLEASE PLEASE STAY AT

HOME IF YOU WANT TO STAY ALIVE'. The picture also reads: 'In case you're still not convinced to stay home for you & ur beloved ones... Here's a picture from Italy!' The post has now been shared more than 2,000 times.

Another Facebook user's post with the same picture has been shared more than 2,800 times. There's nothing wrong with the call to stay home. However, the picture has been taken out of context. It was taken as early as 2013, when numerous refugees drowned off Lampedusa.

The photo has no connection to the current situation in Italy

We have uploaded the picture to the backwards image search engine - Tineye. The first link led directly to the image database of the photo agency Getty Images.

According to this the photo was taken by the French press agency AFP. The caption reads: 'These coffins of the victims were seen in a hangar at Lampedusa airport on 5 October 2013 after a boat carrying migrants sank and more than a hundred people were killed. Another 200 people are still missing.'

On 3 October 2013, a tugboat carrying refugees and migrants sank off the coast of Lampedusa. Almost 500 people from Somalia and Eritrea were on board, according to this media report in the Süddeutsche Zeitung. 339 of them could only be recovered dead from the sea.' [12]

National borders were now being closed. Eventually there were exit restrictions throughout the country, not only in Italy and Austria, but also in Germany, and the restrictions were growing ever more increasingly severe. Police vehicles began patrolling my residential area with loudspeaker announcements, as if an enemy attack were about to arrive any minute and we were all supposed to hurry down into the air-raid shelters. At the beginning I had the idea that this could only be a bad dream from which I would soon wake up. But the dream was rapidly changing into a nightmare.

---

[12] The original German article quoted from appears here:
https://correctiv.org/faktencheck/2020/03/20/dieses-foto-zeigt-keine-saerge-von-menschen-die-in-italien-durch-das-coronavirus-gestorben-sind
An English language site reporting on the same photograph can be found here:
https://factcheck.afp.com/these-photos-show-coffins-victims-boat-disaster-2013
(retrieved 21/08/20)

Back To Myself
Third Article - 20th March 2020

An Open Discussion On The Risk Of Covid-19

Due to the many contradictory interpretations as to what is really going on, I am unable to form my own clear opinion about the danger of the corona virus and Covid-19, so I am withdrawing from any debate about assessing the risk.

What I would like to see, in view of the enormous wide-ranging political measures that are being taken at the moment, the true extent of which cannot be really estimated by anyone, is an open-ended discussion about the health risk of the 'novel' coronavirus. I would like this discussion to take place in the public broadcasting media and mainstream print. Instead of them always consulting the same experts, who then recommend only one single strategy for action, all those who have alternative views and options and plans for action and currently only find a way to share their knowledge and assessments on the Internet and on social media should be brought together to exchange their arguments and points of view. Then it would also become clear which questions are still currently up for debate to which nobody has an answer at the moment.

If, however, the officially adopted strategy of 'avoiding all social contact' becomes dogma and dissenting opinions are suppressed, for example by the forced shutdown of alternative media channels, then what began as just a natural threat from a virus will suddenly turn into a dictatorship of opinion, where the joint acquisition of knowledge and a meaningful, ethical, political, sociological, psychological, philosophical and economic weighing of benefits and harms will be out of the window. At the current moment, there should not be just one, but several options and scenarios for action.

The Corona Crisis As An Opportunity For Society

This would also be a great opportunity, through the course of how we deal with 'Corona', for the societies of this world to counter the already existing formation of camps and divisions with something meaningful instead. In my view, traumas that are not directly caused by human beings are always an opportunity to set processes of solidarity in motion. Man-made traumas, on the other hand, promote social divisions and never-ending perpetrator-victim spirals.

In the near future we will see who was right in their assessment of the actual risk of 'Corona'. Then we will have the actual numbers of those who fall seriously ill and the number of people who die who can be clearly proven to have been infected with the novel corona virus and whose symptoms can actually be attributed to the way this virus works. The immense political, economic, cultural and social costs and damages caused by the current drastic measures are in the meantime becoming more and more noticeable for each of us every day. Whether and for whom it was worthwhile in the end, nobody knows for sure at the moment.

What I wish for all of us, in any case, is that this state of emergency, which for many people is increasingly taking on the character of a traumatising situation and, in addition, is increasingly provoking the emergence of old traumas, should come to an end as soon as possible.

Do Not Create New Perpetrator-Victim Dynamics

I have no interest whatsoever in furthering already existing perpetrator-victim discussions. This is clearly expressed in my book 'Who am I in a Traumatised and Traumatising society?' Therefore, in my public contributions to the 'Corona Crisis' I will now only stick to what I can definitively observe in myself and in my therapeutic practice.

My main contribution to this discussion is my deep conviction, from my experience time and time again, that the emotional processing of traumatic experiences, especially in early childhood, has a profoundly healing effect on the health of every single person. I observe this again and again with physical illnesses of all kinds.

Being, Becoming and Remaining The Subject Of One's Own Health

It is about being or becoming the subject of our own life and therefore also of being the subject when it comes to our own body and our mental and physical health. Through traumatisation, this subjectivity is often lost very early in life and, as a result, our own body is then seen and treated as an object. When it comes to physical disorders, we then immediately feel dependent on experts who are supposed to make us healthy again but who have no idea, and even do not want to know, about our own life story and our current life situation. These experts are then often very committed, but basically always overtaxed if 'the patient' does not take responsibility for his own life.

My idea is that first of all each of us is our own best expert when it comes to our own health. We basically only need the expert from outside in special emergencies situations, and then only when we still retain the possibility to develop our own 'I' and our own 'want'.[13]

Covid-19 And Old Traumas

How far Covid-19 will directly mean that this emergency situation is played out and for whom and for how many, I

---

[13] The healthy 'I' and 'want' is a fundamental in IoPT Theory. For more information please see the chapter on the 'The Theory of Identity-orientated Psychotrauma Therapy' on page 64.

cannot estimate at the current time. All I know at the moment is that what is happening now is feeding old trauma structures in many people I know and that it is seriously affecting their quality of life. And I know that unfortunately many of us carry such unprocessed trauma structures within us. Instead of living our lives, it could be said that, many of us are now, in some ways, merely surviving.

Raising Awareness Through Emotional Clarification

Crises can bring feelings that had previously been well suppressed back up to the surface. If we don't take a closer look at these feelings, they can easily result in narrow thinking based on one-sided ideas and lead us into blindly taking action. Therefore it is advisable to distinguish which of these feelings that are currently bubbling-up belong to my past and are only being reactivated by the current situation. It then becomes possible for us to identify the original situation and understand emotionally how it is linked to the current situation; if we can do this then the mind will also become clear and free again. And then in the current present-day situation, we then usually find that we have alternatives for action that we would never have seen before. This process is, in principle, the secret of every good therapy.

Engaging In Dialogue With Those Who Hold Other Opinions

95% of the reactions I received in response to my article 'The Corona Pandemic Mania' were positive. However, there was one particularly negative reaction and I used it as an opportunity to enter into a personal dialogue with the writer. He has allowed me to publish our dialogue here.

From: IK,
Sent: Thursday, March 19, 2020 10:01,
To: professor@franz-ruppert.de
Subject: KenFM Contribution Daily Dose

Dear Mr Ruppert,

I have just listened to your daily dose contribution on 'KenFM' from 18.03.2020, on YouTube. At first I could not imagine that these were really your words. After some research, I confirmed that they were. How irresponsible, lacking in solidarity and without empathy! The reality in Italy, in Spain etc. shows what can/will happen if we do not act. I don't want to give any further arguments here - there is no need to discuss it. Seeing and hearing should be enough.

I am amazed how many 'likes' you got for it. With your essay you have put yourself on the level of people who say a lot of stupid things in the parks, at corona parties etc.: "solve your traumas and you stay healthy" - ?!?!? HUH????

I don't understand how you can work in an institution whose essence is charity and whose main task is to support the weak in our society.

Until tonight I thought you were a 'very' clever person. This article makes you sound like a 'quack' who quacks from his island of 'Narcissus' - "Listen to me, now I am a virologist too" :-))

Come on, you can do better than this!
Stay healthy.

With kind regards
IK

P.S.: We have taken your books off of our shelves. What, you may ask, qualifies me to comment on your supposedly clever contribution at all - humanity and common sense.

On 19 March 2020, 11:09 +0100 Franz Ruppert wrote <professor@franz-ruppert.de>:

Dear Mr K,

I am a little overwhelmed by your strong emotional reaction. While reading your words I immediately felt a feeling of fear in my stomach, probably because as a child I experienced a lot of rejection from both my mother and father.

Who do you want to be responsible, in solidarity and empathetic towards you? What did you experience from your mother and father in this respect?

Would you also like to get more 'Likes'?

For me, charity depends very much on whether I love myself. If charity is connected with self-sacrifice, then in my experience there is something wrong with this love – this kind of charity is an expression of what I call in my theory the 'trauma of love'.

Stay healthy too!
Franz Ruppert

P.S. If you don't mind, I would like to publish your letter to me and my reply to it, and maybe again your reply to my reply on my website.

From: IK,
Sent: Thursday, March 19, 2020 11:40,
To: Franz Ruppert <professor@franz-ruppert.de>
Subject: Re: AW: KenFM contribution Daily dose

Dear Mr Ruppert,

If you change my name, you are welcome to publish our correspondence on your site. I don't need 'Likes'. I get them anyway every day through my work and particularly from my family and my children. In my life gratitude is the most important thing to me.

My writing does not only refer to just poor little me. If you have children of your own, then you might know that your own perception and focus moves away from you and in these times, the motivation to act, even from the close circle of the family, expands. This is what I mean by solidarity.

If you act now - take responsibility, you don't need to complain about your childhood/parents anymore. That includes accepting yourself as you are - since life is a process, certainly not perfect, but in any case lovable, with all its rough edges ...

Best regards IK
On 19 March 2020, 12:02 +0100 Franz Ruppert wrote <professor@franz-ruppert.de>:

Dear Mr K.,
Thank you very much for agreeing to a possible publication of our correspondence. The expression 'poor little me' now makes me even more curious about what you experienced yourself when you were 'poor' and 'little'. I don't know how old you are. I will be 63 years old this year.

I am also interested in your childhood experience because I wonder with what inner attitude you perceive the needs of your children, who have their own 'poor little me's inside them.

With kind regards
Franz Ruppert

From: IK,
Sent: Thursday, 19 March 2020 12:52,
To: Franz Ruppert <professor@franz-ruppert.de>
Subject: Re: AW: AW: KenFM contribution Daily dose

Dear Mr Ruppert,

'Poor little me' is a hint that the matter and my life is not only about me anymore – and that feels good. I am 59 years old.

My childhood experiences, as well as the experiences of my entire life, are full of negative as well as positive traumas. Being in love - being abandoned - humiliated - cheered - sometimes divine, sometimes diabolic - winning - losing. Just life. And, that is good.

From the lens of these experiences, I experience my environment and I get in contact or not. I think that I and we can extend our experiences with another positive trauma, if we show solidarity - even if not everything is perfectly organised. As I said, life is dynamic in a "universe that is in process".

I am not an expert. But, it is obvious that the virus has a very perfidious characteristic - it spreads unobtrusively, making not everyone sick (hence the sharp increase in the number of infected people) and strikes at the weakest. Although in Mitterteich a child at the age of 9 and a 19-year-old adolescent are both on respirators.

Even if all those who are severely affected by the disease are old and "already ill anyway", I think it is justified to take precautions to ensure that sufficient medical care is available for those affected. In my opinion, that is all that is happening here right now. There is no need to panic. The actions result from the circumstances, which is RESPONSIBLE.

Best regards
IK

On 19.03.2020 at 21:26 Franz Ruppert wrote

Dear Mr K,

When in your life was it really all about you?

Could you say more about the negative and positive traumas?

You can find some information about my life story in my book 'Who am I in a traumatised society?' I'm also attaching an article about my professional development.

Do you know anyone in your life who has such a perfidious quality as you now perceive in the coronavirus?

Have you ever experienced yourself that you were not given enough medical help?

With kind regards

Franz Ruppert

From: IK,
Sent: Thursday, March 19, 2020 23:01
To: Franz Ruppert <professor@franz-ruppert.de>
Subject: Re: KenFM contribution daily dose

Dear Mr Ruppert,

Your first question is quickly answered. Until I became a father, my life was all about me. Devoted to freedom, the desire to experience and to explore my own abilities. Even while saving the world, I wanted to save "my world".

To your second question: Perhaps it is presumptuous for a layman, not a psychologist, to use such terms. In my world there are both negative and positive experiences that have a great influence on my behaviour, my actions, my contact with my environment. It will probably only become apparent at the end of my life which (positive or negative) traumas have opened or closed the doors for me. Was it the warmth and the scent of my mother that saved me from running into misfortune with the next best affair? Or was it this trauma that made me set my standards too high and thus not able to recognise true love. Is it my father's slap in the face that made me a better father, who would never countenance doing the same? Only in the light of my entire life will the consequences of my experiences become apparent.

45

For better understanding: I don't think that only negative experiences - beatings - withdrawal of love - humiliation etc. traumatise us. I see that positive experiences cause similar burdens as negative ones - experienced moments of happiness make us restless seekers - beautiful places make us experience the rest of the world as dreary. The experience of great love is perhaps the most influential of all the positive experiences that a person can experience. This experience, as told in many great poems, has destroyed lives. My most incisive, most positive traumatic experience was the realisation that love never comes from outside - always from within. In that moment I came to the realisation that most of the actions of my life up to that point were wasted energy - and I always looked at the wrong end - what a shock!

I don't know anybody who behaves like the Covid 19. But I am convinced that the virus is not after us, but is most important to itself. And that's its weakness! We can take away its basis for survival by standing together and being in solidarity - that is what we as humans have over the coronavirus. We don't break our backs, even if we do something wrong again. Because, life is a process - a research and experience, always on a knife blade.

In keeping with these sentiments - happy exploring

Yours

Mr K.

On 20.03.2020 at 10:45 Franz Ruppert wrote

Dear Mr K,

Thank you very much for your personal openness. Now I understand better what you mean by 'positive' traumatisation. I was not familiar with this term before.

Being hurt by love relationships is also a central theme in my life and in my theory formation. Therefore I have written the book 'Trauma, Fear and Love'. Which determines our life more, fear or love?

I have come to think that everyone is his or her own best psychologist. But sometimes, when we are emotionally stuck, we need a few impulses from outside. This is the principle of the Intention method I have developed.

I also wish you continued good personal development.

With best regards

Franz Ruppert

Should I Be Scared Now?

At that time I wasn't really feeling afraid of 'Corona', this virus officially called SARS-CoV-2. It seemed to be very important in official language to always designate it 'novel' to emphasise its particular danger, even though word got around very quickly that 90% of those infected with SARS-CoV-2 were showing no symptoms other than a slight sore throat and fever and then, after a few days, were back to health again. So how it was known already, without any comparative studies, that this virus was more contagious than other viruses, was a mystery to me.

I was also feeling relatively calm because last year I had a severe case of flu. I'm not sure which particular strain of pathogen it was because I did not see a doctor. I had gone to bed, had eaten little and drunk a lot, had raised my fever with hot water bottles, had blown my nose a lot, coughed a lot and spat out mucus. When things were more or less okay again, I did another self-encounter IoPT process for myself at my practice and discovered a one year-old part of me in dire need. I was finally, through feeling much pain and shedding many tears, able to take this tiny part of myself back into my heart. Two days later I was fighting fit again.

On 24th May 2020, I received this report which summarised the situation in Italy, and which now makes it clear why people were dying in Italy – they weren't dying because of 'Corona' but because of the implementation of the pandemic measures:

'In the last few weeks, most Eastern European carers, who were working 24 hours a day, 7 days a week caring for those in need in Italy, have left the country in a hurry. This is not least because of the panic-mongering and the curfews and border closures threatened by the 'emergency governments'. As a result of this, elderly people in need of care and disabled people, sometimes without relatives, were left helpless and without carers.

After a few days, many of these abandoned people then ended up in hospitals – hospitals which have been permanently overburdened for years because, among other things, they were chronically underfunded. Unfortunately, the hospitals now also lacked staff, because they had to stay at home locked up in their apartments looking after their children because schools and kindergartens had been closed.

This led to the complete collapse of the care system for the disabled and the elderly, especially in those areas where even harder 'measures' were ordered, leading to chaotic conditions.

The nursing emergency, which was caused by the panic, temporarily led to many deaths among those in need of care and increasingly among younger patients in the hospitals. These fatalities then served to cause even more panic among those in charge and the media, who reported, for example, 'another 475 fatalities' and 'the dead are being removed from hospitals by the army', accompanied by pictures of coffins and army trucks lined up.

However, this army's involvement was the result of funeral directors' fears of the 'killer virus', who therefore refused their services. Moreover, on the one hand there were too many deaths at once and on the other hand the government passed a law that the corpses carrying the coronavirus had to be cremated. In Catholic Italy, few cremations had been carried out in the past. Therefore there were only a few small crematoria, which very quickly reached their limits and the deceased had to be laid out in different churches.

In principle, this development is the same in all countries. However, the quality of the health system has a considerable influence on the effects. Therefore, there are fewer problems in Germany, Austria or Switzerland than in Italy, Spain or the USA. However, as can be seen in the official figures, there is no significant increase in the mortality rate. Just a small mountain that came from this tragedy.'[14]

---

[14] https://swprs.org/covid-19-a-report-from-italy/ (retrieved 17.07.20)

Replacing One Evil With Another
Fourth Article – 23rd March 2020

We Don't Want Talking! Just Action!!

At the present time the political leadership in countries such as Germany, Italy or France will not brook any discussion about their current handling of the corona virus and Covid-19. The sole focus must be the strategy of containing infection rates and increasing the capacity of intensive care beds in hospitals. The aim is to save as many lives as possible from Covid-19. And yes, the situation is already dramatic in some countries, with the number of deaths increasing daily, although it is not clear what these people are actually dying of. And so, out of their fear of this 'novel' virus, the majority of the population is demanding this strategy from their leaders or is at least in support of it.

Covid-19 As A Natural Disaster

Viruses that are potentially highly damaging to us are part and parcel of our natural environment and will always be so. Covid-19 is a natural phenomenon. I do not believe that this virus has been deliberately introduced to mankind by any human intervention. Therefore, the pandemic caused by SARS-Cov-2 is primarily a natural disaster such as an earthquake, a tsunami, a hurricane, a flood, a wildfire etc. but it is happening on a global scale.

Existential Traumas

Natural disasters mean that in a short space of time there are a high number of fatalities and many who are seriously injured. A person feeling that they might die is an experience of existential trauma. The fundamental emotion is that of fear – the fear of the dying process itself and of being dead – and that leads to panic. This causes a lot of stress and there is a tremendous pressure to act and the wish to be supported and helped by others.

If someone is lucky enough to survive such a situation, it is still possible that the fear of death remains unprocessed in his psyche and he can tell his children and grandchildren what it was like to have narrowly escaped death and how much we have to protect ourselves from such dangers.

The so-called 'Spanish' flu of 1919/20, for example, still seems to have a hold on the collective memory of the world population today. Similarly 'Black Friday' – when in 1869 the price of gold plummeted – was still held as an unprocessed memory in relation to the Wall Street Crash of 1929 and more recently in relation to the collapse of Lehman Brothers in 2008, which then caused a worldwide collapse of the financial system and cost many people their jobs or 'professional existence'.

Loss Traumas

When a person dies despite all efforts to prevent it, his death is experienced by others, especially those close to him, as a trauma of loss. The main trauma is the pain of loss and the deep grief associated with it. My mother lost her father in an accident at work and never really got over this pain in her psyche. This is one of the reasons why she was never completely emotionally available for us children.

Many people who aren't directly involved also feel compassion for the deaths they witness, especially if the death is the result of a natural event, for example an earthquake or a tsunami. We then put ourselves in the position of the dying as well as their relatives and suffer with them. Especially when we see pictures of the cruel event, it is hard to distance ourselves. We feel as if it all happened to us.

Covid-19 or the Corona pandemic is currently causing numerous existential and loss traumas and the fear that these could become too many in total and escalate in number.

Triage And Artificial Respiration As A Trauma

If, due to the lack of capacity in intensive care units, doctors and nurses have to use 'triage' to decide who they will put on a potentially life-saving respirator and who they will not, then this is a traumatic situation for medical professionals too. Such situations, in which doctors as well as nurses can no longer help, are one of the basic risks of their profession and are therefore feared accordingly. They would obviously like to get into such situations of helplessness and powerlessness as rarely as possible.

It's also true with us psychotherapists that a similar traumatic situation can occur when a patient in their hopelessness can no longer be reached and is permanently depressed or - at least fortunately for us usually not right in front of our own eyes - takes their own life. Despite all our efforts we cannot help them.

Preventing Existential And Loss Traumas By Any Means Possible

Human beings are social creatures and it therefore makes sense that we want to prevent such existential and loss traumas in any way possible, on an individual as well as on a collective level. Hence the efforts of governments and populations around the world to make a stand against the death and loss from this pandemic right now. Every suitable means should be considered, no costs should be too high. The experience of previous pandemics should be used to teach us so that old mistakes should not be repeated. The science of virology and epidemiology, with its modern knowledge and methods, should now be used to help prevent the catastrophe or at least get it under control.

However, the political measures to combat Covid-19 are currently unable to prevent the fact that there will be existential trauma and numerous loss traumas. Many people are dying and many are already in mourning and many of those in the caring profession are being confronted with their growing powerlessness.

However what is happening is that the measures currently being taken are actually creating a new traumatising situation. All those healthy people who are currently still in full possession of their strength are now made to feel powerless with every new death, defenceless against the impact and the effects of the virus. And nobody from the government or the experts it consults can tell the population when this situation will end and when normality will return or if - as has already been warned as a precaution - it ever will do so again.

It is now just as it was in the definition of the two forefathers of psychotraumatology, Gottfried Fischer and Peter Riedesser: A trauma is an event that leads to an experience of vital discrepancy between the characteristics of the situation itself and the reaction possibilities of the people affected by it, and therefore it leads to a permanent shaking of their understanding of themselves and the world (Fischer and Riedesser 1998). This applies at both the individual and collective level.

Can The Actions Of The Government Be Questioned?

At the moment, the officially adopted strategy of avoiding all social contacts at all costs seems to have become a dogma of faith, underscored by the coffins of the dead, as we wait for our virologists to find a vaccine. Alternative strategies are ruled out, dissenting opinions are devalued and those who do not enthusiastically participate are now at the mercy of social ostracism (we are 'unreasonable', 'lacking in solidarity', 'unempathetic', 'a danger to public safety').

Consequently, there is a very real danger that a natural threat from a new virus could suddenly turn into a dictatorship of opinion and action, in which it seems unsafe to form one's own opinion even though the situation is something that threatens us personally. Let alone expressing that opinion publicly and putting it up for discussion, for fear of being shunted to the side-lines of society and being met with hostility. I am even experiencing this at the moment in exchanges with colleagues from my professorial community.

The fact that the opposition is completely silent at the moment and the press is holding back in its critical enquiries is not, in my view, a positive sign of this being an unparalleled example of social solidarity. The measures taken to prevent new infections are by no means clearly leading to success. There is still a high degree of uncertainty as to whether the whole enterprise will be of any great benefit and whether Covid-19 can really be brought under control on a global scale in this way. We are all paying a high price right now and have no assurance that it will pay off in the near future. Even in China, doubts are now being raised again as to whether the epidemic in the country can be stopped after the temporary shutdown and the resumption of normal social life.

Looking For A Balance Between Damage And Benefit Instead Of A One-Dimensional Strategy

Actually, therefore, there should be discussions and disputes right now. Individuals should not have to bear the burden of these momentous decisions. Rather, it should be about the joint acquisition of knowledge and the striving for a meaningful ethically, politically, sociologically, psychologically, philosophically, legally and economically sound cost versus benefit analysis of all possible alternatives to deal with this traumatising situation of Covid-19. Above all, we need to be ensuring that these existential and loss-related traumas provoked by the virus do not lead to us creating collective and completely new traumatising situations for the whole of society.

Especially in emergency situations, sometimes conscious non-action can often cause less damage than hasty and one-dimensional throwing ourselves straight into an action that has obvious consequences.

If a strategy will achieve foreseeable success, temporary necessary limitations are easier to accept and support. Instead of spreading panic and a doomsday mood and powerlessness, a shared sense of achievement could emerge in the end.

If the situation is indeed as great a threat as the virologists or epidemiologists are currently projecting, then there must be not just one, but several options and scenarios for action. For example, the possibility that the non-risk group of people under 60 years of age could be infected with the virus as unhindered as possible and develop immunity to it, while people over 60 plus could take special precautions, be supported in strengthening their immune system, protect themselves as well as possible against infection and be given the best possible care in case of illness. This has nothing to do with indifference or heartlessness towards these people.

Leaving the thinking and research to the government-appointed virologists/epidemiologists and their model calculations based on many uncertain assumptions as the last word of wisdom may gradually lead to a flattening of the exponentially increasing infection rates and to a reduction in the workload in intensive care units. At the same time, however, this will also lead to a sudden thousand-fold collapse of all social life, transport routes and space for us to move in. Borders should remain closed even if infection rates in a country have been reduced below 1.0 by means of the most comprehensive restrictions.

In any case, the virologists/epidemiologists in their specialist discipline cannot tell us a period of time in which the risk of infection will finally be over. Will it be in three months? Six months? Two years? They too are aware that it is not possible to simply put the entire social life of the world on standby for such a long period of time. So in the end, there can be no 'reasonable', purely scientifically based easing of the lockdown, but only a pragmatic one, based on the motto: "We can't take any more! We can't sacrifice any more for the idea of controlling Covid-19 or we will all perish." Italy is currently tightening its contact avoidance control policy and is even running the entire economy down to almost zero. No one can foresee where such a situation will lead for society as a whole.

Even the promise to make available enormous funds to compensate for the damage caused by such a social shutdown, which a rich state like Germany still believes it can afford at the moment, will not be able to completely eliminate the collateral damage of the lockdown that has already occurred. The control strategies that are now still supposedly helpful could soon lead to a situation in which not only the virus gets completely out of control, but entire social coexistence.

Be Reasonable And Make The Best Of It?

I have just received the following enquiry via email: 'I am a single parent with a 9 year old who is incredibly bored. Must we resort to computers and so on? I am annoyed and he is annoyed. Very few children just follow their parents' lead and do everything they are told. What do you advise to get through this situation so that neither parents nor children will be harmed?'

For one or two weeks such a situation is perhaps still psychologically endurable and maybe even can be used for something good, beautiful and new. Parents could use their work-free time to interact more intensively with their children again, instead of just managing them by taking them to the crèche, kindergarten and school and picking them up again afterwards. In spite of all the restrictions, they could not be prevented from romping around with them outside. This will not work indefinitely, however, when the professional future and the income of the parents become more and more uncertain.

Stress Levels Rise

The lockdown is already causing suffering and possibly even death in places where no one could have foreseen it on this scale. For example, can anyone actually predict and foresee how many people will become depressed while locked up in their apartments, drink more while sitting at home alone, become aggressive to their family and neighbours out of frustration, or perhaps become hopeless and end up taking their own lives because of losing their jobs or having their professional life ruined?

On Saturday at noon my front doorbell rang and a woman, with whom I have been working therapeutically for a long time, stood there completely distraught and confused. Despite the curfew, she had got into her car and driven over one hundred and fifty kilometres, because she couldn't stand the feeling of being locked up at home anymore. So I did an ad hoc therapeutic session with her in my house.

Especially now, when many people's nerves are already on edge after such a short space of time, the people with whom I work regularly in therapy are uncertain whether they should and may come to my practice at all.

Suppressing Stress And Feelings Makes You Sick

The current lockdown is certainly not beneficial to the health of the majority of the population. Otherwise it would not be necessary to keep stressing how much we should all pull ourselves together, be sensible and make sacrifices. How we feel should not come into it right now. But suppressed feelings are, according to widely researched experience, one of the main reasons for illness, both physical and psychological. The rationality of statistical model calculations to flatten the rate for a new Covid 19 infection, which doesn't take into account the basic rate of already existing infections and therefore also any already existing immune protection within the population, has in my opinion only a limited range and in the long run little practical relevance.

Rescue Through Collective Self-Destruction?

Can it therefore be the wisest course of action to react to a given existential and loss trauma situation by creating a social relationship trauma situation? Should we really, out of fear of the suffering and dying of many people and the impending powerlessness of not being able to do enough about it, place ourselves in a situation of collective self-destruction in which nothing is certain and predictable? Should children at the moment, in order to keep their mummy or grandmother or dad or granddad alive for as many more years as possible, put their entire future at risk because there is currently an unbearable number of dead for our psyche to deal with and not enough help available in the intensive care units? Do we have to put all our resources in the balance at the moment because medicine is not fulfilling its perhaps far too ambitious ideal of being able to prevent every possible death?

What is urgently needed here is open ethical discourse. Such questions cannot be solved by scientific rationality alone, in which doctors are trained worldwide.

Are We No Longer Capable Of Mourning?

If, as we now know, over 90% of those infected show only moderate symptoms and mild disease progression, then the question arises as to why Covid-19 has to become an existential risk for everyone right now? Do we not have to accept many existential and loss traumas as we do with other natural disasters? And learn to cope with these traumas emotionally? Or have we already become so accustomed to the idea that we can overcome death with money and technology so that we no longer have to cry and mourn?

The Death Of My Mother

My mother died last November in an intensive care unit at the age of 86. I always wished her as much lifetime as she wanted. In the end, all they had left to help her were their medications and the doctors and nurses made interventions that they themselves were no longer really convinced by. My mother's death and her dying was for me a process that brought a lot of pain up from my unconscious to the surface. At the same time, it gave me the chance to find out a bit more about my own physical symptoms and to become more alive by allowing my pain - and at times my fears and anger.

How Can We Use Money And Medical Technology Sensibly?

So why not plan for the long-term and put all the money that the complete lockdown will now cost, after this pandemic, into a health care system that is apparently working at the limit and that has been forced to fulfil its tasks for years under enormous financial pressure and lack of personnel? That, due to cost calculations, does not have enough capacity to deal with such emergency situations?

Why not offer adequate trauma-therapeutic support to all those people who have lost their relatives and to those exhausted doctors, nurses and carers? Existential and loss traumas can be healed with the knowledge and methods of modern trauma therapy.

Covid-19 And Man-Made Disasters

A virus is a natural phenomenon and is not man-made, unlike things like air pollution, smoking and drinking, exposure to pollutants in workplaces or war. Therefore, no one can be blamed if someone dies from a virus. A virus such as SARS-CoV-2 could well be the straw that breaks the camel's back because a person has accumulated a lot of disease in his or her body due to many other risk factors. Then the question needs to be asked why suddenly this virus alone is now the focus of health care and not all the other conditions that *are* man-made and which can cause a person to become ill and possibly die.

Competent And Well-Intentioned

The accumulated detailed knowledge, the continuous observation, the methodological accuracy of the statistics and the finely graded intervention proposals in the case of identified health hazards by various institutions, like the Robert Koch Institute in Germany, are impressive. Hardly anything is left out here that needs to be considered from a medical perspective. The model calculations of the German Society for Epidemiology are also based on what is currently calculable with a certain probability.

At the moment, however, it is only the same experts who are being asked again and again their view of the situation and to recommend their strategy for action. However, all those who have alternative views and options for action to offer and who currently only find a way to communicate their findings and assessments on the Internet and in alternative media should also be given space in the public media. Those who think they can say something substantial for and against should sit down together at a table to exchange their arguments and points of view publicly[15].

What I would like to see, however, in view of the far-reaching consequences of the strategy of action rather than discussion, which at the moment cannot be assessed by anyone, is an open-minded discussion about possible alternatives for getting out of this double trauma situation – because there is the trauma caused by the virus, but also there is there man-made trauma that has come about as a result of the measures taken to combat the virus – and I would like this discussion to take place amongst the public broadcasters and the mainstream print media.

Then it would quickly become clear what we collectively know and which questions are currently still without an answer and in some cases are being very hotly debated:

- Is Covid-19 really far more insidiously infectious than other viruses? [16]
- What different methods of assessing the risk are available?
- What are the different ways of determining the mortality rate?
- Will it be possible to develop a drug and a vaccine that effectively prevents SARS-Cov-2 from doing its job in the host body?
- Is it worth waiting for?
- Will there be compulsory vaccinations?
- Who might possibly make money from it then?
- Is the WHO a neutral body or is it influenced by lobby groups?

---

[15] https://www.youtube.com/watch?v=N2cn-uI8pDE (retrieved 24/07/20) In German. There is another interview with Sucharit Bhakdi with English subtitles that can be found here: https://www.youtube.com/watch?v=WbWJ4xIPAkA (retrieved 27/08/20)

[16] https://www.youtube.com/watch?v=JaTJyKVVnyo (retrieved 24/07/20) In German

- What interests do the global players in the financial system have in this situation?[17]
- Is infection control now going to be used as a permanent political option for summarily drastically restricting civil liberties?
- Will the virus be used to abolish cash etc.?

Will We Then Eliminate Other Trauma Situations In The Future?

If it should actually be possible to somehow get out of the current traumatic pincer hold - where on the one side we have the trauma of Covid-19 itself and on the other the traumatising consequences of the fight against Covid-19 – then this would be a good reason in the future to try to defuse other traumatic risk potentials for humanity at an early stage before it is too late.

After all, a 'novel' virus is only one of many problems that endanger our health and overburden healthcare systems worldwide. And there will of course be other 'novel' viruses in the future. Will the argument that we must 'save lives at all costs and not have to watch people suffocate in agony' then also apply to all other potentially life-threatening situations? Will we now also ban driving cars or riding bicycles in order to prevent lung-damaging air pollution, traffic deaths and serious injuries? Will the production of weapons and warfare be put on hold because it will cause millions of deaths? What about the civilian use of nuclear energy, which still poses a high risk potential and could once again cause serious damage to thousands of people in the event of another reactor disaster? What should we do about the climate catastrophe? Will an unconditional basic income be instituted worldwide as a preventive measure so that no one else has to starve to death?

---

[17] https://www.youtube.com/watch?v=aYZ2gVs9U7o&feature=youtu.be (retrieved 24/07/20) In German

Together, we could learn a lot in the current situation, when it is really about something in the common interest and not about partial or undisclosed interests, we could say goodbye to half truths and ideas and ask much more far-reaching questions than 'How many will die from Covid-19?' Whether this is possible or not, I don't know, but I am learning something new every day.

Locked Up And Locked Out Of My Practice

As I am locked up at home indefinitely, the reports in the public media become more and more extreme. Fear, fear, fear on every channel on the TV and it's also all there is to read in my daily newspaper, which up until now I had considered fairly liberal. I feel intimidated. My meticulously arranged plans for the year are crumbling. The seminar in Oslo with the Norwegian launch of my latest book 'Love, Lust & Trauma' at the Oslo Concert Hall is cancelled because more than 100 people wanted to come. I am doing one last open men's group and then it is not clear anymore when this and also my open evening groups may ever take place again. My fully booked seminar in Vienna at the beginning of April, which a lot of planning had gone into, has to be cancelled as well. Austria restricts the freedom of movement even more strictly than Bavaria and the usual problem-free back and forth between the two countries has become impossible. Regular visitors to my practice from Austria are missing. Nevertheless I try to keep my practice running with many small groups and try to keep a sense of business as usual. But then people become unsure whether they are still allowed to come to my practice and I also feel uneasy about whether it is actually still legal for more than two people to be here and not to keep a distance of a metre and a half from each other.

Then I also have to cancel my advanced training group - 45 people in a room suddenly seems an unimaginable gathering of people, almost a conspiratorial or even criminal organisation. I also notice that the few people who still dare to come to my practice speak with the few others that are there in a subdued voice. My practice assistant closes the curtains so that no one can look in from the outside. In one fell swoop, a normal psychotherapy practice looks like the meeting place of a conspiratorial association.

The Theory Of Identity-oriented Psychotrauma Theory (IoPT)

Since 2000 I started to develop my own theory based on my practical psychotherapeutic experience. To date I have presented this theory in ten books (for a full list please see the bibliography), all of which have been translated into English.

The development of one's own theory is a comprehensive research project that takes years. It requires numerous opportunities to explore the theory in a real-world setting and, as far as possible, you want reality to appear in all its complexity, with its many dimensions and facets. Experiences have to go beyond one's own educational, cultural and linguistic horizons in order to formulate a universally valid theory. The theory has to be tested in practice and there needs to be a way to evaluate possible changes and interventions for their suitability.

In 1994 I got lucky because I came into contact with a method called 'Constellations'. These constellations were originally developed by Bert Hellinger (1925-2019) in the context of his therapeutic practice (Hellinger 1994). Under the name of 'family' and 'systemic constellations' it gained a lot of attention during this time. Many people followed Hellinger's example and also offered 'constellations' (Weber 1995). In the light of the Corona pandemic, it strikes me that the rapid and worldwide spread of 'constellations' was much too fast for some of those in the psychotherapeutic community at that time. There is a critical book on the subject called 'The Hellinger Virus' (Haas 2009). There were both devout admirers of Bert Hellinger and those who hated him with a passion.

The Beginning Of My Emotional Opening

I felt personally deeply touched by what I experienced in constellation seminars. My 'soul', as I called it then, began to open up. Up until then I had essentially been a person who lived in his head, now I began to become interested in my feelings. In the mirror that the constellation method offered I could see my profound inability to relate. It made me able to better understand my personal and professional life and why so many unresolvable conflicts arose for me.

The constellation method, in which people serve as 'representatives' for family members and, surprisingly, behave exactly like the real people they are representing, opened up unexpected insights for me. My previous experience had been that insights had been difficult to learn from books and empirical research projects often raised more questions than they answered, but here was a method that appeared to prove things quickly and clearly in a straightforward way. Relationship dynamics between parents and children or between siblings, sometimes continuing over several generations, became apparent and comprehensible within minutes. I was particularly fascinated by the fact that even phenomena such as 'psychoses' revealed their psychological origin in a family constellation.

All this was reason enough for me to reorient my entire professional life towards these 'constellations' and to embark on a personal and professional research journey that continues to this day.

The Core Concepts Of IoPT

I do not want to go into a lengthy history of my research, with all its backward and forward steps, its blind allies and detours. At this point I only want to outline the essential core fundamentals of Identity-oriented Psychotrauma Therapy and Theory (IoPT), as I have developed them over the last twenty years, in so far as they have become relevant to my understanding of the Corona pandemic in 2020.

1. From the very beginning, the human psyche is an integral part of the living human organism, used to capture and process the reality that exists outside of the person concerned, as well as his or her inner world, in such a way that it is conducive to self-preservation and to the preservation of the human species in general. This information processing 'tool' is therefore complex, selective, adaptive and constantly evolving.

2. The main activity of the human psyche, namely this reception, processing and transmission of information, occurs in its most optimal state when humans feel secure. As soon as a person is under stress and has to switch to a fight or flight mode, these processes become hyper-selective. Under trauma conditions, the psychological functions inverse - the psyche has to blot out reality instead of recognising it.

3. Trauma lies in the relationship between the external situation and the possibilities a person has to psychologically cope with it. If the external situation is too over-taxing for a person's psychological capacities, this leads to feelings of powerlessness, helplessness and being at the mercy of others. Since the external situation can no longer be changed, only the psyche itself can change. It splits itself into separate parts for its own self-protection.

4. A non-traumatised human psyche is engaged with, and capable of recognising, reality as it is. Perceptions, feelings, ideas and thoughts flow together in this cognitive process in such a way that an increasingly clear picture and an increasingly unambiguous concept of reality emerges. Knowing that one's own perspective is always subjectively limited and possibly distorted, that every person has his or her blind spots, a person with a healthy psyche has the need for exchange, conversation and dialogue with others in order to achieve a correct and mutually harmonious co-consciousness about reality. There will always be questions left open in the process. I like to quote the poet Rilke at this point who said, 'Live the questions now. Perhaps then, someday far in the future, you will gradually, without even noticing it, live your way into the answer.'

5. With a traumatised psyche, it is different. This person was confronted with a reality they could not withstand. Their life was in mortal danger and they could only save themselves by doing the opposite of what a healthy psyche does: i.e. by not recognising reality. Only by blotting out this reality and by permanently splitting off the extreme experience of threat could they live on. The psyche remained, and still remains, stuck in this emergency mechanism, long after the acute threat situation has subsided. They can no longer free themselves from it without outside help. From now on the psyche's inner structure remains basically divided into three fundamental groups: the (still) healthy parts, the traumatised parts and the trauma survival strategies (figure 2).

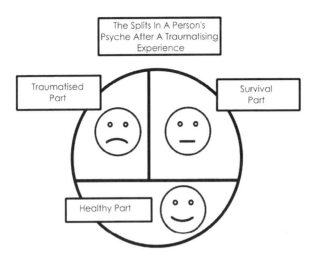

Figure 2: The basic structure of a traumatised and therefore split psyche.

6. For people who have had traumatic experiences, there is a fundamental difficulty in the capture and processing of their life as it really is. If they are relaxed and do not feel threatened, they may be able to do this. However, when anxiety comes, or even the slight beginnings of panic, which means that they are coming closer to their repressed traumas, they can easily and very quickly then slide out of their healthy psychological structures and switch over to survival mode. Then they tend to act rather confused, quickly become aggressive or resort to automated intellectual strategies that are only seemingly rational.

7. To react to a currently experienced threat with the old and ingrained strategies that made survival possible at the time of the trauma, however, cannot achieve much in the current situation and on the contrary can even make the present situation worse. We can see this, for example, when a person tries to numb their anxiety with some form of drug. But they then, overtime, become dependent on the drug and eventually have to deal with the side effects. In my experience, the use of old trauma survival strategies, instead of helping to alleviate or diffuse the internal and external situation of threat, actually leads to the situation worsening and becoming chronic.

8. Events that take place in a person's early history are particularly hard for the everyday mind to access. Since conscious memories only begin from the second or third year of life, the time before that lies in the dark of our consciousness (Figure 3). Experiences from psychotrauma therapy sessions have shown me increasingly and with great clarity that it is precisely there that the key can be found to the countless psychological and physical symptoms of suffering that can plague people throughout their lives. It can make the difference between whether a person is born with a healthy psyche or is already highly traumatised when they come out into the world depending on:

- what occurs after the egg and sperm cell have fused together
- whether there is a welcoming atmosphere or rejection when the fertilised egg implants in the uterus
- whether the growth process within the mother's womb can proceed undisturbed or if there are disturbances.
- whether the mother wants to give birth or not and therefore whether or not there are complications, possibly even violent complications, during the birth process.

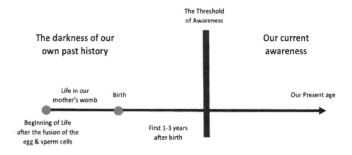

Figure 3: Our own history lies in the darkness of consciousness beyond the threshold of what we can remember.

Even in the first three years of life a lot can happen that is traumatising for a child.

- Isolation and being left alone for a long time,

- Neglect of the basic needs for food and physical closeness,
- Early external care by relatives or in crèches and foster homes,
- Physical and sexual violence etc.

Experiences such as this can damage a person so massively that he has to spend his whole life predominantly in survival strategies without being aware of the origins of his life difficulties. Only a therapy that takes the early development of a person into account can clarify such connections for the people affected and bring them into a process of change and therefore healing. In terms of my model of splitting, healing means to become whole again and to end the division of the psyche into three parts.

9. From a starting point of such early traumatisation, a person can experience his or her entire life as a trauma biography where they have to play their own prescribed part and cannot find their way out of this traumatised state. For this purpose I have developed the model of a four-step developmental logic for traumatisations: From the trauma of identity comes the trauma of love, which in turn leads more often than one would like to admit into the trauma of sexuality. And then the trauma victims themselves eventually become trauma perpetrators, who thereby further traumatise themselves and others (figure 4).

10. What manifests itself as physical symptoms in traumatised people and is then diagnosed by the conventional medical system as a 'disease' is often the expression of the consequences of trauma and the associated survival strategies. Because of the fundamental importance of a bonding connection and love to one's own mother, an 'illness' very often expresses the traumatising entanglement with one's own traumatised mother.

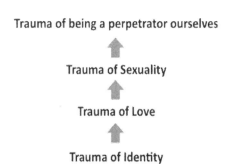

Trauma of being a perpetrator ourselves

⬆

Trauma of Sexuality

⬆

Trauma of Love

⬆

Trauma of Identity

Possible trauma biography from the beginning

Figure 4: The trauma biography in its developmental logic

The Need For Symbiosis And Autonomy

A living human organism has one thing above all: needs. From these arise all those feelings that are linked to the hope of fulfilling our needs and the fear of not fulfilling our needs. An essential building block of my theory is therefore the distinction between two forms of needs. According to this, all human beings have both symbiotic and autonomous needs from the beginning of their lives until their death. Symbiotic needs are listed in Figure 5 using the example of childhood needs in relation to his mother.

Our symbiotic needs

- to be fed
- to be kept warm
- to have body contact
- to be held
- to be seen
- to be understood
- to be supported
- to have a sense of belonging
- to be welcome

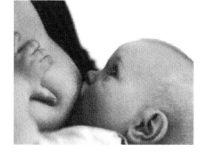

Figure 5: Forms of symbiotic needs

And here is a list of our needs for autonomy:

Our Autonomy Needs

❖ Self perception, feeling, thinking
❖ Standing on our own two feet
❖ Finding support within ourselves
❖ Doing things for ourselves
❖ Being independent
❖ Being free
❖ Deciding for ourselves
❖ ...

Figure 6: Forms of autonomy needs

If the symbiotic needs are not adequately met, especially in that time of primary bonding between the mother and child, this can lead to lifelong symbiotic dependence and to symbiotic entanglements, and therefore to a child-like attachment to the mother. This is usually supplemented by forms of pseudo-autonomy, in which these symbiotically undernourished people pretend that they do not have the needs they have and do not need anyone to give them closeness, love or attention. (Ruppert 2012).

Health And Illness

In the context of IoPT, our physical and mental health are shown to be the direct consequences of our personal life experiences, the associated external life circumstances and in many cases our own trauma biography. Those traumatising, not fully processed, life experiences are expressed in manifold forms of physical and psychological suffering. For this reason, getting well means coming to terms with these traumatic experiences and, as far as we are able, leaving these traumatising life circumstances behind. The forms of expression our suffering takes are indicators and sources of information that should not simply be removed, but should be further explored. Often, especially when the symptoms of suffering are recurrent and chronic, they are incomplete and repeatedly failing attempts at self-healing in the persisting traumatising environment (Ruppert & Banzhaf 2018).

The basic conditions for being and becoming healthy are correspondingly diverse because of the complex kind of organism that we humans are. Figure 7 shows what these conditions are from my IoPT perspective. It may seem surprising why I give the subject of truth such a prominent place in this. In my opinion, this becomes very apparent in connection with the Corona pandemic. If the narrative is untrue that this 'novel' corona virus now requires all personal and social efforts to eradicate it, this will subsequently lead to disease-causing rather than health-promoting actions and measures. The proclamation, by the WHO, that this is a pandemic and all the consequences that entails is what then makes people ill and even causes them to die early.

What do we need to be and stay healthy?

- Clean air to breathe
- Enough good food & clean water
- Protection from heat and cold
- Protection against toxic substances **Truth**
  (e.g. radioactive contamination, chemical
  pollutants, biological toxins etc.)
- Protection from armed violence
- Sufficient space to exercise
- A safe place to live

- A separate 'I'
- A free will/want
- To be able to show our own needs and feelings
- A clear mind
- Constructive relations
- Constructive social systems
- Peaceful coexistence on earth

Figure 7: Basic conditions for being and staying healthy

This holistic understanding of health and illness is contrasted with the reductionist understanding of traditional orthodox medicine, which is the predominant form in most 'modern' societies. In this orthodox view, it is assumed that genes cause physical and mental illness. And, bacteria and viruses are also primarily to blame for the development of diseases. In this way of thinking, illness is defined by the terms in which the physical and mental suffering is being expressed. According to this logic, curing illness is the elimination, or at least the reduction, of the symptoms of illness.

This often leads to radical interventions. The human organism is separated from the person whose 'mere' body is then treated as an object of medical procedures. The subjectivity of the respective person, with their own needs and associated feelings, is ignored, even defined as disruptive to the medical treatment. Being healthy and becoming healthy are then not the consequence of a person's dealing with his life experiences and his current life situation, but rather a question of whether experts from outside can bring this about, especially with physical intervention (including emergency ventilation with oxygen), chemical intervention (medicines, psychotherapeutic drugs, vaccines) and surgery (heart and stomach operations, Caesarean sections etc.).

Such treatments, which make the body of a human being an object and ignore the person's existence as a subject, are often traumatising in their very nature for the person concerned. The often already existing psychological splits that keep us from experiencing our feelings and our own body are thereby further deepened. In this way the inner life of a person becomes further fragmented.

Working Against Reality

Going against the truth and reality of a situation, i.e. thinking and acting counterfactually, is characteristic of trauma survival strategies that are undeterred by the negative effects of their actions. Practised as they are in the tireless fight against the symptoms and accustomed to existing in a chronic state of fear, stress and struggle, they move from one battle to the next. The symptoms (or side-effects) that then further result from this method of symptom control are again fought with the same questionable means. The thinking and acting behind this is hailed as something that has no alternative and in specific areas as very successful. From the point of view of survival strategies the next great breakthrough in the fight against diseases - whether that's 'cancer', 'schizophrenia' or a virus epidemic - is supposedly always just around the corner. In enlightened societies, orthodox medicine has replaced God as the thing we pray to and which promises us salvation. Some doctors indeed believe themselves to be godlike and feel responsible for the life and death of the people they end up treating.

Orthodox medicine's reduced theoretical model is particularly alarming in that it also defines the self-healing attempts that the human organism makes as diseases in themselves and therefore seeks to hinder their development. This is particularly counterproductive in the context of a viral infection. Since potentially harmful viruses are kept in check primarily by the immune system increasing the body's own temperature, then the policy of administering antipyretic drugs (drugs designed to bring down a fever) can be damaging. Instead, the increase in body temperature should be welcomed and further encouraged by the person who is going through this illness, as natural medicine has long recommended. [18]

The same is also true when it comes to inflammations, which also indicate an increased activity of the immune system. Anti-inflammatory medicines counteract the self-healing processes that are taking place in the body. Trying to prohibit any of the results of the body's self-healing processes (mucus, exhalation of pathogens and cytotoxins) by mechanical means (e.g. with masks that cover the mouth and nose) or again with medications (cough suppressants or agents that stop the nasal mucus) in these acute self-healing phases could be looked at as a form of self-disabling or self-harm.

Where the motive of a health industry is to make money out of everything, human needs are commercialised as well, as conventional medicine offers its services to all those who ignore their basic human needs and their associated feelings of joy, fear, anger or shame. From conception through to death, sophisticated technologies are used without any regard to each individual's own human psyche. No thought is given, for example, to how it is for a child whose mother acts only as a surrogate or how these women, degraded to the status of birthing machines (Bachinger 2015), feel; what needs children have in their birth process or what dying people need in order to be able to bid a dignified farewell to their relatives. Whatever is technically feasible is done, whatever it takes, at the psychological cost to all those involved.

The Baby Food Scandal Also Happened In Bavaria In 1957

In my student days (1976-82) I was aware, on my periphery, about the Nestlé milk powder scandal. The Nestlé Company had been advertising its powdered milk products as baby food in developing countries. 'Milk nurses', essentially sales-people dressed as nurses, tried to convince mothers that powdered milk was better than breastfeeding for their children. But these 'nurses' earned money from sales of the powdered milk, so they were anything but

---

[18] The original German page referenced which is entitled 'Fever: Do not suppress, but encourage' can be found here: https://www.heilpflanzen-welt.de/2007-12-Fieber-Nicht-unterdruecken-sondern-foerdern/ (retrieved 21/08/20)

independent consultants. This milk powder was then used by mothers who, in these developing countries, lacked the basic hygienic conditions to boil and sterilise the baby bottles or who diluted the milk powder because it was so expensive. As a consequence the babies became ill and even died. This was the reason that there were serious allegations made against Nestlé. There was a report compiled by development aid groups that looked into this scandal. It was called 'The Baby Killer'. [19]

I only recently learned that breast milk is the best immune protection for babies when I was giving a lecture at a breastfeeding support association in Tuttlingen on 12 March 2020. I bought a book by Regine Gresens (2016) there and read it on the train back to Munich. This book provides comprehensive information on the subject. There is no better food for babies than their mother's milk: 'With every breastfeeding meal, the baby gets millions of ingredients which support its immune system in defending itself against pathogens, protect it against disease, inhibit inflammation and promote wound healing'. (Gresens 2016, p. 17) No substitute food in the world, no matter how sophisticated, can replicate what evolution has optimised over millions of years. Breast milk is a living fluid like our blood.

I know that I myself almost died as a baby when I was 4 months old because my mother stopped breastfeeding me and switched to a powdered milk substitute. In June 2020, in a conversation with my father, I looked into the matter again. He told me that in the community of Workerszell, where I was born in 1957, there had been, during this time, regular mother counselling sessions. At one of these the counsellor recommended a powdered milk substitute diet to my mother. This was expensive and my parents had to buy it in a pharmacy in the nearest town. In this conversation with my father I also learned that my parents lived under primitive hygienic conditions. It was the post-war period and eight families lived together in a two-storey house with an outside toilet and a single water connection at the entrance to the house. In my parents' apartment there was only a wood stove and bowls for washing dishes and personal hygiene. So these were exactly the conditions that probably also in developing countries led to milk bottles being unclean and babies getting diarrhoea and becoming dehydrated.

---

[19]https://en.wikibooks.org/wiki/Professionalism/The_Nestlé_Infant_Formula_Scandal (retrieved 21/08/20)

Only the change to a powdered rice diet saved me from dying. But, because of it, I had digestive problems all my life. Our gut is one of the most important parts of our immune system. Having an immunologically healthy gut is one of the basic prerequisites for health and well-being.

Anxiety, Chronic Stress And Trauma

When I came to properly understanding the 'phenomenon of stress' (Vester 1991) it was, for me, one of those key wake-up moments. I can say that it literally saved my life, otherwise I would probably have stressed myself to an early grave by now.

Originally stress arises in a situation in which we feel threatened:

- The perception of a danger signal sets off a cascade of stimuli in the diencephalon part of the brain (which comprises the limbic system, amygdala, thalamus, hypothalamus)
- Signals from the brain-stem cause the pituitary gland to flood the brain and body with stress hormones.
- The adrenal gland is activated via the sympathetic nerve system; the adrenal medulla releases adrenalin and noradrenalin into the bloodstream.
- These hormones accelerate blood pressure, resulting in palpitations, dilation of the pupils and perspiration.
- Sugar and fat reserves are mobilised, as the muscles receive an injection of glucose.
- Adrenocorticotropic hormone (ACTH) is sent to the adrenal gland via the pituitary gland. Hydrocortisone is then released in the adrenal cortex.
- Hydrocortisone concentrates all the body's energy on dealing with the danger, everything superfluous is switched off (digestion, sexuality, immune defence).
- Red blood cells flood the arteries for a better oxygen-carbon dioxide exchange. Blood coagulation factors increase abruptly, wounds can close faster in case of injuries.
- From the subcortical areas of the brain, fight or flight and avoidance reactions are triggered, which are then interpreted in the cortical structures as having no alternative.

In a stress situation we go through a series of different stages:

- 'Overexcitement', an alarm reaction that affects us into a state of emergency,
- Increased pressure to act,
- Anger which will lead us to attack,
- Fear which will lead to flight,
- The alarm response can escalate,
- We fall into a state of desperation.

The stress response is intended for short-term threat situations. It should return to a state of well-being as soon as possible after the elimination of a threat situation in the following way:

- There is danger present,
- There is a mobilisation of resistance,
- We cope with the danger,
- We calm down.

However, if the danger situation persists, the stress response of the human organism becomes chronic and this has myriad consequences for our psychological state. A permanent state of stress leads to:

- Insecurity, irritability,
- Depression, moodiness,
- Lack of a plan or purpose,
- Inability to make decisions, loss of self-discipline,
- Learning and concentration difficulties,
- Indifference to others,
- Authoritarian behaviour to the point of violence.

The chronic state of stress can also express itself on a physical level, manifesting itself in 'diseases' of all shapes and sizes from asthma, high blood pressure, dementia, fibromyalgia to heart attacks, headaches, cancer, rheumatism, obesity or diabetes and many many more.

In the Adverse Childhood Experiences (ACE) study (Vince Felitti & Bob Anda 1998)[20], researchers came to the following conclusions:

---

[20] http://acestoohigh.com/2012/10/03/the-adverse-childhood-experiences-study-the-largest-most-important-public-health-study-you-never-heard-of-began-in-an-obesity-clinic (retrieved on 22/7/20)

From a sample of 17,500 adults, mostly white and educated

- 67% have at least one ACE (an Adverse Childhood Experience – this includes physical, emotional or sexual abuse, child neglect, parents with mental illness, drug addiction, prison sentences, separation and divorce, domestic violence etc.).
- 12.6% had 4 or more ACEs.
- The more ACEs, the greater the health problems.
- 7 ACEs and more: 3 times more likely to develop lung cancer, 3.5 times more heart attacks.
- Even without health risk behaviour, traumatic stress destroys the brain.

Because the permanent danger situation has become internalised, this then progressively appears as something that is natural and expected and we get used to living or surviving in flight and fight mode. A state of well-being and relaxation appears to us like a distant utopia, which we can only at best achieve momentarily by doing breathing and relaxation exercises, getting a massage, going to the sauna or enjoying a good meal in a nice restaurant. Everyday life is in essence stressful and remains so.

I was particularly shocked by an experiment with treeshrews as described by Frederik Vester (1991, p. p. 54 ff). If the habitat of a treeshrew population is restricted too much, the social tension between the animals increases and then it can even happen that mothers not only neglect their own young, but even eat them.

It was also important for my growing understanding of how the world and human beings work, to understand the difference between what is a stress situation and what is a trauma situation.

Stressful situations lead to the mobilisation of energies

- For fight or flight mode.
- On the contrary, trauma situations make it necessary to block the mobilised energies,
- To freeze emotionally or to split internally ('freeze or fragment' mode).

In contrast to stress situations, when we experience trauma situations it is less easy for us to return to our original state of well-being. The freezing of the psychological processes, especially the freezing of our feelings, and the splitting off and splitting up within our psyche remains present even when the dangerous situation is over. One part of the psychosomatic network remains forever in the danger situation; another continues to fend off the perception of the threat as if it were still acute. The threat situations are therefore in this way permanently internalised. External terror is now joined by internal terror.

Stress then arises not only from when we come into confrontation with the outside world. It also comes from a person's inner world too and is then projected onto the outer world. In this way the outside world is experienced as threatening and dangerous, even if it is calm and peaceful in and of itself. For example, a mother experiences her child as threatening because of her experiences of violence in her own childhood. The mere sight of her child evokes these feelings of threat from her own childhood and puts her in a state of alarm and stress.

A Culture Of Healthy Identity Instead Of Dependence

The orthodox medical model is part of the culture of dependence that we find in traumatised and traumatising societies. The people there are dependent on

- Their respective governments
- Money
- Their partnership relations
- Experts from all disciplines
- Medicines and drugs
- Material things
- The continual validation from others.

Figure 8 shows the components, which, from the point of view of IoPT, represent the alternative to the orthodox model in terms of medical theory and action and can therefore offer us a way out of the culture of dependence. The self-responsibility of human subjects for their own health and the associated processes of awareness is given central importance here.

Basically, the following holds true: No doctor, psychiatrist, psychologist or psychotherapist can be an expert on illness and health if they refuse to deal with their own life story.

Steps towards a new culture of health

- accept that trauma and psychotrauma biographies are very common in a society
- stop constantly traumatising each other
- stop spending large amounts of time and money on social systems that have a limited understanding of the body and psyche and actively demand traumatisation and ignore psychotrauma
- take our health into our own hands

Figure 8: What a new culture of health might look like…

Traumatised And Traumatising Societies

In my experience, every person comes into this world with a huge potential of life energy, a joy in life, a will to live and a heart full of love. Every child loves and wants to be loved. Every child is a new chance for humanity to peacefully coexist on this planet. How can it happen that there are so many frustrated, depressed, aggressive, unfeeling and petrified people on this earth who are just functioning without any connection to their life-force and joy? How is it that these people are in permanent conflict with each other and are fighting to the death? My answer to this is: because these children's hearts that were once full of love met a world of adults who did not want them, did not love them and did not protect them from harm. They were hurt so deeply at an early age that they closed themselves off, withdrew their good sides into themselves and only survive instead of truly living. And these adults who treat them like this have also experienced these early rejections of their own love and joy of life in their own childhood. This has been going on for many, many generations. But every new generation could be a chance to finally do something different and could be an occasion where children are really welcomed and parents could accompany them lovingly into life and protect them from harm. Then these children could become parents themselves who in turn love their children from the bottom of their hearts.

Because this is not yet the case and because many children are currently damaged at an early age by pre-, peri- and postnatal trauma, are overburdened by early external care, and because their relationship with their traumatised parents means that their 'yes' to their own existence is soon lost, traumatised and traumatising societies continue to exist in which most of their members are traumatised.

This is particularly true for patrilineal societies. In these societies, property belongs to men and men also see women and children as their property. This means that women often have no choice but to marry and to give birth to children. It is expected of them almost as if that were the natural way of things. They are also often degraded to the status of sex objects of male sexuality. Likewise, these women are either completely abandoned by the fathers of their children when it comes to bringing up their children, or this is of course delegated to them like all other household duties.

In such societies, men remain sons of mothers and cannot emotionally cut the cord with them, while women tend to reject motherhood - their own suffering and merely functioning mothers are not a shining example for them - and so they are fixated on men.

In patrilineal societies, male thinking also shapes the health system. Orthodox medicine hardly takes the human psyche into account. In gynaecology, for example, this creates traumatising situations for mothers and children. Caesarean section births, which represent trauma for both mother and child, are considered normal. Similarly, in the competitive economy of patrilineal societies, the needs of mothers with small children are ignored. Many mothers, for example, live on the poverty line as single parents. In order to earn money, they are forced or persuaded to place their small children in outside care far too early. In this way, the breeding ground for early trauma is laid for the next generation. As adult men and women, these children then become the traumatising mothers and fathers for the next generation.

In my opinion, this patriarchal way of life even shows itself in the 'fight' against a virus, which is declared a 'war' by some presidents, such as Mr Macron, who appear as if they would like to use their army to destroy as many viruses as possible. These traumatised societies are basically in a constant state of alarm, fear and stress. When one danger is over, the next one is already lurking around the corner.

In a traumatised society, victims are constantly being produced and at the same time victims are forbidden to complain about being victims. They should accept it as their destiny and bear it patiently. And to remember that others elsewhere are much worse off than they are, or that things could possibly get even worse.

Since the victims themselves usually do not want to admit their own victimhood, they develop victim attitudes through which they do not perceive the perpetrators as perpetrators and even protect them and experience themselves as responsible for their own plight.

If the victims then demand something, they do not do it in the name of their own needs. Instead, they demand consideration for others or solidarity with the poor and weak, thus confirming the trauma perpetrators' view that they should not complain about how it is for themselves. Insisting on one's own needs is considered immoral and is essentially ostracised in traumatising societies. It is 'selfishness' to think of one's own needs.

Bonding System Trauma

In my book 'Verwirrte Seelen' (Confused Souls) (Ruppert 2002)[21], I was concerned with shedding light on why people become insane and mad or, as psychiatry calls it, 'psychotic' and 'schizophrenic'. One of my answers was: such people live in a bonding system that traumatises them. Attachment relationships are interpersonal relationships in which there is emotional dependence. Such emotional dependencies exist mainly in the child-parent relationship, but also in couple relationships, in friendships and work relationships. Even in politics we can see that people are emotionally dependent on the parties and politicians they vote for. Here, childlike dependencies that exist towards one's own mother and father are transferred onto the partner, the friendship, work or political relationship. The less someone can break away from their own traumatised parents, the more likely they are to remain in childlike dependency when it comes to future bonding relationships in their lives. Destructive relationship patterns repeat themselves for this person throughout his life.

In my experience, traumatised bonding systems produce the most severe physical and psychological disorders, especially because the truth about what is really going on must not be told. As long as there is no possibility for a person to leave such an ever more delusional attachment system, he can only protect himself from the unbearable reality in which he spends his life through ever more psychological splits. Those whom he loves, in whom he trusts, on whose actions he

---

[21] 'Verwirrte Seelen' is not available in English, however 'Trauma, Fear & Love' is a revising and updating of the ideas contained in it. (SL)

is existentially dependent, reject him, despise him, torture him and are prepared to kill him.

One is usually born into a bonding system trauma. Therefore people often know nothing else but this form of existence. In such a system, one is first of all the victim who is robbed of his original joy of existence and his original will to live. The trauma victims become more often than not trauma perpetrators themselves in the course of their lives. They harm themselves and destroy the lives of others. Masochistic victim attitudes go hand in hand with sadistic perpetrator attitudes in such bonding systems.

Humanity likes to think of itself as the pinnacle of creation. But in reality, there is probably no other living being on this earth which so systematically destroys itself and drags the whole of the rest of nature into its pathogenic and murderous abyss of trauma.

Money And Psychotrauma

Since a psychotrauma often creates an extremely severe disconnect between someone's physical existence and their psychological one, many people in traumatised societies live more in their world of thoughts and ideas than in reality. This is most strongly expressed when it comes to their relationship to what is considered to be of value. Abstract wealth is what counts in traumatised societies. It manifests itself in the form of bank notes, coins and precious metals or simply as account entries with as many zeros as possible. In contrast, concrete actual wealth in the form of natural beauty and people's own resources when it comes to relationships, intelligence, creativity and ability to work, is generally underestimated. In other words, money, in whatever form, has increasingly become the focal point of all social interaction over the last two hundred and fifty years. We do not work in order to live, but we live in order to work, in order to earn money from it and to increase that money. To see money as capital means that we always want it and have to increase it. To make more money out of money becomes an ideal and an obsession of economic action.

Everything else in a society is then subordinated to the multiplication of money. Only if money can be made out of something, does it become something of value. This is why, for example, housework and above all the accompanying of children into their emotional and psychological independence by their parents and relatives are not regarded as something particularly worthwhile. Especially for mothers there is the expectation that they do this for free, because they do it out of love for their children, while at the same time meeting all the demands of a neo-liberal economy (Ruppert 2012).

Therefore, professional childcare by designated educators and childhood specialists is much more appreciated financially because it opens up a new line of business with which money can be made. A mother who places her child in a crèche so that she can then work in a day care centre providing professional pedagogical care for the children of other mothers is, from this point of view, an accepted member of such a money multiplying society and therefore 'important to the system'.

A society which is forced to operate a monetary system or which spends a great deal of time and effort creating such a system for itself becomes more and more entangled in it and fundamentally separates its members from direct access to the wealth of nature and from spontaneous and well thought-out social cooperation. Everything now comes with a cash price, which must first be paid before any desired goods can be made use of.

Contrary to the common assertion of economics and business, money does not help to make life easier, but rather forces its members to earn and acquire money in order to survive within the monetary system. Especially since this system is based on competition and wherever it permeates through every last corner of society, the profit of one side always causes a loss on the other side. Therefore, within a money-competition based system like this it can also be seen that those who are rich get richer and those who have little get poorer and poorer. Everybody who has ever played a game of 'Monopoly' knows this principle. Today, 0.9% of the world population owns 43.9% of the world's money wealth, while 56.8% of the world population owns just 1.8% of the world's wealth[22]. The corona pandemic is further accelerating this inequality when it comes to the fair distribution of financial assets. Because shops are closed, orders at Amazon are increasing. 'The US super rich are happy to see their accounts grow even larger. They are clearly among the winners of the Corona crisis. In particular, Jeff Bezos, Bill Gates, Mark Zuckerberg, Warren Buffett and Larry Ellison. And so once again, the saying goes, 'For whosoever hath, to him shall be given, and he

---

[22] https://de.statista.com/statistik/daten/studie/384680/umfrage/verteilung-des-reichtums-auf-der-welt/ (retrieved 05/07/20) In German

shall have more abundance; but whosoever hath not, from him shall be taken away even that he hath.'[23]

However, abstract wealth in the form of shares, bonds, account balances or even gold can suddenly collapse like a house of cards or melt away like ice in the sun. The Wall Street Crash of 1929 or the banking crisis of 2008 are cemented in the collective memory of capitalist societies. Money that can no longer find a way to multiply is suddenly then no longer capital and becomes worthless. The need for money-based profits makes people greedy and insatiable and even makes the owners of capital trample over corpses in the need to satisfy their desires, because the fear of their money devaluing is constantly breathing down theirs necks, as long as they continue to take part in this system. A capitalist society is a restless and unstable system.

As a consequence of this obsession with making money, in such societies...

- Mothers and fathers neglect their children in order to earn money and have a career.
- Pupils and students are not properly educated and are kept in ignorance by their teachers and professors about the true nature of this money multiplication system and they are sorted into future winners and losers on the basis of the marks they get.
- Men expect their wives to do unpaid housework and to also take on gainful employment if necessary.
- Business owners demand that their workers and employees, under threat of sanctions and possibly even dismissal, hold back from voicing their own truths and do not make any fundamental criticism of this system.
- Businesses buy politicians and scientists to help enshrine their interests in law and give their business practices the appearance of scientific objectivity.
- Deadly weapons are produced in order to make a profit and to eliminate by force 'competitors' across the world for this same abstract wealth.
- States wage wars in their competition for raw materials and market shares and in order not to have to pay their own debts.

---

[23] https://www.rubikon.news/artikel/die-mega-milliardare (retrieved 05/06/20) In German

The conflicting interests inherent in such relationship structures then create perpetrator-victim dynamics on an ever wider scale. Parents become trauma perpetrators against their children, men buy women as their property, companies exploit their workforce, states demand that their citizens participate in this often very violent program of money multiplication throughout every corner of society. Deception, lies, fraud, robbery, corruption and murder are all consequences of this hunt for abstract wealth (Figure 9).

The Costs of Competition/Rivalry/Contest

- Constant time pressure, physical deterioration, psychological stress, frustration, 'burn-out'

- Jealousy, envy, shame, 'narcissism'

- Distrust, dishonesty, opportunism, ruthlessness

- Images of the enemy, military build-up, war

Figure 9: Psychological costs of hunting for abstract wealth

The blind pursuit of money wealth divides relationships and the world community. It produces ideologies in all nations that lead to constant and endless perpetrator-victim dynamics (Figure 10).

Ideologies are mental constructs with which trauma perpetrators try to immobilise and disempower their trauma victims. If the trauma victims adopt these constructs too, there is then agreement between perpetrators and victims. This is what happens in families, and it also happens in a corporate and governmental context and on the world stage.

86

Violent Competitive Ideologies

- There are some people who are higher and some who are inferior ('the master' and 'the servant', 'the leader' and 'the led').
- 'National' and 'racial' affiliation is a determining factor in regards to value and people (e.g. 'White' versus 'Black').
- War is necessary in the struggle between the strong and the weak (it is the 'will of nature'/ 'survival of the fittest').
- 'Morality', 'guilty conscience', 'humanitarianism', 'feelings' etc. are expressions of weakness
- 'Blood sacrifice' is necessary for the national 'resurgence'.
- War in self-defence against 'foreign rule'.
- We the 'people' need the 'greatest leader of all time', the 'shining light' who will bring us out of the darkness
- Without competition and struggle there is no progress

Figure 10: Competitive ideologies

Self Encounters With The Intention Method

In this book, I refer at several points to the Intention Method. I have developed this therapeutic method over the last ten years to translate the theory of Identity-oriented Psychotraumatology into a workable method of psychotherapy.

The current way it works is: someone formulates their Intention for their current piece of work. This can take whatever form they wish - a sentence, a question, individual words, a drawing or a combination of words and drawings. For the practical work the person bringing their Intention should then name a maximum of three elements (or information units) from this Intention (each unit may be a word, a grouping of words, a part of the drawing etc.) for which he then selects people (in a group situation), who then go into resonance with that element. Then he gives a signal for the process to start. Without speaking, the people chosen start to resonate with their information unit. After 1-2 minutes, the Intention Holder begins to talk with his resonators about what they are experiencing. In this way, it gradually becomes clear what his Intention is about.

When I am acting as a therapist, I observe what is shown in these dialogues. If I find it useful and appropriate, I intervene. In principle, I trust in the self-healing potential of the human psyche when it is given the opportunity to resonate with itself in a protected and guided setting. Therefore I consciously limit my interventions in these processes to a minimum.

The Corona Pandemic has also had a very positive side for my therapeutic work in relation to my method. I have to offer Identity-oriented Psychotrauma Therapy (IoPT) online. I also then got an offer from Singapore to do some online teaching and to offer IoPT as online group workshops. Over ZOOM this seems to work wonderfully. It still leads to the necessary processes of emotional clarification. This confirms to me my opinion that the human psyche is, in its core, comprised of: information intake, processing and then release.

IoPT Goes Online

So I am learning how to offer group seminars in English and as I was working out how to run them in German, someone materialised out of nowhere who was willing to prepare and administrate them and now ensures that everything runs smoothly on the technical side. We clarify the necessary safety rules for such events and then I only need to log into ZOOM with my link, which I get from my administrators, and I can do IoPT therapy online from my office at home.

It works incredibly well. The people who go into resonance show their emotional reactions on their screens as they would in real-life seminars. The Intention Holders are psychologically and emotionally involved and at the end of the process they have become more in contact with themselves. I can hardly believe it.

In between I make individual appointments online or in my practice. Some people have sensed the chance to get an appointment during this time, which are normally booked far in advance, and some get one. As always, there are a lot of unresolved early childhood traumas. And as expected, the current traumatising isolation situation triggers old childhood wounds.

Remaining Mentally Clear

Amidst all of this, I sit a lot at the computer and try to sort out my thoughts. What is going on here? Am I crazy and don't recognise the real danger or are others constantly spreading horror scenarios that don't even exist? People in Italy seems to be dying at an unimaginable rate; the bodies could not be removed fast enough. The morgues are overcrowded and the military has to be called in quickly to remove the coffins.

I search the Internet and source information from the alternative media. Jens Wernicke of the Rubikon.news website now supplies me with at least 10 emails every day, crammed with information and content that does not appear in ARD, ZDF and the Süddeutsche Zeitung. I stopped reading the Spiegel many years ago but I quickly realise, through Jens Wernicke and the other alternative news sites, that it also takes part in the panic-mongering. I realise that I urgently need to form my own opinion and therefore I start to write more articles of my own on the Corona pandemic.

Who And What Can I Trust Right Now?

Sixth Article - 25th March 2020

I think that at this point in time a major issue for us is that of trust. Do I trust those who are issuing dire warnings of an extremely deadly and contagious virus or those who say that Covid-19 is pretty much the same as a flu epidemic? Do I have confidence in the restrictive measures that politicians are currently imposing in most countries or do I panic in light of the consequences that these measures are already having (loss of contact, financial hardship, lack of planning security for the near or possibly even distant future and much more)? Do I basically trust in what is promised from outside in the way of help or do I trust more in myself and my own powers of self-healing? In the meantime am I distrustful of any close physical contact or do I trust in our collective powers of self-healing? Do I have faith in the pure scientific rational world of facts and figures and statistics or do I trust my own intuition and emotional intelligence?

Do others trust me that I know and can feel what is best for me and what is not or do they feel that they have to control and supervise me?

Mistrust engenders fear, and only leads to more mistrust. Everyone knows this, everyone feels this. Mistrust makes us ill; it puts a strain on our relationships and poisons social interaction. Mutual trust is certainly the better way of protecting our health.

When We Come Into Contact With Someone Is It Really Only Pathogens That We Exchange?

In an interview yesterday with my IoPT colleague Marta Thorsheim from Norway, I expressed the hypothesis that through physical contact and also by sharing the air we breathe and direct skin contact, we may not only exchange harmful pathogens, but also beneficial information from within our immune system. The closer we get to each other, the more we could perhaps take on each other's successful immune strategies in dealing with pathogens. So if the person I am in contact with is already immunised against a pathogen this would mean that my immune system could benefit and learn from his in a similar way to a vaccination – and a completely natural form of vaccination at that – without any additives – and one for which we don't have to wait. This type of vaccination has been made for humans and has already been successfully tested on the human organism.

Mothers Immunise Their Children

We know that this is true for the mother-child relationship because it has already been well-researched. It is not only the case that the child receives food and oxygen from the mother whilst in her womb and then milk from her after birth, but he or she is also continually supplied with what the mother's immune system has learned about old and new pathogens. This happens before birth via the umbilical cord, during birth when the child passes through the vaginal birth canal and afterwards via skin-to-skin contact with the mother and through her breast milk (Gresens 2016).

Couples Infect Each Other With Good Information

When we kiss someone or hold their hands, surely it's not only germs that are transmitted? Those who stay together as a couple adapt their immune system to their partner and possibly benefit from his or her successful immune defence.

I suspect that this is why frequent changes of partners also lead to increased infections of the mucous membranes because a person's immune system has to cope with them on its own.

Career Choice And Immune Resilience

Furthermore, my assumption would be that people who work very closely in physical contact with others, i.e. doctors, physiotherapists, body therapists etc., have an immune system that is very well trained and can protect the person against infection as it quickly absorbs the immune defence information as it becomes known in the general population. After all, it would not make sense for a haemophiliac to take up a job as a butcher. He would not survive for long.

Our Pets

This mutual exchange of immune information must also exist in the relationship between humans and animals. We have been living here with our two cats for 10 years now and never has one of our cats become sick because of us, nor have we been infected by the germs that our cats carry into the house every day from their trips around the neighbourhood.

Wildlife And Covid-19

So does this mean that Covid-19 is so dangerous because it has managed to jump from a species of wild animal to humans? If we were all bats or pangolins, it couldn't hurt us. So the human species must now learn together to deal with Covid-19 and its mutations as successfully as the bats and pangolins do.

Again, it would be unwise to wait for each and every one of us to do this individually. In fact, that would take too many of us. We need a collective response to this now. If we all take refuge in panic and essentially climb a tree and sit up there on our own for weeks, we are then lacking the direct exchange of information about successful strategies to contain Covid-19 that could pass from human body to human body.

When Foreign Cultures Meet

Epidemics that are transmitted from person to person are therefore probably most likely to occur where one isolated group suddenly encounters another population and is then unable to counteract the pathogens with an immune response fast enough. This is apparently what happened when the Spaniards came into contact with the Aztecs, when the English, Irish and Germans met the native people of North America and the Aborigines in Australia.

A presumable precondition for the rapid dying away of the indigenous people was probably also that the group of conquerors was not willing to deal slowly and in friendship with those 'native' people who already lived there and to share the natural wealth with them.

Xenophobia

Perhaps this is where the deep-seated, unconscious distrust that we humans have towards strangers we do not yet know comes from, on the basis of 'are we able to deal with the germs that you bring with you? It's better that you keep your distance first and see what happens if we approach each other carefully enough and then see if the exchange of information between your and my immune system actually works'.

Being Alone

If a person isolates themselves up in their tree, not only will they not probably benefit from any 'herd immunity', but when they come back down into the community they will be at increased risk of being struck down by an overload of pathogens. A species of living creatures must already have a very robust and fast-reacting immune system in order to survive such a solitary existence in the long run.

Immune Defence Information Goes Viral

Since the immune system often reacts in cycles when dealing with viruses, it could be that I have to go through fewer cycles because I can already receive essential preliminary information from you. It is similar here to the exchange of thoughts and insights: not every one of us has to reinvent the wheel. It is enough if a realisation has come to us at the same time in different places in the world and already this realisation goes - especially today in times of the internet – 'viral'.

It seems conclusive to me that in this way not only the individual, but a whole population - and we humans are herd animals - can be protected against infection relatively quickly. If each individual had to do this on his or her own, it would probably take far too long. After all, new pathogens are springing up all the time.

Contact Instead Of Isolation

In practical terms, this would also mean, in the current situation, that isolation exacerbates the problem; it's not the solution. Good contact instead of isolation would be what's needed and could also be the secret of success in dealing with Covid-19. Anyone who has already learned something about this virus may be hours, days and weeks ahead of me in terms of their immune defences. And I can benefit from that.

People are going to die from Covid-19 right now. But that's true of all natural hazards and risks. We're going to have to deal with this emotionally. We can't be spared from the pain and grief by technical, administrative or pharmacological measures.

Special Solidarity

But we now know who the particularly vulnerable risk groups are and can show particular solidarity with them and give more attention to them than usual. But we do not have to force our aid on these people, however we must provide them with the best possible information. In most cases, their immune system will also find its most sensible response.

Questions To The Immunologists

When I first studied the topic of the immune system in 1992 (Münzing-Ruf 1991), I found it extremely exciting and had many 'light-bulb' moments. I am now curious to see what my colleagues in immunology will say in answer to my hypotheses and conclusions.

The projections and calculations that are currently being done here in relation to Covid-19 are essentially being done whilst ignoring the fundamental ingredient, namely the unimaginably meticulous human immune system itself. We can't therefore just look to virologists and pathologists alone to provide the right answers to the corona crisis. Here, we also need colleagues from immunology, psychology and, above all, salutogenesis – that medical approach that focuses on factors that support human health and well-being, rather than on factors that cause disease (pathogenesis).

I Trust My Immune System, Myself And The People

I have been living in close contact with people for 63 years now. When I made my first trip to North Africa in my student days, I was vaccinated as a precaution. Nevertheless, this didn't spare me a severe intestinal infection whilst I was on this trip. And when I got back home I found I had scabies. Today I travel around the world and have no major problems with infectious diseases, perhaps a good sign that we are already a closely networked world population, which also exchanges its immune defence information quickly.

So I will rather continue to trust my immune system and the immune system of my 'herd', in other words my fellow human beings, which has developed over thousands of years and which carries millions of pieces of information in itself, which probably not even the most powerful computer can manage to even approximately model. This system is extremely intelligent and capable of learning! What's that compared to a handful of people fiddling around in their laboratories to develop a vaccine? I, for one, am not placing all my hopes on that when it comes to my life and death and the life and death of those close to me.

Irrespective of whether my hypothesis of a collective immune system is true - that it is not only individual but systemically built up - there are many options to at least train and support the individual immune system in the context of the Corona crisis, instead of weakening it considerably through fear, aggression and stress.

Expanding Further On My Hypothesis

The idea of a collective immune system came to me because we humans like to be so close to each other and usually no problem arises from this. On the contrary, the problem is loneliness and isolation. In psychotherapy, I experience this again and again as one of the most traumatic feelings for a person, especially when he experiences this in his early childhood. But even as adults, it is only in exceptional circumstances that we feel good for a long period of time when we are completely on our own.

I'm going to throw in another idea: it is essential that the information is passed on from person to person, i.e. it would not even have to be large particles that are exchanged here. It may be that the information alone is enough to produce changes in the state of an organism. I experience this every day in the form of therapy I have developed, the Intention Method. Just asking someone to resonate with a certain word causes a very far-reaching change in the psychosomatic state of the person. At first this seems unbelievable and even exceeds my current capacity of imagination and explanation. But it works for all people that I work with the world over.

But as I said, these are for now only all hypotheses that immunologists could perhaps prove or even completely refute. At the moment, my main concern is to find arguments to put an end to the Corona induced panic state of emergency as quickly as possible, which has such incalculable consequences on the individual and collective level and is currently not only weakening the immune system of many individuals, but certainly also of the entire population. Seen in this light, perhaps this idea of a collective immune system is just a placebo, but even so it could still produce good effects in reality.

Shutdown Of The University

The university, where I have been employed as a professor of psychology since 1992, is also affected by the lockdown. At first it seemed to be only a postponement of the start of the semester, which was moved back from March 15th to April 20th. But then it turned out that all courses were cancelled and we were supposed to switch to a 'distanced learning' mode. The entire campus was declared a restricted area for the university staff and for the students. The campus and my own office could only be entered with the explicit permission of the university president. Those responsible for the running of this small but fine university now have their hands full day and night trying to explore, organise and regulate this new situation. I truly do not envy them this task and am grateful to them for making at least an emergency operation possible for the summer semester. This will not only cost enormous amounts of working time, but an unexpected and unplanned for almost half a million euros from the university budget for the purchase of digital platforms and faster and better servers.

Critical Discourse Becomes A Daring Endeavour

In my probably rather childish naivety I dared to send my first article about the 'Corona Madness Pandemic' to a college at the university, which is currently making a sincere effort to make the summer semester 2020 possible for the students despite the lockdown. I immediately receive an e-mail back from the President of our University saying that this could only be my private opinion and that:

> 'the non-pharmaceutical intervention currently underway to contain the risk of infection with the novel corona virus is receiving full support from the University'.

So does this mean that there are only two alternatives: the pharmaceutical interventions such as vaccinations and medications - and the non-pharmaceutical, just this overall social lockdown? Am I risking my job right now if I start a public discussion at a university that claims to be an opinion leader in social issues? Are they saying that they want no discussion of what is going on in society at the moment? Couldn't students learn a great deal from it about how our society works? How credible am I as a professor if I don't bring in my professional voice in such a situation and choose instead to just keep silent?

For my part, I immediately assure the President that this article is, of course, only my private opinion and give him my sincere appreciation that he is doing his best in the current crisis situation and is in a position of responsibility that now demands a lot of him.

If - as has become more and more apparent over the course of time – the dishonest narrative of the 'novel coronavirus' 'saving human lives', 'solidarity with the particularly threatened old and weak in society' has now already become the official motto, what do I, as a professor at a university for social services, want to object to?

Weeks later, in my first online lecture that took place on the 21st April 2020, I am asked by students whether I think the lockdown is justified and who might be interested in it. I refer to Bill Gates, and his mania for vaccination in relation to 7 billion people and the WHO. Shortly afterwards I received the following email from a student:

'Dear Mr Ruppert,
Thank you very much for your great lecture! I felt I had to get in touch with you directly, as I thought your words were great at the end. I respect you for having addressed the topic, including the financing of the WHO and the Bill Gates Foundation. We need people like you at this time. I really hope very much that some of the students will listen and also inform themselves with alternative views.
Thank you very much and see you next week.'

The reports that my students write about their internships in the following weeks show how massively social work is prevented by this social distancing policy and how their work now cannot provide effective help in social emergencies because direct client contact is not possible.

The (Nonsensical) Logic Of The Perpetrator–Victim–Rescuer Dynamic
Seventh Article – 27th March 2020

There is a treacherous logic in interpersonal relationships, namely that of the perpetrator-victim-rescuer dynamic. It is probably the worst thing that can happen to you in a relationship, in a family, in an institution or on a society-wide level. It is pure psychotrauma. The dynamic basically works like this: I, as the perpetrator, inflict severe damage on you, the victim. Then I come along and present myself as your rescuer and let you reward me for being your saviour.

There are countless examples of this:

- A parent may punish their child because of the child's sheer liveliness and joy. The mother or father then goes on to offer that the child does something in order to make up with them again. I experienced a particularly stark example of this in a therapy session: The client had in her childish joy and curiosity played with a bottle of her mother's perfume and had ended up spraying it over the wardrobe. When her mother saw what had happened she flipped out and stuck her daughter in a bath of scalding hot water. Then she offered her daughter, who was covered in burns, the opportunity to crochet some oven gloves with her so that mummy could feel happy about something again.
- When a father sexually traumatises his daughter he tells her that if she were to tell anyone no one would believe her. So she should be happy that she has him, otherwise she would be totally alone.
- A husband beats up his wife and then comforts her and then offers that if she sleeps with him then everything will be alright again.

- A psychiatrist declares that someone who is suffering from psychological problems is mentally unwell and then sells him drugs to help him recover. But these drugs then cause the patient further psychological and physical problems for which the psychiatrist then offers him more medicines to buy.
- A doctor, because of his interventions, destroys a pregnant woman's own confidence in her innate ability to give birth. The doctor delivers her child and then says that he has saved both her and her child's life. This of course costs a little bit more than a completely normal birth.
- One ruler declares war on another ruler, and in this way massively threatens the life and health of his people. He then demands that his people, for their own protection and in gratitude for his leadership, concentrate all their energies on this war and sacrifice their health and their lives for it.
- A security service spies on everything. It then sets up a company that gets paid handsomely to protect countries and businesses from being spied on. At the same time, it incorporates code into the protection software if offers, that delivers all of its customers' confidential data free to its door.
- A food company damages the population's health with its sugary and high-fat drinks. It then sets itself up as a pharmaceutical company and offers the solution to these health problems with its drugs.
- A supposedly impartial world health organisation declares that there is a virus pandemic. It dismantles entire societies and then offers its aid programmes to save humanity. It then receives handsome rewards from those societies for the vaccines it has developed.

The striking and twisted thing about this psychological dynamic is that the perpetrators manage to be perceived by their victims as their benefactors.

In these kind of situations, as long as a person accepts that the damage wreaked by a perpetrator is natural and inevitable, then that person is only concerned with trying to compensate for the consequences of the damage caused and for the consequences of that and for the consequences of that and so on for ever. In private, as well as in public or political life, a phase of ceaseless activity then begins. And anyone who takes part then becomes trapped in this perpetrator-victim-rescuer system and becomes exhausted in this endless fight against the symptoms. And it's possible that this can go on for someone's entire life.

The only way we can find a way out is by looking at the logic of the whole system. What is actually going on here? Who is playing what cruel game with whom?

In my experience it is not possible to get out of the perpetrator-victim-rescuer dynamic if the victim is still trying to battle with the perpetrator. It is enough to recognise and name them for what they are. This is possible if I pay attention to my intuitive emotional reactions, if I bring my common sense into play and if I am in contact with my basic needs. I can then immediately see, feel and recognise what is going wrong and who means the best for me and who means me harm. In this way, I no longer put myself at the mercy of others as a naive, unsuspecting victim who lacks his own 'I' or 'want'.

An important question is: what do the perpetrators actually want? My answer is: they want to escape their own inner chaos. Because they are not able to get a grip on their inner, trauma-induced chaos, they try instead to create order on the outside. This could be expressed as a mania for cleaning when it comes to a housewife or it could be a policeman who does everything in his power to keep law and order. The more political power or financial means someone has, the more this longing for order can make itself heard in society and assert itself in practice. Then it becomes something much more far-reaching than just a matter of meticulously tidying up the wardrobe. Then it can happen that someone wants to put the whole society or perhaps even the whole world in order. He sees himself entitled to enforce his idea of 'order', by violence if necessary. However, the more extreme someone becomes, the more he isolates himself from 'the others' and society in general and therefore also from his primal need for belonging and genuine contact. He puts himself on an ever-higher pedestal, feels strong and powerful and feels he is the only person who can implement his ideas, plans and projects. The people with whom he surrounds himself and with whom he forges alliances of supposed goodness are usually as detached from their feelings as he himself is. The higher the social climb, the greater the fall and therefore the fear of losing all his power again. As well as this, there is also always the fear of revenge from those whom he has wronged without a second thought in his ascent to power.

Another important question also comes up: do the perpetrators feel guilty when other people have to pay with their health or their lives because of the perpetrator's idea of order? It seems that yes of course they do, otherwise they would not try to hide the consequences of their actions, or to sugarcoat them. With the increasing number and intensity of perpetrator attitudes, however, they are moving even further away from themselves and from the community whose interests they think they are serving.

The effect of what the perpetrators do in a society is to sooner or later create even more chaos. As with any trauma survival strategy, the obsession with 'keeping order' is the sure path to new chaos. Therefore, trauma perpetrators never escape their inner chaos - no matter how many battles they fight or how many wars they win. Unfortunately, the majority of people in societies often suffer enormously from this, until they succeed in freeing themselves from a trauma perpetrator and all their willing accomplices.

They can only do this if they look to their own needs and express the feelings that come with them. By fighting purely on the cognitive level, they are usually inferior to the trauma perpetrators, especially since these are the ones who are sitting at the levers of power.

The Original Health Ideal Of The WHO

Since the importance of the World Health Organization (WHO) in this pandemic is becoming more and more apparent to me, I have started studying it more closely. When the WHO was founded in 1946, it was on the basis of the following constitution:

'Health is a state of complete physical, mental and social well-being and not merely the absence of disease or infirmity. The enjoyment of the highest attainable standard of health is one of the fundamental rights of every human being without distinction of race, religion, political belief, economic or social condition. The health of all peoples is fundamental to the attainment of peace and security and is dependent upon the fullest co-operation of individuals and States. The achievement of any State in the promotion and protection of health is of value to all. Unequal development in different countries in the promotion of health and control of disease, especially communicable disease, is a common danger. Healthy development of the child is of basic importance; the ability to live harmoniously in a changing total environment is essential to such development. The extension to all peoples of the benefits of medical, psychological and related knowledge is essential to the fullest attainment of health. Informed opinion and active co-operation on the part of the public are of the utmost importance in the improvement of the health of the people. Governments have a responsibility for the health of their peoples which can be fulfilled only by the provision of adequate health and social measures.'[24]

This constitution is still valid today. In 1946, WHO was still a supranational association promoting global goals, just like the United Nations (UN). Under the impact of the madness of the Second World War, the states on this earth obviously wanted to come to their senses and put aside their mutual conflicts in favour of common goals such as peace and health. A general prohibition of violence is laid down in Article 2.4 of the Charter of the United Nations and prohibits the member states from the use of military

---

[24] https://apps.who.int/gb/bd/PDF/bd47/EN/constitution-en.pdf?ua=1 (retrieved 24/07/20)

force: 'All Members shall refrain in their international relations from the threat or use of force against the territorial integrity or political independence of any state, or in any other manner inconsistent with the Purposes of the United Nations.'[25]

Of course, this was too good to be true! The UN quickly became, like many before it, a body in which those with the most power and financial resources dictated their interests to others. 'The five permanent members (France, Russia, the United States, the People's Republic of China and the United Kingdom) have an extended power of veto in the passing of resolutions and are therefore referred to as veto powers.'[26]

The nuclear powers USA, USSR (today Russia), France, Great Britain and China are therefore more equal than the other 188 states on earth.

Under this condition, wars were and are still possible, since one of the veto powers can always vote against it even if the rest of the world does not approve of a warlike conflict. The Third World War was therefore able to unfold as a confrontation between the two superpowers, the USA and the USSR, immediately after the end of the Second World War and found and still finds its expression in proxy wars, among others in Indochina, Cuba, Vietnam, Israel, Chile, Nicaragua, Afghanistan, Ukraine, Libya and currently in Syria, because the two superpowers justifiably shy away from a direct exchange of blows with their nuclear weapons. If they did that there would be no winner, only scorched and contaminated earth. The very construction of such weapons is evidence of how confused, and according to my theory - because of how traumatised, the people who would do something like this are. After all, they are digging their own graves.

The WHO Becomes Increasingly Privatised

The WHO has also changed fundamentally from when it was founded until now. One of the main reasons was the gradual withdrawal of the USA from joint trans-national funding, as this opened the doors to financiers with their own interests, who could now make use of the still good reputation of this institution.

---

[25] https://www.un.org/en/sections/un-charter/un-charter-full-text/ (retrieved 24/07/20)

[26] https://en.wikipedia.org/wiki/United_Nations_Security_Council_veto_power (retrieved 24/07/20)

'The Organisation is financed through two main channels: the fixed compulsory contributions of its 194 Member States and voluntary contributions. The level of the compulsory contributions is based on the degree of prosperity of the Member State and its population. Since 1993, the level of these contributions has been frozen - over the years their share of the organisation's total budget has steadily decreased and is now, according to the organisation, about a quarter.

More than 75 per cent of the WHO's resources are therefore obtained from voluntary contributions. A large proportion of this is earmarked for a specific purpose and flows into specific areas of activity of the organisation. These contributions, unlike mandatory contributions, come from both member states and other organisations - such as the GAVI Vaccine Alliance, the World Bank, Rotarians International, and the Bill and Melinda Gates Foundation - one of the largest donors.

For the period 2018-2019, the World Health Organization's approved two-year budget was more than US$4.4 billion. The largest contributor - measured by the sum of compulsory and voluntary contributions - was the United States, which was responsible for just under 15 percent of the payments during this period. The Bill and Melinda Gates Foundation was the second largest donor with just under 10 percent, followed by the GAVI vaccine alliance (8.4 percent), Great Britain (7.8 percent) and Germany (5.67 percent).

Most of the funds went to programs to eradicate polio, improve access to health and nutrition systems, and the vaccine prevention of disease.'[27]

The WHO provide a detailed list of their funding sources on their website, which can be found here[28]. As the Bill and Melinda Gates Foundation is also behind the GAVI (Global Alliance for Vaccines and Immunisation) and owns shares in the big pharmaceutical

---

[27] The original German website referenced is here:
https://www.tagesschau.de/faktenfinder/who-finanzierung-101.html - an English language website setting out the same information can be found here:
https://www.weforum.org/agenda/2020/04/who-funds-world-health-organization-un-coronavirus-pandemic-covid-trump/ (retrieved 24/7/20)
[28] https://open.who.int/2018-19/contributors/contributor (retrieved 24/7/20)

companies and food producers, the WHO is clearly weighted in the direction of the interests of the pharmaceutical industry and its global players like Novartis, Pfizer, Hoffmann-La Roche, Sanofi, MSD, Johnson & Johnson, GlaxoSmithKline etc.[29]

Medical Doctor Bernd Hontschik now considers the WHO to be quite corrupt:

> 'The WHO still denies the terrible health effects of the disasters of Chernobyl and Fukushima. Secret treaties with the International Atomic Energy Agency IAEA in Vienna came to light, in which the WHO was obliged to maintain silence so that it would not disrupt the use of nuclear energy.
>
> But that was not all. Already in the case of the bird flu in 2005, the WHO predicted a worldwide epidemic with at least seven million deaths, and also in the case of the swine flu in 2009, the WHO declared what was this rather harmless infectious disease to be a worldwide pandemic of the very highest danger level. This led to a grandiose market success of ineffective flu drugs and superfluous flu vaccinations all over the world, which were later quietly and silently burned in combined heat and power plants. Before joining the WHO, the then Director of the WHO Vaccine Department was employed by the French pharmaceutical company Transgene, which had partnerships for vaccine production with the Swiss pharmaceutical company Roche.
>
> Another WHO Director of Vaccines joined the Swiss pharmaceutical company Novartis in 2007. Lobbying is as simple as that. In contrast, the WHO looked away for a long, long time, far too long, during the Ebola epidemic in poverty-stricken West Africa in 2014. Because there was nothing to earn there, no medicine and no vaccine were available. Step by step, the WHO lost its credibility.'[30]

Health, which was once very broadly defined in the constitution of the WHO, is, in this way, increasingly reduced to just the medical-biological model of infectious diseases: there are pathogens which must be combated with vaccines and medicines. The self-healing activities of the body's own immune system; the psychological,

---

[29] https://en.wikipedia.org/wiki/Pharmaceutical_industry (retrieved 24/7/20)
[30] https://www.fr.de/panorama/vorsicht-10962409.html (retrieved 24/07/20) In German

social, economic, nutritional and environmental factors that decisively determine a person's state of health can be radically ignored. From now on, large amounts of money are to be invested in the prevention of infections and the research and distribution of vaccines, as if the well-being of the whole of humanity depended on a handful of viruses. Are we all to become junkies waiting on a vaccination needle?

New Definition Of What A Pandemic Is By The WHO

To this end, the definition of a pandemic was changed, meaning that, among other things, a pandemic can be declared immediately, and without a further risk assessment of its consequences, solely based on if infections are present. This came about because of the disaster with the so-called swine flu (H1N1), and the rejection of the criticism of this change by the Robert Koch Institute on August 2, 2010 confirms the suspicion that, from the pint of view of the WHO, pandemics and vaccines are essentially and fundamentally linked and should continue to be linked: 'The accusation that the World Health Organization changed the pandemic phases so that it could declare a pandemic is not true. Even according to the epidemiological criteria of previous pandemics it is a pandemic (see the question 'Was pandemic influenza 2009 a pandemic?'). Measures must be taken against such a pathogen and, *in particular, a vaccine must be offered to the population quickly*, regardless of phase definitions'[31]. As if there were no alternative to vaccination in response to infection.

However, the WHO's views must be incorporated into national and regional legislation. The Bavarian Influenza Pandemic Framework Plan, for example, is very closely based on the WHO guidelines:

'A pandemic refers to a worldwide epidemic. Influenza pandemic is caused by a new type of influenza virus. Since this new pathogen has not previously been present in the human population or has not been present for a very long

---

[31] https://www.rki.de/SharedDocs/FAQ/Pandemie/FAQ20.html (retrieved 24/07/20) In German. Some Information from the Robert Koch Institute does appear in English here: https://www.rki.de/EN/Home/homepage_node.html (retrieved 21/08/20)

time, the immune system is not prepared. And this means that the human being is therefore not protected. Pandemics can thus lead to increased morbidity and mortality rates, which are many times higher than the rates of annual influenza waves. They could thus lead to extreme burdens on the medical care system and the public health service and even pose a considerable threat to public order and the functioning of the entire national economy. [...]

General measures aim to contain the dynamics of infection by reducing social contacts in the general population or in specific groups of people. They can be considered - alone or in addition to individual measures - to counteract the spread of influenza by still healthy or only slightly ill persons. By their very nature, they are accompanied by major restrictions on public life, sometimes have considerable economic or organisational consequences, may conflict with fundamental rights and are therefore reserved exclusively for situations where less drastic measures are not sufficient. Affected are, for example, events or major events (e.g. cultural, sporting or political events, markets, public festivals), which can be restricted, prohibited or subject to infection-minimising requirements. Fundamental rights affected are freedom of opinion, artistic freedom, freedom of occupation; in the case of political events - also freedom of assembly. The closure of public or private institutions in which a larger number of people come together is also possible. [...]

The possibility of vaccinating the population in the event of a pandemic with a novel influenza virus is a key protective measure of any modern pandemic planning. Against the background of the technical framework conditions for the production of a pandemic vaccine, several months are to be expected between the WHO recommendation and the comprehensive delivery of the vaccine by the manufacturer. This must be taken into account in the conceptual planning for coping with a pandemic. The aim is to ensure the vaccine supply for those parts of the population for which vaccination is recommended as soon as possible'. [32]

---

[32] https://www.stmgp.bayern.de/wp-content/uploads/2020/02/influenza-bayern.pdf (retrieved 10/05/20) In German

The importance of this document is to show everyone who reads it that in spring 2020 with SARS-CoV-2 everything was indeed done right, but it is based on the highly questionable logic of the WHO: novel pathogen, no self-immunisation of the population possible, therefore protective vaccination as the main route out of the pandemic is the primary goal. And, of course, to show that this ominous SARS-CoV-2 is supposedly not an influenza virus at all, but something completely different, for whatever reasons.

Even experienced family doctors cannot distinguish between corona and influenza viruses because no tests are normally carried out: Here's an example from the Saar News Programme (a regional news network from the West of Germany) when the editorial team put a question to a local GP, Dr. Zimmer:

'Saar News: What is the difference between this and a normal influenza flu?

Zimmer: Normally it is impossible to tell the difference, patients come to the practice with so-called respiratory diseases, everyone knows that, i.e. with cough, fever, sniffles, sore throat, and we cannot, for reasons of cost alone, because we are budgeted, carry out all the tests.' [33]

In plain language: The pandemic is being declared on the basis of 'well-founded ignorance' of the corona virus SARS-CoV-2!' [34]

As Soon As There's One Pandemic – There'll Be More And More Pandemics

However, the WHO has long since moved on in its thinking. It makes no difference whether it is an influenza or corona pandemic - the main thing is that it's a pandemic:

'WHO today released a Global Influenza Strategy for 2019-2030 aimed at protecting people in all countries from the

---

[33] https://deutungsvielfalt.de/2020/05/07/saarnews-dr-ernst-zimmer-es-wird-keine-zweite-welle-geben/ (retrieved 11/05/20) In German

[34] https://spitzen-praevention.com/2020/05/12/corona-ist-weder-harmlos-noch-die-pestilenz-wie-wohltuend-wenn-fakten-auf-den-tisch-gelegt-werden/ (retrieved 12/05/20) In German

threat of influenza. The goal of the strategy is to prevent seasonal influenza, control the spread of influenza from animals to humans, and prepare for the next influenza pandemic.

"The threat of pandemic influenza is ever-present," said WHO Director-General Dr Tedros Adhanom Ghebreyesus. "The on-going risk of a new influenza virus transmitting from animals to humans and potentially causing a pandemic is real. The question is not if we will have another pandemic, but when. We must be vigilant and prepared – the cost of a major influenza outbreak will far outweigh the price of prevention."'

The WHO's objective is also clearly stated: To monitor people and produce medicines and vaccines for the world.

'The new strategy is the most comprehensive and far-reaching that WHO has ever developed for influenza. It outlines a path to protect populations every year and helps prepare for a pandemic through strengthening routine programmes. It has two overarching goals:

1. Build stronger country capacities for disease surveillance and response, prevention and control, and preparedness. To achieve this, it calls for every country to have a tailored influenza programme that contributes to national and global preparedness and health security.
2. Develop better tools to prevent, detect, control and treat influenza, such as more effective vaccines, antivirals and treatments, with the goal of making these accessible for all countries."[35]

There can be no clearer statement as to what the 2020 corona pandemic will be good for in the long term. In my view, the WHO is in the process of turning the world into a hell and should be rechristened the World Hell Organisation.

---

[35] https://www.who.int/news-room/detail/11-03-2019-who-launches-new-global-influenza-strategy (retrieved 24/7/20)

The idea behind this is also to produce a universal vaccine for all influenza viruses so that we don't have to search for a more or less effective vaccination every year:

> 'Against the background of SARS and MERS, the German government, under the leadership of the Robert Koch Institute, had the worst-case scenario for a pandemic in Germany simulated in 2012: "Modi-SARS". In this simulation, a virus introduced from Asia spreads uncontrolled in Germany and leads to a peak of up to four million people falling ill at the same time.
>
> Although this risk analysis represents a so-called maximum scenario caused by a fictitious pathogen, the real probability of pandemics increases with the increasing destruction of ecosystems and biodiversity.
>
> Rolf Hilgenfeld sees reacting to this as part of a state welfare system.
>
> "We should examine all RNA viruses known to us," he demands. "We should detect unknown ones, sequence them. We should elucidate the structures of some of the key enzymes of these RNA viruses and for each key enzyme, for each virus family, we should develop a drug that we have on the shelf. And when it is ready, it will be quickly brought into testing and produced in large quantities, which would save us years of basic research. This of course costs a lot of money and is a governmental task. It's part of the public service.'[36]

But this is all on the basis that mankind only has this one concern, how do we prevent an outbreak of flu! For this goal, which is coming with a myriad of unproven assumptions, and only starts from an unproven hypothesis that such a vaccine could even be found in the first place, means that catastrophic damage for the entire world population in real terms is accepted. In return, the vaccination industry will plunder the national coffers and the participating states are expected to embark on psychological warfare against their own populations.

---

[36] https://www.deutschlandfunkkultur.de/impfstoffe-der-zukunft-wettlauf-im-kampf-gegen-kommende.976.de.html?dram:article_id=480235 (retrieved 10/07/20) In German

WHO, The G20 And Germany

The WHO's plans are being promoted by Germany at both an international and national level. On 1st December 2016, Germany took on the presidency of the 'G20', (the association of the 20 leading industrialized and emerging countries) for one year. In the first meeting of the G20 health ministers in Berlin on 19 May 2017, the two-day meeting focused on combating global health threats under the banner 'Together Today for a Healthy Tomorrow - Joint Commitment for Shaping Global Health'.

At this meeting 'Federal Minister of Health Hermann Gröhe said, "Dangerous diseases and germs against which antibiotics are ineffective do not stop at national borders. They cause untold human suffering. And they can dramatically set back the social, economic and political development of countries. The fact that we have put the fight against cross-border health threats on the G20 agenda is an important milestone for global health. After all, the G20 represents two thirds of the world's population and three quarters of world trade. Only together can we stand up to global health crises".

In order to be better prepared for future health crises, the G20 health ministers, together with representatives of the World Health Organization (WHO) and the World Bank, will test the emergency response to a cross-border disease outbreak at the meeting. In 'Anycountry', a model low-income country, a fatal respiratory disease breaks out and threatens to spread worldwide. During the crisis exercise, the flow of information and decision-making processes are put to the test. How can it be ensured that dangerous outbreaks are reported promptly by the affected countries? How can international aid be provided more quickly? What can the G20 do to quickly contain global health crises? And how can the World Health Organization be strengthened?

Germany is committed to further strengthening the WHO. For the WHO has a key role to play in managing global health crises. This is also the purpose of the Contingency Fund for Emergencies (CFE), which was set up in 2015 and to which Germany is the largest contributor with 13 million dollars. In addition, in 2017, for the first time, there will be a separate contribution from the budget of the Federal Ministry of Health amounting to 35 million euro as a voluntary additional contribution to WHO. In addition, the BMG provides support in the form of experts in crisis situations on site as part of the Global Health Program and provides assistance in the prevention of disease outbreaks'.[37]

Roadmap On Vaccinations For Europe

At the European level, too, a sophisticated strategy has been in place since 2018 to make global mass vaccination practically and ideologically possible[38]. There are then the following goals:

- Electronic vaccination cards: 'Examine the feasibility of developing a common vaccination card/passport for EU citizens (that takes into account potentially different national vaccination schedules) and that is compatible with electronic immunisation information systems and recognised for use across borders, without duplicating work at national level'.
- Convincing people to get vaccinated: 'Produce on a regular basis a Report on the State of Vaccine Confidence in the EU, to monitor attitudes to vaccination. Based on that report and taking into account related work by WHO, present guidance that can support Member States in countering vaccine hesitancy'.
- Build immunisation coalitions: 'Convene a Coalition for Vaccination to bring together European associations of healthcare workers as well as relevant students' associations in the field, to commit to delivering accurate information to the public, combating myths and exchanging best practice. Convened in March 2019, follow-up meeting in September 2019'.
- Vaccination for all: 'Identify barriers to access and support interventions to increase access to vaccination for disadvantaged and socially excluded groups, including by promoting health mediators and grassroots community networks, in line with national recommendations'.
- Electronic monitoring systems for immunity certificates: 'Develop EU guidance for establishing comprehensive electronic

---

[37] https://www.bundesgesundheitsministerium.de/presse/pressemitteilungen/2017/2-quartal/g20-gesundheitsministertreffen.html (retrieved 01/07/20) In German
[38] https://ec.europa.eu/health/sites/health/files/vaccination/docs/2019-2022_roadmap_en.pdf (retrieved 21/07/20)

immunization information systems for effective monitoring of immunization programmes'.

- Constant research on vaccines: 'Continue to support research and innovation through the EU framework programmes for Research and Innovation for the development of safe and effective new vaccines, and the optimisation of existing vaccines'.

- Forging vaccination alliances: 'Strengthen existing partnerships and collaboration with international actors and initiatives, such as the WHO and its Strategic Advisory Group of Experts on Immunization (SAGE), the European Technical Advisory Group of Experts on Immunization (ETAGE), the Global Health Security Initiative and Agenda processes (Global Health Security Initiative, Global Health Security Agenda), Unicef and financing and research initiatives like GAVI, CEPI, GloPID-R and JPIAMR (the Joint Programming Initiative on Antimicrobial Resistance)'.

- Stop vaccination criticism: 'Counter online vaccine misinformation and develop evidence-based information tools and guidance to support Member States in responding to vaccine hesitancy, in line with the Commission Communication on tackling online disinformation'.

- Financial support for the vaccination industry: 'Consider, jointly with stakeholders, in particular with the vaccine-manufacturing industry, which has a key role in meeting these aims, possibilities for improving EU manufacturing capacity, ensuring continuity of supply and ensuring diversity of suppliers'.

- Psychologically evaluate the opponents to vaccination: 'Consider investing in behavioural and social science research on the determinants of vaccine hesitancy across different subgroups of the population and healthcare workers'.

Germany, together with France, plays an essential role in this vaccination alliance. In their national budgets, it seems that there is money allocated for those who participate in this vaccine alliance and this is the means by which this madness is funded. It is therefore no coincidence that Angela Merkel has already made the decision in advance that the pandemic will only be over when a vaccine against 'Corona' is available. Macron has also sided with the vaccine alliance in drastic words and declared war on the virus: 'Nous sommes en guerre!'[39]

Donald Trump, who is not playing this game, will be opposed by this alliance. With his eccentric personality, it is easy to mobilise people against him, at least in Europe, as the 'spontaneous' demonstrations 'Black Lives Matter' have shown. Here, for example, in Munich, there were no restrictive conditions for the gathering of 25,000 people, in contrast to the restrictions imposed on any demonstrations which were critical of the pandemic.

The Paradoxical Logic Of Possibility

The very logic of the pandemic definition that says there is the possibility that a pathogen could be dangerous, without already knowing how dangerous it is and to what extent it could be dangerous, puts those who initiate the proclamation of a pandemic case in an almost insoluble dilemma. They are taking measures which are in fact only justified in the event of a disaster and which cause considerable social damage. The longer they maintain this situation of a pandemic, the more psychological, social, financial, legal and ethical damage will occur. And so they have to justify what they are doing all the more and have difficulty in withdrawing without losing face and without the risk of being held liable for the damage caused. The proclamation of disaster becomes a disaster in itself. A pandemic definition of this kind is therefore a contradiction in terms and should be reconsidered as a matter of urgency.

I fear, however, that this pandemic definition by the WHO is what the WHO wants, so that it can then use the damage caused to extol 'redemption by vaccine' as the final argument in the fight against the pandemic.

Viruses - Reality And Ideology

Dieter Storl has written a wonderful educational article about viruses on his website. Among other things he writes that:

'even in early evolution, in the primordial ocean, viruses existed. Like other biomolecules, they were integrated into

---

[39] https://www.google.com/search?client=firefox-b-d&q=nous+sommes+en+guerre (retrieved 01/08/20)

the cells of organisms as endosymbionts[40]. At least 20% of our human genome has a viral origin, explains microbiologist Patrick Forterre of the Pasteur Institute in Paris. In ancient times, viruses infected us, introduced their genetic material into our chromosomes and became part of the human genome. Researchers suspect that viruses in the brain cells even influence our thinking and feeling. The cells of all living organisms have mutated under the influence of the viruses. The structure of the DNA [2] (double helix) was invented by the viruses. According to the French virologist Thierry Heidmann, the 'mutilated' viral genes present in our genome help to protect our cells from other viruses that attack from outside. Viruses are our evolutionary sparring partners, they advanced our evolution.'[41]

The reductionist view of conventional medicine can be clearly seen when it comes to viruses. There are an estimated 80 billion viruses present in a human organism. Most of them have useful functions and make an important contribution to the development of more complex organisms. They are an essential driving force of evolution.[42] So to define individual viruses as 'enemies' of mankind therefore seems somewhat presumptuous and arises from the hubris of human thinking that it can place itself above evolution with conventional medical means such as the mass vaccination of all humans. This is not only stupid, but fundamentally hostile to life. In addition, agribusiness and mass animal production create situations that are an ideal breeding ground for bacteria and viruses to spread and multiply rapidly in populations of homogeneous living beings. This is supported rather than critically questioned by veterinary medicine too. You could almost say that, in the Corona pandemic, us humans are being treated more from a veterinary medicine rather than a human medicine point of view.

Where vaccinations against pathogens have been proven to have a positive effect, as evidenced by scientific studies, there would be no

---

[40] An endosymbiont is any organism that lives within the body or cells of another organism most often, though not always, in a mutualistic relationship. (Wikipedia)
[41] https://www.storl.de/gesundheit-phytotherapie/die-krone-der-viren/ (retrieved 03/07/20) In German
[42] https://www.youtube.com/watch?v=w0DMuH44h1Y (retrieved 22/04/20) In German

objection to them (Bakdhi and Reiss 2016). People in their healthy parts would certainly not object to this.

I Am A Layman When It Comes To Virology

A visit to the homepage of Dr. Wolfgang Wodarg makes it clear to me once again how much of a layman I am in the field of virology and how complex the processes are by which viruses are created in an organism and how they continuously mutate in all directions. It also makes it clear to me how unreliable a virus test is. I am now all the more surprised how many people think they are virus experts and know for a fact that this one corona virus is completely new, highly infectious and a serial killer that can be clearly detected by a test and can ultimately only be dealt with by a vaccination. Dr. Wodarg writes this about the corona pandemic:

> 'Everything is initiated by a dilapidated test, hasty measures and a blind trust in some nano part of the evolutionary machine nature, which is digitised in the gene databases and not justified by anything. Science and the politicians believing that advice will have to continue to pursue their self-made crisis. Although it is very doubtful that a virus that causes no (!) symptoms in 50 - 70% of infected people had arrived in Europe at the exact time the tests were started, as some now want to make us believe with the help of the curves for excess mortality. And this in a patient population in which 40% of intensive care patients came directly from the nursing home to the ICU in need of the most intensive care'.[43]

I can strongly recommend studying Dr. Wodarg's website to anyone who wants to learn more about this. Some of his key articles also appear in English.

The Ideology Of 'Mental Illness'

What I do know more about, however, are psychological phenomena. And from my point of view, the World Health Organization (WHO) does not take a very progressive position in the field of the psyche. It still publishes the 'International Classification of Mental Disorders', currently in its 10th edition (Dilling, Mombour

---

[43] https://www.wodarg.com/krieg-gegen-einen-joker/war-against-a-joker-english/ (retrieved 01/08/20)

& Schmidt 1993). In it, conspicuous features in the behaviour and experience of people are bundled into symptom groups, given an overall title and then listed as mental illnesses. No effort is made to show causal connections, only detailed descriptions of symptoms are given.

In this way mental abnormalities are generally transported into an area of human existence that is made difficult to understand – in other words, some people are just like that. Even when it comes to a cause-related diagnosis such as 'post-traumatic stress disorder' (ICD 10, F 43.1), the approach is ultimately only used to include this as a sub- and special form of mental illness. Here, too, the thrust of the approach is clear. Anyone who is diagnosed as mentally ill is a case for medicine and therefore should receive medical measures, essentially anti-psychotic drugs, as the standard treatment. Once started, many people get stuck with them and end up as chronically mentally ill.

Unfortunately, traumatised people who do not want to admit their own victimhood share this reduced view of orthodox medicine. This can then, without contradiction, on the part of the trauma victims, make the medical industry billions of dollars in profits and they of course have a vested interest in spreading this false awareness of mental health and illness.

This is a striking example of how trauma victims and trauma perpetrators share a kind of quasi- innocence. Both are apparently concerned with a higher good, people's health. Accustomed to living separately from their own bodies and in treating them like objects, the assaults by doctors and medical assistants are not experienced as violence and an obstacle to a person's own self-healing, but are instead welcomed by those affected. According to the logic well known in IoPT, the perpetrators appear as saviours and those that call out the perpetrators as perpetrators are made out to be the perpetrators themselves or at least are considered not quite sane and are those in need of psychiatric help. I have already experienced this myself when I was subjected to heavy attack from the pharmaceutical lobby in 2002 after the publication of my psychiatry-critical book 'Confused Souls'.

Surviving in the Asylum
Eighth Article – 28th March 2020

'The Asylum' (Die Anstalt) is a German Political Satire show on the TV channel ZDF, which I love very much because I like to laugh and I like good jokes. And what 'The Asylum' offers is well-researched, witty, humorous, truth telling, which is not often heard otherwise in such a big public medium. The topic of the show is now of course 'Corona' and to comply with the situation it is currently coming from the home offices of the two main actors Klaus von Wagner and Max Uthoff and their comrades-in-arms. It was very imaginative, had many good punch lines and some of it was hilarious. But then there was something shocking. Dr. Wodarg, for me a voice of reason in this sea of panic, was mentioned and then, by below the belt means, he was chastised as an irrelevant lunatic. I couldn't believe it and again it brought up the question in me: who can be trusted, who is still 'normal' and who is already infected by this virus mania?

The next day I wrote to the main people responsible for this show:

Dear Mr von Wagner and Mr Uthoff,

I'm always happy when a new episode of 'The Asylum' comes on. It always takes on very relevant topics that are important to society and gets to the heart of all the connections (e.g. when it was about housing and rent - simply ingenious) and it's also often so funny that I almost fall off my chair. In short: satire and comedy at its best.

At the beginning of the show on Corona I was very impressed. Many good arguments and punch lines.

When you also brought Dr. Wodarg into play, I was happy and excited. But how you then discredited this person, I found deeply shocking:

- He's got long hair: he should go to the hairdresser
- He's already retired: so he's an old bastard, with nothing more to say
- He's insignificant: in addition to that you leave out his Dr. title

- He was with the SPD[44]: therefore belongs to a minority
- He's been disproved: but you don't tell us where and how
- He was head of a health department when a fake doctor registered there, so he has not got a grip on his business, he lets fake doctors loose on mankind.

My spirits were in the dumps afterwards. I wouldn't have expected you to treat a person below the belt like that.

In this case I find it especially serious, because you are doing with it what is done in all instances of war propaganda (in brackets I compare it to the situation before the 2nd Iraq war):

- We have a designated enemy: the virus. (Saddam Hussein)
- This enemy is extremely dangerous: a new type of virus so devious that it doesn't even show itself and then suddenly it will strike and destroy us all (Saddam Hussein and his alleged weapons of mass destruction and anthrax)
- We've got shocking images of how cruel the enemy is: People lie helpless in overcrowded hospital corridors, the military removes the corpses (re-enacted pictures of people allegedly terribly injured and killed by poison gas, soldiers allegedly dragging small children from their beds and throwing them on the ground)
- We must act immediately, the threat situation does not allow any more delay (bombing of Baghdad...)
- Anyone who doubts our story is a conspiracy theorist who has lost his marbles. He is shunted to the sidelines both personally and professionally (e.g. a peace researcher like Daniele Ganser is then no longer employed by his university).

It's like war propaganda. But during the Iraq war it was clear what interests the USA were pursuing. With Corona this is not yet so public. I suspect that those who now want to sell their drugs and vaccines to the governments of this world have a part to play.

I am enclosing some articles I have written during the Corona crisis.

I look forward to your reply.

With best regards
Franz Ruppert

Dr. Wodarg addressed the public once again on 13th April 2020 with a thirty minute statement on the corona

---

[44] The Social Democratic Party of Germany is one of the two major contemporary political parties in Germany along with the Christian Democratic Union of Germany. https://en.wikipedia.org/wiki/Social_Democratic_Party_of_Germany (retrieved 20/08/20)

pandemic via his homepage. He seemed to me to be extremely competent and credible.[45]

---

[45] https://www.wodarg.com/ (retrieved 13/04/20)

Vaccines To Save Humanity?

The research and production of vaccines and medicines is not altruistic, but is based on the profits of those who produce and distribute them. From the outset, national states are the main addressees of this business policy, because only they can support such extensive research with their financial resources. There is no private demand for vaccinations among the general public. Therefore, the states have to buy the products from the vaccine manufacturers at whatever price they set. Whether these products are then actually needed and whether they are administered to people by compulsory vaccination is another question. The vaccine manufacturers may be indifferent to this. They have already made their profit by selling them. Now it is up to the states what they do with them. Back in 2010, for example, vaccines, for the declared Swine Flu pandemic, that had cost Germany 130 million euros, ended up being burned.

'The pandemic was declared over in August 2010. The vaccination programme cost about 1.3 billion euros in Great Britain and 990 million euros in France. An average influenza season costs 87 million euros. As only one dose was needed for vaccination instead of two, as initially assumed, and because of the low vaccination take-up rate, approximately 29 million vaccine doses remained unused in Germany. The health insurance companies only covered the costs for the doses actually injected, thus causing a financial loss of 245 million Euros for the federal states. The expiry date of the vaccine was set at the end of 2011 and it could no longer be used. For this reason, the states destroyed about 12.7 million vaccine doses. Another 16 million doses, stored centrally, were also incinerated.

Switzerland sold 750,000 doses of Celtura to Iran at the beginning of 2010, and another 150,000 doses were distributed free of charge. It also gave away about a tenth of its Pandemrix order to the WHO. 2.5 million vaccine doses had been used, 8.7 million vaccine doses worth 56 million Swiss francs were destroyed by the end of 2011[46]'.

---

[46] The German article detailing the costs & wastage associated with the Swine Flu Vaccine can be found here: https://de.wikipedia.org/wiki/Schweinegrippe-Impfung

This extremely one-sided programme to save the world by giving humanity vaccinations contains so many contradictions that it can only be realised with a great deal of political power and violence. The question is how best to do this. It can't be revealed, of course, that this is all in the name of the selfish interests of the vaccine and drug manufacturers and based on personal interest. So it must be made out to be in the name of something else that can be designated a common good and make sense to the population or can be gradually brought to the attention of the broad mass of people as something good.

Humanity has already been ideologically appropriated under many pretexts:

- In the name of God Almighty
- In the name of the King
- In the name of freedom
- In the name of communism
- In the name of the nation and the people
- In the name of world peace and the fight against terrorism

And now…

- In the name of immunisation health.

Vaccination And Population Control - A Pet Project Of The Moneyed Aristocracy

In his KenFM daily dose on 9th April 2020 Hermann Ploppa talked about the connections between:

- The American moneyed-aristocracy
- The eugenics ideologies of these elites vis-à-vis supposedly inferior sections of the population
- And vaccination programmes in Africa and India, which are linked to sterilisation.

(retrieved 27/7/20) -The associated English page
https://en.wikipedia.org/wiki/2009_swine_flu_pandemic_vaccine has different information to the German page omitting the financial costs and wastage but detailing the adverse effects of the vaccine.

The racism and heartlessness of these are almost incomprehensible. Ploppa calls for such ideas and practices not to be allowed to undermine the constitutional state in Europe too[47]. But the detailed planners, strategists and makers of such madness will always insist that the whole thing has good intentions and is for the good of all.

To get personal here: even if a patron means well, it doesn't mean I should invite him to run my life. This reminds me of my traumatised grandmother, who generously provided us children with sweets and cakes to make herself popular with us. We ended up with tooth decay and cavities and had to go to the dentist from an early age, who filled the holes in our ailing teeth with amalgam fillings.

---

[47] https://kenfm.de/tagesdosis-9-5-2019-wir-haben-noch-die-wahl-neo-feudalismus-oder-verfassungsdemokratie/ (retrieved 10/05/20)

Can This Really Be True?

Ninth article – 28th March 2020

1. In 1975 a young nerd called Bill Gates starts to revolutionise the computer industry. He sets up Microsoft and buys up all the state of the art software available at the time. This gradually makes him the richest man in the world and the world becomes dependent on his Microsoft software.

2. The company GOOGLE creates the necessary conditions for a global information network. Information itself is now sold and becomes a world commodity for the 20th and 21st centuries. It enters into competition with the previous global commodities - steel, coal & oil. The old patriarchal industrial magnates and those quick-on-the-draw old-timer oil company bosses are gradually retiring and the smart sneaker-wearing CEO's of the software companies are dominating the world stage and see themselves as the future. They are the new super billionaires.

3. Since 2007 a new world currency ('Bitcoin') has been making its first attempts to replace the previous world money (the petrodollar and its derivatives YEN, EURO etc. ...).

4. Increasingly intelligent Information Technology is also becoming a new means of power for governance. Anything and everything can be spied on, monitored and controlled down to the last detail. In the West and in Russia, this has been done discreetly and covertly by the secret services. In China, on the other hand, it has already become an official doctrine that the total surveillance of every single citizen is necessary for the sake of maintaining the state.

5. Bill Gates leaves Microsoft and buys into the World Health Organization (WHO) by means of the Bill and Melinda Gates Foundation.[48] He makes 'health' the

---

[48] https://www.deutschlandfunkkultur.de/unabhaengigkeit-der-weltgesundheitsorganisation-

brand to which all our ideas and action in this world should be focused. For this business idea, he wants to be, or has to be at least seen to be, a friendly philanthropist who saves the world with his fortune by killing off infectious diseases. In the end, when it comes down to it, he markets health in just the same way as he would any other commodity from which he makes a profit. But it would be very strange if he actually acted like a sinister dictator rather than a charming communicator when it came to announcing his 'health-cure' to the world.

6. In 2017 Bill Gates presents his plan to save the world at the Munich Security Conference. The old enmities between countries should be abandoned in favour of a common global war against infectious diseases, or in other words, to boost his business. Let's turn swords to plough blades and shovels, was once a saying in the peace movement. But for a better business idea, how about we now convert tanks into vaccination needles?

7. On 18th October 2019, the Bill Gates Foundation together with the Johns Hopkins Centre for Health Security conducted a simulation exercise called Event 201 based on a hypothetical 'coronavirus' pandemic. The starting point of this pandemic was Brazil.[49]

8. At the beginning of January 2020, a virus designated as 'novel' spreads across the globe from China.

9. On 11th March 2020, the WHO proclaims a pandemic because of the SARS-CoV-2 virus, which is immediately equated with a disease: Covid-19.

10. All counter-arguments that SARS-CoV-2 is no more dangerous than previously known influenza viruses are consistently ignored. The supposedly clearly defined disease Covid-19 is now the test case in an attempt to reinvent governance, economy and society.

gefaehrdet.976.de.html?dram:article_id=423076&fbclid=IwAR1Dk8rf65AvYPS17X8 UHERM2_ZkJOO_dcK8NCm2MBZxuT2FMbrInzXQqZY (retrieved 28/03/20) In German

[49] https://www.centerforhealthsecurity.org/event201/scenario.html (retrieved 01/07/20)

The question of whether and how involved Germany is in this is becoming a very important yardstick for the success of the whole campaign.

11. At a meeting on 25th March 2020, the G20 countries devolved themselves of power in favour of the WHO, which therefore acquired a kind of world government status. In the future 'health' should come before the 'economy', which means 'health' should become the new world commodity that can be bought and sold on a global scale. If Big Food and Big Pharma come together you can earn twice as much: You can make money from what makes people sick and then make it again from something that claims to make people healthy again.

12. The Western states are possibly getting involved in this deal because their financial system is on the brink of its next crash. In this way, the liquidation of the monetary system and the rebuilding of a new currency are not perceived as just the logical consequence of the ever-exponentially exploding search for investment opportunities, but can be declared to be a consequence of 'Corona'.

13. The infection protection laws are designed to ensure that during this transitional situation the populations of the world remain well under control at every level.

In summary:
Bill Gates donates a lot of money - to himself, tax free!
Bill Gates gives money to MasterCard so that they can expand their business in developing countries - tax-free!
Bill Gates donates millions to rich companies, which he co-owns - tax-free!
Bill Gates gives millions to media companies to get favourable coverage of his activities - tax free! [50]

[50] https://www.thenation.com/article/society/bill-gates-foundation-philanthropy/ (retrieved 01/08/20)

The True Cost Of This New Supposed Form Of Health

Since March 2020, under the supposed pretext of saving human lives and creating security the world has witnessed:

- Human rights to free movement being suspended, who we choose to have social contact with, our professional practice, expressions of opinion and demonstration – all being overruled.
- All private, cultural, educational, religious and economic systems being taken control of from above and being severely disrupted.
- People being robbed of their sources of income and put into a state of existential distress.
- People being degraded to the status of 'charity cases' dependant on state benefits.
- The health system itself not being permitted to perform its normal activities.
- People dying because they are being treated with emergency ventilators too quickly.
- People dying because they are no longer have access to normal medical treatment.
- People being put under such a state of fear and stress that they become physically and mentally ill, and:
  - Aggressively attack each other.
  - Denounce each other.
  - And some even kill themselves.

The countries that implement this programme, which is driven by the prospect of private profit in the name of health, are not just sawing through the financial branch on which they are sitting but are cutting down the whole societal trunk which supports them. In Germany, for example, even the automobile industry, which contributes a major part of the gross national product, is subject to restrictions that have meant it has had to stop entire production lines. Supply chains are interrupted by border closures and controls. A wide-reaching economic recession is accepted willingly.

In order to calm the unrest in the population, those who are now losing their jobs or who are no longer able to obtain work in a self-employed capacity are promised financial compensation, which will result in a massive public debt that will run into the trillions of euros. The entire model of state funding through tax revenues with its focus on monetary stability, will be put at risk and has been from the time this pandemic started. Deflation, hyperinflation, the collapse of the stock markets or of the leading currencies, the dollar, yen or euro - no economic argument seems to frighten those who now pursue interest-driven politics for the vaccine manufacturers in the name of health.

This is all so confused and contradictory that it cannot come from people's healthy psychological parts. We've got to therefore ask ourselves, what makes people so blind to reality that they end up harming themselves and dragging others down with them. I know such behaviour only too well from working with people who are traumatised.

Trying Not To Get Lost

Everyday I vacillate back and forth. Sometimes I feel very clear that this whole pandemic must be a production that's been long in the planning, although it is not by any means clear who's orchestrating it, what for and who stands to benefit. Then I watch the talk shows on the television again – the leading German TV current affairs programmes like Hard but Fair, Anne Will, Markus Lanz – and they're all filmed in these spookily empty studios, where everyone is sitting around obeying the rules with their 1.5 metre minimum distance between them. The danger of death that is constantly being conjured up by this malicious virus is so insidious, that it is impossible to judge how dangerous it really is!

And anyone who isn't now cooperating with all this and making the required sacrifices, both idealistically and materially, is an evil, unreasonable and selfish person. I feel caught because I am not 100% in agreement with the prevailing narrative. How long before they find out about me? After a restless night, I open up my computer in the morning and new messages offering alternative points of view to the mainstream await me. Many people praise my courage in this situation, in which apparently the majority are still supportive of the drastic measures of restricting their own freedoms, suppressing their economic activities and rapidly dismantling democratically legitimised decision-making processes. And, if we can trust the opinion polls, people are calling for even tougher measures to be imposed. But I'm increasingly doubting everything I read in the mainstream media - why should they start reporting the full truth now when it comes to these opinion polls?

Strengthened by a growing community that apparently sees things differently, I go back to work on my latest article, post it on the home page of my website and let it go viral. Now I understand what a good idea it was a few months back to add that section 'Comments on Current Affairs' onto my homepage. Now there are indeed a lot of comments to make, especially from my IoPT point of view.

It is a constant up and down. Late at night I'll post a new article about the pandemic on my webpage, and then by the next morning I've already discovered fresh information on the subject and new thoughts start to go through my head. I'll revise the article or write a new one straight away.

I get many requests for interviews. And at each one I get to learn what I am sure about and what I am not. Essentially, my confidence is growing as I am able to draw from my existing knowledge base and see how it relates to the many pieces of this information puzzle that I'm collecting.

What has so starkly and suddenly happened around me is for me 'Who am I in a traumatised society?' in an intensified form. I can no longer withdraw into the niche I have created for myself over the past few years with a well-meaning community here in Munich and my numerous IoPT contacts worldwide. Now I have been plunged right into the middle of a system that makes the central method of IoPT therapy impossible: namely - to meet each other (both psychologically and physically) - to look into each other's eyes, to touch each other's hands, to hug one another and cry on each other's shoulders. None of this is now allowed. Every contact is now portrayed as contact with the enemy.

What Game Is YouTube Playing?

Because the mainstream media (here in Germany that's ARD, ZDF, Spiegel, Süddeutsche Zeitung or Focus) are increasingly devoting themselves to the Corona narrative, alternative journalistic media such as Rubikon or KenFM and social media like WhatsApp, Twitter and above all YouTube are becoming more and more important for the dissemination of alternative Corona news and dissenting opinions. But on which side are Google or Facebook then in this debate? Basically it seems, on the side of power and money.

My article 'The Corona Pandemic Mania', was published as a 'Daily Dose' on KenFM's YouTube channel on 18th March, but apparently it received too many clicks over too short a period. There were more than 110,000 when I found it there for the last time. Then it disappeared. It was quickly uploaded again by other YouTube channels. On 24th April I tracked it down again. It now had 165,332 hits.

I started to hear more and more reports about the deletion of critical YouTube contributions. Anything which spoke out against the governmental corona control measures was being taken down, because they do not comply with the YouTube guidelines - whatever they consist of. Then follows the usual game of cat and mouse: the contributions are uploaded again and blocked by YouTube again and so on.

The longer the lockdown lasts the more the resistance to it grows and so, to save their own hides an appeal is launched by those spearheading the lockdown on the campaign platform Avaaz, which is subsequently published by way of a full-page advertisement in the New York Times on 7th May 2020. It comprises a letter signed by 100 doctors around the world including Christian Drosten (Director of the Institute of Virology at Charité Hospital in Berlin) and Melanie Brinkmann (from the Technische Universität Braunschweig) Colin Hutchinson (The Chair of Doctors for the NHS), The EveryDoctor Team in the UK & Ron Waldman (Professor of Global Health, George Washington University & President of Doctors of the World – USA). The goal is to: Take 'immediate systematic action' to delete from Facebook, Twitter and Google conspiracy theories which claim, among other things, that Bill Gates is 'involved in the spread of the pandemic'. The Frankfurter Allgemeine Zeitung[51] which reports on the story, then writes:

'The measures taken so far by the corporations, like Facebook, to delete reported content and provide the WHO with free advertising space are not enough. Instead the signatories make two concrete demands: the tech companies should 'publish corrections to the health misinformation'.

---

[51] The report on this in the Frankfurter Allgemeine can be found (in German) here: https://www.faz.net/aktuell/wirtschaft/digitec/corona-virologen-legen-sich-mit-tech-konzernen-an-16757974.html?printPagedArticle=true#pageIndex_2 (retrieved 08/05/20). Here is the original campaign letter on Avaaz in English: https://secure.avaaz.org/campaign/en/health_disinfo_letter/ (retrieved 27/08/20)

Whoever has seen this misinformation on the platforms should then be shown these corrections retroactively. They should also 'detoxify' their algorithms. These currently help lies to spread quickly and are designed to 'keep users online rather than protect their health'. Overall, the tech giants should 'stop fuelling the lies, distortions and fantasies that threaten us all'.

Again it becomes clear that Google and also Facebook are trying to undermine alternative views on the Corona pandemic by deleting posts and references that are overly critical to the allegedly correct view. And under 'dubious' YouTube contributions there appears a link that takes you to the official guidance saying: 'COVID-19 - Current, scientific information can be found at the Federal Centre for Health Education'[52] (This seems to be the same around the world – videos offering alternative viewpoints on Covid 19 when viewed in the UK, for example, appear with a link under them pointing you to the official NHS England site).

An article in the Süddeutsche Zeitung on 11th May 2020 shows what kind of counter-propaganda and repression of opinion is going on behind the scenes:

'When fact-checkers like the research organisation Correctiv or the German Press Agency identify these kind of false statements, it influences the algorithms that the networks recommend. This kind of content is then less often automatically suggested to users or not suggested at all and is harder to find. The problem with this is: most people who want to watch such videos have long since switched to messenger services like Telegram anyway. There people are able to send the links directly to each other, the algorithms of the platforms then no longer play a role.' [53]

How insecure the pandemic makers must be to be driven into hysteria by a few critical dissenting voices! Or do they just feel caught out?

---

[52] The German link takes you direct to:
https://www.infektionsschutz.de/coronavirus-sars-cov-2.html - The UK one to:
https://www.nhs.uk/conditions/coronavirus-covid-19/
[53] https://www.sueddeutsche.de/politik/im-feindbild-vereint-falsch-aber-faszinierend-1.4903960 (retrieved 10/05/20)

Stop The Pan(dem)ic!
Tenth article - March 29th 2020

War Propaganda

The weekend edition of the Süddeutsche Zeitung (28th/29th March) is like a non-stop panic-mongering piece of war propaganda, fighting the good fight against 'Corona'. Of course the supposed killer virus is not affected by this, but I am. I feel like someone who, because I have a different opinion on this subject, can be classified as the enemy that now has to be eradicated. I would never have thought that all the official media in this country could be brought into line so quickly. How can this be? Is there a secret conspiracy going on here, and the fourth power, the press, which is so highly praised in a democracy, is now becoming solely the mouthpiece of the government, which no longer has any opposition because everyone is in favour of declaring an emergency and a disaster?

Who Is Benefiting From All This Fear?

One thing I do know for sure, however, is that even if there is a virus that is possibly more dangerous than I can imagine at the moment, the last thing that helps promote the health of the population is to stir up fear and spread panic. Fear makes people blind and stupid. Fear causes stress and undermines the immune system. Fear makes people suspicious and poisons relationships.

In this context it was important for me to watch, together with my wife, the film, 'Profiteure der Angst' (Profiteers of Fear) – a 2009 documentary about 'Swine Flu.'[54] I would appeal to everyone to please watch this film as a matter of urgency. Also this article by Dr. Wodarg[55], who was involved at the time, is really eye

---

[54] https://www.youtube.com/watch?v=ECO4FzFP6Nk (retrieved 01/08/20)
[55] https://franz-ruppert.de/de/downloads/send/2-uebergreifende-informationen/514-pandemie-als-geschaeftsidee (in German) - Here is another link to

opening (Wodarg 2015). It is uncanny to see how the scare tactics of that time are being repeated today. Everything from 10 years ago is being played out again now.

The leading players in that situation, unlike the general population and their political leaders, seem to have learned from their defeat. It seems as if the coup d'état of Big Pharma is much more systematic today: Now they are using the propaganda of panic to bring the public television stations and daily newspapers into line. They are closing down the universities, putting workers on shorter working hours, and best of all, they are locking up everyone at home in order to nip any discussion or hint of resistance in the bud. The people, deprived of their gainful employment and income, are reassured with state compensation payments, and any natural immunisation of the population is prevented from taking place by prohibiting any possibly infectious social contacts. State funding for corona drugs and compulsory vaccinations is already made available.

It will now take some time before the pharmaceutical industry announces the availability of the Corona vaccine - in view of the emergency, of course, this can happen without major testing and approval hurdles. Bill Gates now talks of 18 months in which this can be achieved. So does that mean 18 months of this state of emergency?

The Internet As A Place For The Opposition

All people who think their own thoughts, wish for an open-ended discussion and express themselves in a manner critical of the mainstream are denounced and threatened across the board as incompetent, lacking in solidarity, unempathetic, irrelevant, a minority,

the article 'Google-translated' into English:
https://translate.google.com/translate?hl=en&sl=de&u=https://www.wissenschaftsl aden-dortmund.de/wp-content/uploads/2020/04/2020-03-25-Wodarg-Die-Schweinegrippe.pdf&prev=search&pto=aue

conspiracy theorists or sometimes even radical right-wingers. How would it be if the Internet, the alternative media and the engagement of individuals in these forums and forms of contradiction did not exist?

This is another reason why I appeal to all of us here, and especially to those who are creating panic about the Corona virus and therefore creating chaos everywhere: this is not good for your health, it makes you sick!

It is not worth it, whether out of idealism, or out of the interests of power or profit, or in order not to have to deal with your own fears from your childhood, to wage a psychological war against the whole of humanity. We already have to pay dearly for this war and we will all lose out in the end. Health cannot be forced and is not something that a vaccination can provide.

My Website Administrator Gives Me Notice – Temporarily

Over the next few days, I keep on writing my articles about the Corona Crisis and putting them up on my homepage. Then suddenly an email arrives from the administrator of my website, saying that she plans to terminate our working relationship on the grounds that I am posting links to articles which represent AfD-near views (Alternative for Germany – a far right political party). This is the last criticism I would have expected. We email back and forth a few times, exchange views and further links about our information sources and finally have a personal conversation. From this I find out that she considers Ken Jebsen (a journalist on KenFM – to whom I provide links on my website) to be affiliated to the AfD. Now, I've met Ken Jebsen personally several times and I consider him to be a very perceptive and sharp-tongued critical person. For me, he is clearly assigned to the left spectrum of political thinking. I don't want to get involved in discussing our opinions of him any further and so ask my system administrator to call Ken Jebsen herself directly and clarify with him whether he really has something to do with Pegida (a pan-European anti-Islam far right political movement). After a fifty-minute telephone conversation with him and an intensive exchange of arguments, she decides to continue to maintain my website.

The Personal Conversation Is Crucial

If someone is sitting alone at his computer, trying to distinguish fact from fiction, he is encouraged to divide people into friends and enemies, with the majority of the population made out to be the good dutiful citizens. Therefore I seek out a personal discussion each time someone emails me criticising what I've said. Then it turns out within a short time that this is coming from someone who is also, like me, an unsure person looking for the truth, who has his own views and reliable sources that back them up. And in the end we always say goodbye with politeness and respect and sometimes even laugh about the absurd situation in which we have landed together seemingly overnight.

Even during conversations on the street, the ice is quickly broken as everybody has to struggle in his own way with the imposed restrictions. One of us now has to stay at home working reduced hours, the other is not allowed to visit her mother anymore, even though her father has just died and her mother needs special support...

A great help in adopting this open attitude is the brilliant case study of the famous communication psychologist Paul Watzlawick. He tells the story of a man who wants to borrow a hammer from his neighbour. But then suddenly doubts begin to set in, he starts to question whether this neighbour will really be so kind as to actually do him this favour and lend him his hammer. He becomes more and more suspicious of his neighbour, so that when he finally goes over and rings his neighbour's doorbell to ask him for the hammer, he's in a blinding rage. And so when the neighbour answers his door, before he can even speak, the man yells at him: "Keep your hammer, you bully!"[56] (Watzlawick 2019)

I'm also really benefitting right now from many other great teachers of communication theory:

- Carl Rogers with his principles of active listening, mirroring and basic empathic attitude (Rogers 1994)
- Michael Lukas Möller and his basics of couple conversations on equal terms (Moeller 1988)
- Schulz von Thun and his four sides model and his listing of different communication styles such as devaluing, questioning, appeasing, interpreting, comforting (Schulz von Thun 1992)[57],
- Marshall Rosenberg and his non-violent communication with jackal versus giraffe language (Rosenberg 2010).

In my family of origin there was often only shouting or scolding in the place of real communication. My mother and father demonstrated to us what we children then enacted against each other: that the stronger is right and the weaker must give in, even if they are right.

On the other hand, in difficult conversational situations, my theory of what comprises 'Identity' can help me stop compartmentalising people into boxes like left or right or stupid or

---

[56] https://www.youtube.com/watch?v=FExI1gNST3Y, (retrieved 02/04/20)
[57] https://medium.com/seek-blog/the-art-of-misunderstanding-and-the-4-sides-model-of-communication-7188408457ba (retrieved 31/08/20)

intelligent. Everyone has their own life story, which has brought them, physically, emotionally and psychologically, to the place where they are now. Everybody has their burden to bear and everybody has learned something in their own way, has special qualities and abilities which they can develop in different fields of social life. It is important for me to understand what the trauma survival strategies are of the person I am in dialogue with and to not to get caught up in any discussion with these parts. This only leads to the dispute escalating.

Corinna Busch, a journalist who lives in France, has become an important link with the public for me in terms of reaching people who are not already aware of my IoPT ideas. Therefore, in an interview with her, I don't have a dig at the crazy toilet paper buyers and hoarders. These people have their own good reasons for their behaviour. And if anyone is to be blamed, it is those who are now talking up the danger or writing things that drive these people into such panic, lock them up in their houses from one day to the next and exile them into working from home, so that even toilet paper becomes an existential question: how long will this state of emergency last, and am I well equipped for it with the things I need every day? After all, everyone has to go to the toilet several times a day. Before Corona you could still use the toilet at work.

Psychology In Times Of Crisis
Eleventh Article - 29th March 2020

Risk Taker?

I am participating in this discussion about the 'Corona' crisis because, in my own way, I am affected by the pandemic measures. I am no longer able to carry out my work as a university lecturer and as a psychotherapist in the way that I think is right and sensible. I'm lucky, I live in a house with a garden and from there I can easily take walks to a nearby park. And because of the crisis, I have learned to do Identity-Oriented Psychotrauma Therapy in online groups instead. As a psychotherapist, I am, seen in this light, more of a winner from this crisis than others - at least for the time being.

I don't deny that there are viruses, bacteria, fungi and so on that can overwhelm a person's immune system, cause severe symptoms of suffering - especially as an expression of exuberant counter-reactions on the part of the immune system - and can even lead to death in some people. However, I am convinced that it is not only these biological micro-organisms on the outside that lead directly to the endangerment of their host bodies, but it is the relationship between what comes as an external burden and the fitness of the immune defence to cope with it.

In addition, our entire lifestyle and life history plays a significant role in how well our organism copes with external threats. From my psychotherapeutic experiences I know that unresolved traumas, especially from early childhood, lead to permanent stress conditions that chronically overload the organism and also impair the immune system and its ability to function. Therefore it is enormously healing on all levels, rather than looking for material or spiritual answers, to seek out emotional solutions to our own inner conflicts. Being healthy requires above all being able to be a subject, to be in constructive relationships, to know the truth, to have freedom, good food, fresh air and trust in our own potential and abilities.

The Declaration Of The Pandemic Is The Risk

My concern in the current pandemic situation is that I will be made an object by reducing the good direct personal contact I have in my relationships with lots of people, so that these all take place on a purely virtual level. Other people throw questionable projections and one-sided views and panic-mongering at me, my freedom of movement is extremely restricted and I have to work every day on trusting myself more than what is imposed on me as presumably well-intentioned help from outside.

The official line seems to be: we don't know exactly what this new SARS-CoV-2 is and only afterwards will we probably be more clued up about it and how dangerous this virus really is. But for now we are simply assuming the worst-case scenario and declaring a pandemic as a precaution. We are already paralysing everything, based on the logic that to stop any infestation we are best off burning down our house, because an infestation is bound to happen sooner or later. This is the same mentality as thinking that in order to stop myself being frightened of dying, I'm best off killing myself.

If a protective measure against danger, as is now becoming increasingly clear, causes more damage than it benefits, then something is fundamentally wrong. If, in order to stabilise the health system, the whole of society is brought into disarray, then questions must be asked about the cost-benefit balance of the measures taken.

'Corona As A Trauma Trigger'...

A personal breakthrough for me was when I did my own IoPT self-encounter process with the Intention: 'I' 'SARS-Cov-2'. It resulted in me being able to better connect with

myself and it clarified my feelings and my thoughts on
this subject.

My Self-Encounter With SARS-CoV-2

Twelfth Article – 1st April 2020

'I' And 'Sars-CoV-2'

Yesterday (31st March) I did a self-encounter process for myself on the topic of the Corona crisis using my Intention method. My Intention consisted of two elements: 'I' and 'SARS-CoV-2'.

I chose one resonator for 'I' and one for 'SARS-CoV-2' and when we started the 'I' got up from his chair, walked towards me and looked at me briefly. Then he took a blanket, went to 'SARS-CoV-2', who was still sitting on his chair, coughing and breathing heavily, and threw the blanket over him. SARS-CoV-2 put up with this and continued breathing heavily under the blanket.

The person resonating with my 'I' came back over to me, looked at me and said: "I am tired of it."

This really landed with me. The evening before I had the feeling that I had now said everything I wanted to say about the Corona crisis, and that all the arguments from those opposed to the lockdown had been put on the table sufficiently to initiate a turnaround in the policy of curfews and the prevention of all social contact. But if they are not listened to, then there is nothing I can do. I must then try to continue to do what I think is right for me and make the best of this traumatising situation that is happening in the outside world.

After a while, the resonator for SARS-CoV-2 slid off his chair onto the floor. Still buried under the covers, he said, "But I'm also a part of you!"

This aroused my curiosity and I went and knelt on the floor in front of him. The resonator said that he was the little child in me that I did not want to see. He was very ill. He felt some heat in his chest, but otherwise he was so very cold.

I now began to remember how it was for me in my first year of life. According to my mother I cried a lot after my birth. And then, one evening, my father came over to my cot and yelled at me violently. And from that point on I was always calm and well-behaved. In addition, my parents informed me that I had lost more and more weight when I was six months old and almost died until the family doctor changed my diet from milk powder to rice gruel. After that I put on weight again. My mother had probably breastfed me for only 6 weeks after my birth.

Suddenly I could resonate with the crying of this child inside me. More and more sadness and despair rose up in me. I was able to get closer and closer to the person resonating with SARS-CoV-2, who was huddled under the blanket. I let my feelings run free more and more, felt the desperation of this baby, cried and screamed together with him at times. My 'I' had now also come over and I felt very supported by him in this very painful process. What I had suspected for some time was confirmed by the person resonating with SARS-CoV-2. As well as yelling at me, my father had also put a pillow over my face to stop me crying when I was in my cot.

After a while I asked another woman and a man to go into resonance with my mother and father. They both turned their heads away from me and from my other parts.

The person resonating with my mother said, "I feel I have to support my husband because he feels so weak. I see what is happening on the ground over there, but I cannot do anything about it. I wonder what we've done to this child, but he's best when he's calm".

My father said, "I can see that our child is in some distress there. But I can't get emotionally involved in this any deeper. It would bring up too many of my own feelings that I can't handle."

That was my experience of my parents. My mother, born in 1933, grew up on a small farm together with 7 brothers and sisters in poor circumstances. I always experienced her as overburdened and constantly busy with cleaning, cooking and working. With my father I felt a little more emotionality and had a hope of being noticed by him. But that usually did not come to anything. As a child, born in 1934, he had grown up in the Sudetenland during the war, was driven from house and home, together with his extended family and had to make his own living as a shepherd in Bavaria at the age of 14.

The resonator for 'SARS-CoV-2', or rather my early childhood part, still felt that he was not wanted by his parents and did not know how to deal with that. Now that he is there, he feels like he is a burden for our mother and is ashamed of this. He has an unbearable fear of her rejection.

I remained inwardly in contact with this child part of me and my 'I'. Further waves of despair and pain came up, I imagined holding the child wrapped in the blanket on my lap, opening the blanket by his head and touching him with my hand. I was more and more consumed by emotions and in the end I had the feeling that I could now breathe more freely and deeply.

After about 45 minutes I finished the process, which had been therapeutically accompanied by a colleague.

What Did I Learn From This Self-Encounter?

The basic model of my Identity Oriented Psychotrauma Theory (IoPT) states that there are three different psychological parts: healthy parts, traumatised parts and trauma survival strategies (see Figure 2).

1. SARS-CoV-2 is for me a trigger for my own personal trauma.
2. Therefore, if I only deal with it externally, I deepen the split within myself.

3. My view of the current situation is shaped by my early life experiences, as it probably is with everyone else.
4. The current crisis is therefore a chance to come into contact with myself in a deep and meaningful way.
5. There can be no objective view of the situation here, which could be proved by numbers, statistics and comparisons of figures. Everyone interprets such numbers on the basis of the current state of their own psyche.
6. Even the actions of those who now make decisions that affect the general population are not only influenced by superficial power, money or career interests, but also by their early childhood psychological states, of which they are usually not aware.
7. It is important that any far-reaching political measures and decisions, that affect the whole of society and our lives as we know them, should be taken as unencumbered as possible from anyone's own unconscious psychological states that have resulted from their unprocessed traumas.
8. Perception, feeling, thoughts and action shaped by our own unresolved traumatic experiences lead to different forms of survival strategies. These are characterised by emotional defence and do not do justice to the complexity of life situations. They consist for example of:
   • Being only in your head.
   • Juggling and manipulating numbers and statistics.
   • Acting without thinking.
   • Being resistant to information that does not fit into your own concept of how things are.
   • Talking about mortality rates without letting the suffering behind them get to you.
   • Thinking in simple black and white terms of friend versus enemy.

- Becoming more vague or more and more radical in one's views in the face of opposition.
- Becoming more and more unempathetic when confronted with the real suffering that comes as a result of decisions you have made.
- Making out that the victims are the real perpetrators and much more.

9. Trauma survival strategies can try to counteract trauma in an extreme situation by creating more trauma. This does not solve the old emotional problem; it creates new problems all the time. The trauma survival strategies do not help by their actions when it is urgently necessary.

10. Rational decisions are only possible when they are connected to our own healthy emotionality. Feelings (emotion) and thoughts (rationality) are not opposites when we are in our healthy parts.

11. Nobody is to be blamed for his early childhood traumas. Responsibility arises when I have the chance to deal with my trauma but do not use it and others then suffer from my trauma survival strategies.

In my personal case, my parents - as the ones actually responsible for me as a baby - clearly did not act from their healthy parts, but were mainly coming from their trauma survival strategies. They brought about my distress, then ignored this distress and because of my emergency reaction also saw themselves as victims of me. My trauma-emergency reactions were suppressed by a further traumatisation against me - shouting at me and almost suffocating me with a pillow.

What Is The Model Of Thinking That Underlies Our Understanding Of Illness And Health?

In the current crisis situation it should be important to discuss the underlying model of illness and health. Which model makes more sense? Model A, which defines illness on the basis of symptoms and wants to create health by eliminating these symptoms? (see Figure 11).

Traditional Model

- Pathogen (P)
- Causes Symptoms (S) = Diseases (D)
- Diseases are combatted by eliminating symptoms

P ⟶ S=D

- The means of fighting the symptoms are: operations, drugs, vaccinations, mostly with side effects that create new symptoms.
- The person is an object for treatment by specialists.

Figure 11: The traditional model of disease and health

Or model B, which understands symptoms of disease as reactions of the living organism to external threats (as in my case where the cough, fever and heat in the chest was a reaction to the emotional coldness I felt from my parents, being fed the wrong food as a baby and being neglected)? (see Figure 12).

Holistic Model

- Pathogens (P) stimulate the Organism (O) to take countermeasures
- Symptoms are expressions of Reactions of the physical & psychological Immune System (RIS)
- Health results from the strengthening of the physical & psychological defences

- Possible ways of strengthening these are: fresh air, clean water, healthy food, constructive relationships, reducing stress, trauma work, truth
- The person concerned remains a subject and receives support from experts in the specialist fields when needed.

Figure 12: The holistic model of health and disease

The Current Strategy In Dealing With SARS-CoV-2

In the current situation, a pathogen (SARS-CoV-2, popularly known as 'Corona') is being dealt with in the way it is because politicians are relying on doctors and epidemiologists, who adhere to the traditional model of disease. This means that the pathogen should be prevented from spreading and the infection chains should be interrupted. This strategy would certainly make sense if a pathogen that is actually highly dangerous is identified in a contained environment and its further spread can be prevented by protective measures. However, if its worldwide spread has already occurred, which is why a 'pandemic' has been declared in the first place, then such measures are no longer effective. On the contrary, they become counterproductive because they paralyse the whole of society, causing enormous damage to the economy and to our health.

Perhaps I can throw one more thought into the mix on the subject of the charts and statistics that are currently being hotly debated and form the basis of this traditional model of disease and health. One of the things I learned in my statistics foundation course that I took as part of my psychology studies was: never trust statistics that you have not falsified yourself!

The second stage of the traditional understanding of disease, i.e. the treatment of the diseases themselves, is already coming from a state of emergency because of the threat the pathogens pose. Many countries have hardly enough hospital beds or intensive care units anyway and, even in the richer countries, the hospital system is under financial pressure to save money and suffers from staff shortages. Attempts to overcome these bottlenecks in turn lead to gaps in other areas, so that in the end even normal operations in hospitals such as doctors' outpatient departments are no longer able to function properly. This leads to new suffering, symptoms of other illnesses go untreated and in the end some people even die.

Because, in my view, this strategy is a trauma survival strategy - the health system must survive the stampeding rush of sick people - the ever more visible sacrifices that this strategy costs are dismissed as a necessary evil in order to achieve the ultimate goal. What exactly is this ultimate goal and when will we achieve it - one, two, three years? The players in this strategy cannot say. In any case, the question to be asked here is, what will be won when this battle against SARS-CoV-2 is over? Who's to say we won't have to declare war on another 'novel' virus like 'Mers-CoV-20' next year and employ similar tactics all over again?

The political dimension within this traditional model of disease control can be seen clearly in the current Corona crisis. The ban on contact in order to interrupt chains of infection must be implemented by force, because it is fundamentally contrary to human nature. The pictures burn themselves into the memory – images from India, where people are beaten and humiliated by policemen in the streets; the pictures from Africa, where bulldozers simply clear away vendor's market stalls and people now have to spend their days crammed together in their huts - without money to buy food, without clean water, and so on. Under the banner of disease prevention, new diseases are then created, possibly even epidemics. It generates distress and desperation, people's economic livelihoods are destroyed, people starve and die or possibly may end up killing themselves in their distress, as seems to be the case with the Hessian Minister of Finance Dr. Schäfer.[58] The external situation has a traumatising effect because it prohibits direct interpersonal contact, which is an elixir of life for us humans, as essential as food and drink - it is worth remembering here the convincing experiments of Harry Harlow[59] with rhesus monkey babies. This current lack of contact therefore evokes old traumatic situations, especially those that were split off in early childhood, and it now leaves countless people unprotected in states of retraumatisation.

Here, too, political leaders can only stick to this strategy if they are not compassionate about the plight of others, but strike a heroic pose in the fight against the virus and make themselves out as saviours of all human life, with the mantra: the main thing is that as many people as possible survive; their quality of life no longer matters. This also applies to life-saving measures such as forced ventilation. Although in some cases this can ensure survival in that moment, they are at the same time a traumatising experience for the person concerned, which will remain etched in his psyche for the rest of his life.

The one-sidedness and blindness to reality that is inherent in trauma survival strategies also becomes

---

[58] Here's an English article detailing the story: https://www.dw.com/en/german-state-finance-minister-thomas-sch%C3%A4fer-found-dead/a-52948976 (retrieved 31/07/20)
[59] https://en.wikipedia.org/wiki/Harry_Harlow (retrieved 31/07/20)

apparent in their contradictory nature: people sit in traffic jams and car exhaust fumes for hours, live in smog-covered cities, and therefore put extreme stress on their lungs. And suddenly, the only problem that is supposed to be damaging to our lungs is a virus. And yet this virus is probably, if at all, only the infamous straw that breaks the camel's back. In this respect, the lockdown with less air and car traffic may even have a positive effect on air quality.

When we are in our trauma-survival parts, there always seems to be only one possible course of action for us. And power-driven people think that they have to enforce this, if possible as the sole ruler, by force. The temptation to abuse this traditional model of illness for political autocracy is then given to some politicians, such as Mr. Orban in Hungary.[60]

The Holistic Model For SARS-CoV-2

If the holistic model of health and illness were to be applied now, there would be different strategies for action available:

- General education on how the human immune system works.
- Special support and guidance with measures such as healthy food, clean air, clean drinking water, getting out in the sun a lot, possibly taking additional vitamins,
- Supporting constructive interpersonal relation-ships, both currently and in the future
- Stress reduction in various areas of life,
- No further stirring up of fears, but education about these fears and showing people ways to deal with them with professional support,
- Supporting the immune system when there is an infection, not suppressing it by anti-fever drugs.

---

[60] Here's an article detailing Viktor Orban's actions in the wake of the 'Corona Crisis': https://balkaninsight.com/2020/07/29/hungarian-militarisation-under-orban-stirs-concern/ (retrieved 01/08/20)

- Coming to terms with our old traumas from our life histories.

It's not up to me to list all the strategies that make sense. There are certainly countless possibilities for special 'at risk' groups of people to be offered suitable means for looking after and strengthening themselves and measures for primary and secondary prevention. The basic principle should be that people should always remain subjects and therefore the main person responsible for their health should be they themselves. No one should be coerced or arbitrarily assigned to an age-group which is then forced into doing a certain thing. After all, I am already 63 years old and know my own ways and means of keeping myself healthy.

We All Have A Choice

If we are in our healthy parts, we have a choice, even in the current crisis, because in our healthy selves we are open to dialogue and to the realisation that complex realities and even crises can only be overcome through co-consciousness and constructive cooperation.

Reactions To This Article

In response to the publication of my personal experience with 'the virus' I received only positive reactions. Many people describe to me their own self-encounters with 'Corona', in which this virus or actually this word 'Corona', has very different meanings, depending on their personal biography. In one case 'Corona' was even the expression of liveliness, which was then suppressed by the person's own mother, who could not bear a 'lively' child because of her own trauma biography.

Even without a therapeutic setting, many people now experience their everyday life as a trauma trigger and apparently IoPT helps them to correctly classify what then happens inside them. Here is an example from an e-mail I received:

'I watched Markus Lanz [61] this evening. There was a situation during the discussion that triggered me, which I would like to tell you about briefly. I don't actually feel personally threatened by this virus and I was surprised that I suddenly got this surge of trauma feelings whilst watching this talk show. At first I could not explain why. A recovered patient reported about having moderate symptoms of the disease and that she was alone at home with her three children before she had to go to the clinic.

While she was telling us this, I noticed that I suddenly found it difficult to breathe and I felt this vague fear. These were clearly trauma feelings. When the show was over, I suddenly had to cry and it came from deep inside myself. It really shook me up. That's when I realised what the trigger in the show was. My mother had cancer when I was in the womb and my whole childhood was over-shadowed by my mother's illness. The trigger was that the mother here was also sick and threatened with death and the children had to fear for their mother's life. I felt my own pain and my fear that my mother might die. I cried for a long time after that. Up until now, actually.

Thanks to you and your IoPT, I am now able to recognise and interpret such triggers and trauma feelings, and

---

[61] A German TV talk show/discussion panel hosted by Markus Lanz: https://en.wikipedia.org/wiki/Markus_Lanz (retrieved 01/08/20)

in the meantime, I am often able to assign them without the need for a constellation. This is invaluable. I really hope that soon more people can have these kind of healing experiences.'

Many people who have already had their own experiences with IoPT now share their experiences and assessments of the situation with me. I am very happy that in this global trauma situation IoPT is an anchor for many people to remain stable and with themselves.

'The present events have shaken me up quite a bit. Not that I'm afraid of the virus, but the madness going on around the world is frightening. Especially how willingly people follow the fear-mongers and politicians without criticism, like lemmings.

I see this all as a worldwide collective war traumatisation, something that has never been seen before on this scale. It's like a Third World War. But the common enemy is a tiny living being, how grotesque, how absurd! But from my point of view this irrational reaction just confirms this. People do not want to hear the truth about the virus, they just wallow in this 'we can do it together' survival strategy. Critics are dismissed as deniers, YouTube posts are censored and deleted.

Unfortunately, I have a lot of experiences of re-traumatisation. What I noticed is that I do feel better for a while after the trauma gets triggered. Like feeling better after throwing up. It will be interesting, I think, whether this will also be the case in a collective sense now. My son, who lives in Graz, said that the people in the city seemed to him as if they were relieved by the collective projection of their fearful dreams onto the virus and the government's taking the responsibility for their lives. Same as always - doctors heal me, only this time on a global scale.

I am so glad that I have become immune to the insanity. You've contributed a good part of that with your work. The truth has never been popular, and it will probably always stay that way. Through my work with your method, my true self-confidence is growing more and more, enabling me to fearlessly go my own way and shape my life. Immune means untouchable.

Yes my dear, perhaps you will find the time for an answer and if so that would make me very happy. You have become an important person in my more and more happy life. Thank you for that.

I send you my greetings from the bottom of my heart.'

I'm still receiving more e-mails now with references to interesting studies, statements, articles and blogs that contradict the government's official line. More and more people are waking up and taking an active stand.

What is also not reported in the official media either are horror scenarios like this one, which I learnt from a colleague in Barcelona. He wrote to me:

'In Spain, the people affected usually die alone, without their families being able to visit them in the nursing homes and hospitals. The impotence and despair of the relatives is clear to see. Even the wake ritual in the mortuary is forbidden! The relatives can collect the ashes two weeks later (in case of cremation).' (07/04/20)

The Power Of Images And Propaganda

In the German public broadcast media, especially on ARD and ZDF, in the formerly liberal press such as the Süddeutsche Zeitung and in the tabloid press, the fear of 'the virus' continues to be stirred up by every means available. In Italy and Spain they are drowning in wooden coffins stacked in cold stores, because there are too many to be buried, and in the USA, with its completely inadequate health care system, the same is about to happen. Hospitals in Germany, too, are still overburdened and are frantically preparing for the coming onslaught of Corona patients. Individual cases that do not come from the high-risk group of the very old and already seriously ill are now being sought out and paraded before the cameras.

ARD and ZDF have a clear advantage in the battle for the sovereignty to interpret how great the current or still imminent catastrophe is. They can broadcast horror pictures that will become etched in the memory of the population. They can broadcast talk shows not only with the new stars of virology, but also with the health experts popular with the people, such as Eckart von

Hirschhausen[62]. Serious, well known scientists can get in on the act like Harald Lesch[63], whom I otherwise appreciate for his critical view of the world (Lesch 2019). In his programme 'Was weiß die Wissenschaft?' (What does science know?) on 24th March 2020, Lesch predicted the horror that would be coming next weekend: in Germany, too, it will be the case that in overcrowded clinics, doctors and nurses will have to use triage and decide who gets one of the precious few ventilators.[64]

On April 3rd 2020, the Chancellor addressed the people again in a televised broadcast, asking them to stay at home over Easter and to refrain from the usual 'getaways' to the lakes, the mountains and to their dear relatives.

On April 4th a leaked strategy paper from the Ministry of the Interior came to public attention, which assumes a worst-case scenario of one million dead[65]. The paper states that to avoid this catastrophe it is therefore recommended to create fear in the population by:

- Presenting evidence of torturous suffocation (*'suffocation or not getting enough air is a primal fear in everyone'*).
- Making children feel guilty that they can infect others, who could then die.
- Pointing out the possible long-term damage of a virus infection that could suddenly break out.
- Also the connection between 1919 (Spanish flu) and 1929 (world economic crisis) is to be made again and again to increase the general level of fear and to illustrate the seriousness of the situation.[66]

---

[62] https://en.wikipedia.org/wiki/Eckart_von_Hirschhausen

[63] https://en.wikipedia.org/wiki/Harald_Lesch (retrieved 01/09/20)

[64] https://www.zdf.de/wissen/leschs-kosmos/corona-was-sagt-die-wissenschaft-102.html, (retrieved 04/04/20)

[65] https://www.focus.de/politik/deutschland/aus-dem-innenministerium-wie-sag-ichs-den-leuten-internes-papier-empfiehlt-den-deutschen-angst-zu-machen_id_11851227.html (retrieved 04/04/20) - Here's an English article referring to the 'Project Fear' Agenda as expressed in the Leaked German document: https://faith-and-politics.com/2020/04/05/coronavirus-project-fear-exposed-by-leaked-secret-government-document/ (retrieved 01/09/20)

[66] https://fragdenstaat.de/dokumente/4123-wie-wir-covid-19-unter-kontrolle-bekommen/ (retrieved 04/04/20) Here's another English article (originally published by Rubikon) quoting the leaked document: https://midtifleisen.wordpress.com/2020/04/06/the-state-deliberately-wants-to-frighten-us/ (retrieved 01/09/20)

This confirms my intuition that the public media are deliberately propagating fear.

The extent to which my intuition that scientific chairs at universities are interspersed with professors close to the pharmaceutical industry is also proving to be true and can be seen in an interview with Professor Ulrike Protzer, Director of the Institute of Virology at the Technical University of Munich. 'If we hadn't done anything, this would have cost a million lives in Germany so far', he said.[67]

In order to stir up the panic, the media can't just use statistics of people over 80 who die of corona. There must also be examples of how even young and healthy people can suddenly find themselves in mortal danger. A report in the Süddeutsche Zeitung of 16th April 2020, p. R4, fulfils this purpose. A forty-year-old man ends up in an intensive care unit. However, he had previously done everything wrong that can be done wrong in a situation of a viral infection. He had been taking antipyretic, anti-inflammatory medication that blocked his cough whilst trying to carry on as normal in his stressful life.

A look at the 'propaganda key' offered by the Swiss Policy Research Project, which is made up of independent experts who are not externally funded, could create urgently needed critical awareness here[68]. Especially in Germany with its unspeakable propaganda during the 'Third Reich' and the continued indoctrination in the former socialist East of the country after World War II, people would do well to learn from this history.

In an interview with Corinna Busch on 4th May 2020 she and I also talk about the psychology of propaganda.[69]

Jens Wernicke And The Rubikon

Jens Wernicke, the founder and publisher of the alternative media platform Rubikon, tirelessly collects all the figures and statistics that contradict the mainstream and it acts as a counterweight to the official corona horror narrative. In a contribution by Jens Bernert, 62 sources are mentioned in which professors from virology, epidemiology, intensive care medicine, communication science, linguistics, law, economics, psychology, doctors, hospital chief

---

[67] Deutschlands größte Corona-Studie, Münchner Merkur from 04/04/20

[68] https://swprs.org/the-propaganda-key/ (retrieved 14/10/20)

[69] https://youtu.be/-mvwOZt44A8 (In German) (retrieved 09/05/20)

physicians from Germany and abroad (Italy, England, USA, Sweden) comment on the risk of Covid-19.[70] All of them came to the same conclusions:

- That the risk potential of Covid-19 cannot be estimated to be higher than that of an influenza virus, and is in any case much lower than that of the great wave of influenza that occurred in 2018
- That for a scientifically based assessment of the risk, counting cases of infection alone is not meaningful,
- That it is not clear which deaths are attributable to Covid-19 and which are not,
- That there is no reliable data on the already existing level of infection and immunisation in the population
- That there is no prior harm-benefit analysis with regard to the measures taken to prevent infection,
- That the economic, cultural, social and psychological damage already caused is enormous
- That democracy has been virtually abolished by coercive measures based solely on regulations.

Heribert Prantl, former editor-in-chief of the Süddeutsche Zeitung, also makes this urgent point in a podcast broadcast on n-tv on 5th April 2020.[71]

Every day I receive new information on the Corona situation from Jens Wernicke. Here is the status as of April 21, 2020. In the original he provides numerous links to the original sources of the respective information. I have left these out in this list.[72]

---

[70] Original German article here: https://www.rubikon.news/artikel/weltweite-warnungen (retrieved 05/04/2020) On 20th April Jens Bernert's article is expanded to now include testimony from 120 experts. This version can be found in English here: https://normanpilon.com/2020/05/15/120-expert-opinions-on-corona-high-ranking-scientists-doctors-lawyers-and-other-experts-worldwide-criticize-the-handling-of-the-corona-virus-jens-bernert-rubikon/ (retrieved 01/09/20)

[71] https://www.n-tv.de/21689999 In German - (retrieved 05/04/20)

[72] A lot of this information (with links) can be found here:
https://www.rubikon.news/artikel/120-expertenstimmen-zu-corona (retrieved 01/09/20) (This is the article that appears in English in footnote 70. By the end of May the Rubikon article is expanded further to comprise 250 experts critical of the handling of Corona.

21ˢᵗ April 2020 - Medical Updates

- Stanford medical professor John Ioannidis explains, in a new one-hour interview, several new studies on Covid-19, which, according to Professor Ioannidis, show that the lethality of Covid-19 is 'in the range of seasonal flu'. For people under 65 years of age, the mortality risk even in the global 'hotspots' is comparable to the daily car ride to work, while for healthy people under 65 years of age, the mortality risk is 'completely negligible'. Only in New York was the mortality risk for persons under 65 years of age in the range of a professional truck driver.

- Professor Carl Heneghan, Director of the Centre for Evidence-Based Medicine at Oxford University, warns that the damage caused by the lockdown could be greater than that caused by the virus. The peak of the epidemic had already been reached in most countries before the lockdown.

- A new antibody study in Los Angeles County concludes that already 28 to 55 times more people than previously thought had Covid-19 without showing severe symptoms, which reduces the danger of the disease accordingly.

- In the city of Chelsea near Boston, about one third of 200 blood donors had antibodies against the Covid-19 pathogen. Half of them reported having experienced a cold symptom in the last month. In a homeless shelter near Boston, just over a third of the people tested positive, with no symptoms.

- Scotland reports that half of the (upgraded) intensive care beds remain empty. In the meantime the admission of new patients with other complaints has ground to a halt.

- The emergency room in Bergamo's municipal hospital was completely empty at the beginning of this week for the first time in 45 days. In the meantime, more people with other diseases were again treated than those who had 'Covid-19'.

- An article in the specialist magazine Lancet already came to the conclusion at the beginning of April that school closures to contain corona viruses have no or minimal effect.

- A nine-year-old French child with corona infection was in contact with 172 people, but did not infect any of them.

This confirms earlier results that corona infection (unlike influenza) is not or hardly ever transmitted by children.

- The German emeritus microbiology professor Sucharit Bhakdi gave a new one-hour interview on Covid-19. Professor Bhakdi believes, among other things, that most of the media have acted 'completely irresponsibly'.

- The German Initiative for Care Ethics criticises blanket bans on visits and painful intensive care treatment of nursing patients: 'Even before Corona, around 900 old people in need of care died every day in German homes without being taken to hospital again shortly before. In fact, palliative treatment, if at all, would be more appropriate for these patients. (...) According to all we know about Corona so far, there is not a single plausible reason why the protection against infection should continue to be valued higher than the basic rights of citizens. Lift the visiting bans! They are inhuman and unnecessary!'

- The oldest woman in the Swiss canton of St. Gallen died last week at the age of 109. She survived the 'Spanish flu' of 1918, was not Corona-infected and 'for her age she was very well'. The 'corona-induced isolation', however, had 'very much affected her': 'She atrophied without the daily visits of her family members.'

- The Swiss cardiologist Dr. Nils Kucher reports that in Switzerland currently about 75% of all additional deaths occur not in hospital but at home. This certainly explains the largely empty Swiss hospitals and intensive care units. It is also already known that about 50% of all additional deaths occur in old people's homes and nursing homes. Dr. Kucher suspects that some of these people die of sudden pulmonary embolism. This is conceivable. Nevertheless, the question arises as to what role the 'lockdown' plays in these additional deaths.

- The Italian health authority ISS warns that Covid-19 patients from the Mediterranean region, who often have a genetic metabolic peculiarity called favism, should not be treated with antimalarial drugs such as chloroquines, as these can lead to death in the case of favism. This is a further indication that the wrong or overly aggressive medication can make the disease even worse.

- Rubikon publishes 120 expert opinions on Corona. Worldwide, high-ranking scientists, doctors, lawyers and other experts criticise the handling of the corona virus.

Classification Of The Pandemic

In 2007, the US health authorities defined a five-step classification for pandemic influenza and related measures.[73] The five categories are based on how lethal a pandemic is according to the case fatality rate (CFR) of the pandemic, from category 1 (less than 0.1%) to category 5 (2% or higher). According to this scale, the current corona pandemic would probably currently be classified in category 2 (0.1% to 0.5%). For this category the main measure at the time was only envisaged as being the 'voluntary isolation of sick persons'.

In 2009, however, the WHO deleted lethality from its pandemic definition, so that since then, in principle, every worldwide wave of influenza can be declared a pandemic, as happened for the first time with the very mild 'swine flu' of 2009/2010, for which vaccines worth around 18 billion dollars were sold.

The documentary 'Trust WHO' which dealt with the dubious role of the WHO in the context of the 'swine flu', was recently deleted by VIMEO.[74]

Chief Physician Pietro Vernazza: Simple Measures Are Enough

In his latest contribution to the debate, the Swiss head of Infectious diseases, Pietro Vernazza, uses the results of the German Robert Koch Institute and ETH Zurich to show that the Covid 19 epidemic was already under control before the 'lockdown' was introduced:

'These results are explosive. Apparently these two studies now show more or less the same results: that the simple measures, the renunciation of major events and the introduction of hygiene measures were highly effective. The population was able to implement these recommendations well and the measures could almost bring the epidemic to a halt. In any case, these measures are sufficient to protect our

---

[73] https://en.wikipedia.org/wiki/Pandemic_severity_index (retrieved 01/09/20)
[74] The makers of the documentary talk about their video being removed from Vimeo here: https://www.youtube.com/watch?v=9MvB5hoIQok (retrieved 05/05/20)

health system in such a way that the hospitals do not become overburdened'.

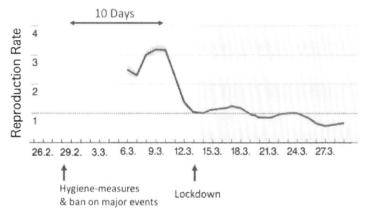

Figure a: Reproduction rate of the virus in Switzerland (ETH/Vernazza)

Switzerland: Cumulative Total Mortality Is In The Normal Range

In Switzerland, the cumulative total mortality in the first quarter (until 5 April) was at the mean expected value and more than 1500 persons below the upper expected value. By the beginning of April, the total mortality rate was more than 2000 persons below the comparative value from the severe flu season of 2015 (see figures b & c).

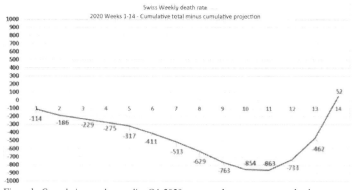

Figure b: Cumulative total mortality Q1 2020 compared to mean expected value

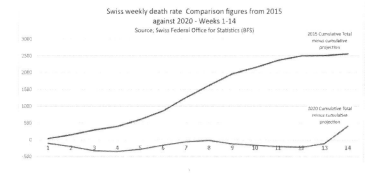

Figure c: Cumulative total mortality Q1 2020 compared to the severe flu epidemic in 2015

Sweden: Epidemic Ends Without Lockdown

In Sweden, the latest figures on patients and deaths show that the epidemic is coming to an end. In Sweden too the excess mortality occurred mainly in nursing homes that were not well protected, according to the country's chief epidemiologist, Anders Tegnell.

The Swedish population now also benefits from a very high natural immunity to Covid-19 compared to other countries, which will better protect them from a possible 'second wave' next winter.

It is expected that Covid-19 will not be visible as a major cause in the Swedish total mortality figure for 2020. The Swedish example shows that 'lockdowns' were medically unnecessary or counterproductive, and socially and economically devastating.

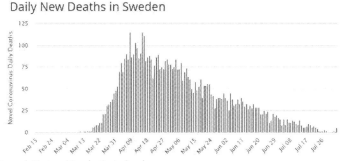

Figure d: Test positive deaths in Sweden

Anecdotes Vs. Evidence

In the face of a lack of scientific evidence, some media increasingly rely on gruesome anecdotes in order to maintain fear in the population. The typical example is the 'healthy children' who are said to have died of Covid-19, but who later turn out not to have died of Covid-19 after all, or who had underlying serious health conditions.

Neurological effects such as the temporary loss of the sense of smell or taste are also frequently cited. Here too, it is usually not mentioned that this is a classic symptom of cold and flu viruses too, and Covid-19 has so far seemed milder in this respect.

Other reports highlight possible effects on various organs such as the kidneys, liver or brain, without mentioning that many of the patients affected were already very old and had severe chronic conditions.

Political Updates

- Die Wochenzeitung'[75]: When Fear Rules. 'In the wake of the Corona crisis, fundamental freedoms are being eroded - with the advent of drones, apps and bans on demonstrations. If we don't watch out, these will remain in place even after the lockdown - but the extreme situation also offers reason for hope.'

- Multipolar[76]: What Is The Agenda Here? 'The government is congratulating itself, spreading slogans of perseverance and at the same time slowing down the collection of basic data that would allow the spread and danger of the virus to be reliably measured. Meanwhile the authorities are acting quickly and decisively to expand questionable instruments such as new 'corona apps' for collective temperature measurement and contact tracing. What is the agenda here?'

- Professor Christian Piska, expert for public law and legal tech in Vienna, comments critically on the current developments: 'Austria has become different. Very different, even if most

---

[75] www.woz.ch An independent national newspaper in German-speaking Switzerland – literal trans. The Weekly Newspaper – According to Wikipedia: 'it doesn't belong to either a political party or association or media company, and attempts to deliver critical, unique, quality journalism'

[76] Multipolar (https://multipolar-magazin.de/) An online magazine dedicated to 'multi-perspective journalism' as opposed to 'the oppressive political and media formation of recent years'. A selection of their key articles appear in English.

people seem to just accept it. Step by step, whether the economy is booming or not, we are suddenly living with police-state conditions and severe restrictions on our basic human rights, which would be a perfect breeding ground for dictatorial regimes. (…) This is Pandora's box, which once opened, may never be closed again.'

- More than 300 scientists from 26 countries warn of an 'unprecedented surveillance of society' by non data protection compliant corona apps. Several scientists and universities, including ETH Zurich and EPFL Professor Marcel Salathé, have now withdrawn from the European contact tracing project PEPP-PT[77] due to a lack of transparency. Recently it became known that the Swiss company AGT is involved in the project, which previously set up human monitoring systems for Arab countries.

- In Israel, about 5000 people (at a distance of 2m each from each other) demonstrated against the measures of the Netanyahu government: 'They talk about an exponential increase of Corona cases, but the only thing that increases exponentially is the number of people who stand up to protect our country and our democracy'.

- Madrid-based Irish journalist Jason O'Toole describes the situation in Spain: 'With the military visible on the streets of Spain, it's hard not to describe the situation as martial law in all but name. George Orwell's Big Brother is alive and well here, with the Spanish police monitoring everybody using CCTV or by flying drones overhead. A staggering 650,000 people were fined and 5,568 arrested during the first four weeks alone.... I was shocked when I watched one video clip of a cop using heavy force to arrest a mentally ill young man who was apparently just walking home with bread..'[78]

- US investigative journalist Whitney Webb writes in a new article entitled 'Techno-Tyranny: How the US National Security State Is Using Coronavirus To Fulfil An Orwellian Vision: 'Last year, a government commission called for the U.S. to adopt an AI-driven mass surveillance system far beyond that used in any other country in order to ensure American hegemony in

---

[77] https://www.pepp-pt.org/ (retrieved 01/09/20)
[78] https://www.rt.com/op-ed/486350-spain-tough-rules-covid-19-lockdown/ (retrieved 01/09/20)

artificial intelligence. Now, many of the 'obstacles' they had cited as preventing its implementation are rapidly being removed under the guise of combating the coronavirus crisis.'[79]

- In an early April paper, Whitney Webb already addressed the central role of the Johns Hopkins University Health Security Centre in the current pandemic, its involvement in previous pandemic and bio-weapons simulations, and its close ties to the U.S. security and military apparatus.

- 'The Truth About Fauci': in a new interview, US virologist Dr. Judy Mikovits talks about her very negative professional experiences with Dr. Anthony Fauci, who is currently playing a major role in shaping the US government's Covid 19 measures.

- Aid organisations warn that 'far more people' will die from the economic consequences of the measures than from Covid-19 itself. Forecasts now predict that 35 to 65 million people will fall into absolute poverty as a result of the global recession. And many of them are threatened with starvation.

- In Germany, 2.35 million people are expected to be on short-term working contracts in 2020, more than twice as many as after the financial crisis of 2008/2009. This 'short work' (or Kurzarbeit) is Germany's equivalent of the UK furlough scheme and allows employers to reduce a worker's hours with the state helping compensate the worker for lost earnings.

---

[79] https://citizentruth.org/techno-tyranny-how-the-us-national-security-state-is-using-coronavirus-to-fulfill-an-orwellian-vision/ (retrieved 22/08/20)

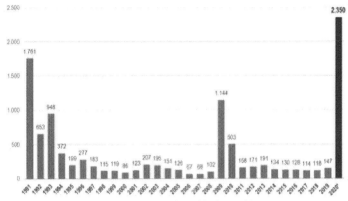

Employment in Short-term work in Germany 1991-2020
Annual Average in 1,000s

2020 = Forecast from the Federal Government on the basis of the Corona crisis
Source: The Federal Agency for Work

Figure e: Projected short-term contract employment in Germany

On 4th May 2020, Dirk Ginzel (MSc) recalculated the available figures and came to the conclusion: 'The RKI and the Federal Government had to know that there was no serious danger before any measures were taken. The extent of the wave and the danger of the disease were in the range of a medium flu wave, which cannot be contained and does not have to be contained. [...] Especially the number of those who tested positive says almost nothing. Its course, both the absolute magnitude and its derivative, which corresponds to the R number, can be modelled almost arbitrarily by appropriate testing activity'.[80]

---

[80] https://multipolar-magazin.de/artikel/bundesregierung-gefahr-ubertrieben (retrieved 08/05/20) - A link to their English articles can be found here: https://multipolar-magazin.de/?locale=en

Figures, Statistics And Theoretical Models
Thirteenth Article – 3rd April 2020

Epistemological Foundations

Collecting and evaluating figures and interpreting statistics only makes sense if the underlying theoretical assumptions are sound in the first place. A theory is correct if it can explain real phenomena without contradiction. Collecting data for a statistic where the basic concepts are insufficiently clarified and still contradictory becomes scientifically nonsensical. Serious science involves not only proving one's own hypotheses with empirical figures, but also finding counter-arguments that allow a different interpretation of the figures. At least 'critical rationalism' and 'falsification', as formulated by Sir Karl Popper, still has prestige at universities worldwide[81]. Hypotheses are therefore only considered scientific if they can be refuted (Chalmers 2001, p. 51 ff.).

SARS-CoV-2 And The Pandemic Are Unchallengeable

The theoretical model on which the corona crisis is based is as simple as I believe it is wrong and basically sets itself up as incontestable:

- A pandemic is declared when a virus spreads globally
- Unlike other viruses, and even already known corona viruses, SARS-Covid-2 is denoted 'novel' to claim that mankind has not yet developed immunity to it. It is basically classified as highly dangerous and highly infectious, even though there cannot yet be any empirical studies or even comparative studies

---

[81] https://www.simplypsychology.org/Karl-Popper.html (retrieved 22/08/20)

with other viruses that prove this because it is only now emerging – it is still 'novel'. There are also no pathological or post-mortem findings substantiated by scientific studies as to whether and how people actually fall ill and die from this virus. Instead of providing scientific studies, SARS-CoV-2 is being put by its designers on an equal footing with the case of the so-called Spanish flu or even the plague in order to illustrate its high level of danger.

- Every case of infection with SARS-CoV-2 is therefore considered in and of itself a high-risk case. Every infection with SARS-CoV-2 is automatically defined as a threatening case of illness.
- It is not necessary to prove that the infection actually causes symptoms of suffering for the person actually affected.
- Tests make SARS-CoV-2 visible, quantitatively detectable and countable. Therefore, the higher the number of positively tested persons, the more cases of illness, the more risk is supposedly expressed in increasing numbers.
- The number of infections detected in the laboratory are therefore counted in absolute terms and not in relation to a population of possibly existing but untested cases of infection. Even people who are healthy again after an infection with disease symptoms are still counted in this total of infections.
- To make the risk posed by SARS-CoV-2 even more plausible, as many deaths as possible are attributed to the virus. Corpses are even, as in Italy, tested for SARS-CoV-2 after death. At the same time, it is systematically ruled out that non-SARS-CoV-2 cases are not included in these statistics by claiming that an autopsy would be too dangerous, that one could also be infected with the virus from corpses. [82]
- On the other hand, in order to be able to set the ratio between cases of infection and deaths as high as

---

[82] https://www.youtube.com/watch?v=gSn_YaOYYcY (retrieved 01/05/20)

possible, not too many SARS-CoV-2 tests should be carried out. It is best to limit these tests to people who are already ill.

- If the numbers then turn out to be nothing so dramatic as has been made out, then the argument can be made that this is only the beginning and that it will get worse later, because the virus can hide for a long time in an infected person unnoticed before they go on to infect other people.

So in this case, what is said in basic statistics courses to the students as a mantra by their teachers who are already experienced in dealing with statistics is very clearly valid: 'Don't trust any statistics that you haven't falsified yourself!'

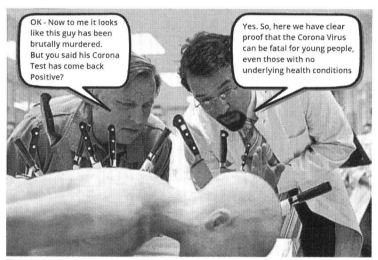

Figure 13: A little satire in humourless times

The Simplified Orthodox Medical Model Will Be Simplified Even Further

The theoretical model behind the pandemic that has been declared by the WHO and been implemented by national governments is contradictory. The majority of infections with SARS-CoV-2 do not cause massive physical suffering, and the mortality rate is not significantly increased. Even the auxiliary argument that the health system cannot cope with the rise of respiratory diseases requiring ventilation does not correspond to reality in most countries. Every wave of influenza causes peak and overload operations, but in the intervening years the hospital system has been extremely underfunded as a result of government cost-cutting measures. In addition, there has been no global increase in the death rates amongst the populations of the various countries beyond what would be expected with a wave of influenza.

The fact that this WHO model is not concerned with the phenomenon of 'health' is also shown by the fact that the logic of preventing infection takes no account of the harmful consequences it has for health.

A Strategy To Avoid One Specific Risk Leads To A High Risk Situation For Everything Else

This model has the fundamental contradiction of pretending to be a model for minimising the risk of SARS-CoV-2 but, because of its very nature, it represents a high-risk situation not only for national health systems but for all other systems across society (from social, educational, economic, and cultural to family systems and partnerships and so on).

Ideology Instead Of Science

The model of disease outlined here can be seen to be guided by those involved's own interests and therefore is an ideology. Despite reference to high ethical values (solidarity with the elderly, sick and weak), it all comes down to the fact that there should only be one proven antidote to infections caused by Sars-CoV-2, namely vaccination. This vaccination must then of course be prescribed as compulsory for everyone in order to protect public health.

What Is Going On In Nursing And Intensive Care?

Dr. Matthias Thöns, a specialist in anaesthesiology, emergency, pain and palliative medicine, draws attention to an important detail regarding the spread of infections:

> 'We know from Spain that 12 percent of medical staff are currently infected. In China the figure was 3.4 percent, and they were well protected at the beginning. In Italy it was 9 percent. We know that infections occur during respiratory procedures such as intubation, suction or bronchoscopy. All procedures which result in the virus being carried into the air are highly infectious. And we cannot protect ourselves sufficiently in Germany at the moment. Not only because the material is missing, but also because the highest level of protection, the FFP3 masks have a 5 percent leakage rate. You can tell this by the fact that, for example, glasses fog up when you wear the mask.'

Basically, he describes the situation created by the pandemic as follows:

> 'If you are honest, Covid-19 is not an intensive care disease. On average, patients over 80 years of age are severely affected, and in the vast majority of cases they are multimorbid, (i.e. they have multiple chronic illnesses at the same time). They get pneumonia as a result of this virus and that is then fatal. The majority of those affected by pneumonia in the past have always been treated by palliative care - pneumonia at the end of life was called the old person's friend. And now they go and diagnose the Corona infection and turn it into an intensive care case and of course they still can't save the patients. They're just too sick and they can't be saved.'[83]

Even in emails to me, some people express confusion about the current conditions in hospitals and nursing homes. Here is an

---

[83] https://www.dud-magazin.de/2020/04/03/corona-sprechen-wir-über-ethik-und-gerechtigkeit/ (retrieved 10/04/20) In German

assessment by a woman who sees how the nursing staff are currently completely overtaxed and feel abandoned:

'I just watched your latest video on your site. The questions you raised touched me. From where I am today, I agree with you on every point. But I used to be a nurse and I notice how it triggers me that the crisis is being played out at the expense of the nursing staff. I know that fundamentally, of course, this is all triggering me because I myself had to take responsibility for my mother who had cancer from the moment I was conceived and, since my early childhood, I was also responsible for an aunt in need of care who lived with our family and whom we nursed for 25 years. In this respect I have been severely overburdened from an early age. No wonder I became a nurse and then my brother became a nurse.

Nevertheless, I am currently in contact with many people who still work in nursing - my husband, my brother, some very good friends. I don't know why the impression is being created that our hospitals are currently not overloaded. There is chaos in many intensive care units, because on every level materials are missing and are not being delivered and because the nursing staff is increasingly exhausted and is absent due to illness.

In Tübingen, people are having to work 12-hour shifts due to a lack of personnel. And everyone is worried about how long the staff will be able to cope. On top of this, there is also the knowledge that ventilation only allows a small number of patients to survive and is only done to prevent people from suffocating. In the palliative wards and nursing homes, people are allowed to die, but it is true that they suffocate in agony and are therefore put to sleep with morphine. Everyone in the hospital I speak to says they have never experienced anything like this.

From this point of view I can understand why people are frightened by politics. Although of course I don't think that's right and proper. But most people know nothing about inner healing. I often ask myself how one could bring it to people at large.

Perhaps it is also that socially, sick and old people, those needing care and those that are dying are a split-off part of society. This is true of disabled people too, which I experience on a daily basis in my work now as a special needs teacher. Hospitals, nursing homes and special schools are reception centres for people who have no place in society and whom we do not want to see because people cannot stand it. This part of the population is almost analogous to the traumatised parts of the psyche that are split off in our inner psychological world. Do you think it's valid to make this comparison?

From where I stand today, it is clear to me that I could only work as a nurse because I had the ability to split. Otherwise, what one experiences in hospital is unbearable. Fortunately, I recognised this early on and gave up the profession after a few years. Also because orthodox medicine always left too many questions unanswered for me and I always had a holistic view of the human being. For me, conventional medicine is emergency medicine and I haven't had to use it for a long time, not least thanks to your IoPT.

I am therefore very interested in bringing your method into wider society. I recommended you to ZDF TV for their programme 'Markus Lanz'. The ZDF thanked me by return of post with the remark that they had passed on my suggestion to the editorial staff responsible for guest planning. It was good to be heard. I very much hope that you too will be heard by an even wider audience than is already the case.'

I received this email from this lady on 12th April 2020. As part of my reply, I sent her the following article that I had recently come across about the causes of the current chaos:

'A doctor from the Ruhrgebiet is now criticising the coronavirus strategy. Do old and weak patients with Covid-19 belong in intensive care? […]

Palliative physician Thöns also has an opinion with regard to the issue of patient will. 'We are now prescribing intensive care here, buying expensive equipment, running weekend courses for medical staff to serve a group that in most cases doesn't want this at all'. The current actions of many decision-makers are described by experts as being in 'panic mode'.

Currently (as of 8th April), intensive care beds in Germany are still relatively empty. Respirators are free. According to Thöns, hospital managers may soon come up with the idea of admitting old people for reasons of turnover. In 14 days, the wards will be full of non-rescuable, multimorbid old people. And once they are on the machines, the question arises as to who will switch them off again. 'That would be a homicide,' says the doctor from Witten. An 'ethical catastrophe' is imminent due to greed for money.'[84]

To this I received this reply from the woman I'd been in touch with (13/04/20):

'Thank you for your answer. It is true that the beds must currently be kept free for Corona patients and small hospitals are afraid of being ruined by this. This shows how sick our system is. All operations and treatments that are not essential to life have had to be cancelled. It is also true that people currently avoid going to hospitals, even if it is necessary, because they are afraid of getting infected.

It saddens me that many people who may never have seen the inside of a care facility and probably have never cared for a sick person and/or accompanied a dying person are now suddenly writing a lot on the subject,. It has become clear to me that the groups of sick people and the groups of carers are currently being abused by both sides of this Corona War – by those that are hysterical and the deniers. But both groups (the sick & their carers) are not really seen and neither side is looked after. Since it sets strong triggers off in me, I will do a self-encounter process about it.

My friend, who works in a palliative ward, told me yesterday that corona patients always reminded her of feverish little children lying neglected in their beds, waiting for someone to come. You and I know who they are waiting for.

---

[84] https://www.ruhr24.de/ruhrgebiet/coronavirus-behandlung-intensivstation-nrw-lungenentzuendung-matthias-thoens-witten-zr-13645038.html?fbclid=IwAR2HvGIAbswNmydbDF9Wtd6qNchNH-bjTikjQvVzhI0k5ZF0gTV-pX2Lilk

She also said that it would be no problem to care for these patients if there were enough staff and material available. They could have brought in retired staff for that.

My hope is that the current crisis will make more people aware of themselves, their traumas and their inner healing ... Best wishes'

Gradually this woman became aware of why she was so personally touched by the situation in the intensive care units:

'When I was in the womb, my mother was operated on because she had an ovarian tumour. That was in the fourth month of pregnancy, in 1976, and I once felt in a constellation that I was severely deprived of oxygen during the operation and almost died. Probably also from the anaesthetic, as my mother was also ventilated during the operation. What nobody noticed at that time was that there was another baby in her belly that did not survive. My twin was quasi-euthanised during the operation, or at least that is how I perceive it.

Now it has become clear to me why the subject of shortness of breath, respiration and euthanasia are such strong triggers for me. I have often mourned the loss of my twin after constellations in which he appeared. Perhaps I am now a little closer to integrating the loss of my twin.

My hope is that all people, especially those who are currently making decisions for the population, would look more at themselves and their own biography and understand why they are making decisions from their unconscious that put others into difficulty ... warm greetings'.

(email from 13/04/20)

Here is another personal report from someone working within a nursing department (dated 17/04/20):

'The question of where we would now be without Corona, made me angry at first. Then immediately came feelings of abuse, which were already coming when I wrote you the questions about nursing care in society. I find it so shameful that the care industry is not properly seen.

When I woke up yesterday, I was crying and the trauma came up. When my mother found out that she was pregnant with me, she frequently stroked and squeezed her stomach very hard, over and over again. She did not want to have a child. It was supposed to go away again. For me in the womb this was really threatening, a life and death struggle. I was defenceless and exposed to the danger without being able to do anything about it. That part of me that stands up for itself, that defends itself.

I was a remarkably affectionate child, who was overburdened with many tasks such as looking after other children, taking on the role of mother, and not least having to take care of myself. This constant overtaxing of me and crossing of my boundaries has left me with these feelings of abuse. I was also sexually abused by my grandfather when I was 8 years old, which is not directly being triggered at the moment, but the feeling of being at the mercy of others and of being defenceless is.

In my profession as a nurse, which I love to do, there are of course always excessive demands. It is simply too much work for one person to do. And there is no way to say no in this situation. I simply cannot just not take care of three patients if they are there in front of me.

The problem is the high economic pressure the system is under, which seems to be getting higher all the time. The work rotas can only be planned to a very limited extent and it is not getting any better with the new 'lower personnel limit'. What are we supposed to do when suddenly five patients are admitted late on in the day, or when a patient suddenly feels really bad and needs one-on-one care over a prolonged length of time. What about the other patients that you are meant to be covering on that shift? We have a dementia area, and if a patient slips into delirium there, he will need intensive care over a longer period of time. On these shifts, you feel like you've been left alone. You get help from your colleagues, but they have their own 10 patients to look after. 20 years ago, when I started this profession, there were stressful shifts, but also quiet ones. Now you have the feeling that there are either stressful shifts or very stressful shifts, often without a break.

Now in the Corona crisis, the pressure is enormous. We currently have 20 Corona patients in our hospital and 10 of them on our ward. We have expanded the area on our ward to take another 7 beds. The new arrivals that display symptoms are isolated in single rooms until their test results come back. If they are positive, they come to us and are placed in group isolation. The care of corona patients requires twice as much staff because it is incredibly strenuous to work with these FFP 2 masks on. The test results will come in the afternoon at 16:00. Only then can I decide whether I need the 3rd person (2 qualified nurses need 1 non-qualified support person) at night and the 7th person (3 qualified and 3 practical nurses need an additional qualified support person) the next day or not. This person does not know until 4 p.m. whether he/she has to work the night or the next morning at 6.30 a.m. or not. Sometimes you have planned one person too many because 4 patients are suddenly discharged, then a person who is ready to work has to be cancelled.

In order to be able to provide this level of staff at all, we had to resort to students who have done their training and were still at college and to colleagues who are already retired.

And at this point I come back to my question about society. What am I to make of the debate on television yesterday about the gradual re-opening of schools. They say that teachers of at-risk age do not have to teach. In my profession, at the beginning of the Corona crisis, there was a special call to bring colleagues out of retirement. There is a debate about how it should work if everyone wears a facemask at school. Does anyone ask how we communicate with our hearing impaired or those patients suffering from dementia? Does anybody care how stressful it is for us to be exposed to the danger? Among teachers, it is certainly a political issue.

There's a lot of fuss being made about how they're going to run the whole thing. I have never experienced group isolation either and my colleague and I had four hours AFTER the normal early shift to set up this area. It is a political decision because if staff in the nursing sector become scarce, we may/must end up working 12-hour shifts! Is this being considered for teachers too?

I have 2 children (16 and 13 years old) and I am currently forced to keep them at home and school them. I think it is presumptuous that the teachers are currently receiving their regular pay for doing nothing. When I'm having to do twice as much work and am getting nothing! I have the feeling that the care industry is a split off part of society, which must not be looked at, because otherwise so much pain would come to the surface. And society would really have to look at what parts of itself are not working.

Of course I see how this all connects with my personal life and to the traumas that I have experienced. But now the question arises for me, what to do in the current situation? Is it about getting out of the job because I have recognised my trauma and no longer want these triggers all the time? Or is it about fighting for the visibility of care? When I empathise, I always get the answer, I should just stay with myself. It'll all work out. I see the Corona crisis as an opportunity for everyone and for society as a whole.'

Highly competent physicians from intensive care units are now speaking out. They are aware that people will die at their hands if they treat them according to current orthodox thinking. However, if they respond to the individual needs of their patients, give them care, increase their fever and offer them vitamins, they then recover without having to endure the ordeal of artificial respiration, although whether the people treating them are able to effectively evaluate the objective data in front of them is uncertain because they are so locked-in to the orthodox model..[85]

Level-headed people who have been working in intensive care units for a long time should not be encouraged to misuse the pictures of intensive care units to put innocent people into a state of trauma.[86]

The argument that there are too few ventilators for this virus, which mainly infects the lungs and therefore starves people of oxygen, is gradually collapsing. When pathologists disregarded the warning of the Robert Koch Institute not to autopsy those who had died as a result of Covid-19, the following became apparent:

---

[85] https://m.youtube.com/watch?v=JWlouv9QafU&feature=share (retrieved 13/04/20) – The video has since become private.
[86] https://www.freitag.de/autoren/elsa-koester/menschen-sterben-immer (retrieved 13/04/20)

'In Switzerland, pathologists have already performed autopsies, depending on the equipment in the autopsy rooms and 'depending on courage', as Alexandar Tzankov, head of the autopsy department at the University Hospital of Basel, says. So far, twenty Covid-19 deceased have been autopsied there, and Tzankov can already identify patterns in the diagnoses. "All the patients had high blood pressure," says the professor, "the majority of the patients were also severely obese or at least significantly overweight. And they were mostly men", he says. "More than two thirds of the patients had damaged coronary arteries, one third had diabetes."

In addition to clarifying the pre-existing conditions, Tzankov's team of doctors also examined damage to the lung tissue of the deceased. "Very few patients had pneumonia," he says, "but what we saw under the microscope was a severe disturbance of the microcirculation of the lungs". This means that oxygen exchange is no longer functioning, and explains the difficulties in ventilating Covid-19 patients in intensive care units. "You can give the patients as much oxygen as you want, it just won't circulate". It is unclear whether the findings could have been taken into account earlier in the treatment of ICU patients.' (Süddeutsche Zeitung, April 22, 2020, p. 2)

On 25th April 2020 I receive the following report from an Italian doctor, who also thinks that the treatment of Covid-19 patients in intensive care units with ventilators is contraindicated. It is venous microthrombosis, not pneumonia, that is leading to a higher risk of mortality. Therefore, home treatments with anti-inflammatory drugs would help just as well and just as quickly:

'Fernando Otero De Navascues: THE LAST HOUR

About the coronavirus: it seems that this disease has attacked the whole world. Thanks to the autopsies carried out by the Italians, it has been shown that it is not pneumonia but disseminated intravascular coagulation (thrombosis) that leads to mortality. The way to combat this is with antibiotics, anti-inflammatory and anticoagulant drugs.

Protocols have been changed here since midday. According to the valuable information from Italian pathologists, neither ventilators nor intensive care units should be needed. If this is true in all cases, we will be able to find our way out of all this sooner than expected.

Important and novel about the coronavirus:

Worldwide, COVID-19 has been mishandled due to a serious diagnostic error.

A video was made of a Mexican family in the USA, in which it was confirmed that they were cured with a home remedy: three 500mg aspirin tablets, dissolved in lemon juice boiled with honey, are taken hot and the next day they were well as if nothing had happened to them! Well, the following scientific information proves that they are right!

This information was published by a medical researcher from Italy:

Thanks to 50 autopsies performed on patients who had died of COVID-19, they found that, strictly speaking, it was not pneumonia that had caused their deaths - since the virus not only kills pneumocytes of its type, but also triggers a rapidly progressing inflammation to produce an endothelial vascular thrombosis. The corresponding diffuse thrombosis of the lung has been the most common as the lung is the most inflamed, but it has also caused heart attacks or strokes and many other thrombotic diseases. In fact, these records have exposed the antiviral therapies as useless and have shown that it is necessary to focus on the anti-inflammatory and anticoagulant therapies instead. These therapies can also be carried out straight away at home, as patients respond very well to the treatment. Later they are less effective. They are almost useless during resuscitation. If the Chinese had found out, they would have invested in home therapy, not intensive care! The solution to WIDE INTRAVASCULAR COAGUALATION (THROMBOSIS) is to use antibiotics, anti-inflammatories and anticoagulants.

An Italian anatomical pathologist reports that the hospital in Bergamo has performed a total of 50 autopsies and that in Milan there have been 20, meaning that the Italian rate of Covid-related autopsies is the highest in the world, the Chinese have performed only 3, but these autopsies seem to fully confirm the information above. In short, the success of the treatment is determined by the disseminated intravascular coagulation activated by the virus. Thus, interstitial pneumonia would have had nothing to do with the cause of death, but would have been a major diagnostic error. We have unnecessarily doubled the number of resuscitation sites in intensive care units at exorbitant cost. Looking back, I have to reconsider these chest x-rays, which were discussed a month ago as interstitial pneumonia. In fact, they may be entirely consistent with the said disseminated interstitial coagulation.

People go to intensive care units for generalised venous thrombotic embolism, predominately in the lungs. If this were the case, intubation and resuscitation would be useless if the thrombosis embolism is not corrected first. If you are ventilating a lung where the blood is not flowing, this is useless. In fact, nine out of ten die because the problem is cardiovascular, not respiratory.

It is venous microthrombosis, not pneumonia, that determines mortality.

Why do thrombi form? Because, according to conventional medicine, inflammation triggers thrombosis through a complex but known pathophysiological mechanism. In the scientific literature, especially from China, it is therefore stated that no anti-inflammatory drugs should be used and this was the situation at least until mid-March. Now, in Italy, therapy with anti-inflammatory drugs and antibiotics is used, as in the case of influenza, and the number of hospital patients has been reduced.

Many deaths, including those of forty-year-olds, had a history of fever for 10 to 15 days and were not treated adequately. The inflammation destroyed everything and created the ground for the formation of thrombi, since the main problem is not the virus but the immune reaction that destroys the cell into which the virus enters. In fact, patients with rheumatoid arthritis were never admitted to the Covid departments because they receive cortisone therapy, which has a great anti-inflammatory effect. This is the main reason why hospital stays in Italy are decreasing and Covid is becoming a treatable disease at home. Good treatment at home not only avoids hospitalisation, but also lowers the risk of thrombosis. It was not easy to understand, as the signs of micro-embolism have faded even in the echocardiogram.

This weekend the data of 50 patients were compared between those who have trouble breathing and those who are breathing fine and the situation seems to be very clear.

With this important finding, it is not possible to immediately return to normal life and open quarantined shops. However, it is time to publish this data so that the health authorities of each country can carry out their respective analyses of this information. In this way they can avoid more needless deaths and the vaccine may come later.

In Italy, as of today, the protocols are changing.

According to valuable information from Italian pathologists, respirators and intensive care units are not required. So we need to reconsider what measures are being put in place to adequately treat this disease.' [87]

The intensive care physician Stefan Kluge makes a similar argument:

'"This is dramatic and was new for us". This is how intensive care physician Stefan Kluge, professor at the University Hospital Hamburg-Eppendorf, reacted to the latest evaluation of autopsies of more than 170 people who died of Covid-19:

More than half had venous thrombosis in both legs;

One third suffered a fatal pulmonary embolism (blocked blood vessel in the lung).

"As practicing clinicians, we can only suspect causes of death", explained Kluge in the programme 'ARD Extra' on 7th May. "Only autopsies can provide proof." Almost all of these patients had never been treated for thrombosis or pulmonary embolism before.

"In our university hospital, we now treat all admitted patients suffering from Covid-19 with the anticoagulant heparin," said Kluge. "It is important to remember to treat all Covid-19 patients [with more severe symptoms even outside the hospital] with heparin prophylactically. Heparin is injected intravenously (during the acute phase) but also subcutaneously (prophylaxis, longer therapy). Studies would have to investigate the extent to which blood-thinning drugs

---

[87] Since I could not find the link to this article on the internet despite intensive research, here is a link to an Italian study that points in the same direction: https://youtu.be/-mvwOZt44A8 (retrieved 09/05/20)

are most effective without causing complications due to an increased risk of bleeding".[88]

This report in the Tagesspiegel of 20th April 2020 is also on similar lines:

'There is currently growing evidence that it is not only the so-called 'shock lung', the Acute Respiratory Distress Syndrome (ARDS), that causes death, but also pulmonary embolisms - the clogging of vital lung vessels with blood clots.'[89]

So does this mean that the panic-mongering that we have too few ventilators in intensive care units is barking up the wrong tree and is basically superfluous, even fatal?

It gets worse. In May, a study by the Allgemeine Ortskrankenkassen (AOK) (General Local Health Insurance Funds) reveals that many people with symptoms of serious illness are no longer going to hospitals.

'Most recently, on the 'National Day against Strokes', the Association of Statutory Health Insurance Physicians in Lower Saxony (KVN) stated that people with stroke symptoms should still immediately alert a doctor or clinic despite the Corona epidemic. Otherwise, it could lead to fatal or serious consequences. Medical specialists had been saying that the number of patients reporting stroke-like symptoms has decreased by 30 percent in the past few weeks. And that even chronically ill patients often do not come to the practice for regular check-ups.'

Does this mean that people are dying not because of the corona virus, but because of the lockdown measures?[90] This might be one of the reasons why the death rate in Germany has increased despite the fact that the flu/corona wave had already passed through the

---

[88] https://www.infosperber.ch/Artikel/Gesundheit/Alle-Corona-Patienten-mit-Blutverdunnern-behandeln (retrieved 09/05/20)

[89] https://www.tagesspiegel.de/wissen/woran-sterben-corona-patienten-wirklich-ein-schweizer-forscher-macht-hoffnung-im-kampf-gegen-covid-19/25750666.html (retrieved 09/05/20)

[90] https://www.focus.de/gesundheit/news/drastischer-rueckgang-erste-studie-zeigt-wie-viele-patienten-sich-wegen-corona-nicht-behandeln-liessen_id_11988988.html (retrieved 14/05/20)

population.[91] This is almost too monstrous an idea to contemplate: People are not dying from 'Corona', but from the consequences of the unjustly declared Corona pandemic.

What's Going On In The Nursing Homes?

On the 8th May 2020 an insider source writes to Jens Wernicke of the Rubikon with the following report:

'For information purposes. This may be passed on anonymously. Living in a care home means anything but feeling at home, even after the so-called relaxation of the previous restrictions on visits. Everything here is more like being in a prison with conditional release. The residents feel that too. Some have complained from the beginning that they want to get out of this prison. The excess mortality due to loneliness and lack of human contact has certainly long outweighed the risks of all the viruses in the world put together.

Bill Gates is certainly going to be pleased about the now massively increased use of video calling in care homes. But the elderly also need physical closeness. People are not androids who only communicate digitally. All in all, the Corona emergency legislation is primarily directed against the old, sick and poor in our society. And that seems to be the state's raison d'etre, judging by the pattern of Merkel/Spahn's government: to run away from all this. But at the moment you can't get any further than the border of the country anyway but even so we've long since passed the border of what's tolerable.'

---

[91] https://www.faz.net/aktuell/gesellschaft/gesundheit/coronavirus/sterblichkeit-in-deutschland-durch-corona-ueber-dem-durchschnitt-16760063.html (retrieved 14/05/20)

Everyone's A 'Conspiracy Theorist'

Meanwhile, Dr. Wodarg and countless experts from Germany and abroad and the alternative media channels - here in Germany for example the Rubikon or KenFM - are not valued in the public media as critical dissenting voices, in the search for a factual explanation of the risk potential of Covid-19, as should be the case if this were actually a natural phenomenon. Instead, there is an attempt to dismiss all critical dissenting voices by every method of propaganda possible ('Monitor' TV programme broadcast on 02/04/20) [92]. Supposedly serious scientifically fact checkers, that are paid for by, amongst others, the ARD (Germany's group of public-service broadcasters), support the continuing Corona propaganda machine.

For some time now, the catchword 'conspiracy theory' has been used to devalue any objection to the prevailing politics. [93] It is then no longer the point itself that needs to be argued, instead all argument becomes centred on the person themselves. This means that person concerned can be accused of having sinister intentions, and that personal mistakes they've made in the past or shady contacts they've had with other persons or institutions, which have already been excluded from society, are all brought up in order to undermine them and so therefore dismiss their arguments. So past contact with the broadcaster Russia Today can be a welcome opportunity to accuse someone of collaboration with the still main political enemy number one. No distinction is made between whether the counter-arguments come from the left or the right of the political spectrum. Conspiracy theorists are basically made out to be unworldly crackpots, they are people wrapped up in their own fantasies, who are actually more in need of psychiatric help than any serious examination of their arguments.

Carsten Forberger, in his extensively researched article on the history and current practice of using the term 'conspiracy theory', comes to the following conclusion:

'Anyone who accuses others of spreading 'conspiracy theories' when it comes to complex and politically explosive

---

[92] https://www1.wdr.de/daserste/monitor/sendungen/corona-fake-news-106.html (retrieved 04/04/20)

[93] https://off-guardian.org/2020/06/03/a-conspiracy-theorist-confesses/ (retrieved 07/06/20)

events is therefore unintentionally revealing that he is trapped in the same thought constructs in which the 'conspiracy theorists' are allegedly to be found: in simple dualisms of black and white or friend and foe (the virus is evil and must go away), in simplistic explanations of complex contexts (the virus is novel, highly contagious, particularly dangerous and therefore, until the introduction of a vaccine, every means of destroying it is right), and in the exclusion of all medical and legal facts that contradict one's own dogma. In psychology this is probably called projection. I call it a framework in which facts are arbitrarily reinterpreted into outlawed opinions. It is highly unscientific and ideologically dangerous.'[94]

Since fear of the AfD (a far-right political party in Germany – the German equivalent of the British National Front) is more widespread among the critical part of the German population today than of left-wing revolutionaries, an attempt is being made here to catch two birds with one stone. When people from the left spectrum criticise not only the governing parties but also the media close to the government (Wernicke 2017), they are lumped together with right-wing parties for the sole reason that they too speak of things like the 'lying press', because they feel that they are not sufficiently represented by it. A term such as 'Querfront' (the 'Third Position'[95]) is then created for this in order to seal an alliance in spirit between left-wing critics and right-wing radicals.

I first heard the term 'conspiracy theorist' a few years ago when I was studying the lectures and books of Dr. Daniele Ganser[96]. He is a historian and his specialist field is the period after 1945, especially dealing with the different wars that have taken place since then. He comes to the conclusion that the respective reasons for starting wars in violation of international law were to impute hostility on the part of the opponent, but that this hostility was started by their own side. In English this is called a 'false-flag' operation.[97]

The start of the Second World War was also justified on the part of the Third German Reich by the fact that Polish nationalists had undertaken an attack on a radio station in the border town of

---

[94] https://multipolar-magazin.de/artikel/wenn-fakten-zu-verschworungstheorien-werden (retrieved 28/05/20) In German

[95] https://en.wikipedia.org/wiki/Third_Position retrieved 10.08.20

[96] https://en.wikipedia.org/wiki/Daniele_Ganser retrieved 10.08.20

[97] https://en.wikipedia.org/wiki/False_flag retrieved 10.08.20

Gleiwitz on 31st August 1939, but in reality this was carried out by SS soldiers disguised as Polish guerrillas. In an address to the supreme commanders of the Wehrmacht, Hitler already said on August 22, 1939: 'I will provide a propagandistic casus belli[98]. Its credibility doesn't matter. When we are victorious, we will not be asked whether we told the truth.'[99] Therefore, as planned, on August 31st, Hitler was able to announce to his people: 'Since 5:45 a.m. shots have been fired back!'

Daniele Ganser has also shown that the beginnings of the Vietnam War by the USA on August 4th 1964 followed a similar pattern, through an attack on the US warship Maddox, faked by the American military themselves (Ganser 2016, p. 135 ff.). In his book 'Illegal Wars' Ganser presents the result of his historical research by describing conflicts from the Cuban crisis through to the Syrian war. In these conflicts, the aggressors have always given themselves the justifications for the alleged necessity of starting these acts of war. From the perspective of IoPT, these are typical perpetrator strategies. The victims are declared as perpetrators and the actual perpetrators present themselves as the victims.

The USA and its allies in NATO don't find it easy to read Ganser's findings. What particularly earned Daniele Ganser the reputation of being a 'conspiracy theorist' was his analysis of the reasons for the 'war on terror', which the American president G.W. Bush Jr. started with the attack on Afghanistan. This war against states which, in the opinion of the USA, supported terrorist groups such as Al-Qaeda was justified by citing the attack by 16 terrorists on the two buildings of the World Trade Centre in New York, on the Pentagon and the White House in Washington. One of the numerous mysteries of this event, which is still unsolved today, is that a third building in New York – the WTC 7 - also collapsed that day, apparently as a result of an explosion, although no aircraft had crashed into it, as allegedly had happened to the north and south towers of the WTC.

On what unstable foundations the story that 'terrorists have steered two airplanes into the two WTC towers' stands, is not only proven by numerous counter-opinions from architects and pilot associations both inside and outside the USA. Even a Year 10 school student can seemingly effortlessly list a whole range of hard to refute

---

[98] A Casus Belli is a Latin expression meaning 'an act that justifies war'.
[99] https://en.wikipedia.org/wiki/Gleiwitz_incident retrieved 10/08/20

concrete arguments in his term paper that basically rules out the possibility of the WTC buildings collapsing due to airplanes and a fire that melts the massive steel beams of the buildings (Hühler 2018)[100]. Rather, it makes most sense that all the buildings were blown up from the inside.

Even almost twenty years after 9/11, all alternative explanations for the collapse of the WTC buildings, which deviate from the official line that the then Bush administration presented as true and valid in its final report, are called 'conspiracy theories'.

The argument of a 'conspiracy theory' was already being used in relation to the assassination of American President John F. Kennedy in 1963, if anyone questioned the official narrative:

'John F. Kennedy, the 35th President of the United States, was assassinated on Friday, November 22, 1963, at 12:30 p.m. Central Standard Time in Dallas, Texas, while riding in a presidential motorcade through Dealey Plaza… He was fatally shot by former U.S. Marine Lee Harvey Oswald firing in ambush from a nearby building… Oswald was arrested by the Dallas Police Department 70 minutes after the initial shooting… Oswald was fatally shot in the basement of Dallas Police Headquarters by Dallas nightclub operator Jack Ruby.

The Warren Commission appointed by Kennedy's successor Lyndon B. Johnson came to the conclusion that Oswald was the sole perpetrator. A committee of inquiry convened later by the House of Representatives (HSCA), on the other hand, found that there had probably been several perpetrators. There is no clear forensic evidence for this; rather, recent investigations of the available material have confirmed the single perpetrator thesis. However, the question is still controversial today. The assassination attempt polarized the public in a lasting way. The majority of Americans believe that Kennedy was the victim of a conspiracy. A number of conspiracy theories continue to be considered. From the very beginning, the investigation of the murder case was hampered by mishaps, omissions and mistakes by the investigating authorities, doctors and

---

[100] https://www.siper.ch/assets/uploads/files/zeitungsartikel/Martin-Luther-Gymnasium%20Hartha%20(2018)%20-%20Die%20ungeloesten%20(physikalischen)%20Raetsel%20des%2011.%20September%202001.pdf (retrieved 09/04/20) In German

investigative commissions. Historians tend to favour the single perpetrator theory'. [101]

'Conspiracy theory' in this sense is a relic from days gone by of twentieth century political agitation, when it was still easy to isolate and sideline unpopular opinions and critics. Today however, thanks to the Internet and social media, no one has a monopoly on opinion. This is one of the reasons why dictatorial regimes try to bring the Internet and social media under their control.

This strategy is based on anonymity, also in this sense it is a sniper mentality. For example, with Wikipedia, you cannot trace who inserts comments on the pages of unpopular people, this person could be spreading conspiracy theories.

Figure 14: Should we automatically dismiss conspiracy theories? [102]

Basically what I do know for sure is that there are people and institutions that secretly influence political, economic and social events and shun the light of publicity. These include, for example,

[101] https://de.wikipedia.org/wiki/Attentat_auf_John_F._Kennedy (retrieved 25/04/20)
[102]

https://wirrklich.files.wordpress.com/2011/01/verschwoerungstheorie.jpg?w=500&h=364 (retrieved 25/04/20) the secret services, lobbyists and commissioned think tanks that keep their clients anonymous.

It is makes sense that trauma perpetrators like to cover up their actions and do not want to be seen. It makes me think of the saying: He who points a finger at others is pointing three fingers at himself.

It is impossible for me to verify all the assumptions and opinions as to what is true about the staging of the pandemic. For example, an apparently highly qualified American medical doctor thinks he knows facts that indicate that research has been done in America on corona viruses to make them more infectious. When this was prohibited by the American government, officials from the Ministry of Health channelled funds into China so that research could continue on this virus programme in Wuhan.[103] In Wuhan, the institute where the corona virus research was being carried out and the market where the virus is said to have jumped from animal to human are within sight of each other.

At the very least the following does seems plausible to me: if a pandemic is to be staged, by whomever, it needs a virus or bacterium that is less dangerous than Ebola or the plague pathogen, but produces more infections and deaths than seasonal influenza. A 'novel' corona virus in combination with SARS, a lung disease that has caused fear and anxiety in Asia in the past, has a good chance of being a candidate for this. But this is just speculation.

Conspiracy theories should not be considered good or bad in and of themselves. What matters is whether they are true or not.

A Community Of Conspirators

From the perspective of my Identity-Oriented Psychotrauma Theory (IoPT), I find that when perpetrators and victims exist within groups of people they often become a community of co-conspirators. Victims hold on to communities that are destructive to them such as family, partnerships, companies or states because they do not want to admit their victimhood, they have existential fears or are ashamed of what has happened to them. The perpetrators also do not want to clearly see and feel that they have been perpetrators, because otherwise they would also be ashamed of this and would have to fear the anger and indignation of their victims.

---

[103] https://www.youtube.com/watch?v=mSH_NI9FA9k&feature=youtu.be (retrieved 25/04/20)

In this way, the victims spare the perpetrators and the perpetrators carry on as if their physically, emotionally and psychologically abusive actions only fulfilled the victims' most ardent wishes for safety, security and well-being. Victims and perpetrators, with their respective victim and perpetrator attitudes, then feel trapped in a delusional 'we' in which the truth about what is really happening must not come to light and therefore the traumatisation can continue unhindered.

It makes me happy when people wake up and see through such connections, as in this letter that someone sent me recently:

'I find it impressive how calmly and clearly you name facts and perpetrators. First I felt shyness and uneasiness, then I felt relief. Now, for the first time, I have really understood the perpetrator-victim-rescuer dynamic. And I see in my immediate environment how survival strategies have become radicalised – it is all highly emotional and not very rational. It is exciting to see that these are exactly the dynamics I read in your books. Right now I feel like part of a big human experiment.

I am irritated by the fact that people try to push other people to the sidelines by calling them conspiracy theorists. Because for me I associate conspiracy with something that is 'carried out in secret'. Therefore, the appropriate term for me would be 'attempted fraud'. Every day I get to observe how not taking responsibility goes hand in hand with accusation. I think then, oh yes, I have already read that as theory – and now I experience it in practice.

Unfortunately, I observe an increasing devaluation of my fellow human beings because of their opinions. The devaluation of people, especially in media reports, without any apparent desire to deal with the content of what they are saying, scares me. For it is precisely the media, in the use of language and in the way discourse should take place, that I see as a role model, which they do not currently live up to. The linguistic devaluation is the beginning of a spiral which, in my opinion, if it is not stopped, can lead to material damage and physical abuse.

I find your clear position in the current situation courageous, refreshing, and very important for me, it serves as a role model!' (e-mail, received on 16/05/20)

Perpetrator-Victim-Rescuer Dynamics In Conventional Medicine

In the following email, which I received on the same day (16/05/20), the writer expresses that she too is currently experiencing the perpetrator-victim logic at close quarters, this time in hospital:

'Unfortunately, I am lying in hospital after a serious operation and this is not a good time to be ill - in every respect. I could write a book straight from Corona hospital hell. Here everything that can be is pathologised, and that pathologisation is really intensified and is a breeding ground for the perpetrator-victim dynamic. But then I remember it's actually called a 'house for illness' (this is what the German word for 'hospital' 'Krankenhaus' literally means) not a house for health.'

I'd also like to share this letter from a former nurse about her experiences with conventional medicine (e-mail from 23/03/20):

'As a paediatric nurse I have many years of experience in intensive care and palliative care of both children and adults and both inpatient and outpatient. Recently, I have changed my field of work, as I could no longer support many decisions that were leading to medical treatments. I did not want to be continually giving up on myself and supporting the overburdened health care system by abandoning myself more and more.

Large parts of the currently influential orthodox medicine and pharmaceutical industry have the attitude that they must exhaust all medically feasible treatment options. The economisation of the health system, in which medical treatment is recognised as the main criterion for cash benefits, feeds this situation. The natural limits of life, the inherent wisdom of every life to accept that growth, healing and dying are all natural processes, is hardly possible within conventional medicine. Nowadays this has been replaced by a highly sophisticated machine-based medicine, which is capable of keeping every life technically alive through drug therapies, which can suppress, deceive or manipulate the function of whole body systems; through the ability to transplant many organs or to build artificial spare parts into the organism itself. All this technology leads to the attitude that we are the masters over life and death. The number of people with complex illnesses who need care is growing. The quality of life of those affected is of secondary importance. The suffering inflicted on patients and their relatives is immense. The lack of specialists and the fact that fewer and fewer people are able to care for their relatives at home also has an effect on this. This permanent chronic overburdening of the health care system leads to an insidious self-abandonment from everyone concerned. As people abandon themselves this leads to ever greater 'efficiency' in the nursing care sector, and, not infrequently, this working attitude is valued as 'heroic'.

When making decisions at the crossroads of life, the fact that someone can go on living has become the most important thing. But at what price for all those involved and with what drastic consequences and effects on the quality of life, social coexistence and everyday life, is often glossed over. In outpatient care, this dilemma is perceived and endured as a fact that is difficult or impossible to change. This includes support by outpatient nursing services that does not evolve with the patient, as there is a great shortage of skilled workers. Chronic lack of time in care is normal, since the services provided in the field of treatment care and basic care are billed in lump sums from an economic point of view, independent of the current condition, or help that the 'client' actually needs. The care provided by relatives is not remunerated at all. Many caregivers are responsible for the care of their own family in addition to their professional activities, which is an immense overburdening, especially since the sleep rhythm is often interrupted by the needs of the person being cared for. Necessary outpatient visits to therapists/specialists, applications for grants for the costs or treatments, nursing costs, materials, etc. also contribute to this chronic overburdening. When it comes to the decision to terminate life-prolonging measures, and if the consequence of this is death, this is also a burden too far for many people, especially when close relatives are involved.

Conventional medicine uses therapies that treat the symptoms. Pathogenic germs are fought, malignant cells are destroyed. The side effect that healthy parts of the body's immune system are also destroyed or impaired is accepted as normal. The body's natural defences are neither strengthened nor utilised. Triggers and causes of the disease patterns are not looked into. Conventional medicine can only, with difficulty, let its patients die, even if life itself considers it appropriate and sensible. And a large part of the people in this society cannot allow dying, because it happens so separated from everyday life. Ignorance about dying and the fact that many of us do not witness the dying process gives rise to many fears, including fear of great suffering. In this society, we do not own death as part and parcel of human life.

I have the perception that this attitude towards life and the actions that result from it have a direct influence on the current far-reaching political decision making. The complex contexts of life, the manifold possibilities of action that can be available to our lives even in times of crisis must be perceived and exploited in order not to let ourselves be dominated by this state of emergency.'

And here's a letter to me from a surgeon at a small hospital in the Lower Rhine region (e-mail from 24/03/20):

'You are certainly right that our conventional medicine models maintain our traumas. I often wrestle with my job, but I have not yet found another way to do it and I do try to treat as 'atraumatically' as I can as often as I can. But every patient chooses his own therapy. Our patients are primarily people who do not want to do anything for their health themselves, but come to us expecting to be 'repaired'.'

Gerd Reuther sums it up in a Rubikon article where he explains how conventional medicine originally set out to put a stop to quacks with a scientific approach and standards. However, in 2020 the situation looks bleak in this respect:

'For 2,400 years this was the medical standard: bloodletting, enemas, emetics and opium for everyone and against everything. Is this to be the case again now, when the injection of RNA fragments in the form of a 'vaccination' with fake proof of efficacy, which would otherwise sit unused on the shelves of the pharmaceutical industry, is declared the standard of treatment?

This is what Big Pharma wants. For some years now, the companies have had the authorities bring in accelerated approval procedures to meet their specific needs. Initially only for drugs for rare diseases, but now also in other cases without adequate scientific research.'[104]

Response To My Publications

If I use Wolfgang Wodarg, the Rubikon and KenFM as my sources of information, it is inevitable that I will also be suspected of being a conspiracy theorist. When this happens, wherever I can I try to pick up the phone and seek out personal contact with those people who have got in touch. Most of the time, I find that the person on the other end of the line has not yet thought about what exactly they mean by 'conspiracy theory'.

Sometimes I am faced with resistance from people I didn't expect it from. A participant in my training group last year is a doctor who is confronted with people who suffer from severe lung infections. He does his best to help these people. He does not share my fundamental criticism of the proclamation of a corona pandemic:

'In view of the hundreds and thousands of corpses piling up in France, Italy, New York, Ecuador, Brazil, I find your comments today on your website outrageous. My dear Franz, I'll say it to you one last time: I think you are completely misunderstanding the situation! Please open your eyes and stop denying reality.' (email dated 07/04/20)

His advice of essentially 'Si tacuisses, philosophus mansisses!'[105] really affected me. The idea that I mustn't raise my voice when my needs are ignored, was something I learned very well from my father.

---

[104] https://www.rubikon.news/artikel/lugen-ohne-limit (retrieved on 16/05/20)
[105] This quote is often attributed to the Latin philosopher Boethius of the late fifth and early sixth centuries. It translates literally as, 'If you had been silent, you would have remained a philosopher.' In the British TV series 'Yes, Prime Minister', Sir Humphrey Appleby translated it to the PM as: "If you'd kept your mouth shut we might have thought you were clever"
https://glosbe.com/la/en/si%20tacuisses,%20philosophus%20mansisses

When I was a child he'd stand over me and yell at me. When I was a baby he put a pillow on my head to stop me crying and screaming. Even later, he'd always batter me with verbal threats and abuse: 'As long as you're living under my roof, you do what I tell you!' Although I offered this doctor who wrote to me a personal conversation, he has still not accepted my offer.

At the moment I don't want to be a philosopher who sits safe in his ivory tower, tossing out the odd clever remark about current events. In this crisis situation it feels essential that I must raise my voice in public. If I simply ducked away and kept a noble silence, I would not have learned all that I know today. I would not have had so many interesting conversations with people who are also searching and trying to understand this strange and confusing situation. I would never have gone through all the highs and lows, from places of feeling safe to times I felt unsafe, that have challenged me both psychologically and emotionally during this time.

That is why I am happy about correspondence like this, which a woman sent to me when she ordered the first German language PDF edition of my Corona Pandemic Book from me on 15th May 2020:

'As I read your book 'Who am I in a traumatised society?' it really interested me and gave me a growing awareness of my own trauma biography. In the 50s I grew up in a village in east Bavaria. As girls we had to curtsey and kiss the priest's hand when we met him on the street. How's that as an example of an abusive method of demonstrating and manifesting your power? I'm writing to you now as I would like to purchase your new Corona book as a PDF.

Incidentally, I am experiencing something like a re-traumatisation right now with what I consider to be these arbitrary measures that are being imposed. It is horrible. When will we understand that no human being can protect life from life itself?'

Even feedback like this (email from 23/05/20) related to my educational work makes me feel better:

'Dear Prof. Ruppert,
Thank you very much for adding me to your mailing list. It is a great help and support for me to hear from other people and get their take on what is going on, particularly people

who are definitely not conspiracy theorists or right-wing radicals! But rather, like me, interested, committed, critical, feeling people from the centre ground of society. Being excluded from the mainstream triggers me in many ways. It stirs up old fears, increases my feelings of loneliness and throws up the age-old question of life: Am I wanted?

Apparently I am not alone in feeling like this. I find it striking that especially older, already emeritus, retired or highly paid academics have become the face of resistance. Luckily, they have the reputation and networks to withstand criticism or damage to their reputation. For many others, it is now becoming difficult to even ask critical questions without having to bear negative consequences.

As you make clear in your Corona publication, I personally see this time as a blueprint, that can show up the patterns in my life that still have a lasting effect and want to be seen'.

I would also like to share the following feedback from the 25th May on the updated first German edition of this book:

'Dear Prof. Ruppert, many thanks for the updated version. I would like to give you some feedback. I spent last Sunday sitting in the garden - at my laptop - and read the whole version. Once I had started, I couldn't stop reading. In between I got up and walked around again and again, because a lot of things stirred me and moved me.

Mostly I sat nodding in front of your words and sentences and said to myself: 'Yes, that's exactly how I experience it,' or 'I have these questions too'. Some of your words spoke to my soul and gave me many answers. Thank you very much for letting people share in your thoughts, your research and also in your own process. Such a valuable book. One can feel your inner journey, your doubts, your struggle for knowledge and truth, resignation and then again courage - and then how this all links to the trauma explanations as well as your own trauma feelings, in the context of Corona, government (parents?) etc.

I think I will read these pages again. On Sunday I went through it all very 'fast' because I wanted to experience it all and put it together and understand it. In the next few days I will take more time for this in some way.

I often feel that I am standing looking at this desperate situation and can hardly believe all that is going on. Sometimes I think that I will wake up from this nightmare. I experience this division in society and the poisonous tone, the denunciation and degradation. I am horrified. And it just doesn't stop. I am almost speechless.

In my work in psychiatry (I am an art therapist) I meet doctors and psychologists who have jumped on the panic bandwagon and praise the government. We are warned against so-called 'conspiracy theorists' (those who demonstrate and seriously top-class scientists and professors). It is downright crazy. I also experience that many colleagues pretend that nothing is wrong. 'It will be alright!' they say. And that becomes really fascinating if we look at it in terms of your explanation of personal traumas.

I personally often feel fear of something that I can't quite grasp yet. It feels like an atmosphere, a mood. It's like in the book 'Momo' by Michael Ende, when the men in grey come and this veil comes down that covers everything. I also feel cold. I don't want a new normality and at the same time I feel that the old normality can't exist anymore either, after all that has happened and what is happening.

I have a tendency to deny it. Surely no government or those with power and money can be so evil? But I know from my own history that I prefer to believe in the good in people. But in this case it is now so blatant that you have to really look at it. This is why it is good to understand that it is about trauma. The actions of those in power can probably only be understood through your theory. At least that's how it is for me, I can understand it all better having read your book.

In this whole process of the last weeks and months I tried again and again to sort myself out and orient myself somewhere. At some points only my own physical and psychological experience helped me. As soon as I heard Prof. Bhakdi speak, it opened up something in me. The tension in my stomach relaxed and everything became a little brighter. As soon as I read a story in the press, it immediately became tight inside me again, I was left frozen and fearful. From then on, I almost only dealt with people who were kind to me and I tried to concentrate on myself: through feeling (the tension in my stomach) and understanding (with the help of your book).

And when I glance at the news today and see that the Thuringian Prime Minister is feeling under pressure and has done a U-turn, inside I start to feel frozen again. And then there's this: 'The vaccine is coming soon'.

It's a pity, but I'd love to be part of a group with you at the moment, in a protected community with people who want to meet themselves. Yes, that's what I really miss at the moment. Encounters and contact with real people and with myself.'

Here too is some more feedback that reflect the sad reality of the consequences of the pandemic:

'I really appreciate your Corona book. It confirms what I myself see is happening. In my opinion, the psychological peak of the Corona crisis is what we in the hospital are having to deal with. I would sometimes like those who have decided on the measures to be taken to be forced to see that.' (email 26/05/20)

Dialogue With A Denunciator

The following letter from 14th April 2020 has made me very sad:

'Dear President Prof. Dr. XXXXX and Sirs & Madams of the Presidium of KSH (Catholic Foundation of Applied Sciences Munich),

In the course of looking into the Corona Pandemic, I stumbled upon Prof. Dr. Franz Ruppert and his conspiracy theories. Example here: https://franz-ruppert.de/de/9-startseite/106-warum

In addition to statements like 'this pandemic is a business game, causally linked to the richest man in the world, Bill Gates', Prof. Ruppert provides links to Dr. Wodarg, who obviously has been spreading theories that have long been proven wrong. In his text Prof. Ruppert also shows that, apart from the dangerous spreading of misinformation, he cannot master the simplest scientific methods of quoting others or he deliberately puts wrong words and statements into Mr. Bill Gates' mouth. Both are unworthy of a professor.

As a professor he is associated with your university and is also listed on the homepage of the KSH. How do you explain to students of your university that a conspiracist is allowed to teach? When can I expect a statement from you in which you will distance yourselves from these crude theories? Will Franz Ruppert still be allowed to call himself professor at your university? I look forward to receiving an answer soon.

Yours sincerely, Dr M.'

I immediately offered Dr. M. the opportunity to have a conversation, which we managed to have the next day via ZOOM. He is a 33-year-old man from Germany, who is currently living with his family in America, where he is on a scholarship from the German Research Society. We talked for about 90 minutes about various topics on the subject of Corona. He then wanted to end the conversation. The next day he sent me another email. I responded to his statements by noting my statement below it (plain text = Dr. M, **bold = Franz Ruppert**).

Prof. Dr. Ruppert, it was interesting and sobering talking to you.

Yes, it was for me too.

How would you feel if people were to seek help from an epidemiologist or virologist instead of a psychotherapist or psychologist in dealing with trauma and how to cope with it?

I would like to see virologists, epidemiologists and psychotraumatologists sitting together and advising each other from their different perspectives and their specialist fields. It would be very exciting for me to see what the results would be.
What would be your current Intention if you were seeking help? If you like, I can work on it online with you using my Intention method.

So far I have been very concerned about scientific scepticism and thought that this is mainly a problem of lack of education. Now I have come to realise with you that even education will not protect us from misinformation making people feel insecure.

You are right about that. Education is usually cognitive. It avoids dealing with personal emotional issues. What about you and your education? Did you have the opportunity during your school education, during your studies and since then to 'educate' yourself emotionally, i.e. to make further progress in your psycho-emotional development and deal with your own insecurities and fears? Even when I was studying psychology there wasn't the possibility of furthering my emotional education. It was only afterwards, in my psychotherapy training, that this was offered and even expected. But even there, there are still possibilities to avoid coming into contact with oneself. Cognitive education does certainly not provide emotional stability.

You criticise me for reporting your conspiracy theories to your employer?

Yes, what you have done is, in my view, a form of personal denunciation. I have been in contact with the university administration and have told them that my statements on the Corona pandemic are my private opinion. Even a university administration is not in possession of 'the' truth, but has to adapt as best it can to the circumstances of an outside situation like this. I do not know what understanding of science and university you have. For me, science is the examination of different facts, views, possible interpretations of statistics, possible alternative plans of action ... In short: dialogue instead of dictating one particular viewpoint. This may be a challenge both psychologically and emotionally. But if we are prepared to listen to the other person, we can all learn something from each other. For me, consciousness development is always the development of a co-consciousness.
Especially because of what has happened in German history (National Socialism, the GDR Stasi and so on) I am personally very concerned that a young man like you

is not ashamed of this action of denunciation to the authorities. Rather than first seeking contact with the person involved, you have approached his employer straight away, demanding the dismissal/professional annihilation of this person whose views you do not agree with - I am totally shocked by this. Education obviously does not protect against the tendency to denounce.

With catchwords like 'conspiracy theory' you also leave the field of actual argument behind. 'Conspiracy Theory' is an annihilator of argument. People have been using the phrase 'conspiracy theory' to devalue any objection against the ruling politics across the world. There is then no need to argue the point but only the character of the person - Conspiracy theorists can then basically be written off as crackpots and people trapped in their own fantasies who are actually a case for psychiatry.

You are a scientist who is making unfounded assumptions about other scientists from a completely different field, but you are saying that your own statements should not be checked by the university president or governing body?

There are different scientific assessments of the corona pandemic, both in Germany and around the world. Here is a summary: https://www.rubikon.news/artikel/weltweite-warnungen

If politicians decide on a path that here in Germany is based primarily on the opinions of Mr Drosten and Mr Wieler, then in my view this no longer has anything to do with finding the truth, but with political decisions. A university administration is also a political role. Are you saying, then, that at a university, too, the decisions on what is scientifically true should be based primarily on political considerations? I think you are confusing power with truth here. Especially when it comes to highly complex problems, we mustn't rely on monocausal theories, but rather a concert of voices, all of which can contribute something to the clarification of a complex situation.

Your own basis from which you derive your article 'Why? Because Bill Gates wants it that way!' is hair-raising. You write your text based on information from a KenFM video.

No, that's not true. I only put the link to the KenFM video there afterwards, after I had presented my thoughts on the role of Bill Gates in the two articles I had written before. I did this in the interview on the subject of Bill Gates on the 'Tagesthemen' show because I was so shocked that he seriously believes that the lockdown must continue until a vaccine is available for 7 billion people. How would you intervene here, who would you get in touch with as his employer to denounce such an insane idea?

All of this out of a motivation that came from a 'feeling', when you saw too much panic in the media.

My feeling is that there is panic in the media right now about this Corona virus, yes. It scares me and makes me feel very uneasy. And many people I know feel the same way. That's what these reports are all about isn't it, the piling up corpses and the stories of working in intensive care units?
So I then use my mind to try and clarify for myself, is this fear-mongering justified or not? I have personally experienced an education based on fear and violence. Arguing with my parents was almost impossible. This was also one of the reasons why I turned to science. What is your experience in regards to this?

I can only recommend the book on conspiracy myths, compiled by climate scientists. It's available here in many languages including German:
 https://www.climatechangecommunication.org/conspiracy-theory-handbook/
Maybe you will question one or the other YouTube videos on the basis of the 7 criteria / traits of conspiratorial thinking (on page 6 in the book): Contradictory, Overriding suspicion, Nefarious intent, something must be wrong, persecuted victim, immune to evidence, re-interpreting randomness.

Yes, I agree with you. Self-reflection and constant checking of one's own views are also part of science. I've been doing that ever since I started dealing with this Corona pandemic. That's why I'm looking for people like you who disagree with me. I want to know what you, for example, know differently or know that I don't. I have written a contribution to this on my website: https://www.franz-ruppert.de/de/aktuelles/anmerkungen-zum-zeitgeschehen/91-corona-diskussion

We all want to hear good news right now. But we still have to be realistic about the situation.

Yes, I completely agree with you. However, as a psychologist I know that the perception of reality is always selective and is determined by the state of the psyche of the individual. We can only ever grasp reality subjectively despite all our attempts to put it into objective parameters. That's where we have got to in the broad field of cognitive science. That is why gaining knowledge is always guided by interests. At this point we can only do one thing: to disclose our interests, as far as possible, for ourselves and for others. What is your current interest in this Corona pandemic?

Before our conversation, I asked you to take a look at the homepage that Dr. Wodarg was still praising as a 'safe source' a month ago. You said that you did not see any unusual trends in the death figures shown.
Please see here the long term weekly fluctuations:
https://www.euromomo.eu/outputs/number.html

As I see it, the peak in the 15-64 year olds has gone down again, and the peak in the over 65 year olds is also going down. How do you interpret the peaks in previous years? What was going on there?

You are wrong that in the figures, the annual peak of dying people in 2020 is still within usual figures for winter. You can see at the end of the time period that the line goes up there, right? ... but yes, for 'many people death is also a release' as you say.

On this point you have not understood my argument. I said that I had read a report by a physician who has experience in intensive care and palliative care units that an infection with a germ - whether corona or something else - is then the last straw that breaks the camel's back. My mother also died last year in November in an intensive care unit and she had previously decided against intensive care measures in a living will she made. A relative of mine is a doctor and responsible for a nursing home. He says that in the current situation he is glad that the people he is looking after have made their own decision whether or not they want intensive medical treatment. This is particularly problematic for dementia patients.

I'll just work through the Rubicon points: ....

Thank you very much for going into such detail. At the moment this is your genuine contribution to the current situation. What kind of message do you want to get across to the public at the moment?

All the best to you,
Dr. M.

**Best wishes,
Franz Ruppert'**

Dr. M. then received the following reply from the university management on 17.4.2020:

'Dear Dr. M,
Unfortunately, your message did not reach me until today due to a technical problem. Enclosed you will find the position of the university management regarding private opinions on the subject of the Corona Pandemic.

Dear Sir or Madam,

We are all currently affected by the challenges posed by the corona crisis. As President of the KSH Munich, it is my intention to inform you that the non-pharmaceutical intervention currently underway to contain the risk of infection with the novel coronavirus is receiving full support from the university management, the university and its sponsor.

We take note of any private opinions of members of the university on issues related to the complex topic of corona, in which different positions may be taken, as an expression of the right to freedom of speech, but these do not in any way represent the position of the university.

Like all other Universities of Applied Sciences in Bavaria, we at KSH Munich are adapting to the changed conditions of our studies and teaching, research and development, and in academic continuing education. We will continue to address the challenges of our time in a serious, science-based manner.

With best regards, Prof. Dr. ...".

Encouragement

Mostly though I receive confirming and encouraging messages via email and WhatsApp like these:

'Dear Franz, Thank you so much for your open and informative website'

or

'Dear Prof. Ruppert, thank you very much for the wonderful article about the self-fulfilling prophecy'. (emails from April 8th 2020)

I was also pleased to receive the following message on the 22nd April:

'With this email I would like to thank you very, very much for your invaluable educational work during this time! Your contributions and links show with so much objectivity, level-headedness and clarity what is really going on behind the scenes. What my feelings have told me about all the dramatic and frightening images in the public media is reinforced by your statements. While my feelings are confirmed, it is of course actually very frightening what is happening now (or has been happening for a long time) in politics, medicine and the media.

I wish you - from the bottom of my heart - much strength and courage to continue on this path and therefore to enlighten and shake people up! We all wish that truths will finally come to light and that all the machinations will come to an end'.

Here's a letter dated 27th April :

'Dear Franz, I just wanted to write to you to say how grateful I am that you are so involved in the current Corona situation, one could also say in the current Corona madness (in the literal sense). The feeling that something is not right here kept nagging at me until, after much research (both on an emotional and intellectual level) I stumbled across Bill Gates' involvement. I didn't dare to tell anybody, they'd think I was crazy. And then I read it on your site! I cried with relief. My inner compass is right. I want to thank you for that with all my heart. And I thank you for your courage to speak out clearly here!!

Now I would like to write to you about the theory I've arrived at concerning Angela Merkel. Now that she is weaker and at the end of her power, she re-stages the childhood trauma she went through growing up in the GDR. i.e. closed borders, forced medical interventions, denunciations, censorship, propaganda, nationalisation of the economy etc. I vacillate from despair, to anger, to hoping that truth will prevail.

But the ominous marriage of Gates' morbid 'I'm saving the world' and Merkel's 'I must and will control everything and everyone' frightens me greatly. I hope very much, enough healthy parts in many people (many feel that something is wrong here, even if they can't put it into words) can bring light into this collective delusion and the truth can show itself!

I'm sending you hugs for your supportive clarity. Hopefully see you soon in freedom and open discourse, C.'.

With many people, a growing loss of trust in the public media can be observed:

> 'I won't turn on my radio (WDR 5), which I loved, because I can't stand the enforced conformity – it's so painful ...' (email from 13/05/20)

Sars-CoV-2 Produces Millions Of Corpses?

I keep getting messages that make the whole idea that there are piles of corpses seem questionable. Forensic scientist Prof. Klaus Püschel says in the Hamburg Morning Post on 4th April:

> 'So far, there has not been a single person who was not previously ill, that has died from the consequences of Covid-19. All those we have examined so far had cancer, chronic lung disease, were heavy smokers or severely obese, suffered from diabetes or had cardiovascular disease'.

So the virus was the last straw that broke the camel's back. He also does not see any excess mortality due to corona in Germany at the moment.[106] The mortality rate in Austria is also not above the average of the last few years, according to the Centre for Medical Statistics at the University of Vienna:

> 'We are analysing the age and gender distribution of the reported COVID-19 deaths in Austria. Consistent with international studies, the Austrian data also suggests that the risk of death increases sharply with age. The observed age is consistent with the general annual mortality risk in Austria.'[107]

What's Going On In Sweden?

There is at least one country in Europe whose health minister dares to go his own way. There is no lockdown, only special precautions for people in the high-risk groups. And this gives us a chance for a comparison to see what is the better strategy in dealing with SARS-Covid-19.

---

[106] https://www.pressreader.com/germany/hamburger-morgenpost/20200403/281487868456736 (retrieved 08/04/20)
[107] https://cemsiis.meduniwien.ac.at/ms/ (retrieved 08/04/20)

What seems to be the picture, as of 14th April 2020, is that it makes no difference whether a state imposes curfews or - like Sweden - does not. This apparently has no effect on mortality rates.[108]

The example of Sweden is then an excellent point of reference for a leading opposition politician in the Austrian parliament to ensure that the lockdown, which Austria has also carried out, is not seen as without alternative. In an emotional and explosive speech, the FPÖ politician Herbert Kickl put forward all the counter-arguments against the Coronoia.[109] The fact that I end up posting a link to a speech by an FPÖ politician on my own website would have seemed completely absurd to me just a few days ago (The Freedom Party of Austria is a far-right populist and national-conservative political party). Herbert Kickl is an extreme agitator and violent propagandist with regard to migration and asylum. My wife, when she sees what I have done, immediately reads me the riot act. This will completely relegate me to the sidelines, she says. I suggest to her that if she can find me a similarly enlightening speech by another opposition politician, then I would gladly put that up on my homepage instead. As more and more Corona-critical voices appear, I take the video with Kickl's speech in the Austrian parliament off my website again on 6th May.

Surprisingly, on May 1st, there is even praise from the WHO for the special way Sweden is handling things:

'After the frequently expressed criticism of Sweden's way, it is now surprising that the Scandinavians get praise from the leadership of the WHO. Mike Ryan, the Executive Director of the WHO's Emergency Health Programme, has now said according to focus.de: 'We can possibly learn from our colleagues in Sweden'. how to 'return to a society without lockdown'. Ryan also reiterated that it was a misunderstanding that Sweden had not taken action. The difference, he said, was that in Sweden they had not relied on bans but on the insight and willingness of citizens to regulate themselves and keep their distance.

According to Ryan, this is a 'model for the future' because: if we want to put an end to the measures and closures that

---

[108] https://www.youtube.com/watch?v=Q3GzBbmnI10&feature=youtu.be (retrieved 15/04/20)

[109] https://www.youtube.com/watch?v=3gH4zH4Cp9Q (retrieved 22/04/20)

have been taken, society must adapt its 'physical and social conditions' to the virus. And this change in lifestyle may have to be maintained over a long period of time. Ryan sees Sweden as a pioneer in this.' [110]

I think that's very calculating praise for the Swedes: Basically it says 'you didn't question our pandemic, you were still part of it. And since we want to continue to maintain this pandemic until the vaccines and the obligation to vaccinate are in place, without ruining the countries to which we want to sell these vaccines, we will have to grudgingly recommend that there should at least be a return to something like normality in everyday life.'

Why is there this unreasonable stubbornness?
Meanwhile, the government is stubbornly sticking to its policy of controlling the infection. Even frightening figures, which say that it would need the horrendous sum of more than 1.3 trillion euros to compensate for the economic damage already caused within a few weeks, or that states, local authorities and large cities are warning that they are already deep in the red, do not seem to be able to dissuade them from their course. On the contrary, even the Oktoberfest in Munich is now to be cancelled as a precaution because a second wave of infection is expected in autumn. Who is driving this close-your-eyes-and-hope-whatever-the-cost course of action?

From IoPT, I am well aware that such behaviour comes from trauma survival strategies: just carry on regardless, even if you or the whole world goes under in the process. Just don't look at the real causes, because then you might have to face the truth of your own traumatisation. Just stay in your head, deny everything, pretend to be stupid – anything just to avoid feeling and staying in relationship with people who are hurting you. In this way, children can maintain the illusion that they have a mother and a father who love them. In this way, a sexual trauma can be denied and kept out of consciousness for someone's entire life. I know from numerous case studies how difficult it is to overcome such strategies of denial and

---

[110] https://www.merkur.de/welt/coronavirus-schweden-who-sonderweg-regeln-lob-mike-ryan-anders-tegnell-stockholm-news-zr-13746997.html (retrieved 02/05/20). You can read a complete transcript (in English) of this WHO press conference. Mike Ryan's comments about Sweden appear on Page 8.

illusion. What determination it takes to open the door to the split-off trauma feelings and to free oneself internally from one's perpetrators.

So am I saying that all those who are now making themselves immune to all reason and ignoring every objection, are they severely traumatised? We can say at least that those people who here in Germany are sitting at the levers of power, were all born after the Second World War and most likely had the experience of having traumatised parents.

Before all this, and because of his obvious trauma survival strategies, I looked into Donald Trump's history and it was clear to me that he was traumatised in early childhood and probably passed this on almost directly to his son Donald Trump Jr. Even with Boris Johnson, it wouldn't surprise me that he was traumatised when I consider his childhood spent at boarding school. Whatever the case, the people currently in power across the world seem to be so psychologically unstable that they immediately cave in when they are made to feel fear and pressure, so only the most rigorous measures can prove that they are determined to do everything possible to prevent deaths in the population.

Despite all the counter-opinions and refuting of the statistics that supposedly support the Corona narrative, the government in Germany, together with its panic-mongers in the press, remains adamant: the measures we are taking are helpful and necessary. Paul Schreyer therefore writes in an article on 21st April 2020:

'Despite a continuing stable health care system, the political tunnel vision concerning the Corona case numbers leads to 'side effects', such as mass fear (Merkel's "We must not, for a second, allow ourselves to be lulled into a sense of security"), extreme stress for millions of families and tens of thousands of company bankruptcies and social suicide because of our fear of dying.'[111]

Just how seriously those in Germany who keep the pandemic scenario going actually take their own scare tactics is made clear by this picture, which then soon went viral:

---

[111] https://multipolar-magazin.de/artikel/die-massnahmen-wirken (retrieved 21/04/20)

AA   🔒 mobile.twitter.com   ↻

Figure 15: The panic-makers closely packed together in the elevator

Sexual Traumatisation Is The Real Pandemic

Fourteenth Article - 7th April 2020

To Be Made An Object

If a person is made an object in order to satisfy someone's sexual needs, then there is a high probability that he or she will be traumatised by this. This has far-reaching consequences on both a psychological and physical level. It can have a massive impact on this person's entire life when it comes to being in relationships.

I do seminars all over the world, and during everything that is going on right now in the world, I am receiving more and more requests to participate in online conferences. It seems that my main expertise as a psychotraumatologist is much in demand at the moment. From my experience at these seminars and workshops, I see that sexual traumatisation occurs across the world and is by no means rare or exceptional. For me, the suffering caused by sexual trauma is pandemic. This would be good grounds on which to actually declare a pandemic. Then we could further clarify the causes of sexual traumatisation and develop meaningful measures to contain it.

In an interview with Angela Bittl, who has started a permanent online conference on this topic, I talk about my experiences with sexual traumatisation.[112] What are the causes? Which symptoms can be read to indicate a sexual traumatisation? What forms of perpetration are there? What ways are there to help and what are my experiences with Identity Oriented Psychotrauma Therapy (IoPT)?

---

[112] https://missbrauch.seiduselbst.info/galerie/franzruppert/ (retrieved 09/09/20)

Will Prostitution Now Disappear Forever In Germany?

In a country where sex work is legal if it is handled like normal gainful employment, I was surprised how silently the closure of brothels in Germany was carried out in the course of the Corona pandemic. I am curious to see how things will continue after the pandemic has been called off, especially in this sphere where millionfold massive sexual traumatisation happens on a daily basis. After all, it is mainly those who have been victims of sexual traumatisation as children who end up in prostitution.

Child Prostitution Amongst The Highest Echelons Of Finance And Politics

The scandal surrounding Jeffrey Epstein shows just to what extent the people who strut around in the highest circles of the financial world and politics can also be involved with sexual exploitation and child prostitution.[113] Based on my experience with perpetrator and victim attitudes in the many therapy processes I have accompanied, it is no wonder that especially rich and powerful people are deeply unhappy because they did not receive love from their mothers as children and were often humiliated by their fathers. It is then obvious for them to use their wealth and power to re-stage their own traumas by making children into objects because this is what happened to them when they were children.

Moreover, such networks are also well suited to create dependencies. Anyone who operates in such circles can be blackmailed at any time and be made to serve any purpose.

---

[113] https://en.wikipedia.org/wiki/Jeffrey_Epstein (retrieved 09/09/20)

Overt And Covert Lobbying By BIG PHARMA

But who is working behind the scenes, who is masquerading as this so called 'voice of the people' to ensure that pressure is put on those in government? We can see that countries such as England and the USA, who initially embarked on a course of protecting people by allowing them to develop immunity, did a swift u-turn and joined the majority with a course of protecting people from infection. Was there systematic lobbying? Are the governments worldwide interspersed with lobbyists whose clients are set to profit if we go the route of 'protection from infection instead of protection by immunity'?

It is well known from past experience that the pharmaceutical industry has also tried before to capitalise on viruses and other pathogens and make them the basis of pandemic scenarios: Bird flu, swine flu and mad cow disease (BSE) ... I have often thought in recent years, what's it going to be this time? But after all the repeated failed attempts by the WHO to bring about a global pandemic, I would never have thought that I'd actually find myself in the middle of such a scenario. I thought enough people had seen through the pharmaceutical and vaccine industry's game. But it seems that's not true after all?

My brother-in-law recently told me an example he'd personally witnessed of how cynical the actions of people and companies are when they are only focused on profit. He was involved in the development of an HIV test that could be used on stored blood. The institute in Göttingen, where he worked in administration, offered the test to the blood banks for next to nothing. But this offer met with unanimous rejection, until one day a company brought a test onto the market which could be sold to the hospitals at a high price. Now overnight it suddenly became extremely important to test stored blood so that everyone concerned was kept safe. However, how much damage had already occurred in the meantime because the free test was not accepted can only be guessed.[114]

Hermann Ploppa, a German political scientist, tries to bring together the threads that bind the WHO, the Bill & Melinda Gates Foundation, the World Economic Forum, representatives of national

---

[114] https://www.newscientist.com/article/mg14018961-600-hiv-scandal-rocks-german-ministry/ (retrieved 05/04/20)

governments, pharmaceutical industry, vaccine cartels, Johns Hopkins University, hedge funds, Robert Koch Institute and others in an op-ed article from 28th March 2020.[115] It seems as if the current Corona pandemic had been meticulously prepared for in business simulations and then turned into reality. Despite apparent lofty goals such as health, solidarity and saving human lives, on a base level it's actually all only about one thing: making more money out of money, in other words capitalism in its purest form. The handful of super-rich are once again plundering the state coffers and using the state authorities as the only remaining guarantors for their financial speculations. The population is expected to suffer mass unemployment and further impoverishment in return. This is class struggle from above, as Warren Buffet, one of these mega-super-rich people himself has called it.

---

[115] https://www.youtube.com/watch?v=dTlNf3xT22A (retrieved 08/04/20)

A Strategy To Prevent Infection Or A Strategy To Protect Immunity?

What Do We Want: To Live Or Just To Survive?

Fifteenth Article – 8th April 2020

Infections Are Part Of Everyday Life

Human life means living together, with our bodies in close contact. This means that the mutual exchange of pathogens is happening almost all the time and it's happening everywhere: between mothers and children, between lovers, between teachers and students, doctors and patients, social workers and their clients, bosses and their employees and so on. Usually this isn't a problem because every person has an immune system, that has from the beginning of their life learnt to cope with and continually adapt to any new hazardous situation.[116]

A Pandemic Should Only Be Declared As A Last Resort

The extreme prevention of interpersonal contact, because a pathogen that instantly causes severe damage or is immediately fatal, can only be a last resort, used as a final chance for at least some of the population to survive. It's questionable anyway whether this would even help.

Declaring a pandemic, with all the consequences that brings, must therefore be carefully thought through, and all the pros and cons must be weighed up across the board.

---

[116] https://www.rubikon.news/artikel/der-betrug-mit-der-epidemischen-lage (retrieved 02/09/20)

'Corona' And A Logic Based On Possibility

Many experts from different disciplines do not believe that this evaluating happened in the case of 'Corona.'[117] After all one shouldn't create a pandemic as quickly and easily as that and then argue essentially only with the logic of possibility:

- That the Covid-19 virus [118] _could_ be far more contagious than other viruses
- That is _could_ cause far more lung disease than 'common' flu
- That it _could_ overwhelm the health care system completely
- That it _could_ cause 1 million deaths in Germany alone (500,000 deaths in the UK)[119] and 50 million deaths worldwide.

The reality continues to be somewhat different

- The Covid-19 virus is no more contagious than other influenza viruses
- The rate of severe lung disease is also not much higher than in recent years during outbreaks of influenza.

---

[117] https://www.rubikon.news/artikel/weltweite-warnungen (retrieved 08.04.20) – Although in German - in the footnotes to that article there are various English language source articles including: https://www.statnews.com/2020/03/17/a-fiasco-in-the-making-as-the-coronavirus-pandemic-takes-hold-we-are-making-decisions-without-reliable-data/ & https://www.spectator.co.uk/article/The-evidence-on-Covid-19-is-not-as-clear-as-we-think (

[118] The WHO officially named the disease COVID-19 and the virus that causes it SARS-CoV-2. (https://www.who.int/emergencies/diseases/novel-coronavirus-2019/technical-guidance/naming-the-coronavirus-disease-(covid-2019)-and-the-virus-that-causes-it) To avoid confusion when technically referring to SARS-CoV-2 I have referred to it more simply as the virus that causes COVID-19. (translator's note)

[119] The figure quoted in the original article was for Germany (1 million). https://www.infosperber.ch/Artikel/Gesundheit/Am-Ende-kann-man-Corona--nicht-von-Grippe-Toten-unterscheiden (retrieved 07/04/20). The 500,000 UK projection was from the Imperial College London model cited here: https://www.bbc.co.uk/news/health-51979654 (retrieved 08.04.20) (translator's note)

- The mortality figure rates have not increased in different countries, nor is it currently possible to distinguish between who dies of flu and who dies because of, or with, the Covid-19 virus present in their system.[120]
- The people who are dying now are at the average age that people die anyway, regardless of the cause.
- The younger people who are being infected and dying of Covid-19 already have serious pre-existing health conditions.
- Health systems are overburdened because they have been working at their limit, overstretching their financial and human resource capacity for many years. Because the health system cannot deal with Covid-19 in the way it does the common flu virus, but has to put in place a high-risk management strategy to which everything else is subordinate, it is reaching its limits even more quickly. How would this have been different if the Corona-pandemic had not been declared?

Obviously now we can carry on arguing with a logic based on possibility: the peak of the pandemic may still be ahead of us, it could start up again in the autumn and then there may be another burst next spring. The reality of all this however means that we are all, in a very real sense, locked up in our homes. The police are standing on our streets and we are actually being punished if we do not respect the rules about going out. Because the whole thing will probably drag on for some time, will we then be temporarily released on probation from our home offices, then locked up again when it is deemed necessary? Are we going to be left at the mercy of this possibility like guinea pigs until one day we might be saved from our predicament by a vaccination provided by Mr Bill Gates and the vaccine industry?

---

[120] https://www.infosperber.ch/Artikel/Gesundheit/Am-Ende-kann-man-Corona--nicht-von-Grippe-Toten-unterscheiden (retrieved 07/04/20)

Flu Epidemics Are Terrible

I don't want to trivialise flu epidemics. Anyone infected with a virus goes through a period of suffering. And if someone dies from it, it causes severe trauma to those who love them.

Last year I myself got a severe flu infection, and I was suffering for weeks on end. I had to lie in bed, support the work of my immune system by doing a lot of sweating it out and finally overcame the infection through my own trauma-therapeutic work.

The Strategy Of Controlling The Infection Is Like Sawing A Branch While You're Sitting On It

In the current situation, where this virus has already spread across the globe, an infection control strategy is no longer the best option. Controlling chains of infection now means monitoring everyone's lives down to the last detail. In fact, however, such a policy of apparent strength is nothing more than an admission of weakness and helplessness. Everyone is now like a rabbit staring at the snake, waiting for the virus to bite again. The politicians can only think they are powerful as long as their people obediently obey everything the police strongly encourage them to do.

The strategy of infection control has no exit scenario in place. Professor Christian Schubert, an expert in the field of psychoneuro-immunology, has said: 'When the curfews then stop, the antiviral immune activity of many people will have been so severely compromised by the stress they have experienced whilst in isolation that they will be caught full-force by the so-called second corona wave. ... What we are witnessing now is a brutal social experiment with no known outcome.'[121]

---

[121] https://www.alpenmag.de/medizin-professor-so-belastet-die-corona-quarantaene-koerper-und-geist/ (retrieved 09/10/20)

The Damage That Results From Paranoia

This way of thinking based on possibility that underlies this declared pandemic has the characteristics of someone who is paranoid and has within itself a fundamental contradiction. It claims to be a model for minimising the risk of the resultant damage from the Covid-19 virus. However, it is precisely this model that creates a high-risk situation for everything else. It is not only the national health systems that can no longer function as normal. All other systems in our society such as educational, economic, social, cultural, family, partnerships - simply everything has become severely affected.

Within a matter of days, democracy has also fallen by the wayside. In Germany, the basic rule of law was suspended indefinitely by the Infection Protection Act and its associated legislation. Heribert Prantl, former editor-in-chief of the Süddeutsche Zeitung, illustrated this scandal in a podcast broadcast on n-tv on 5th April 2020.[122]

The damage that has already been caused to families, schools, universities, hospitals, the self-employed, small businesses and larger companies after just a few weeks of 'lock-down' is on a catastrophic scale. Not to mention the massive damage to the psyche of every individual concerned. The supposed solution to the problem of 'Corona' is already causing more damage than the actual problem it claims to solve.

Basically, the infection control strategy leads to systemic collapse. I am certainly not a fan of this capitalist competitive system, but to find myself instead in a neoliberal health care dictatorship is a place I have no desire to be.

---

[122] https://www.n-tv.de/21689999 (retrieved 05/04/20)

Vaccine Manufacturers Hope For Extra Profits

The only ones who can hope to profit in a big way in a situation such as this are the vaccine manufacturers. They are now pulling out all the stops to be the first to get their vaccine on the market - ideally in one or one and a half years at the latest. This promises a monopoly that could make billions in profit.

I would like to say to these people: the human immune system is capable of researching, virtually in real time, and producing within the space of a few days and weeks, exactly what it needs to contain, reduce and block the activities of this Covid-19 virus. The self-vaccination is already here! And there are no financial costs involved, it doesn't cost anything to store it or transport it to exactly where it is most effective: the individuals affected!

Once again Bill Gates is leading the way with his idea to save the world through vaccination. I would like to say to him: Dear Mr Gates, a holistic understanding of health and illness, especially in regards to their psychological aspects, does not really seem to be part of your skillset. Why don't you program something useful for us all again instead - Maybe you could make an app that helps democracies be protected against dictatorial attacks in the name of public health?

A Strategy To Protect Immunity – An Alternative Way

The alternative to the strategy of controlling the infection is obvious. It is the strategy of immune protection that has proven itself for tens of thousands of years across human history. We all have a fantastic tool inside us: our immune system. It is well worth getting better informed about this, namely that the real help is within ourselves and that we are not dependent on doctors and BIG PHARMA. Experts can support our self-healing powers, but in the long run they can never replace them. Many of us will sooner or later also be infected with 'Corona', especially if this virus is as highly infectious as it's supposed to be. Some will suffer less and others more. Some of us will die, as in every flu epidemic. The strategy of trying to control the infection will not prevent this.

If you don't know much about the immune system, use your free time to learn about it. Many years ago, I learned some very basic things about it in a paperback book by Mrs. Münzing-Ruef (1991) [123], which I found enormously helpful and enlightening.

All of us together could take this opportunity to learn some fundamentally important things for our life and how we live together:

- What our immune system is and how it works.
- How we can strengthen it and how we can weaken it. [124]
- Who is telling us the truth and who is lying and manipulating us. [125]
- Who boosts our self-confidence and who undermines it.
- Who sticks by us and who, caught up in their own fears, immediately turns their back on us as soon as we have tested positive.
- Who gives us courage and hope and who makes us fear and panic.

---

[123] Ingeborg Münzing-Ruef's book 'So stärken Sie Ihr Immunsystem' (How to Strengthen your Immune System) does not appear to have been translated into English.
[124] Even the British royal family is more likely to use homeopathy: https://m.facebook.com/story.php?story_fbid=10222357681835184&id=1361551829 (retrieved 07/04/20). Though this story has been disputed since and has been declared untrue (https://www.altnews.in/prince-charless-coronavirus-wasnt-cured-with-ayurvedic-homeopathic-treatment/ (retrieved 01/09/20)) the British royal family have long been rumoured to use homeopathy:
https://www.express.co.uk/news/royal/1260443/queen-coronavirus-news-prince-charles-phillip-royal-family-health-homeopathy-queen
[125] https://www.nachrichten-fabrik.de/news/harald-wiesendanger-ueber-die-massenmedien-waehrend-der-corona-krise-ich-schaeme-mich---meines-berufsstands-152103 (retrieved 07/04/20)

- When we are ill, who really helps us to get well again and who makes us dependent on their help and undermines our own self-healing powers.
- Who leads us through a crisis with a clear head and who leads us to the edge of the abyss because of their own fears, ignorance and blind need to act.

Extra Contributions To The Discussion From My Trauma Research

As a psychotherapist and trauma specialist I can also contribute the following to what we can learn from this crisis:

- Our individual perceptions of the danger of 'Corona' out there in the world are shaped by our unresolved inner fears. The virus is only a blank screen onto which we project these fears. Fear then blocks our ability to think freely and makes us susceptible to manipulation that further fuels these fears.
- These fears often originate in our early childhood, possibly even before birth, or during the birth process or from our first year after birth. We are not aware of all this, but it continues to work in our inner life and in our body.
- Threats from the outside world trigger these old primal fears in us and put us into high stress. They can quickly push us back into the old sense of helplessness we experienced as infants.
- The restrictions engender in us a situation of powerlessness, which now re-traumatises many of us.
- It will not help us if we just concentrate on trying to ward off the dangers from outside. We must work at finally defusing these fear-trauma bombs inside us, which can be so easily set off at any time.
- The strategy of controlling the infection is in itself traumatising for many people. It creates new traumatic situations within many relationships and

families and leads us to experience further psychological trauma.

There could be great opportunities in this crisis, one of which would be: to come to accept ourselves again. I'll give my own example: a few days ago, during my own examination of Covid-19, I discovered a baby part of me, half a year old. When I was that age I almost died of loneliness and rejection. So the heat in my chest was an attempt to survive the emotional coldness outside of me. My cough was the symptom of being fed a disgusting powdered milk diet that I almost died of.

In the past few days I have come across cases in my practice where the fears in the current pandemic situation have brought back memories. In some clients these have manifested as violent inflammatory reactions, which are linked to traumatic birth processes or feelings of guilt associated with the fact of being unwanted.

A Holistic Model Of Health Takes Us Forward

At the moment, we could learn a lot from the fact that such a simple model as 'here's the pathogen and there's the disease' does not do justice to the complexity of what is actually happening in our body and our psyche. Together with the doctor Harald Banzhaf and 25 other colleagues I wrote the book 'My Body, My Trauma, My I'. It contains numerous examples of how unresolved emotional and relationship conflicts lead to physical symptoms of illness. These disappear as soon as the underlying psychological conflicts are resolved.

Vaccinations are only a minimal component for a good and healthy life. If there is someone, for example, in whose psyche the parts are constantly working against themselves because they have for a lifetime turned the original rejection from their parents against themselves, then vaccinating that person is never going to change that and lead to a good state of health for them.

The Crisis Could Create A New Common Awareness

The corona pandemic crisis could therefore, unlike the outbreaks of flu in years before, not simply be something that we get through and survive. This time it could make a valuable contribution to our greater awareness of viral dangers, to greater democracy, to more openness and honesty, to the education of the population, to the strengthening of our life skills, to a clearer awareness of our psyche and its relationship to the outside world. We could all learn to deal with our fears in a life-affirming way.

Together we could have the experience of how to successfully defend ourselves against our individual tendency towards totalitarianism. We could learn how to cultivate a lively culture of discussion and learn how not to get caught up in friend-enemy dynamics. No single individual has acquired wisdom on their own. True consciousness is always co-consciousness. And everyone who wants to take responsibility for something greater should learn to understand that he must first take full responsibility for his own inner life. Otherwise he will not be able to cope with the demanding tasks that will be placed before him. The person who does not know himself does not understand the world either. But anyone who can be completely with himself is automatically a blessing for the rest of humanity.

If we employed the strategy of immune protection, the money we would save by the end of the crisis, would mean that we could give everybody a free bottle of champagne.

Bill Gates: The Visionary And Prophet For Vaccination

Bill Gates apparently has many supporters in the mainstream media. For example, he can publish an article with the headline 'Coronavirus will accelerate three major medical breakthroughs', in April in the Economist Magazine, which is then reprinted in its entirety on 15th May in Focus online, without any comments, inquiries or critical objections. He is apparently considered a visionary worthy of being listened to:

> 'In most of Europe, East Asia and North America the peak of the pandemic will probably have passed by the end of this month. In a few weeks' time, many hope, things will return to the way they were in December. Unfortunately, that won't happen.
>
> I believe that humanity will beat this pandemic, but only when most of the population is vaccinated. Until then, life will not return to normal. Even if governments lift shelter-in-place orders and businesses reopen their doors, humans have a natural aversion to exposing themselves to disease. Airports won't have large crowds. Sports will be played in basically empty stadiums. And the world economy will be depressed because demand will stay low and people will spend more conservatively (…) My hope is that, by the second half of 2021, facilities around the world will be manufacturing a vaccine. If that's the case, it will be a history-making achievement: the fastest humankind has ever gone from recognising a new disease to immunising against it.
>
> Apart from this progress in vaccines, two other big medical breakthroughs will emerge from the pandemic. One will be in the field of diagnostics. The next time a novel virus crops up, people will probably be able to test for it at home in the same way they test for pregnancy. Instead of peeing on a stick, though, they'll swab their nostrils. Researchers could have such a test ready within a few months of identifying a new disease.

The third breakthrough will be in antiviral drugs. These have been an underinvested branch of science. We haven't been as effective at developing drugs to fight viruses as we have those to fight bacteria. But that will change. Researchers will develop large, diverse libraries of antivirals, which they'll be able to scan through and quickly find effective treatments for novel viruses.

All three technologies will prepare us for the next pandemic by allowing us to intervene early, when the number of cases is still very low. But the underlying research will also assist us in fighting existing infectious diseases—and even help advance cures for cancer. (Scientists have long thought mRNA vaccines could lead to an eventual cancer vaccine. Until Covid-19, though, there wasn't much research into how they could be produced en masse at even somewhat affordable prices.)

Our progress won't be in science alone. It will also be in our ability to make sure everyone benefits from that science. In the years after 2021, I think we'll learn from the years after 1945. With the end of the Second World War, leaders built international institutions like the UN to prevent more conflicts. After Covid-19, leaders will prepare institutions to prevent the next pandemic.

These will be a mix of national, regional and global organisations. I expect they will participate in regular "germ games" in the same way as armed forces take part in war games. These will keep us ready for the next time a novel virus jumps from bats or birds to humans. They will also prepare us should a bad actor create an infectious disease in a home-made lab and try to weaponise it. By practising for a pandemic, the world will also be defending itself against an act of bioterrorism…'[126]

'Philanthropist' literally means 'lover of mankind'. Bill Gates is often referred to as such because he donates money. In reality, however, these donations are more of an investment in his own

[126] https://www.focus.de/politik/ausland/analyse-unseres-partner-portals-economist-die-welt-nach-covid-19-bill-gates-ueber-die-bekaempfung-kuenftiger-pandemien_id_11993365.html (retrieved on 15/05/20). The original article in The Economist is here: https://www.economist.com/by-invitation/2020/04/23/bill-gates-on-how-to-fight-future-pandemics (retrieved 04/08/20)

megalomaniacal plans for the future. How great can his compassion for humanity really be when he speaks so seemingly unmoved about the fact that these pandemics, with all the horror and suffering they cause, will occur more often in the future? When it does not seem to concern him that people will be afraid of being close to other people in the future, afraid of approaching them physically? That they will become poorer and poorer and more depressed? That children will learn their socialisation skills in this regime of 'social distancing'? To me this seems extremely heartless and cold. In my opinion, he only sees people as objects for his vaccinations. I do not see any sympathy in him for the people who are harmed by the measures. Those who are now living in unreasonable mortal fear of a virus, those who are now losing their jobs, whose livelihoods are being destroyed by the lockdown, for the children who are now shut up with their parents in small apartments and terrorised by them, for the old people in nursing homes who can no longer be visited by their relatives and who are now dying of loneliness.

In another article Gates summarises his view in this way:

'When I made the transition from my first career at Microsoft to my second career in philanthropy, I didn't think that my success rate would change much. I was now putting money into new ways to reduce poverty and disease. Discovering a new vaccine, I figured, would be just as hard as discovering the next tech unicorn. (Vaccines are much harder, it turns out.)

After 20 years of investing in health, though, one type of investment has surprised me—because, unlike investing in a new vaccine or technology, the success rate is very high. It's what people in the global-health business call "financing and delivery." Decades ago, these investments weren't sure bets, but today, they almost always pay off in a big way. [...] Over the past two decades, my wife Melinda and I have put a total of $10 billion into organizations that do this challenging work, including three big ones: GAVI, the Vaccine Alliance; the Global Fund; and the Global Polio Eradication Initiative. Each of them has been extremely successful, but most people don't know their names or what they do.

Even fewer are watching out for them, making sure they have the money they need to do their work. Without more funding over the next 18 months, all three of these institutions will have to dramatically scale back their efforts to fight disease and keep people healthy. This shouldn't be allowed to happen. These organizations are not trivial or expendable. In fact, they are probably the best investments our foundation has ever made.'[127]

In my experience, these kind of ideas of making the next really big breakthrough are pubescent fantasies of success to impress your own parents. Which in turn raises the question of what early traumatisation Bill Gates experienced in his childhood, which he is now running away from through his manic actions of manipulating people across the world into a regime of continual vaccination? Mr Gates' focus is directed towards his money and the increase in his wealth, because he can then use this money to pull the strings globally as he wishes, even though no one has elected him to any political office. That people can be corrupted with money is no secret in a world in which almost everything revolves around money and professional careers.

From the point of view of the small child that still lives inside this man, this translates as: with my money I can buy your attention! In a recent interview Bill Gates shows almost a devilish delight in the fact that when the next virus comes after 'Corona' even countries like New Zealand, Australia or Taiwan, which were not so far involved in this pandemic, will have to give this new virus their full attention. [128]

The same applies to politicians. These people, usually very neglected in their childhood, are finally getting the attention they missed out on because they are now in positions of power. They can even force other people to show an interest in them. But this money and power is never going to bring about any development or maturation of their personality.

You don't have to be an investigative journalist and do heaps of research and digging around to uncover the truth when it comes to Bill Gates. The truth about his intentions and actions is out in the open. The conspiracy he is orchestrating with his multiple alliances to vaccinate all of humanity is quite public. What would be needed, instead of merely working through the myriad symptoms of the current Corona pandemic, is for us to take seriously his very open

---

[127] https://www.wsj.com/articles/bill-gates-the-best-investment-ive-ever-made-11547683309 (retrieved 16/05/20)
[128] https://www.youtube.com/watch?v=fWQ2DsHWrQE&feature=youtu.be (retrieved 03/07/20)

intentions and plans. This Corbett Report basically gathers everything one needs to know about Bill Gates and the goals and activities of his Bill & Melinda Gates Foundation.[129]

Bill Gates has no medical qualifications whatsoever that would merit him interfering so massively in the interests of all of us in the field of health. In my opinion, he lives completely in his own thought constructs and has completely lost touch with the real world. He turns the reality in his head to fit into his grand master plan, for which he forms strategic alliances all over the world.[130]

I would find it so exciting if he did a self-encounter process with my therapy method in order for him to find out what 'vaccination' and 'injection' mean for him on a personal level. For example, 'injection' often has associations of lethal injection or abortion. For me, injections are in no way associated with positive feelings, but with fear and pain.

It is not my intention to demonise Mr Gates. He is also no more than an exponent of a widespread 21st century mindset which believes that everything is feasible through application of careful management and technology, and is in a perpetual state of war, against something, it does not matter what. He says as much in his 2015 TED talk:

'But in fact, we can build a really good response system. We have the benefits of all the science and technology that we talk about here. We've got cell phones to get information from the public and get information out to them. We have satellite maps where we can see where people are and where they're moving. We have advances in biology that should dramatically change the turnaround time to look at a pathogen and be able to make drugs and vaccines that fit for that pathogen. So we can have tools, but those tools need to be put into an overall global health system. And we need preparedness.

The best lessons, I think, on how to get prepared are again, what we do for war. For soldiers, we have full-time, waiting to go. We have reserves that can scale us up to large numbers. NATO has a mobile unit that can deploy very rapidly. NATO does a lot of war games to check, are people

[129] https://www.corbettreport.com/bill-gates-plan-to-vaccinate-the-world/ (retrieved 18/09/20)

[130] https://www.gatesnotes.com/Health/Pandemic-Innovation (retrieved 01/07/20)

well trained? Do they understand about fuel and logistics and the same radio frequencies? So they are absolutely ready to go. So those are the kinds of things we need to deal with an epidemic.'[131]

As if something like human health, of all things, could be strategically planned for and that the only way to protect it is by chemical means. Where does that leave the people themselves? Their personal responsibility, their feelings, their need for freedom. Their own ability to cope with suffering and death? For the sake of our health, do we have to resort to waging war against infectious pathogens? Aren't there more peaceful and gentle ways of doing this? Natural and holistic medicine has long since been aware of the alternatives. And the improvement of living conditions - clean water, healthy food, peaceful coexistence, etc. - is what prevents the spread of epidemics anyway.

A firewall against computer viruses is something completely different from a vaccination! But it is this black-and-white thinking: viruses are bad so vaccinations are good. It is this fixation on technocratic solutions to health problems, but health problems are primarily of a social and psychological nature, and so technocratic solutions become, in my opinion, something of pure horror and not an expression of philanthropy. In this black-and-white way of thinking, people are just objects that you can do with what you wish. Therefore, such technological and chemical 'solutions' cause more health problems than they get rid of. But they fit in well with the capitalist thought pattern of supposed human happiness, and, in this thought pattern, there is obviously no alternative to these solutions. Also in this system, 'health' is just one of many possible things people could invest in to make even more money. Such false assumptions about reality and such profound delusions can ultimately only be imposed by force against the interests of the majority of those affected.

[131]

https://www.ted.com/talks/bill_gates_the_next_outbreak_we_re_not_ready/transcript#t-361601 (retrieved 01/08/20)

Why? Because That's What Bill Gates Wants!

Sixteenth Article – 12th April 2020

There are two ways to deal with any problem:

1. **Question it**: Ask about the causes, try to find out what they are and, if possible, eliminate them.
2. **Battle it**: Deal with the manifold effects that this problem brings with it and work on its symptoms.

Experience shows that the second strategy of fighting symptoms usually results in new symptoms. So let's look at the problem using the first strategy and ask questions. Why does this corona pandemic exist? I have divided it into several sub-questions:

- Why is a 'corona' virus considered 'novel' but also immediately known to be 'highly infectious'?
- Why are there immediate comparisons with the Plague and with Ebola?
- Why is the grim picture being painted of horrific figures of millions of dead ('mountains of corpses')?
- Why is the focus on a painful death by suffocation?
- Why is the idea of triage always being brought into the discussion?
- Why is no risk assessment of the pros and cons of pandemic measures allowed?
- Why does the WHO, as an institution funded to a large extent by the Gates Foundation and pharmaceutical and food companies, even have this power to declare pandemics?
- Why are historical examples such as the 2009/2010 pandemic of swine flu not carefully evaluated?
- Why can Bill Gates, although he holds no political office, present his idea of all countries waging a

common war against viruses at the Munich Security Conference 2017?

- Why in particular, does this billionaire call for more money to be invested in research into new, safe and effective vaccines?
- Why did the German government investigate a theoretical scenario in 2012 in which a new type of SARS corona virus from Asia spreads in Europe?
- Why did the Bill and Melinda Gates Foundation organise a simulation scenario with a Corona virus – 'Event 201', on 18th October 2019 in New York - which, in this simulation, started in Brazil and led to a pandemic with an estimated 65 million dead?
- Why is the Johns Hopkins University in Baltimore such a prominent player in all this?
- Why is the Robert Koch Institute so closely linked to Johns Hopkins University?
- Why do heads of state actually talk in terms of a war against Corona?
- Why are alternative views immediately discredited in the public and mainstream media?
- Why are no meaningful scientific studies commissioned to shed light on the actual risk of SARS-CoV-2 and Covid-19?
- Why are projected death figures constantly bandied about as much as possible?
- Why are studies that could reduce people's fear around all this immediately questioned?
- Why is the risk even extended into years (1st, 2nd, 3rd wave)?
- Why are state aid funds decided on on an almost unlimited scale?
- Why should EU aid to countries like Italy and Spain only be used for the health system?
- Why is Bill Gates now initiating a huge campaign to make vaccines available as quickly as possible?[132]

---

[132] https://www.youtube.com/watch?v=0CCWlYyVV1A In German (retrieved 11/04/20)

- Why are people who ask these kind of questions immediately condemned as 'conspiracy theorists' and presented as people that we should no longer take seriously? [133]

In a conversation with Katharina Popper from Austria I discussed these questions in detail and published them on my website.

Questioning The Causes Goes Viral

At the same time I see that other people are also asking very similar questions[134]. As if perhaps now is the time to wake up from the shock that this pandemic has temporarily caused in all of us and to use our minds again and put two and two together.

Bill Gates also has a vision right now: 'Things won't go back to truly normal until we have a vaccine that we've gotten out to basically the entire world... Activities, like mass gatherings, may ... until you're widely vaccinated ... not come back at all.'[135] So the curfews can only be lifted if a vaccine is available for the entire world.

In order not to be considered a conspiracy theorist, I had not yet said what Bill Gates officially announced on April 12th 2020 at about 10:15 pm in an interview with the ARD Tagesthemen (one of Germany's main daily television news programmes) presenter Ingo Zamperoni: This pandemic with all its limitations will only be over when a vaccine for 7 billion people has been found and distributed. There will then be further pandemics in the coming years, which in turn will need these vaccines. That is what the global economy of the future will be and we must all prepare ourselves psychologically for this brave new world now. Bill Gates tells us this, not because

---

[133] https://www.youtube.com/watch?v=8TUv07vNZAA&app=desktop (retrieved 11/04/20) Video is no longer available.

[134] https://www.youtube.com/watch?v=8TUv07vNZAA&app=desktop (retrieved 11/04/20) Video is no longer available.

[135] https://www.youtube.com/watch?v=umfxaCjYS5E (retrieved 01/09/20)

he was democratically elected by anyone for this, but simply because he is so fabulously rich and has bought the WHO. He tells us nonchalantly and with a smile on his face what - he also names the main companies in the pharmaceutical industry - the world will be about in the future. That is why all the traumas - he even use the word - that people around the world are suffering at the moment are easily worth the sacrifice, aren't they?[136]

The Global Consequences Of Bill Gates' Vaccine Mania

The following list, compiled by Robert F. Kennedy Jr., shows the disaster Bill Gates has already caused in recent years with his vaccination mania:[137]

'Vaccines, for Bill Gates, are a strategic philanthropy that feed his many vaccine-related businesses (including Microsoft's ambition to control a global vac ID enterprise) and give him dictatorial control over global health policy—the spear tip of corporate neo-imperialism.

Gates' obsession with vaccines seems fuelled by a messianic conviction that he is ordained to save the world with technology and a god-like willingness to experiment with the lives of lesser humans.

Promising to eradicate Polio with $1.2 billion, Gates took control of India's National Advisory Board (NAB) and mandated 50 polio vaccines (up from 5) to every child before age 5. Indian doctors blame the Gates campaign for a devastating vaccine-strain polio epidemic that paralyzed 496,000 children between 2000 and 2017. In 2017, the Indian Government dialled back Gates' vaccine regimen and evicted Gates and his cronies from the

---

[136] https://www.tagesschau.de/ausland/gates-corona-101.html (retrieved 01/09/20)
[137] https://www.instagram.com/p/B-s-9ZjH0YP/?igshid=s27c7sis7n1s (retrieved 01/09/20)

NAB. Polio paralysis rates dropped precipitously. In 2017, the World Health Organization reluctantly admitted that the global polio explosion is predominantly vaccine strain, meaning it is coming from Gates' Vaccine Program. The most frightening epidemics in Congo, the Philippines, and Afghanistan are all linked to Gates' vaccines. By 2018, ¾ of global polio cases were from Gates' vaccines.

In 2014, the Gates Foundation funded tests of experimental HPV vaccines, developed by GSK and Merck, on 23,000 young girls in remote Indian provinces. Approximately 1,200 suffered severe side effects, including autoimmune and fertility disorders. Seven died. Indian government investigations charged that Gates funded researchers committed pervasive ethical violations: pressuring vulnerable village girls into the trial, bullying parents, forging consent forms, and refusing medical care to the injured girls. The case is now in the country's Supreme Court.

In 2010, the Gates Foundation funded a trial of a GSK's experimental malaria vaccine, killing 151 African infants and causing serious adverse effects including paralysis, seizure, and febrile convulsions to 1,048 of the 5,049 children.

During Gates' 2002 MenAfriVac campaign in Sub-Saharan Africa, Gates' operatives forcibly vaccinated thousands of African children against meningitis. Between 50 and 500 children vaccinated developed paralysis. South African newspapers complained, 'We are guinea pigs for the drug makers.' Nelson Mandela's former Senior Economist, Professor Patrick Bond, describes Gates' philanthropic practices as 'ruthless and immoral.'

In 2010, Gates committed $10 billion to the WHO promising to reduce population, in part, through new vaccines. A month later, Gates said in a Ted Talk that new vaccines 'could reduce population'. In 2014, Kenya's Catholic Doctors Association accused the WHO of chemically sterilizing millions of unwilling Kenyan women with a phony 'tetanus' vaccine campaign. Independent labs found the sterility formula in every vaccine tested. After denying the charges, WHO finally admitted it had been developing the sterility vaccines for over a decade. Similar accusations came from Tanzania, Nicaragua, Mexico, and the Philippines.

A 2017 study (Morgenson et. al. 2017) showed that WHO's popular DTP vaccine is killing more African children than the diseases it pretends to prevent. DTP-vaccinated girls suffered 10x the death rate of unvaccinated children. Gates and WHO have refused to recall the lethal vaccine which WHO forces upon millions of African children annually.

Global public health advocates around the world accuse Gates of hijacking WHO's agenda away from the projects that are proven to curb infectious diseases: clean water, hygiene, nutrition, and economic development. They say he has diverted agency resources to serve his personal fetish - that good health only comes in a syringe.

In addition to using his philanthropy to control WHO, UNICEF, GAVI, and PATH, Gates funds a private pharmaceutical company that manufactures vaccines, and a massive network of pharmaceutical-industry front groups that broadcast deceptive propaganda, develop fraudulent studies, conduct surveillance and psychological operations against vaccine hesitancy and use Gates' power and money to silent dissent and coerce compliance. In his recent nonstop Pharmedia appearances, Gates appears gleeful that the Covid-19 crisis will give him the opportunity to force his third-world vaccine programs on American children.'

Addendum 10/05/2020: A collection of the quotes in which Bill Gates advocates a reduction of the world population can be found in this video.[138] In the meantime, Bill Gates has probably convinced himself that improving health automatically leads to families with two children, as he said in a discussion with the presenter Markus Lanz on 4 July 2011.[139]

---

[138] https://www.youtube.com/watch?v=k1a2EuQWVR0 (retrieved 27/08/20). Here is a English language 'mash-up' of Gates' quotes on Population Reduction: https://www.youtube.com/watch?v=knIkw3KJzrY (retrieved 01/09/20)
[139] https://www.youtube.com/watch?v=7MF4wzi1QZU (retrieved 27/08/20). An English language video containing similar thoughts and ideas from Bill Gates appears here: https://www.youtube.com/watch?v=ozlbeXrb_5A (retrieved 01/09/20)

The Protectors Of Gates In The Media

Ever since Bill Gates began being increasingly criticised as one of the most publicly visible masterminds behind this crisis, the 'fact checker' website, which ARD (the joint organisation of Germany's regional public-service broadcasters) has set up in light of the Corona pandemic, has been trying to protect him. In this context, what I had already suspected, his close friendship with Angela Merkel, comes to light:

> 'Again and again Gates sat together with Chancellor Angela Merkel in the past years, campaigned in the Chancellery for greater efforts in this area. Speaking to confidants, Gates once said that he knew hardly anyone else in politics who was as interested in this topic as Merkel, the scientist. In the Chancellery, it is said that the appreciation is mutual'.

In any case, the conclusion of the fact-checker is clear: Anyone who doubts the magnanimity, helpfulness and farsightedness of this Mr Gates is a conspiracy theorist:

> 'The Corona pandemic is accompanied by a worldwide wave of disinformation - and Bill Gates has become the global scapegoat of conspiracy ideologists'.[140]

To me this is a clear expression of what I call the perpetrator-victim-reversal. The perpetrators and their collaborators in the media present themselves as victims and identify their victims, who are just beginning to defend themselves, as the actual perpetrators.

In Germany the situation is acute, because besides Angela Merkel, we have the Minister of Health Jens Spahn, the director of the Robert Koch Institute Lothar Wieler and the virologist Christian Drosten. They are like the dream team for Bill Gates. They all receive money from his foundation and Lothar Wieler has been a member of many WHO committees for years.[141] It is also interesting to take a look at the political career of Jens Spahn:

---

[140] https://www.tagesschau.de/faktenfinder/feindbild-gates-101.html
[141] https://www.youtube.com/watch?v=L_w1hbu5_i4&feature=youtu.be

'In 2012, he was elected one of the '40 under 40 - European Young Leaders' by Friends of Europe, a European 'think tank in which lobbyists and representatives of the EU institutions work together'. Spahn completed the American Council on Germany's Young Leader Program, a partner project of the German think tank Atlantik-Brücke and the American Council on Germany for aspiring political and economic leaders. In June 2017 Spahn attended the Bilderberg Conference in Chantilly, Virginia.

Since April 2013, Spahn has been working with the journalist Daniel Funke, chief lobbyist of Hubert Burda Media and previously head of the Berlin office of the magazine Bunte'.[142]

In a meeting on 9th April 2018 between Bill Gates and Jens Spahn, the latter praised the vaccination lobbyist in the highest terms. This promotional video seems like an alliance of hearts between these two men.[143]

Even before the declaration of the Corona pandemic, Federal Health Minister Jens Spahn tried to disempower the self-administration of the health insurance companies in the debate on organ removal and measles vaccination and he bypassed the Federal Joint Committee (GBA), to set himself up as the minister to which services have to be paid for by the health insurance companies.

A YouTube video from 15th May 2020 reveals the entanglements of Health Minister Spahn with companies and individuals in the pharmaceutical industry. [144] It is based on an article published by Lobby-Control on 24th January 2013. [145] A lot of this Corona pandemic has been planned for a long time.

The Bavarian Minister President Markus Söder also seems to have been a member of the Global Alliance for Vaccines for quite some time. Already during the time of the swine flu in 2009, when he, who at that time was still Bavarian Minister for Health, had himself demonstratively vaccinated and praised the 'people's vaccine' Pandemrix in glowing terms in an article in the Mittelbayerische Zeitung. 'No other vaccine has fewer side effects and has been tested

[142] https://de.wikipedia.org/wiki/Jens_Spahn
[143] https://www.youtube.com/watch?v=pAKu5NnXZw4 (retrieved 01/07/20)
[144] www.youtube.com/watch, (retrieved 15/05/20)
[145] https://www.lobbycontrol.de/2013/01/ein-abgeordneter-mit-lobbyagentur-jens-spahn-antwortet-nicht/ (retrieved 19/05/20)

more extensively than this product of the pharmaceutical company GlaxoSmithKline', he said. [146]

The Children And Grandchildren Of War-Traumatised Parents

Many of today's German politicians have parents who were traumatised by war. Sabine Bode deserves the credit for having described and analysed the psychological consequences for the generations born in Germany after 1945. They are the offspring of mothers and fathers, some of whom have been massively traumatised and who have experienced Nazi terror, bomb attacks, or had family members killed or had to flee or were subject to expulsion (Bode 2004, 2009).

There are many in my therapeutic groups whose parents or grandparents have been through unspeakable experiences and could never talk about them. Their childhood and youth, which was overshadowed by Hitler and war, was surrounded by a cloak of silence. This meant that their children were then confronted with parents who seemed completely unemotional on the outside, because they did everything to hide the split-off trauma feelings that were going on inside them. They functioned, organised, threw themselves into reconstruction with a restless activity. To them, it felt that their manifold illnesses could not be cured by dealing with their biography, but only with tablets, injections or operations. Conventional medicine, which promised to make them free of pain and therefore basically free of emotions, was just the right thing for these people. It spared them having to really look into the abyss of their war experiences.

It was as if having this germ-free and sterile environment on the outside felt like it could act like a cleansing cure for the chaos inside their traumatised bodies. This is probably why detergent advertising with slogans such as 'washes whiter than white' were so well received by the post-war generation. The obsession with cleanliness and the ideal of the perfect housewife were well regarded in this society of the 50s, 60s and 70s.

The children of the war children generation therefore had no choice but to adapt to this lack of emotion on the part of their parents as best they could. They suppressed their own liveliness and

---

[146] https://www.mittelbayerische.de/bayern-nachrichten/schweinegrippe-die-zweite-welle-ist-unterwegs-21705-art473808.html (retrieved 19/05/20)

reduced their needs and feelings, so that it did not exceed the survival level of their parents. Too much liveliness, joy and fun, wanting too much of life, all this would be beyond what their parents could have tolerated. It would have reminded them that they themselves had not had a childhood in which there was real joy and lust for life. For them, life had always been a survival programme in which they had to participate in what others were doing. They were good at it, perhaps even perfect. Wanting something of their own, being free and independent, were realms for which they lacked the imagination. Such a thing did not exist in their childhood, and even after the end of the Second World War it was not available to them. To be regimented, to be subordinate, to be obedient, to make sure that others were doing well, to stand together in times of need, these were their guiding principles. Anything else would be insubordinate egoism and despicable selfishness.

My mother always reproached me for her terrible childhood ("We didn't have proper shoes to go to school; we had to sleep with our siblings on a lice-infested straw bed") in order to dismiss my own needs as unreasonable demands. In this way I learned to join in with my mother's incessant doing and doing, so that I too found it very difficult to just stop and do nothing. I learned to endure her emotional outbursts of fear or anger, her constant whining and suffering. She did not have an easy childhood! Neither did my father, who was driven from his homeland and then set out on his own at the age of 14. Only if I operated on this same level of being undemanding and being happy to exist at all was something like a loving and caring relationship with my mother and father possible. Any more than this, or any alternative, was not on the cards.

Therefore, it would interesting to see what is going on in Mrs Merkel, for example, when she, as Federal Chancellor, says in her speech to the German people on 18th March 2020: 'This is serious. Take it seriously too. Since German reunification, no, since the Second World War, there has not been a challenge to our country where it depends so much on our joint action in solidarity'.[147]

Angela Merkel's father was born in 1928 and her mother in 1926. If you compare the self-dramatised pandemic situation with the end of the Second World War, you might say that what people are saying here on an unconscious level is: 'Look at this, Mummy darling, look

---

[147] https://www.n-tv.de/politik/Merkels-Rede-im-Wortlaut-article21652668.html (retrieved 14/06/20)

at this, dearest Daddy, I now understand how serious it was for you in the war and afterwards! I feel deeply connected to you!'

Two Stories
Seventeenth article – 13th April 2020

Story 1: I, Bill Gates, Save The World

I, Bill Gates, one of the richest men in the world, tell you that: 'A new and malignant virus has been spreading across the globe since early 2020. It is killing millions of people, many of whom are suffocating in agony. It is overwhelming the health systems of the whole world, even those of the highly developed industrialised countries.

So for the time being, the only thing that can help is to interrupt chains of infection. Social contacts must therefore be limited to only what is absolutely necessary! The governments and experts of each respective country must make their population aware of the seriousness of the situation as drastically as possible. The trivialisation and downplaying of the gigantic danger must be countered by every means possible. It must be made clear to everyone that there is only one way to end the pandemic and that is with the Sars-Cov-2 vaccine! It must be developed as soon as possible. We will be successful in 18 months at the latest. Together we can do it!

If we do this, 7 billion people of the world will then be able to be vaccinated and the curfews and shutdown of social life can be lifted. Until the next pandemic, for which we will then be better prepared than this time. Fortunately, all politics, the global economy and all social life will then already have geared themselves up to this new prime goal for the existence of all of us on this earth.

I, Bill Gates, am helping humanity, the rulers, the scientists, the journalists and their populations with my money in this colossal task. To do so, all the countries of the world must also be prepared to put all their wealth on the line. As a patron and philanthropist, I am completely selfless and only concerned for the whole of humanity'.

Story 2: I, Bill Gates, Save The World

I, Bill Gates, have long had the splendid and brilliant idea of contributing to the welfare of all humanity by eradicating all infectious diseases through vaccination. Polio, measles, now Sars-Cov-2 and all future dangerous viruses are the focus of my projects.

I buy the World Health Organisation (WHO) to use it for my idea. I set up various organisations that spread the idea of vaccination around the world and lobby for it (including GAVI). For this purpose I finance the best possible universities in the world (e.g. Johns Hopkins Baltimore) and the relevant national institutes for health (e.g. Robert Koch Institute in Germany). I meet with governments all over the world, bring my world-saving vaccination idea to them, personally accompanied with financial gifts both large and small. I gather the most brilliant scientists around me. I talk openly with the press about my vaccination idea and make no secret of it. I conduct, openly for all, a business game that plays through the Sars-CoV-2 pandemic in all its details, including the narrative of story 1 as mentioned above, which is necessary for the implementation of this plan.

I am completely transparent. People trust me. I have given them Microsoft and Windows. I care about their health and I work for the poorest of the poor. I am a philanthropist!

I earn money through my involvement with the vaccine manufacturers, who will of course support me in this out of their own business interests. At the same time, I can realise my idea of monitoring and controlling the whole of humanity through intelligent software and earn a lot of money from that.

But this side effect of making me even richer should not prevent anyone from believing that I am not a friend of humanity. I only want to use my money to relieve humanity of its suffering, especially the populations in the poor developing countries.

Even though I may be the richest man in the world, I live as modestly as anyone else. So you won't see any designer suits, just my simple clothes, trousers, open shirt and pullover. I am now even calling for donations to the WHO.

Unfortunately, there have been a number of futile attempts by the WHO in recent years (e.g. 2009 and 2015) to declare a pandemic. Now finally in 2020 it is working. To do so, of course, people will have to be persuaded and, if necessary, also forced so that I can make them happy. We must not be too squeamish in our choice of how to do this until everyone else has internalised my fantastic world rescue programme. We must now hold out for a few more months and continue to make sacrifices for this world rescue project. Everyone in his place and with his own means! The current Sars-CoV-2 pandemic is a milestone towards the realisation of my vision. I am very happy about the way things are going at the moment'.

So What Is The Real Story Now?

Is a self-immunisation of 95% of the people infected with Sars-CoV-2 pure utopia? There are, after all, some voices that are already attacking Bill Gates and his attitude of practically defining world health. This is the title of a SWR-2 report on 22.1.2019 by Thomas Kuchem: 'The WHO with the begging bowl - Bill Gates determines what is healthy'.[148]

---

[148] https://www.swr.de/swr2/wissen/aexavarticle-swr-42488.html (retrieved 31/04/20)

The Divide That's Happening In Partner Relationships

Even partnerships are now being put to the test in this pandemic situation, as this e-mail, which reached me on 28th April 2020, shows:

> 'I have decided that in future my husband should go shopping. He thinks the course of action being taken is good, that Mrs Merkel is great and he has no problem with masks. It's as if I'm the only one who feels differently.
>
> I am reading the new book by Hans-Joachim Maaz: A Land Divided[149]. It reads like a prophecy. If I had read it before Corona, I probably would have thought he was exaggerating, with a tendency to paranoia. Now the realities are even more extreme.'

My wife and I spend hours discussing this or that particular detail of the Corona pandemic and often find ourselves far from being in agreement. A person's relationship with the political leadership or the 'authorities' is presumably shaped by their relationship with their own parents. At least that is certainly the case with my wife and I. My wife had parents who were severely traumatised by their family of origin and the Second World War. Her parents were often emotionally unavailable, but at least they were not physically violent. My wife's mother, who I always experienced as having a real leaden heaviness coupled with an anxious irritability, tried to convince her daughter with arguments and supported her in her intellectual development to the best of her ability. Her mother's father was a research doctor and her mother would have liked to become a doctor too. Therefore, my wife now assumes that the decisions of the current German government are based on the assumption that, for the time being, they only want to avert greater damage to the country and the population. When I accuse Mrs Merkel, Mr Spahn, Mr Wieler or Mr Drosten, in conjunction with Bill Gates, of nefarious intentions and business interests, she vehemently defends them.

---

[149] Maaz's book '*Das Gespaltene Land*', has not been translated yet into English. However this article with an interview with him was in the New York Times: https://www.nytimes.com/2019/11/08/world/europe/germany-identity.html (retrieved 01/09/20)

My parents, on the other hand, were not very well educated and their method of trying to win conflicts would usually be with the threat of violence or with actual physical beatings. On an external level, I therefore had to submit as long as I lived at home. But inwardly, I rebelled and would seek out good, logical arguments that could demolish my parents' views lock, stock and barrel. That's probably why I'm always very critical of authority of all kinds, and I'm quick to sense when something is up and stinks to high heaven. In the course of my life I have developed an analytical mind that tries to get to the heart of the relationship between cause-and-effect without getting lost in too much detail. Nevertheless, for a long time there was still a rebel in me, who hoped that those I was criticising would come to their senses and then there would be peace and harmony again and those I had been criticising would then take on their proper role as parents or superiors. Today I know that this too is only a trauma survival strategy.

Who Dares To Raise Their Voice Right Now?

Every voice that now demands the lifting of the state of emergency gives me hope. My wife, who was previously still anxious to see the statistics of deaths and the individual reports of the tragic deaths of younger people, now feels that this is not just about the health of all of us. We are now sharing the alternative voices and insights with each other. I'm sitting at my computer at 5.30 a.m. on 2nd April and she shows me an article in the Münchner Merkur. The Wagner tenor and opera star Günther Groisböck talks in plain language about his assessment of the curfew and the overall social shutdown. In all his arguments, he exactly expresses what I feel.[150]

Even Professor Dr. Drosten from the Berlin Charité, in his skill-set actually only a virus researcher, but in the meantime has seen himself appointed as a key figure in politics and the press, now feels used for something he doesn't mean at all, and timidly announces his withdrawal from the public stage.[151] He could get support from his predecessor in his chair, Professor Emeritus Detlev Krüger. He

---

[150] Ich habe Angst vor Aktionismus" Opernstar Günther Groissböck über Corona, Grundrechte und Jürgen Klopp, Münchner Merkur, Kultur & Leben, 1. April 2020, S. 15

[151] https://www.t-online.de/nachrichten/panorama/id_87625188/corona-krise-virologe-drosten-denkt-an-medien-rueckzug-mir-wird-schlecht-.html, (retrieved 03/04/20)

considers the SARS-CoV-2 virus to be less dangerous than other influenza viruses and advises calm:

'It is said that one should not compare corona and flu waves. But in many respects they can be compared, both in terms of how the viruses are transmitted and in terms of risk groups, with pregnant women and children being added to the list of influenza cases. And it is a fact that we have more deaths due to influenza every year on average than is the case with the new Corona virus, at least in Germany'.[152]

Michael Hüter, author of a comprehensively researched book about childhood suffering in the past and today (Hüter 2018), makes a personal appeal to Angela Merkel and Sebastian Kurz in his guest commentary in the Rubicon :

'Dear Chancellor Angela Merkel. Dear Federal Chancellor Sebastian Kurz, [153] You are both childless, why that is does not matter here. But in 'peacetime' I don't let you tell me when and if I go to a playground with my children. Especially since the coronavirus is in fact and officially - see reports from China, Italy and elsewhere - not a 'killer virus' that kills every second or fourth person, even though most of the media currently suggest it is. Strictly speaking, the mortality rate for the coronavirus is in the per thousand range.

---

[152] https://de.sputniknews.com/interviews/20200425326953541-corona-gefahr-virologe/ (retrieved 25/04/20)
[153] https://www.rubikon.news/artikel/totaler-krieg-gegen-das-virus, (retrieved 04/04/20)

Figure 16: I am stunned on my Sunday bike ride: Going on the swings is prohibited across the whole city - because of Corona.

On 11th May 2020, a letter from an employee of the German Ministry of the Interior makes the rounds, in which he points out with concern that the entire corona pandemic essentially consists of misjudgements of the risk situation.[154] The reason he gives for 'sending this information directly without prior consultation with other competent authorities' is because we are in a state of emergency:

> 'There is imminent danger! At the moment, supposedly protective measures are causing more serious damage every day. There is material damage and damage to our health which is leading to a large number of avoidable deaths'.

He is of course promptly reprimanded by his superiors and relieved of his post. [155]

---

[154] https://deutungsvielfalt.de/2020/05/11/zeit-warum-ein-beamter-in-der-corona-krise-den-aufstand-wagt/
(retrieved 11/05/20)
[155] https://www.ichbinanderermeinung.de/Dokument93.pdf (retrieved 12/05/20)

Mark Twain Got It Right

Eighteenth Article – 15th April 2020

I feel myself drawn in and exploited for the trauma re-enactments of those who have the power and the money to do it.

The pandemic narrative of 'novel corona virus, highly infectious, piles of corpses, death by suffocation, solidarity with the old and weak, health systems are hopelessly overburdened' has the purpose, on a pseudo-rational level, of producing and administering vaccines to the population. In point 17 of the decision of the 'Telephone conference of the Federal Chancellor with the heads of government of the German Federal States on 15 April 2020 Decision, TOP 2 Restrictions on public life to contain the COVID-19 epidemic', this is literally spelled out for all to see:

'17. Timely immunity in the population against SARS-CoV-2 without a vaccine can not be achieved without overburdening the health care system with the resultant risk of many deaths. This is why vaccine development is of central importance. The Federal Government supports German companies and international organisations to support the development of vaccines as soon as possible. A vaccine is the key to a return to normal everyday life. As soon as a vaccine is available sufficient vaccine doses for the entire population should be made available as soon as possible.' [156]

Now something that had been missing from the prevailing corona pandemic narrative can be added: no one can be sure of developing immunity to SARS-CoV-2. Even those who have already been infected and recovered

---

[156] https://www.bundeskanzlerin.de/bkin-de/aktuelles/telefonschaltkonferenz-der-bundeskanzlerin-mit-den-regierungschefinnen-und-regierungschefs-der-laender-am-15-april-2020-1744228 (retrieved 18/04/20)

are not 100% immune to the virus and may continue to infect others. We will soon see this addition to the pandemic narrative become more widely publicised.

Here is a well-researched article that critically examines the lobbying and vaccination activities of the Bill and Melinda Gates Foundation.[157]

At the moment all I can think of is the writer Mark Twain (1835-1910) who said:

> *'It is easier to fool people*
> *than to convince them*
> *that they have been fooled.'*

Mark Twain was the author of 'The Adventures of Tom Sawyer'. One day Tom Sawyer gets the order from his aunt Polly to whitewash a thirty metre long garden fence. He hates it and would rather go and play. But he manages to convince another boy that painting the fence is actually so much fun. Then more and more boys from the village come and want to paint the garden fence too. While all the other boys are painting the fence, Tom is free to go off and play. In fact some of the boys even pay Tom for the privilege of painting the garden fence.[158]

To those who now rather than saying goodbye say 'Stay healthy', I would now like to say: 'Stay with yourself, your needs, your feelings and your own mind'.

---

[157] https://multipolar-magazin.de/artikel/the-gates-foundations-vaccination-activism (retrieved 07/09/20)

[158] https://medium.com/@thenthgen/the-most-important-life-lesson-from-tom-sawyer-e92f86f6afb3 (retrieved 07/09/20)

Where Does The Law Stand?

The Infection Protection Act, which is now being applied in Germany during the corona pandemic, undermines all civil liberties: Freedom of movement, occupation, assembly and demonstration. The specialist law firm Beate Bahner is one of the first to publicly issue a legal challenge against the lockdown of society, using arguments that have been disseminated in the alternative media[159]. On 9th April I am forwarded the following group email from Ms Bahner:

> 'A thousand thanks for your feedback and support!
> Please share this mail - share share share, forward, distribute - that's what we need now! And organise a demonstration in your city or community yourself! Please register with the relevant office beforehand, simply in accordance with § 14 of the Assembly Act, it's easy online... No one can forbid you to hold assemblies and demonstrations in a constitutional state! The right of assembly according to article 8 GG is one of the most fundamental basic rights of all citizens in Germany! In a police state and a dictatorship you are no longer allowed to assemble - and websites are blocked.
> With best regards from Heidelberg:
> WE CREATE THIS!!!
> Yours Beate Bahner' (email from 09/04/20)

After her emergency appeal was rejected by the court, Ms Bahner throws in the towel and probably gives up her resistance. In return, the public prosecutor's office in Heidelberg accused Ms Bahner of violating the infection control law by calling for a demonstration.

On 13th April 2020 she was, according to her own statements, transferred by the police to a psychiatric hospital in Heidelberg. In a telephone conversation with her sister she made this course of events public[160]. This incident shocked me deeply. During this

---

[159] http://beatebahner.de/lib.medien/aktualisierte%20Pressemitteilung.pdf, (retrieved 04/04/20)
[160] This phone call was uploaded to Youtube. It has since been taken down. An article in English detailing what happened to Ms Bahner, her case & arguments and her subsequent violent committal to a psychiatric institute can be found here: https://www.ukcolumn.org/article/coronavirus-lockdown-german-lawyer-detained-opposition (retrieved 10/09/20)

corona pandemic, what is crazy is considered perfectly normal and the normal is portrayed as crazy. I remembered that this was also the way the GDR government dealt with dissidents. Anyone who objected to the socialist state could not be right in the head and had to be re-educated.

However, over the next few days Ms Bahner behaved very contradictorily and it is no longer clear what actually happened when she was admitted to the psychiatric ward. A letter on her homepage dated 5th June is so shocking that I leave it up to the readers to form their own judgement.[161] In June she appears again as a speaker at a demonstration in Miltenberg and appears mentally clear again[162]. Many people approach her directly and thank her for her courage.

It has become one of the key issues in this pandemic: Can the Infection Protection Act really override the civil rights guaranteed in the Basic Law of the Federal Republic of Germany? Does this separation of powers between the legislature, the judiciary and the executive, which is so often invoked in a democracy, still exist? Prof. Dr. David Jungbluth, holder of a deputy professorship at the Frankfurt University of Applied Sciences and a lawyer in Frankfurt

---

[161] The letter which can be found in German here:

(http://beatebahner.de/lib.medien/Stellungnahme%20Unterbringung.pdf - retrieved 09/10/20) runs as follows in English:

The German state uses the following three methods to silence politically unpopular opponents:

1. You are made out to be a 'right-wing extremist'.

2. You are branded a 'conspiracy theorist'.

3. You are 'forcibly detained' in the secure ward of a psychiatric hospital.

Beate Bahner was deprived of her freedom for a total of four weeks from Friday, 24th April 2020 up to and including Friday, 22nd May 2020, in the psychiatric ward of the LVR Clinic in Cologne, against her will, on the basis of an accommodation order by the Cologne Local Court. In the secure unit, she experienced massive physical violence, gagging (so-called "fixation") and multiple instances of confinement in an isolation room. Beate Bahner also received compulsory medication. She had no strength to defend herself against the decision to detain her. The reason for the detainment was an alleged theft of ice cream and chocolate rolls at a petrol station in the centre of Cologne (Beate Bahner was on foot), the knocking over of a flower pot and an alleged violation of the smoking ban. These incidents are alleged to have occurred on the night of 24th April 2020. Access to the file on these proceedings has been requested. Beate Bahner has been at liberty again since 23rd May 2020. She continues to work as a lawyer in her law firm. In order to maintain the ongoing operation of the law firm, it is requested to refrain from making any calls regarding this notice. Emails will of course be answered. Many thanks for your understanding! Beate Bahner

[162] https://www.bitchute.com/video/kMoCpARXSg4J/ (retrieved 29/11/20) (original taken down from Youtube)

am Main specialising in constitutional law as well as foreigners and migration law, comments on this in an interview with Rubikon:

> 'What we are dealing with here is a complete failure of all three state powers, or at the very least a failure of the demarcation and balance functions between these three powers, which can only shock those who have so far been unshakably convinced of the undamaged solidity of the rule of law in this country.
>
> Against this background, it can be stated that a development is emerging which could lead to a case of Article 20 (4) of the Basic Law, which describes the right to resist, since an absolute state of emergency exists in the event that the three state powers - and incidentally also to a large extent the so-called fourth power, i.e. the press/media, and here in particular those of public broadcasting - fail. It is to be hoped, however, that the state authorities will be able to fulfil their responsibility in time and thus avert the occurrence of the emergency situation under Article 20 (4) of the Basic Law[163].

---

[163] https://www.rubikon.news/artikel/angriff-auf-verfassungsmassige-ordnung (retrieved 01/09/20)

Waking Up From The Trauma Trance

Nineteenth Article – 18th April 2020

To all those who now feel that they have to do everything they can to control everything with all their power, wealth and high intelligence, I would like to ask the following questions: When and under what circumstances did you lose control of your own life? When did you give up your own self? When did you lose confidence in your own self-healing powers? To whom did you have to orientate yourself instead? Can you still use your will to satisfy your own needs? Or do you always have to be there for others? To take care of their needs? Even protect them from viruses? Day and night? Who is this virus in reality for you? Your mum, your dad, your...

What would you rather do? When would things finally be about you? When will you start living instead of just surviving?

I know this for sure by now: anyone who wakes up from his trauma trance, a state which we've usually been in since our early childhood, and arrives at himself, is a world saviour. None of us actually need do anything more than this.

Statements And Initiatives By Groups And Individuals

Juli Zeh, whose novel 'Unterleuten'[164] kept me company throughout a long bicycle holiday, makes a clever argument in her recent article in the Süddeutsche Zeitung:

> 'In the case of Covid-19, large sections of the scientific community agree that so-called herd immunisation must take place, i.e., that at least 60 to 70 percent of the population must be infected until the pandemic subsides'.[165]

Because of this, she strongly opposes the changes to the constitution imposed by the Infection Protection Act.

A group of six high-ranking experts from the health and care sector under the leadership of Professor Dr. Matthias Schrappe present a 30-page thesis paper calling for scientifically sound data to assess the risk of Sars-CoV-2. They consider the data published daily by the Robert Koch Institute to be completely inadequate.

An acquaintance of mine is carrying out a small-scale rebellion. She and a friend sit down in front of the town hall of their town. She then writes me the following field report:

> 'It felt very lively. We got into conversation with many different people and also with each other. We had mainly friendly reactions along the lines of 'I see it that way too', many critical thinking people whose view of the financial system and other things was enriching, and we also had conversations with people who started out attacking us, but in the end they all turned to understanding, when I said: 'I was so panicky tonight because the WHO has called for the military to be allowed to storm homes and take out individual family members for compulsory tests, compulsory treatment and compulsory vaccinations', as it is already happening in Denmark. 'I don't want this, it makes me panic!' Many people

---

[164] This novel (Unterleuten is the name of the fictional village where the story is set and would translate as something like 'Underclass') is not yet available in English, though some of Juli Zeh's novels have been translated including 'The Method' (*Corpus Delicti: Ein Prozess*) set in a future 'health dictatorship'

[165] Süddeutsche Zeitung from 4th April 2020

didn't even know that yet and wanted to research it as a matter of urgency.

In the end, after two and a half hours, the public order officer came and declared that we were not allowed to do what we were doing. I asked why, because in my opinion it was only a meeting of two people, which is allowed. They then said that it was not allowed to hold a meeting on a given topic, and certainly not if it aroused interest. I said that I didn't get that and that I was beginning to forget what was actually allowed. We wanted to go home anyway. When I mentioned the problem of breaking into the flats, the woman from the public order office said: 'I can understand that, I don't want that either. Fortunately that's not the case here yet. No one is allowed in there, not even if the neighbours report something. All in all it was an exciting day. Love K.'

From April 18th onwards the activities in the alternative press increase enormously. More and more people are putting their heads over the parapets and putting forward arguments against the lockdown. The statements that Bill Gates made on the Tagesthemen TV show (on 15th April) of how seven billion people will be vaccinated against Corona are making the rounds. The singer Xavier Naidoo initiates a poster campaign on his YouTube channel 'Don't give GATES a chance!' based on the German Health campaign slogan 'Don't give AIDS a chance!'

Lothar Hirneise with his 'ichbinanderermeinung' campaign (Literally – 'I am of a different opinion' – The English section of their website is: https://ichbinanderermeinung.de/en) and Bodo Schiffmann, who disseminates pandemic-critical news and statements every day via his website 'www.schwindelambulanz-sinsheim.de' talk of founding a political party in Germany, which would harness all those who disagree with the course of the current government and provide a voice for the silenced opposition.[166]

On 29th April 2020 Bodo Schiffmann reports that the party he has now founded, widerstand2020.de (Resistance2020) has more than 35,500 members.[167] By 8th May there are already over 100,000 party members. As expected, the supposed 'quality press' attacks this

---

[166] https://widerstand2020.de/ (retrieved 22/04/20)
[167] https://www.youtube.com/watch?v=Cmf5jRUAqxA (retrieved 01/05/20)

protest party with equal vigour. Deutschlandfunk Nova, for example, reports:

> 'The 'Resistance 2020' group is a diffuse pool, says sociologist Matthias Quent of the Institute for Democracy and Civil Society. Its members include conspiracy theorists, right-wing populists, left-wing anti-vaccination activists, but also insecure citizens. This mixture is dangerous.'[168]

Even when this party then loses momentum and Bodo Schiffmann founds his own association, 'Mediziner und Wissenschaftler für Gesundheit, Freiheit und Demokratie' (Doctors and scientists for health, freedom and democracy), which also includes Sucharit Bhakdi and Wolfgang Wodarg, the resistance against the madness of the pandemic continues to organise and grow. As the resistance grows so too does the nervousness of those who then immediately throw mud at everything that threatens to contradict the lies and deception of the Global Impact Alliance with their 'fact checkers'.[169]

The situation becomes more and more absurd when, for example, the panic-makers in Germany apply the protection of the constitution to those whose explicit aim is to protect the German constitution from being destroyed by this corona pandemic. In the former GDR, it was the task of the Stasi to break down popular resistance to the socialism mania of the SED, the unity party. They even had their own university in Höhenschönhausen, where they taught psychological techniques that were particularly suitable for this purpose.[170]

The chairwoman of one of the regional associations of the Ecological Party of Germany (ÖDP) called me and lamented the lethargy in her party and sought scientific arguments that supported her point of view so she felt able to go public with corona criticism. After our conversation she dared to make a critical statement on her Instagram account.

A lawyer called me whilst I was in Berlin for an interview, asking what I could contribute as a trauma expert to help her reach people.

---

[168] https://www.deutschlandfunknova.de/beitrag/protest-gegen-corona-ma%C3%9Fnahmen-widerstand-2020-versammelt-esoteriker-impfgegner-und-rechtspopulisten (retrieved 08/05/20)

[169] https://www.tagesschau.de/faktenfinder/mwgfd-101.html (retrieved 01/07/20)

[170] https://en.wikipedia.org/wiki/Zersetzung (retrieved 01/09/20)

I suggested that she expressed what needs she had that would now be harmed and also that she gave those she was talking to space to recognise their own needs that are being affected by the lockdown. I strongly advised her against entering into perpetrator-victim dialogues.

On the YouTube channel Punkt.Preradovic, the finance scientist Professor Homburg announces that the virus epidemic actually peaked back on March 14th, when the lockdown measures were started in Germany. Today, on 18th April, the epidemic wave has already subsided and is actually over.[171]

Christof Kuhbandner, professor of psychology and chair holder at the Faculty of Human Sciences at the University of Regensburg, also said the same thing:

'After a closer methodical examination of these figures, it is very clear that none of the measures taken can really be scientifically justified:

On the one hand, in reality the number of new infections has never increased rapidly, on the other hand the number of new infections has already been declining since about the beginning to mid-March - this was only masked by the fact that the number of coronavirus tests has increased so much over time and the time lag between the actual time of infection and the time of testing was not sufficiently taken into account. In particular, none of the measures taken can explain the decline, because the first measure (cancellation of large events with more than 1,000 participants) was not taken until 9th March. Similarly, there are no signs of overcrowding in intensive care units or a higher number of deaths in Germany compared with previous years, so that none of the measures can be justified on this basis either'.[172]

However, the other side of the corona narrative is continuing to weave its web. A Mr. Richard Edelmann writes on his website:

[171] https://deutungsvielfalt.de/2020/04/17/punkt-preradovic-prof-dr-stefan-neuerki-zahlen-die-corona-welle-ist-vorbei-es-braucht-sich-keiner-mehr-sorgen-zu-machen/ (retrieved 19/04/20)
[172] https://scilogs.spektrum.de/menschen-bilder/von-der-fehlenden-wissenschaftlichen-begruendung-der-corona-massnahmen/ (retrieved 26/04/20)

'I spoke with Dr. David Nabarro, World Health Organization Special Envoy for Covid-19, about the communications challenges of returning to work as the pandemic begins to ebb. He was clear in his response. "We must remember that the virus will not go away in the foreseeable future: it will remain a threat to us all and we need to find ways to live with it. Every company needs to think now about how to do more physical distancing, and how to manage requests for sick days for those who feel ill. It is a huge mistake to wait when it comes to thinking about these issues until the local authority decides that it is safe for staff to return to work. The time to get ready for new ways to work and to discuss them with each other needs to begin happening now. Communication matters: do not go silent."'[173]

In plain language: whether or not the virus still has any visible consequences for anyone does not matter. It is simply there and everything we do must be in reference to it - until the vaccine is available. That is just the way it is with such a novel virus.

It also continues to leave shrouded in doubt, I think deliberately, whether someone who was already infected with Sars-CoV-2 and is therefore immune-protected is actually no longer infectious. I received a letter from 19th April 2020 to this effect:

'Dear Prof. Ruppert,
The narrative you predicted of 'even after recovery there is no immune protection' is already being brandished about and is causing further uncertainty, fear and isolation. Despite the positive result of an antibody test, the public health department has informed me that all regulatory measures still apply to me. This means that I am still not allowed to visit my mother in a nursing home, I am only allowed to run my practice to a limited extent, I am not allowed to visit my friends and I am also requested to wear a facemask. After I had also asked my representatives in the regional and federal parliaments for legally valid information, I was informed that there were probably no different regulations for people who had already had the virus.

---

[173] https://www.edelman.com/insights/going-back-to-work-the-next-big-challenge-for-communicators (retrieved 19/04/20)

With this context in mind, it is strange that my son, who is working as a medical student in a hospital, was informed by his employer that he could be given preferential treatment in his nursing work after a positive antibody test.

I have high hopes for my clients, who in the future will be wise according to the Robert J. Sternberg 'Balance theory of wisdom': 'intelligence, creativity and common sense' combined with character, commitment, passion and ethical responsibility. Only then can one speak of intelligence when it is truly altruistic and is focused on finding a truly common good. Highly educated, highly talented, highly paid scientists and/or politicians are not saving the world at present. They act 'intelligently', but not 'wisely'.

Thank you very much for your 'wise' contributions. They encourage me in many ways and give me the strength to believe in my own perception.

Best regards G.'

Slowly, voices of reason from the political establishment are beginning to emerge too. On 25th April 2020, for example, Wolfgang Schäuble, President of the Bundestag, makes comments on the Tagesschau (a major ARD Television News programme) about the restrictions on basic rights resulting from the measures to contain the coronavirus.

"'When I hear that everything else is subordinated to the protection of life, I have to say that this is not right to have this absoluteness. If there is an absolute value in the Basic Law, it is the dignity of the human being. That is what is inviolable. But it does not exclude the possibility that we have to die," stressed the President of the Bundestag. "The state must guarantee the best possible health care for everyone. But people will still die of Corona," said Schäuble.'[174]

Even the Catholic Church raised its voice against the Corona coercive measures at the beginning of May, when, in a dramatic move renowned cardinals such as Cardinal Robert Sarah, Cardinal Janis Pujats, Cardinal Gerhard Müller and Cardinal Joseph Zen, as

---

[174] https://www.tagesschau.de/inland/schaeuble-corona-101.html (retrieved 08/05/20)

well as dozens of bishops, priests and intellectuals issued an 'Appeal for the Church and the World' to stop the setting up of totalitarian practices, which were being introduced in most countries under the pretext of Covid-19 containment.

> 'Let us not allow centuries of Christian civilization to be erased under the pretext of a virus, and an *odious technological tyranny* to be established, in which nameless and faceless people can decide the fate of the world by confining us to a virtual reality.' [175]

Even the tabloid Bild Newpaper, which has not been on quite the same panic-mongering course as the Süddeutsche Zeitung, the Münchner Merkur or the Abendzeitung from the outset because it was more concerned with economic decline and rising unemployment, has the headline on 8th May 2020 of 'Lockdown was a huge mistake - Germany's smartest corona sceptics criticise the tough measures'. [176]

---

[175] https://www.ncregister.com/blog/cardinals-bishops-sign-appeal-against-coronavirus-restrictions (retrieved 10/09/20) - It seems that Cardinal Sarah initially signed the open letter but then changed his mind and withdrew his name – this is covered in the updated English article quoted here.

[176] https://www.bild.de/bild-plus/politik/inland/politik-inland/lockdown-war-ein-riesen-fehler-wissenschaftler-kritisieren-corona-massnahmen-70517342,view=conversionToLogin.bild.html (retrieved 08/05/20)

To Enlighten Or To Panic?
Twentieth Article – 19th April 2020

The following report appeared in the Süddeutsche
Zeitung Newspaper on 16th April 2020:

'It all started on 14th March. It was the day before
the local elections, in which Erol Akbulut had put
himself forward as a Social Democratic Party
candidate for the city council. On that morning he
felt a bit feverish. He didn't think much of it at first
– probably just a cold, he thought. Akbulut made
himself some hot lemon and took some Aspirin. The
next day, the Sunday before the election, he had a
full on fever and a temperature of 38.5 degrees. He
tried to lower it with a strong 600 milligram dose of
ibuprofen, but his condition worsened. On Monday
he had diarrhoea and started to vomit. The fever
rose to 39 degrees. Akbulut began to suspect that
he might have caught the Corona virus. He had no
idea what else was in store for him.

Erol Akbulut is 44 years old, he's a sporty guy
who likes to go to the gym. He has had no previous
illnesses. When his symptoms worsened, he called
116117 – the non-emergency doctor on-call service
hotline. Callers get through to medically trained
staff who ask about symptoms, previous illnesses
and risk factors. They will then direct callers to
their family doctor or the nearest hospital,
depending on the urgency. At least that is the
theory, that's how it should be in the Corona
period. In practice, says Erol Akbulut, there was no
getting through on that number. He didn't know
how to help himself other than to call a friend who
is a doctor. His doctor friend sorted him out a test,
Akbulut's wife picked it up for him. He then took
the swab from his throat himself. On 18th March he
got the result: Corona positive. In addition, there

was a high rate of inflammation. His temperature continued to rise, to over 40 degrees. He also had an 'extremely dry cough'. He could hardly speak, there were times when he could not get his breath. And then there was this severe pain in his limbs.

That's how he tells it on the phone, five days after he was discharged from hospital. His voice sounds thin, again and again he is interrupted by coughing. He still feels quite weak.

Erol Akbulut has no idea where he caught the virus. He is a works council member at BMW, in a department with 2800 employees' and then there was the 'election campaign', he says. He was constantly meeting people. He has many contacts. The day before he got his test results, his wife had called an ambulance for the first time. The paramedics came without protective clothing, and then they left. They said he probably had the flu. The next day, knowing that he was Corona positive, his wife called an ambulance again. 'Please let me be picked up, he had said to her. Also because his cough was now so bad. Even the Paracodin drops he was taking didn't help. 'I've never experienced anything like it,' says Akbulut. But they didn't take him away until the next day. Third call, third ambulance. This time his oxygen saturation was below 80 percent - so low that there is a danger to his life.

He spent twelve days with pneumonia in the intensive care unit of the Schwabing hospital, followed by a few days in the normal ward.'[177]

What struck me when I first read this is that this person undermines the work of his own immune system with anti-fever and anti-inflammatory agents and suppresses, with medication, the cleansing function that his cough performs. From my point of view this is normal behaviour

---

[177] Süddeutsche Zeitung, 16.4.2020, S. R4

for people who are not informed about their immune system and its self-healing powers. The body is seen as a machine that is constantly put under stress and is still supposed to perform. That is why he cannot help thinking that he has to be saved by orthodox medicine, which makes him believe that the reactions of his immune system are diseases.

However, this report in the Süddeutsche Zeitung has not been written with the idea of being a kind of health education for the general population. It is written instead to illustrate the corona pandemic narrative with a case study: 'Look, everyone, this new/unpredictable virus can basically hit healthy people hard who would die if they weren't given intensive care'.

In this case, it is not at all clear whether it is a specific Covid-19 related pneumonia or whether this lung symptomatology is the result of other possible influenza viruses or even a bacterial infection. So the corona narrative is once again confirming itself. If we've hidden the Easter eggs ourselves, we're always going to find them.

By the way, this article also makes it clear that not only in Italy, but also in Germany, people who do not fit into the corona narrative are rejected by the health system and do not receive adequate help. If they die and have been tested corona-positive, the enormous risk of death caused by Covid-19 can be pointed out again.

Will Any Publisher Take My IoPT Analyses Of The Corona Situation?

As the volume of my articles continues to grow, the idea comes to me of publishing them in book form. I therefore ask the publishers who have published my previous books. An editor is kind enough to reply to me straight away.

'Dear Mr Ruppert,

There is a fundamental problem in preparing a text that is directly related to current affairs into the medium of a book at short notice. That's why I find it difficult to find another book publisher for this in the short term. All the more so in the current situation, in which the publishers are also mainly concerned with handling the Corona crisis. Time and capacities for 'quick turnarounds' are now even less available than in normal times.

Nevertheless, I understand that you would prefer to publish your current text right away. I can only recommend again what I wrote yesterday: Perhaps you would like to look around for a magazine, a journal or something similar, which might want to publish the article in a somewhat shortened form? Or you could simply put it on your homepage?'

This answer gives me the opportunity to become aware of why I think a book publication makes sense. I therefore write the following answer to my editor:

'For me personally this has less to do with a rush job. For me, the current situation is more a living example of what I wrote in 'Who am I in a Traumatised society?' and which is therefore predictable and understandable by Identity Oriented Psychotrauma Theory (IoPT). It is the same principle as when trauma survival strategies are at work in a society.'

I realised that the Corona pandemic is also hitting the publishing industry hard when my Spanish publisher 'Herder' had to postpone the publication of 'Love, Lust & Trauma', which was planned for this year, until next year or possibly even the year after.

Therefore, for the time being, I decide to make this book available as a PDF file, in order to keep it up-to-date. I will publish it later as a printed version and probably self-publish it.

Help comes promptly. A colleague from Berlin, who has experience in publishing, diligently corrects my manuscript very carefully and helps me enormously. An old acquaintance contacts me out of the blue and helps me to realize this book in a printed edition and an e-book.

And then on 16th May I receive this totally unexpected email:

'I have heard you, Mr Ruppert, speaking about your theory and the practice of IoPT as a guest on one programme or another. I have also read some of your books. I have always had the desire to translate one of your books into Japanese.

Recently, two days ago, I saw you on the Nuoviso programme with Robert Stein and another programme. I was so deeply impressed by what was said there that I immediately bought and read your digital book 'The Corona Virus in a Traumatised Society'. I quickly read the book and decided to translate it into Japanese in order to make it readable for the Japanese people as quickly and widely as possible. The book is so interesting and exciting and enlightening. Your process of perception and thinking about this corona pandemic, which you describe chronologically in the book in individual articles, I can also understand very well, because I myself have experienced a similar process of thinking and feeling.

So here is my question to you: Are the translation rights into Japanese still available? If so, is it possible to obtain the rights to translate this book?

I see it as my duty to present what you have written in the book to as many Japanese readers as possible in order to open their eyes, awaken their consciousness, bring them closer to truths about this whole story, and last but not least to possibly bring their souls to a place of peace.'

The author of these lines has his own publishing house in Japan and is a professor of German and linguistics. I gladly agreed to his request.

A few weeks ago, a small German audio book publisher also approached me. We quickly came to an agreement and soon you will be able to listen to this book as well.

Real, Traumatic Or Made-Up Fears
Twenty-First Article – 1st May 2020

In an interview with Elena Pfarr, she and I talk about fears and their significance in this Corona pandemic, which I believe is staged.[178] Creating fear is an old technique of domination, especially in Germany: fear of the devil, fear of the Jews, fear of communism, fear of unemployment, fear of terrorists, fear of CO_2 emissions, and now fear of an alleged killer virus. In East Germany for many years the Stasi used the fear of capitalism and the class enemy to bring its population into line and to terrorise it.

Rulers ascribe attributions onto the population:

- Everyone is basically sinful and must now prove that he is a God-fearing person. Through baptism we are redeemed from our original sin at least once.
- Everybody is a potential enemy of the system or a possible defector and must prove that he is not by his loyal towing of the line.
- In principle, everyone is a suspected terrorist and everyone must prove through totalitarian surveillance measures that he is not a terrorist.
- Everybody is potentially a conspiracy theorist and must prove that he is not by stating publicly that he does not hold those views and preferably does not reference anyone who does, so that he is not considered suspect in terms of his background or connections.
- Everyone is infectious and must now prove that he is not. The best thing to do is to have a vaccination just to be on the safe side.

Those who create fear make themselves out to be the saviours and the population must pay a price for their

---

[178] https://www.youtube.com/watch?v=SnQmUR1Gv0w (retrieved 01/05/20)

salvation: follow the given rules, do not think for yourself, believe only in the right prophets and not in the wrong ones, let yourself be monitored and controlled, denounce each other and go to war. In short: allow yourself to be traumatised in the name of an invented danger.

Therefore, in view of the waning flu/corona wave, wearing a mask is not now intended for health protection. It serves to give further validity to the narrative that a threat exists and to make the supposed threat visible to everyone.

The whole thing works so well because the unresolved fears from the darkness of one's own early history as a traumatised child are projected into the present. If we were traumatised in our early childhood, these fears from our pre-history are transferred to the here and now and can easily be triggered by panic-mongering.

Here is an illustration (drawing on Figure 2 and Figure 3, earlier in the text) that shows the different kinds of fears in reference to the split psyche.

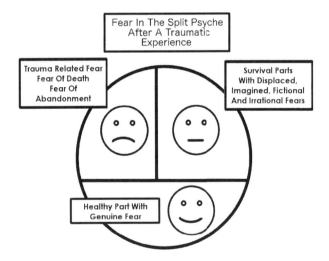

Figure 17: Real, traumatic and perceived fears

Another Day Of Confusion In The Search For Clarity And Truth

<u>Diary entry 19/04/2020:</u> Today is another one of those days that seems governed by extreme emotions. When I get up, I read the Süddeutsche Zeitung over a cup of tea, this time from cover to cover. Corona is everywhere, the greatest threat to humanity in every country of the world and right on our doorstep too. And there's no light at the end of the tunnel.

Then I get an email from a colleague, with a link to an interview Ken Jebsen had yesterday with Professor Sucharit Bhakdi. Whilst radiating such dignity, Professor Bhakdi rejects the Corona horror scenario that is being painted everywhere. He knows he is a competent scientist in this field and calls for clear scientific research on Covid-19. The empirical evidence already available clearly indicates that this virus is no more dangerous than other corona and influenza viruses. Moreover, the epidemic is probably already over. So there is no reason to maintain the lockdown, no reason to drive so many people into personal and professional ruin by these measures.

In a conversation with my wife, I then realise what a psychological dilemma we find ourselves in. It is clear that those who are currently in power and those who advise them with their Corona narrative cannot be trusted under any circumstances. Their statements are too contradictory and confusing, the numbers of infections and alleged corona deaths too unclear. It is impossible to truly predict the personal, social, economic and political consequences that the control strategies that they impose on society will result in. Why don't they just get all the experts together, who are now coming forward, but who can still only be heard in the alternative media? Why do they so stubbornly continue to only take one side? Why do I, as an ordinary citizen who has no idea about virology and epidemiology, intensive care and respiratory care, have to deal with all these things myself, try to get clarity and assess which source is trustworthy and which is not?

In the afternoon, I have a telephone conversation with a 58-year-old man who is in a similar situation to me, who also feels abandoned by the government and the press and who has as a result set up an resource for information online to spread his findings on social networks. Our conclusion is that this corona crisis shows that the entire political, economic, health and media system has, in a sense, pre-existing illnesses and is therefore in great danger of failing because of this virus. The virus only reveals how susceptible our system is to infection by dictatorial tendencies, how wide open the door is to totalitarianism and the mania to control, how prone it is to collapse, and how pronounced is the attitude of turning away in fear and not looking throughout the population.

The crowning glory comes on this day with an e-mail from a friend in Barcelona, who sends me the link to an article by Charles Eisenstein entitled 'The Coronation'. I have never before read such a profound, horizon-widening and warmly human article. I immediately post it on my website and warmly recommend it to everyone.[179] It becomes clear that the objective truth about this virus will never exist. What matters in the end is what each of us makes of it, so that perhaps we can finally become the subject of our own lives.

I feel that my IoPT informed stance has been completely confirmed by Mr Eisenstein's reflections.

The Reproduction Number 'R'

It is only gradually becoming clear to me - and I assume to many others as well - what a major role the so-called basic reproduction number plays in justifying pandemic measures and maintaining them.

'The 'Reproduction Number' indicates the rate of increase or decrease in the number of newly infected persons. If R=2, then on average each infected person infects 2 more people within the infectious period. This is the dreaded 'exponential progression', because after each period of infection, the number of newly infected people is twice as high: 2, 4, 8, 16, 32, 64, so if the number of newly infected persons is 64 times as high after 6 infectious periods, then the reproduction rate was R=2. If R is less than 1, then the number of new cases falls. R=0.5 means that two people on average only infect one person. So if there are currently 1,000 new cases and after 3 generation periods only 125, then the Reproduction Number would be said to be R=0.5.

[179] https://charleseisenstein.org/essays/the-coronation/ (retrieved 01/09/20)

Reproduction numbers play a crucial role in the debate on how to deal with the Corona crisis. Only once R has fallen below 1 does it seem politically possible to talk about easing. Since the 8th April, the RKI (Robert Koch Institute) has included the reproduction rate in its daily reports. At that time, before Easter, there were tough announcements from those in charge. At that time, the R was reported as 1.2, the exponential course was still present, any relaxation would, it was said, lead to a higher R number and was therefore dismissed as irresponsible. When, on 13th April, the R Number dropped to 1 and the rulers met for consultations, nobody wanted to be 'unreasonable', all restrictions were to remain in place in order not to endanger the success that had just been achieved. Schools remained closed, contact or curfew restrictions remained in place and many people remained in tension or fear because of the predicted terrible situation of a continuing and worsening pandemic in Germany.

As correct and understandable as this course of events and the decisions made seem: on closer analysis, the judgements made must clearly by corrected. An argument based on R alone is manipulative. As the RKI itself writes, other relevant aspects must be included in order to avoid falling for the same misconception. [...]

'According to RKI data, the daily reported R number is only a rough estimate and can only be calculated more precisely in hindsight after several weeks. Since one cannot wait that long, one would have to consult the current case numbers and the number of intensive care patients - as the RKI itself recommends. For a more accurate assessment, the RKI would have to regularly publish the more accurate - and not just estimated - reproduction numbers after a few weeks and list them in the report, for example. This has not yet been done. [...] If test capacities are suddenly increased, R will be systematically overestimated, as the RKI also indicates. So if the test capacities are reduced now because of the slowing down of the wave and are increased again significantly in a few months because of a new outbreak, then you will have more absolute case numbers and an overestimated R, without the situation actually really being as critical as it seems. [...] Therefore, the current illness and intensive care figures must be considered instead. This is shown in the section on assessing the course of the pandemic (see below). Those who argue only with the currently reported R number alone act dishonestly and make themselves suspect of panic-mongering (or inappropriate appeasement). This must be understood by every viewer or participant in a discussion, classified accordingly and rejected.

It is also not clear what rate of change R itself has. After all, the 29 days doubling time mentioned above are only present if R remains constant during this time. But this is only the case as long as there is no dynamic development. The time interval without 'dynamic developments', however, does not require short-term decisions and therefore R is of little help there'. [180]

In summary, this means that the reproduction number depends on various factors:

- How it is calculated.
- Which projections are included in its calculation until the actual numbers of infected persons are available – this has a time delay of anything from 3 days.
- How many tests are carried out.
- Who is being tested.
- How much of the population is there that can be possibly infected.
- What the genuine number of infections is.
- Ultimately also how valid the SARS-CoV-2 test procedure itself is.

R is at best a tautology, as Dr. Patrick Grete, the graduate physicist, from whose contribution I am quoting here, puts very succinctly. What comes out on the left side of the equation as a number is only dependant on what was previously given on the right side of the equation. R is not an absolute number, but a ratio, i.e. a relative number, and therefore a number construct. R is not a mathematical number that objectively represents physical realities. It is dependent on human subjects, their assessments, their activities, their fears and

---

[180] https://multipolar-magazin.de/artikel/mythos-reproduktionszahl (retrieved 15/05/20)

their hopes. R can therefore be of a varying high or low value. And therefore is also dependent on who has what interest in using such a number as a basis for argument when it comes to their power decisions.

Is it simply a lack of intelligence to orientate oneself on such factors as 'R', or is there a different kind of calculation behind it? Is 'R' being used to end the pandemic as soon as possible or to prolong it as long as possible?

In view of the immense collateral damage that the pandemic continues to generate on a daily basis, it should actually be in the interest to use this number R to end the pandemic as quickly as possible in order to act in the public interest.

My feeling is that certainly up until this point (7th June 2020) the opposite is happening. The R Number is being used to make the relaxation of measures appear dangerous and to keep the message of a 'second wave' alive. Is it therefore more important for those interested parties to prolong the state of the pandemic until it can be ended by the announcement of mass vaccination, which then also becomes longed for by the majority of the world population who have been suffering from the pandemic state and will welcome it as a release from all its agonies?

Power And Money Traumatise The World In The Name Of Health

Twenty-Second Article – 8th May 2020

The Dark Ages

Who would have imagined back at the beginning of 2020 that a super-rich businessman disguised as a philanthropist would be traumatising the world in the name of health, aided and abetted by virus and statistics mythologists disguised as scientists and pharmaceutical lobbyists disguised as politicians and alarmists disguised as journalists? But that reality is here and they are all working together to undermine people's health in such a fundamental way that it is destroying social, economic, cultural and political structures. With an almost religious zeal, they are staging a crusade against a supposed killer virus, branding anyone who speaks out in the name of real science, such as Dr Wodarg, as a heretic who would be best off burned at the stake.[181] It's all about shock, divide and rule in the name of supposed good against evil – and that's a well-known formula used to make a population compliant. The only question is, for what purpose?

You = Infectious

'Who am I in a Traumatised Society' was the title of my book which I originally published in 2018. In 2020 I receive the answer from the society I live in: Who am I? You are infectious! From now on, I am attributed the status of being a person who is basically infected or infectious with viruses and can therefore infect other people.

That people are infected with pathogens and can then infect others is not a new truth. This has always been the

---

[181] https://www.wodarg.com/2020/05/04/corona-was-always-here/ (retrieved 01/10/20)

case and will always remain so as long as people exist. What is new is that this banal wisdom is now being linked to whether or not people are subject to basic civil rights. Only the citizen who can prove that he is immune to the viruses that lobbying politicians define as highly infectious will continue to have access to civil life and to fundamental rights such as freedom of movement, freedom of occupation, freedom to travel, freedom of assembly, etc. If there was a real danger, people would notice it themselves and would want to protect themselves out of their own interest. Then they would not have to be frightened and socially isolated, the two factors that most affect our powers of self-healing. But these are not supposed to matter anyway in this staged corona pandemic planning game.

The Goal Of The 'Corona' Pandemic From The Beginning

According to its organisers, the Corona pandemic, announced back in March of this year, should not be declared over until there is a vaccine against Covid-19 and sufficient test kits to prove immunity. The German government, in close cooperation with Bill Gates, his WHO, the Robert Koch Institute, Professor Drosten, the so-called 'quality media' and the vaccine manufacturers, has committed itself to this idea from the outset. Since at least 24th April this has no longer even been a secret to the German people. In a press statement during the WHO donation video conference, Chancellor Angela Merkel announced:

"We all know that we have to live with the pandemic until we have found a vaccine. So the development of such a vaccine is of central importance, including of course therapeutics and diagnostic methods.

I agree with the UN Secretary-General - it is a global public duty to produce this vaccine and then distribute it to all parts of the world. It will be a major effort once we have such a vaccine. That is why we are fully committed to supporting the conference on 4th May.

We know that there is still a fairly substantial financial gap to be filled. That is why I would also like to call on everyone, whether from politics or the private sector, anyone who is in a position to support us to close this financial gap of €8 billion, as the Global Preparedness Monitoring Board has told us, and then to really be on the safe path to development".[182]

What a breathtaking handshake between power and money: The German Chancellor, citing a supposed knowledge of us all ("we all know!"), is helping one of the richest men in the world to get even more money to involve the German as well as the world population in his vaccination programme! Everyone who has any money spare should now help to finance this madness! So that this married couple Melinda and Bill Gates, as exponents of the global money-making machine, can make even more money. Allegedly in the name of the health of us all.

What Do Vaccinations Help?

Vaccinations have been criticised for many years and research over the last twenty years into vaccines against the various corona viruses have proved fruitless. It is also up for debate whether vaccinations are of any use at all, and whether they even cause additional diseases and deaths. In a Rubikon article, Gerd Reuther, a specialist in radiology, looks at the history of vaccinations and the

---

[182] https://cvd.bundesregierung.de/cvd-de/pressekonferenzen-briefings/pressestatement-von-bundeskanzlerin-merkel-im-rahmen-der-who-spenden-videokonferenz-1746960 (retrieved 24/04/20)

various diseases and the corresponding vaccination campaigns. His conclusion is sobering. For no disease (TB, Polio, Ebola etc.) have vaccinations brought about a positive influence on the overall health of a population.

'The hubris of those who now appear in Corona's staging of lies as the ultimate fighters for every human life is unmasked in any case when a vaccination against Covid-19 or even an effective drug is postulated as the key to lifting social restrictions. Bill Gates is neither a physician nor a biologist, and he has not completed any studies or vocational training. He is an entrepreneur. And quite unscrupulous, if you look at the vaccinations his foundation has carried out in India, Afghanistan and Africa. Here, vaccinations were used as a pretext for birth control and new vaccines were tested, costing thousands of children their health or lives. The vaccines killed more children than the diseases.'[183]

How this may be in detail for each individual type of infection I cannot make a generalised judgement. This would have to be done by a board of experts, independent of the vaccine manufacturers and their profit interests, according to purely scientific criteria.

The damage vaccination can cause is not unknown in Germany either:

'In Lübeck in 1930, 256 babies (about 84 percent of all newborns in that area) were orally vaccinated against tuberculosis. This mass vaccination was preceded by major advertising campaigns to convince the children's parents that they would be acting negligently if they decided against it.

The consequences of the vaccination campaign were devastating: 131 vaccinated children fell ill

---

[183] https://www.rubikon.news/artikel/der-pseudo-heilsbringer (retrieved 24/04/20)

and suffered from chronic secondary symptoms (e.g. severe hearing loss), some of them for the rest of their lives, and 77 babies died. The resultant legal trial turned out to be particularly difficult, as lawyers had to decide on a matter on which even the medical experts did not agree.

In the end, out of five defendants, only the manufacturer and tuberculosis researcher Georg Deycke was sentenced to two years in prison for negligent bodily injury and negligent homicide. The internist Ernst Altstaedt, on the other hand, who was also involved in the case, was sentenced to only 15 months in prison for the same offences, and he was released after only seven months and was allowed to continue to pursue his profession as a doctor. The conviction was based on the fact that the vaccine had been cultivated in an unsuitable laboratory and animal experiments had not been carried out.

It should be mentioned that the then county court councillor Wibel sympathised with the socially well-off and socially recognised defendants and that without pressure from the outraged public, a trial or conviction would never have taken place. Wibel committed suicide in 1932'. [184]

Where Is The Expertise?

An objective risk assessment based on scientific criteria of Covid-19 and possible vaccine damage is not currently being carried out in the context of SARS-Cov-2 and Covid-19. And there are warnings about the risks of these new RNA-based vaccines.[185] However, there is no scientific board where the leaders in the fields of virology, epidemiology, pulmonary medicine, pathology,

---

[184] https://www.zentrum-der-gesundheit.de/impfschaden.html (retrieved 04/05/20)
[185] https://deutungsvielfalt.de/2020/05/03/biologe-clemens-arvay-genetische-impfstoffe-gegen-covid-19-hoffnung-oder-risiko/ (retrieved 06/05/20)

psychology, sociology, jurisprudence and ethics combine their expertise to find the best possible strategy to deal with a pathogen like 'Corona' in such a way that in the end the health of mankind will actually be promoted.

Since the beginning of the Corona pandemic, only one view has been violently pushed through: 'novel', 'highly infectious', 'causes millions of deaths', 'overburdens the health system', 'solidarity with the old and weak'. This narrative is repeated daily by the apparently 'respectable media' with horrific accounts, terrifying images and people's individual horror stories, so that this pandemic case appears plausible to everyone and it is perpetuated for as long as possible.

There can hardly be a more reduced logical understanding of human health than the current 'one virus = one disease'. Neither the immune status of the people concerned, nor their living conditions, nor the psychological connections are even remotely taken into consideration.

All those who speak out in the supposed 'quality press', or who express different scientific views which are in the best interests of the wider community, are immediately branded as dubious or selfish and placed on the political, scientific or even human sidelines, as has already happened with Dr Wodarg, Professor Bhakdi, Professor Streek or Mr Laschet.

Self-Immunity Is The Major Exception

As predicted, in this business game, a wording for a change in the law is now being brought into play, which will require vaccinations unless someone can prove their immunity has been officially confirmed. Therefore, from now on, (in Germany) the amendment to Section 28 (1) sentence 3 of the Infection Protection Act (Article 1 No. 20 letter a) will read as follows:

'Section 28 is amended as follows: a) Paragraph 1 sentence 3 is inserted

"When ordering and implementing protective measures in accordance with the first and second sentences, due account shall be taken of whether and to what extent a person who, in the light of the state of medical science, is unable to transmit or is no longer able to transmit a particular communicable disease for which the protective measures are being taken, because of existing vaccination protection or immunity, may be exempted from the measure in whole or in part without jeopardising the purpose of the measure. Insofar as individual-related measures are to be dispensed with or exceptions are generally provided for, the person concerned must prove by means of vaccination or immunity documentation in accordance with § 22 or a medical certificate that he or she is unable to transmit or can no longer transmit the specific communicable disease'.

The logic contained in this text is tricky. Applied to Covid-19 it basically says: We assume that there is already a 'vaccination protection' against Covid-19. This is initially put on a par with a possible 'existing immunity' in a human. If this is the case, i.e. if a person has either been vaccinated or has acquired an immune status of his own accord, he can be 'exempted, in whole or in part, from the 'ordering or implementation of protective measures' which the state decides to take. However, this is only possible under certain conditions, namely 'without jeopardising the purpose of the measure'. Which presumably means: there must not be too many exceptions, so as not to undermine the objective of general mass vaccination. In order to avoid this state of emergency of not needing to be vaccinated in individual cases, special efforts must be made to obtain a medical certificate that officially certifies this. Among other things, this certificate should also state how long the immunity will last. In the case of Covid-19, this is simply impossible to assess scientifically due to a lack of empirical studies.

Even if Health Minister Spahn has to back pedal on this point under the pressure of numerous protests, this proposal for a change in the law shows us his way of thinking.

The Infection Protection Act Overrides The Basic Rule Of Law

Not to be vaccinated should therefore be the exception in the future, and vaccination should become the rule. Because those who are not vaccinated are potential social pests. Someone's basic civil rights can/could therefore be suspended for him until he can officially prove his non-infectiousness and his non-infectivity or until he eventually gives up at some point, annoyed and fed up, and voluntarily allows his vaccination doses to be administered.

The possibility of self-immunisation protection is also systematically prevented at the moment, in the case of the infectious disease defined as 'Covid-19', by the social distancing rules and the policy of isolation and the wearing of facemasks. Presumably, therefore, there are now also less infected people and therefore less immune-protected people than is usually the case, for example, with a wave of influenza, which usually causes a so-called 'herd immunity' in a population within one to two months. Therefore, the potential for a possible further wave of Corona infection next autumn may be higher and the mass of people to be vaccinated or tested is correspondingly large, to the delight of the vaccine and test kit manufacturers and their supporters.

How Can You Argue With The Logic Of Possibility

To ensure that the total number of people to be vaccinated does not become too small, as was the case with the 'swine flu' back in 2010, and that the Corona pandemic scenario continues to appear credible, the corona narrative is embellished with another horror idea: At present, 'there is no proof that people who recover from COVID-19 and have antibodies are protected from a second infection, warns the World Health Organisation (WHO)'[186].

To claim such a thing no longer has anything to do with scientific empiricism. It is only possible with the associative thought pattern of the 'logic of possibility'. I claim that something is real because it is theoretically possible. But since everything can be thought as theoretically possible, everyone can think and assert whatever they want. Whether one's own view then carries weight is decided in reality and in practice, not by a fair contest of arguments, but by the question of power and money: whoever has the reins of power defines what is considered possible and what is not. Whoever has the money buys the politicians and scientists who are talking about things that could affect their ability to increase their money.

This then has nothing to do with politics for the common good or actual science. It is just the enforcement and dissemination of ideologies, i.e. of interest-based views of the world and human beings.

The logic of possibility is already the starting point for the WHO to define something as a pandemic. It is only because there is a worldwide *possibility* of infection that a pathogen is classified as dangerous, regardless of any proof of its actual harmfulness.

To attempt a comparison here: it's as if I press the button and set off the alarm system in my house, without knowing whether a burglar is actually trying to break into my house or not. Then I hide myself away in the corner of the smallest room in my home and wait in a

---

[186] https://www.deutschlandfunk.de/covid-19-unklarheit-bei-immunitaet-nach-corona-infektion.676.de.html?dram:article_id=475609 (retrieved 04/05/20)

panic for an indefinite period of time until the police and fire brigade come to rescue me.

Even operating and deciding everything on the basis of infection numbers and their possible increase or decrease by a hypothetically assumed Reproduction Number is the logical consequence of this false, interest-led thinking. And all these numbers and probabilities can be manipulated as required to fit the narrative.[187] It is basically a nuisance for the protagonists of the pandemic that they have to try and prove with mortality rates that a dangerous disease like Covid-19 exists at all and that this disease is actually the cause of many deaths. Ultimately, all they want is to get this SARS CoV-2 virus accepted as a case for treatment by the pharmaceutical industry to support their money-making interests.

This is why such death rate statistics are invariably calculated inadequately and then extrapolated to produce terrifying figures to show the population the seriousness of the situation, so that their fear fantasies can be given enough substance and panic to feed off. But, in the eyes of the pandemic constructors, it should not really be necessary for them to have to do all this. People should just accept that the virus is highly contagious, nobody can protect themselves sufficiently from it on their own, health care systems are overburdened - that should be enough to make the population long for vaccinations and tests as a release from the coercive measures.

This benefits everyone who's playing this game: the vaccine manufacturers are guaranteed their profits for years to come, the state can finally return to its normal way of being, promote exponential money growth everywhere and stop harassing its population with corona measures. And people know in what direction the future is headed and to what extent they will be the object of state health protection measures from now on.

---

[187] https://www.journalistenwatch.com/2020/05/11/professor-brief-das/ (retrieved 11/05/20)

'Corona' As A Test Case For A New World

Once this principle that 'vaccination and testing is a citizen's number one priority' has been legitimised in law, it can then be implemented with any other virus that comes along, after Corona. It can also be retrospectively implemented for any virus that existed before too. If a virus is defined as highly infectious, most people then, by definition, have no immune protection against it and so will go voluntarily for vaccination/testing simply to maintain their civil liberties. At least that is what the initiators of this masterplan hope. In this way, they can avoid having to say the ugly phrase 'compulsory vaccination'.

> 'For the time being at least, the Federal Health Minister Jens Spahn does not expect that if a vaccine against the coronavirus becomes available, vaccination will be compulsory. The CDU politician said in Berlin on Wednesday that his impression was that the vast majority of citizens would want such a vaccination. "Wherever we can reach our goal through willingness and good sense, there is no need for a compulsory vaccination in my view," he said'. [188]

It seems plausible to me that right from the start this was about more than just 'Corona' and that 'Corona' is only just a test case for developing a new 'normal way of doing things', because otherwise Bill Gates would not be demanding that as many vaccine research laboratories and production facilities as possible be established. For him, these are the factories of the future, where modern vaccines will be produced for each respective virus that comes along, which the WHO will then be able to

---

[188] https://www.berliner-zeitung.de/politik-gesellschaft/impfpflicht-durch-die-hintertuer-li.82643 (retrieved 03/05/20)

propagate again as 'novel' and 'highly infectious' and 'highly lethal', if necessary without any further scientific proof.

The political processes will then already have been well-rehearsed and possibly in a few years' time will be available as a default reflex action. People will then have become accustomed to the fact that no time needs to be wasted anymore on lengthy testing when it comes to developing vaccines. The possible side effects of such vaccines are anyway at the expense of the state coffers that pay for the vaccines and not at the expense of the vaccine manufacturers. So is this the much-vaunted 'new normality' - a world which, because of Corona, is supposed to be different from the world before?

I hadn't really thought about all this until the evening of 3rd May when someone forwarded me an article in the Berliner Zeitung that brought it all into really sharp focus. In that article a Mr Dominik Spitzer, who is the health policy spokesman for the FDP parliamentary group in the Bavarian state parliament, made the following statement on vaccination.

According to the Bayerische Staatszeitung, he 'is of the opinion that the flu vaccination should be compulsory for the winter of 2020/2021. For this purpose, millions of vaccine doses would have to be bought now. People should be vaccinated against influenza in order to "prevent a possible overload of our health care system", Spitzer said. "Despite a variety of campaigns, Germany, with a vaccination rate of about 35 percent, does not even reach half of the target set by the World Health Organisation of 75 percent for the over-60s - i.e. the group most vulnerable to the Covid-19 virus. In order to raise this rate and to build up a certain herd immunity against influenza, a one-off compulsory vaccination as a last resort would be a radical step, but definitely a sensible measure because less-severe influenza sufferers would relieve our valuable intensive care resources'. [189]

Hang on a minute, Mr. Spitzer: so are you saying that I should be compulsorily vaccinated against influenza in the future, because there is *a possibility* that hospitals may become overburdened and that there is then *a possibility* that people who *possibly* get Covid-19 may not *possibly* receive the artificial ventilation they *possibly* might need? This is foolishly deceitful thinking based solely on propagating the logic of possibility: it's basically saying 'what are the necessary conditions of possibility to determine possibility'? The only thing that is certain in all of this is that the vaccine manufacturers make their profit and that the state pays for it with our tax money. As long as health is essentially linked to the system of money multiplication, bankers in their capacity as health ministers are perfectly at home in such a confused and fundamentally wrong system.

Is Identifying With This New Attribution The Only Way To Survive?

There is agreement in Germany it seems at the moment between politicians of all political parties that vaccination is the primary civic duty. And if you are a good citizen, you will not shirk your state duty. Because it is only through this act of self-chosen identification with state attributions that the 'good citizen' believes he can move away from being the object of state protection measures and become once more a subject. But he is only a subject in terms of the survival strategies of a traumatised and traumatising society. A genuinely good and self-determined life looks quite different in my opinion.

---

[189] https://www.berliner-zeitung.de/politik-gesellschaft/impfpflicht-durch-die-hintertuer-li.82643 (retrieved 03/05/20)

Making Money Does Not Make You Happy

As we can see from the Corona pandemic: money and the compulsion to multiply money does not make anyone happy or mean that they are intelligent or socially minded:

- The super-rich are becoming more and more excessive, and greedy for even more. They act profoundly a-socially in the ways that they implement their strategies of 'money multiplication'; they have the craziest ideas of how to achieve these schemes including corrupting other people and walking over corpses if need be. They are like a highly dangerous virus themselves – a virus that destroys from within the human communities of which they themselves are a part.

- The ordinary-rich are petrified of losing their wealth and therefore they serve the super-rich and help them act out their strategic games wherever they can. They too squander their intelligence by battling others in competition for supposed personal gain in order to get the biggest slice of the money cake. They too degenerate ethically in the process.

- The poor who are the majority are kept ignorant and inferior. They patiently keep their mouths shut for fear of losing the minimal income opportunities granted to them by the rich and super-rich. They restrict their horizons and adapt to whatever is offered to them as an 'opportunity' not to starve, so that they can get on and raise their children without ending up in unemployment or on social welfare. They develop an attitude as if all this did not really matter to them at all and what the rich and powerful did is what they wanted anyway.

- And the powerful? They too are basically powerless in this system of money multiplication and are at the mercy of the intrigues of the rich and super-rich.

They are at their service and eke out a lonely existence in their exclusive circles, always living in fear of losing their power. The money that they do manage to make does not really make them free or happy either.

Know Yourself

Γνῶθι σεαυτόν 'Know thyself' is one of the Apollonian wisdoms from the ancient sanctuary of Delphi, inscribed on the pillars of the Temple of Apollo from sometime in the 5th century BC.

To realise that I have been betrayed and sold out by the very people I trust most – first of all my parents and now the politicians I elected · is a very painful process of realisation. It is unbelievable: these parents and parental substitutes, from whom we expect love and care, who are supposed to give us support, orientation and protection, are themselves so traumatised that they are not with themselves at all and their trauma survival strategies from which they operate only cause chaos and confusion. Ultimately all they do is drag us into their own trauma abyss with their power and money.

Experience shows that this leads to various defensive reactions because we essentially do not want to admit the truth of this. It makes us both depressed and aggressive. But if we have the courage to face this truth we gradually realise that, with our traumatised psyche and its survival and adaptation programmes, we are standing in our own way of leading a truly happy life. As a result, the willingness to change this grows.

This highly emotional process of self-knowledge is, in my opinion, and in my experience, deeply healing and beneficial to health. It is a very meaningful way to find our way out of the personal and social trauma trance-state in which we have collectively landed. Once we do this, we can then work together to understand why we do not use our emotional and psychological potential for a good life. Without this self-knowledge, we, in our emotional numbness, get lost in our mental constructs, traumatise each other and constantly put ourselves into coercive relationships. We support or tolerate the kind of society in which the increase of money is an end in itself, which degrades us to the status of objects at the whim of its machinations.

When we start to understand all this, we no longer think of ourselves as better than anyone else, we no longer want to dominate, manipulate, coerce or blackmail other people into giving us their services. Our only wish is that others can also become similarly self-determined and inwardly free people. In this way, everyone can work together to use their intelligence and energy to create an empathic, common-interest led community.

If we all did this, then, by the end of 2020, humanity would have taken a good step forward in terms of consciousness and we all would have, in real terms, become closer to each other.

Face Masks And The Obligation To Wear Them

On top of restricting contact and the social distancing requirements, the wearing of face masks is now also being added to the list of things we supposedly have to do. In some states, such as Hesse non-compliance can be punished with a €50 fine. The man who sends me the following e-mail says he now feels like he's living in a madhouse:

'Dear Prof. Dr. Franz Ruppert,

This morning I looked at Ken Jebsen's interview with Prof. Dr. Sucharit Bhakdi, which you have put on your homepage. In it he emphasises once again that face masks are useless. And now the Hessian state government has ordered that face masks be made compulsory as of next Monday: In particular when on public transport or in shops.[190]

The reasoning is based on the recommendations of the RKI. Scientific advice and even the advice of the President of the German Medical Association has simply been ignored! That is unbelievable! In view of this highly contradictory situation, I feel like I'm living in a madhouse! And this insane requirement is of course enforced again with power or violence: fines, penalties and so on are threatened if you don't follow the rules!

This is really not good - it stirs up fear, and this is highly detrimental to a healthy immune system, as you have shown very clearly! I was very pleased to receive a book today about the immune system and how to strengthen it more intensively: 'Your Unknown Superorgan' by Dr. Hauch.

This is a very intense situation right now.

Best regards H.R.'

I was first personally confronted with the face-mask regulations on 21st April, when I drove to a DIY store with my wife. When we got there I realised how seriously everyone was taking this. You could only get into the store if you had a face-mask. My wife had one with her, I did not. So I was already on the verge of turning round and going home again. Then I discovered two cardboard face-masks in

---

[190] https://www.hessen.de/presse/pressemitteilung/landesregierung-beschliesst-maskenpflicht (retrieved 22/04/20)

298

the shopping trolley. How clever of the DIY store management, I thought to myself. I took one of them and clamped it over my mouth. I had no idea whether anyone had used it before. But I did see that there were two of those cardboard things in every shopping trolley. So I assumed that my two were still fresh and unused. Anyway, I left this cardboard thing in the shopping trolley after we'd finished shopping.

If I wear one of these things for a long time I get stressed and start sweating. I get the feeling that not only is this extremely unhygienic but that if I wear it for any prolonged length of time my breathing becomes restricted.

The human organism wants to get rid of waste from its lungs (including carbon monoxide and metabolic waste products) and replenish itself with fresh air, but, by wearing a mask, this is hindered. This is another example of where trauma survival strategies lead us. Our lungs protect us from getting infected by the corona virus by performing this normal healthy function, but it is precisely this measure of mask wearing that then severely limits them in this. I therefore feel regret when I see, for example, the cashier at the DIY store checkout who has to spend her whole working day wearing a face mask. How sick will this make her in the long run?

Professor Pietro Vernazza, the head physician of the Infectiology Department in St. Gallen, summarises studies on the effectiveness of mask wearing as follows:

'These results show that the recommendations of the Federal Office of Public Health continue to be useful and that our findings, which have been established after years of research on viral diseases of the respiratory tract, can also be applied to corona viruses:
- If you do not have any symptoms (cough, cold), you do not need to wear a mask to protect others.
- Masks reduce the risk of transmission of a sick person when they cough.
- In the hours before the onset of symptoms, when a person can be contagious through contact alone, wearing masks does not prevent this infection.
- For other people, from what we know, wearing a mask does not seem necessary.

- The most frequent virus transmission occurs through contact. Hygiene measures remain the most important preventative measure.

Could wearing masks be counterproductive?
There are now more and more people wearing masks simply for their own peace of mind, without any good reason. It could be that masks prevent us from touching our faces. But we must also ask the question does wearing a mask mean we don't carry out other regular hygiene measures – because we're thinking 'I am wearing a mask, I am protected'. I know of no proper study on this matter. But there is at least one observation I can see from everyday hospital life: I see some people who now wear a mask all the time. But I also regularly observe that most of the staff take lunch without washing or disinfecting their hands after removing the mask. Your sandwich is putting the virus in your mouth! With or without a mask: we must get used to changing our hygiene behaviour. Everything else is secondary.'[191]

In his Rubikon article 'The Obedience Test', Roland Rottenfußer concisely expresses my thoughts and mood on the subject of compulsory masks.[192] Rottenfußer writes:

'The current 'King of Germany', Professor Christian Drosten, spoke out clearly in favour of this in an interview: 'This presupposes that really everyone, everyone, everyone in society, in public life must wear these masks', said Drosten. This statement alone ('everyone, everyone, everyone') reveals an alarming tendency towards totalitarianism. It allows neither exceptions nor even gradations of mask duty'.

I am reminded of Gessler's hat from William Tell. In the story, the brutal ruler Gessler erects a pole in the market square and places his hat on top of it. He then orders that everyone in the town bow down before it. William Tell, whose marksmanship and pride are legendary, publicly refuses. Gessler's cruel wrath is tempered by his curiosity to test Tell's skill, so he gives Tell the option of either being executed or

---

[191] https://infekt.ch/2020/04/atemschutzmasken-fuer-alle-medienhype-oder-unverzichtbar/ (retrieved 22/04/20)
[192] https://www.rubikon.news/artikel/die-gehorsams-probe (retrieved 22/04/20)

shooting an apple off his own son's head in one try. Whoever does not wear a mask now is easily identifiable as a dissident of the corona narrative that comes from on high.

In another recent article on the Rubikon website, Gerd Reuther summarises the arguments against the wearing of masks - basically saying face masks are pointless, useless and counterproductive when trying to prevent infection from coronaviruses. He also draws attention to something that is getting lost in the widespread 'Coronoia', something which would have warranted serious attention if it were happening at any other time. In Chernobyl the radioactively contaminated forests are burning!

'Nevertheless, many people are already wearing masks. Premature obedience? Of course, the German likes to do his duty 150 percent. But there is also the illusion of protection. Aren't air pollutants everywhere and aren't the radioactive forests around Chernobyl burning now?'[193]

The real reason for the obligation to wear masks has therefore nothing to do with meaningful protection of the individual and the community. It is about maintaining the climate of fear by means of the mask. Masks signal a danger, no matter whether it is present or not. In this way submission and obedience to the official corona narrative is enforced.

Even people who are officially exempt from wearing masks because of their disability are finding themselves excluded from their everyday lives:

'Severely disabled people are exempt from wearing a mouth and nose protector for good reason. The shop store chain 'L---' has decided to deny these people access to its shops. The reason for this is that fellow people feel harassed if someone enters the shop without a facemask. According to an employee, several complaints have been received by the Chemnitz public order office. L--- fears that it will have to close its branches if it grants severely disabled persons permission to enter the shop without mouth and nose protection.

---

[193] https://www.rubikon.news/artikel/das-vermummungs-gebot (retrieved 22/04/20)

I can only hope that this behaviour towards severely handicapped people does not belong to the ' New Normal', because then I see a very clear discrimination of this minority group'.[194]

The longer the pandemic lasts and the more its devisers and participants start to lose when challenged with rationally comprehensible arguments, the more aggressive and radical the pandemic propaganda becomes. It reminds me of the time of National Socialism (Nazism), when people who did not participate were immediately labelled as 'asocial' or 'enemies of the people', against whom action must be taken with all severity. The people who go along with the campaign are literally incited by so-called journalists against the few who do not wear masks in the underground or do not put them on correctly according to the regulations. Will there soon be 'blockwarden'[195] guards in every house again?[196] I'd like to ask a question of those people who are fanatical about wearing masks: why don't you cover your eyes as well, because viruses can also enter the body that way too?

As a result of all this, more profiteers from this crisis are created: mask manufacturers, glove producers, manufacturers of automatic measuring devices for body temperature, manufacturers of disinfectants, etc. In addition, this is leading to a growing mass of non-biodegradable mask and glove waste across the whole world.[197]

Mandatory And Compulsory Vaccinations?

I wrote a separate article on the subject of immunisation and compulsory vaccination back on 5th May 2020. Afterwards someone directed me towards the website of the paediatrician Dr. Martin Hirte. On his site, he lists in a very clear-cut way, with reference to

---

[194] https://www.facebook.com/katja.strubing.1/posts/2867227483390565 (retrieved 15/05/20). Disabled people in the UK have also faced discrimination since the introduction of compulsory face masks:
https://www.thecanary.co/opinion/2020/07/25/disabled-people-being-abused-for-not-wearing-masks-is-peak-2020/ (retrieved 21/11/20)
[195] The 'Blockwarts' or blockwardens duties included spying on the population and reporting any anti-Nazi activities to the local Gestapo office - allowing a Nazi terror state https://en.wikipedia.org/wiki/Blockleiter (retrieved 14/09/20)
[196] https://m.tagesspiegel.de/berlin/ruecksichtslos-in-der-bahn-maskenverweigerer-ich-verachte-euch-zutiefst/25950318.html (retrieved 01/07/20)
[197] https://www.heise.de/tp/features/Covid-19-Neues-Geschaeftsfeld-fuer-Ruestungsfirmen-4706142.html (retrieved 22/04/20)

many sources, everything that needs to be said about SARS-CoV-2 and Covid-19 in terms of the risk of infection, the risk of death, the deaths and the lockdown in Italy, Spain and the USA, etc. On the subject of vaccination, he writes the following:

'A vaccine against SARS-CoV-2, which has been at least rudimentarily tested for safety, is not expected before mid 2021 according to experts' estimates - if it ever gets that far. Some scientists, including Prof. David Nabarro, one of the leading COVID-19 experts and special representative of the WHO, considers it doubtful: 'You cannot develop a safe and effective vaccine against every virus'. Nabarro criticises the importance ascribed to the vaccine and believes that we should rather learn to live with the virus (today 20/04/20) The virologist Prof. Hendrik Streeck has also spoken out expressing this same opinion (Merkur 25/04/20).

Because of the similarity of viral proteins to human proteins, a coronavirus vaccination could trigger a potential autoimmune response. Previous SARS coronavirus vaccines led to severe lung disease in animal tests a few days after they received a targeted infection with the corona viruses (Tseng 20/04/12). Most potential vaccines involve risky new technologies for which there has been no clinical testing on humans: Vaccines with messenger RNA or viral vectors ('gene shuttles'), which are introduced into human cells, start the production of the vaccine-antigens which then trigger the desired immune response. The approval of such vaccines that bypass the established safety standards ('fast-track approval'), which was made possible by the latest amendment to the German Infection Protection Act, is irresponsible. Nevertheless, the suspension of regulations demanded by virologists and politicians has already been put into practice: In the USA, people were vaccinated for the first time before animal testing was even carried out (SPIEGEL 17/03/20).'[198]

It is becoming increasingly clear to me that for Bill Gates and the pharmaceutical industry, vaccination is just another business model. It's also a particularly attractive one, especially if there is a disclaimer against any possible damage that the vaccinations may cause. In the

---

[198] https://www.martin-hirte.de/coronavirus-2/ (retrieved 05/05/20)

USA, on 17th March 2020, the Department of Health and Human Services declared a disclaimer for medical countermeasures in relation to COVID-19 with retroactive effect from 4th February 2020. According to this declaration, manufacturers, distributors and administrators of vaccines that are made available by 1st October 2024 are completely exempt from liability.[199]

On 5th May 2020, Robert F. Kennedy Jr. from the USA spoke out with a video message to the German resistance against the compulsory vaccination plans of the Gates Alliance[200]. He says that while he received 3 vaccinations as a child, his 6 children already have had to endure 72 vaccinations. For criticism of the oral polio vaccination in India, see also this English language podcast. [201]

Prof. Bhakdi also clearly warns that mRNA vaccinations infect healthy cells, which are then killed by the immune system's killer cells. In this way the infection means that the normal activity of the immune system leads to self-destruction.[202]

In any case, this pandemic threatens the principle of voluntary vaccination. The thinking is everyone should be obligated to have such a vaccination. Those who refuse to do so will then pay the price of the permanent restrictions on their freedoms.

Why Are So Many Taking Part In All This?

One reason why this contradictory and absurd programme of i money making as a be all and end all of life is accepted, is, I think, that so many people lost their self-confidence and their ability to stand up for their own needs at a very early stage of their development. There are so many who were unwanted from the very beginning, so they adapted to their parents by hook or by crook in order to get confirmation from them of their right to exist. 'Look,' they say, 'I am making myself useful to you, please love me!' However, as children they did not receive the love from their already traumatised parents that would keep them healthy. Instead, their fundamental needs for contact and love went unmet. This is how these children learn that money is more important to their parents than they are. That is why they later strive for money too, because

[199] https://www.federalregister.gov/documents/2020/03/17/2020-05484/declaration-under-the-public-readiness-and-emergency-preparedness-act-for-medical-countermeasures (retrieved 10/05/20)

[200] https://t.me/EvaHermanOffiziell/13311 (retrieved 05/05/20)

[201] https://www.corbettreport.com/gatesvaccine/ (retrieved 10/05/20)

[202] https://www.youtube.com/watch?v=yrzgV_2juQQ (retrieved 01/07/20)

for mum and dad money was more important than them, even if by this stage they are no longer aware of this connection. Money and what you can buy with it is usually a substitute for the parental love and recognition by the community that you have not received and it remains a substitute for the rest of your life. And so the guiding principle of all entrepreneurial thinking in profit-oriented organisations is to capitalise on these unmet needs for love, contact and protection, which people have compensated for with a need to consume and that can be exploited when it comes to the sale of goods and services.

I myself come from a poor working class farming family. Up until when I reached puberty there was always a shortage of money. Therefore I wanted to earn my own money as soon as possible and thought that I could impress my parents if I earned a lot of money myself. But this was not the case. Even with my professional successes I could not emotionally reach my parents. In other areas of relationships, too, I found that talking about money stood in the way of good relationships rather than promoting them. What I always found immoral was receiving money for nothing in return. If you grow up in a family where there is wealth and it seems to multiply by itself, you probably see things differently and emulate your parents in this respect.

Who Am I In The Capitalist World Of 2020?

Twenty-Third Article – 10th May 2020

It's All Based On The Principle Of Money Multiplication And Competition

Capitalism, which has been practised for more than 200 years, is the idea of turning money into more money. Money is therefore not only a means of payment and circulation, but a means to an end: more and more money is to be made from money. Simply having money, putting it away and hoarding it like a gold treasure is considered a completely antiquated way of behaving under capitalism. The term capital already contains within it the claim that it will multiply.

The principle of capitalism can take the form of private enterprise, as in America and Europe, or state or collective capitalism, as in Japan or South Korea, or of state controlled capitalism by a single communist party, as in China.

Whether in free enterprise or in a state controlled system, capitalist money multiplication is always a project based on competition. Companies compete against other companies, states against states, private individuals against private individuals.

For this idea to work, everything that serves this purpose of money multiplication must be given a monetary value. Mineral resources, water, air, plants, animals, people - everything is assigned a number: 5 Euros, 10 dollars, 100 pounds, 1000 yen etc. Everything must then be able to be bought and sold. For example, I sell you my used car for €3,000, I buy a haircut from you for €50.

Credit And The Inherent Crash

Since this system is always about the future profit, money in capitalism is in principle always credit money. In other words, a promise to pay, built on profits that will only be realised in the future. Therefore, new loans can be granted on the promise of future payment, and so on, until in the end it is no longer clear what the original business is supposed to be in the first place. Because this system is then increasingly based only on profit speculation and unfeasible promises to pay, it can also quickly collapse if suddenly one of the big players loses faith in a certain promise to pay. Then in one fell swoop the big crash comes, the money loses its value and the whole game must somehow start all over again with adjusted balance sheets. The so-called world economic crisis of 1929 or the banking crash of 2008 are well known to many people living today.

The Actors In The Capitalist Game

If I am a citizen in a capitalist society, there are different roles that I can play:

- I can be a labourer: I can sell my labour to an entrepreneur or to a company for say €2000 a month.
- I can be a consumer: I buy what my monetary income allows me to.
- I can be a patient: I take my body to a doctor who does something about it and earns his money from that.
- I can be a data source: I use apps for free and accept that the software companies behind them collect and resell my data.
- I can be an entrepreneur/businessman myself and buy goods, services and labour.
- I can offer my labour, nowadays often in the form of sitting in front of a PC using my intellectual abilities, to the institutions that support and create the capitalist framework: I could work for

parliaments, for schools, for universities, for the courts, for the police, for the prison service, for the military etc.
- I can act as someone who affirms the capitalist principle of competition or sets an entertaining counterpoint to it: as a sportsman, as a musician, as an artist.

The capitalist principle of the multiplication of money contains a number of contradictions:

- In a competition there are always winners and losers.
- Businessmen want to buy their labour force as cheaply as possible.
- Businessmen want to buy the raw materials for their production as cheaply as possible.
- Businessmen want to dispose of the waste products of their production as cheaply as possible.
- Businessmen want to sell their goods at the highest possible price.
- Businessmen want to be able to have consumers at their disposal.
- Workers want the highest possible wage for the hours they work.
- Consumers want to get as much as possible for their money.
- Political supervision wants to keep control over businessmen and workers.

These contradictions are evident at different levels of social coexistence, including

- Where people are comprehensively transformed into a commodity, into workers who can be bought and who are willing to be bought.
- When mothers are working full or part-time, separating them from their babies and infants.

308

- In their role as 'patients' people become separate from their body and are made the object of treatment.
- When intensive work processes destroy the health of the workers.
- When people in a society are mutual competitors, rivals, opponents, enemies.
- When the whole society is broken down into the rich and the poor.
- When everything ultimately becomes a means to the end of money multiplication: living to work instead of working to live.
- When the competition for mineral resources, markets, labour and credit leads to permanent conflicts and wars.

This System Needs An Ideology

A society that is locked into this principle of capitalist money multiplication with all its inherent contradictions and instabilities is not in itself a united society. It has to be held together on every level by force and ideology.

Ideologically, this system is supported, among other things, by the logic of the perpetrator-victim-reversal. The providers of jobs - the employers - are the benefactors. Anyone who does not take advantage of the opportunity to be an employee, or refuses to do so, is a perpetrator within this system or is simply stupid and is himself to blame for being destitute. This is why people do not like to talk about capitalism, but rather about a 'social market economy' or a 'free market'. Even the term 'neo-liberalism' is less off-putting, because after all it still contains the concept of freedom within its name.

Anyone who questions the system is once again a malicious perpetrator or one caught up in his own illusions. Even the victims of this system, with their victim attitude, defend it as something for which there is no alternative.

Pitting Brother Against Brother

These days the various spheres in which even more money can be made from money are primarily:

- Agricultural corporations
- Energy companies
- Arms companies
- The financial sector
- Pharmaceutical companies
- Information technology companies.

By buying shares across the board, someone who has money can make himself richer still. For their own sake, the individual sectors compete for the money available in the world and for assured credit, especially for the money that is in the national budgets.

For the world's population, each of these sectors brings corresponding catastrophes onto the horizon:

- Poisoning of food with herbicides, pesticides, medicines used in factory farming.
- Nuclear power plant accidents and the production of radioactive waste that contaminates forever.
- Atomic bombs both big and small, which hover like a sword of Damocles over the heads of the 7.5 billion inhabitants of the earth.
- Total economic collapse and stock market crashes with compulsory purchases and mass unemployment.
- Insidious poisoning of the human organism with chemicals that it cannot completely break down.
- Monitoring and spying on every aspect of our privacy.

In 2020, there is now a new particular development in this system and it is happening across the globe. Bill Gates and the pharmaceutical and medical industry want to have all the people of the world available as potential vaccine takers. In doing so, they are disrupting the usual process that goes on of buying and selling in all the other money multiplication industries across the world. It is astonishing how these other sectors of the economy are watching on spellbound, seemingly offering no resistance as their own ways of money multiplication are thwarted as they allow themselves to be hindered by the lockdown measures without a fight. Even Donald Trump, the American president, who is obsessed with economic growth and coal and oil, and who promises the masses new jobs in abundance, is looking on doing nothing as the army of unemployed in his country explodes in a matter of weeks.

'The US has seen a massive increase in unemployment due to the Corona pandemic. The unemployment rate soared from 4.4 per cent to 14.7 per cent in April - the highest level since the post-war period. Before the crisis began in February, the unemployment rate had been 3.5 per cent.

Since March, more than 33 million people applied for unemployment support for the first time. Due to a delay in data collection, the unemployment rate for April only covers the situation up to the middle of the month. [...]

The actual number of unemployed in April is, according to the government, probably some seven million more than officially reported. In the survey for the month, 8.1 million people were registered as 'absent for unspecified reasons', the Ministry of Labour stated. However, this figure is usually only 620,000.

'Our assumption is that these 7.5 million workers should have been reported as 'unemployed due to temporary lay-offs',' said an annex to the official labour market report. Had they been so classified, the unemployment rate would have been 19.5 per cent. The current rate therefore probably does not yet reflect the full extent of the US job crisis.

A leading economic advisor to US President Donald Trump, Kevin Hassett, warned in an interview with CNN that the official rate could reach a value of more than 20 percent or even up to 25 percent in May.'[203]

There are also gloomy forecasts for Germany on the part of the Federal Employment Agency and the Institute for Employment Research (IAB) in Nuremberg.

'The head of the institute, Professor Enzo Weber, expects drastic consequences for the German economy: "If the aforementioned two and a half months of absence were to occur, the unemployment rate could temporarily exceed the three million mark. [...] This is the annual average number of unemployed people in Germany in 2010.'[204]

However, the IT sector is one of the winners of the vaccine industry's 2020 coup. Home offices and virtual meetings are causing the share prices of companies like ZOOM to skyrocket. Companies that develop tracing apps for tracing infection chains are also in high demand.

The Model Of The Bank Rescue Package

Even during the so-called banking crisis, which began in 2008, the view was already being expressed that governments could use their national budgets to

---

[203] https://www.tagesschau.de/ausland/usa-arbeitslosigkeit-corona-101.html In German (retrieved 9.5.2020). Here's a similar English article covering the state of US unemployment as of May 2020
https://www.theguardian.com/business/2020/may/28/jobless-america-unemployment-coronavirus-in-figures (retrieved 14/09/20)

[204] https://www.express.de/news/politik-und-wirtschaft/duestere-prognose-drastischer-anstieg-der-arbeitslosigkeit-durch-corona-krise-36444752 (retrieved 09/05/20)

guarantee loans more securely than private moneylenders. This is why unbelievably high promises of credit protection could be made in the course of the so-called bank rescue package by the German government. This rescue package seems to have cost the Federal Republic of Germany somewhere in the region of 50 billion Euros.

'The Law on the Establishment of a Financial Market Stabilisation Fund' - under this unwieldy title the National Parliament in Germany created a rescue package for the banks in an emergency move, after the shock of Lehman Brothers. Decided on 17th October 2008, the Special Fund Financial Market Stabilisation, or 'Soffin' for short, was launched just one day later. The state provided it with guarantees of up to €400 billion and equity capital of up to €80 billion. The rescue fund was therefore larger than the whole federal budget available to Angela Merkel's government.

The Soffin was managed by the specially created Federal Agency for Financial Market Stabilisation (FMSA), whose offices were at the scene of the financial crisis in Frankfurt am Main. From then on, it supported credit institutions such as the nationalised Hypo Real Estate (HRE), the now dissolved Westdeutsche Landesbank and Commerzbank. In the end less than half of the available funds were actually used. According to the Federal Ministry of Finance, the fund had €168 billion in guarantees and equity investments of €29.4 billion outstanding in the 'peak phase'.

At the beginning of 2018, the FMSA was merged into the German Federal Financial Market Agency. In the view of many politicians and bankers, this marked the end of the financial crisis. The agency now manages the 'normal' debts of the Federal Government.

But what did the bank bailout actually cost overall? In its last balance sheet, the FMSA made clear that by the end of 2017 all guarantees had been repaid without default. Fees of 2.2 billion euros were collected for this.

Only 'capital measures' amounting to EUR 14.6 billion were still outstanding – mainly this was related to the stake in Commerzbank.[205]

But the official figures are deceptive. In a recent interview, Peer Steinbrück, who was Minister of Finance back in 2008, did not contradict the interviewer when it was stated that the bank rescue had cost the taxpayer a sum of up to 50 billion euros. In response to a question by the Green party, the German government estimated the losses at 59 billion - or 3000 euros for every family of four.[206]

All Money Comes From The State

At the moment, the pharmaceutical and vaccine industry takes it for granted that the money for their vaccines and test kits, and all the other masks and respirators and health services in the wake of the corona pandemic, will have to be paid for out of national budgets.

No wonder then that the other sectors of the economy are following suit and also want to be able to claim limitless compensation out of national budgets because of the enormous financial damage they are suffering as a result of the corona pandemic. The airline Deutsche Lufthansa, for example, is now approaching the Federal Minister of Economics with demands running into billions.

'Lufthansa has been particularly hard hit by the corona crisis. The airline is now flying just under 1 per cent of the passengers compared to this time last year, the daily number of passengers fell from an average of 350,000 to around 3,000. Despite a massive cut in working hours for employees under the short-time working scheme, many fixed costs

[205] https://www.deutsche-finanzagentur.de/en/financialmarketstabilisation/ (retrieved 14/09/20)

[206] https://www.neues-deutschland.de/artikel/1100361.rettungsschirm-fuer-banken-was-kostet-uns-die-bankenrettung.html (retrieved 09/05/20)

continue to run on, so that the company is losing around 800 million euros in cash reserves every month.

When giving a mandatory report to the Frankfurt stock index DAX, Lufthansa reported a first quarterly operating loss of 1.2 billion euros for 2020 and predicted even higher amounts for the current months. The company could no longer save itself on its own, it said when presenting its preliminary quarterly figures.

Now the state is to help the ailing company out of the crisis with a package that amounts to a total of nine billion euros. In addition to the silent participation of the Federal Economic Stabilisation Fund (WSF), the package includes a loan of an undisclosed amount and a direct participation of the Federal Government of up to 25 per cent plus one share in the share capital on the DAX index.

However, the state apparently only wants to pay the nominal value of the share of 2.56 euros – rather than the current share price of around 8 euros. The discount is intended to ensure that the taxpayer will benefit financially in a later sale, unlike, for example, in the case of the former rescue of Commerzbank.'[207]

Will there be more of this state-capitalism to come in Germany? Is this coming in to replace the neo-liberalism model we've seen before? The motto 'the profits are privatised, the losses are socialised' has long been the way of things anyway. But where is all this money supposed to come from, when all future sources of income - be that from corporation tax, value added tax and income tax - have all dried up because of the lockdown?

---

[207] https://www.manager-magazin.de/unternehmen/artikel/lufthansa-group-sollte-der-staat-den-vorsitz-im-aufsichtsrat-uebernehmen-a-1306828.html In German (retrieved 09/05/20) An English language article detailing the state of play is here: https://www.dw.com/en/lufthansa-loses-spot-on-germanys-dax-stock-index/a-53694211 (retrieved 14/09/20)

Local government treasurers are already thinking about raising admission fees for swimming pools, museums and public transport. The savings measures that will have to come over the next few years can already be heard rumbling in the distance.

Is There No Alternative To Mere Survival?

Of course, we can all protest against the state subsidisation of Lufthansa AG in the name of environmental protection or whatever else[208]. But this kind of criticism still remains inherently linked into the system and does not fundamentally question the blind actions of this money multiplication machinery.

As long as this system of a money multiplying machine with exponential growth is seen as without alternative, the next disaster will surely come along after Corona, which will continue to force a state of 'survival' upon us all, preventing us from determining our own existence with dignity. For a short time, after the collapse of the Russian-style Communist dictatorships in the Eastern Bloc and the integration of the European states, I hoped that a new era of freedom and intergovernmental cooperation might dawn.

The disappearance of the socialist alternative system, however, apparently only made the West's capital multipliers more demanding on the broad masses of the have-nots. The latter adapted themselves as best they could to the prevailing conditions and tried to make peace with them. But as the Corona pandemic now shows, we are simply not left in peace by this system, because it cannot itself ever rest. As Warren Buffet, one of the richest men on earth says, "There's class warfare, all right". And he adds: "But it's my class, the rich class,

---

[208]https://aktion.campact.de/rettungsgelder/appell/teilnehmen?utm_campaign=%2F rettungsgelder%2F&utm_medium=recommendation&utm_source=rec-lc&utm_term=inside_flow (retrieved 09/05/20)

that's making war, and we're winning,"[209] I often ask myself, what sort of crazy world do I live in?

This corona pandemic is making the handful of very rich even richer and the mass of the world population even poorer:

'Jeff Bezos (founder of Amazon) is currently worth $147.4 billion. The 56-year-old is one of the biggest beneficiaries of the corona crisis, as a new analysis shows. According to the report, the super-rich of the USA have increased their wealth significantly since March.

There are only a few stocks that are higher today than before the Corona crisis. Amazon is one of them. Since mid-February the share price has risen by around 11 percent. This is not surprising, after all, a mail-order company profits enormously from the closure of the bricks and mortar retail stores during the Corona crisis. The Governments themselves are eliminating his natural competition'. [210]

How Would It Be If ...?

How would it be if I didn't have to waste any more of my energy thinking about money? It would mean that I would only work if I thought it made sense or if it felt right to do so. Thinking about this lets me imagine a world where the focus was not on abstract money but on real concrete wealth. Where we value the richness of nature, its bounties of food that are there for us all, the wealth that lies within each and every one of us: our

---

https://markets.businessinsider.com/news/stocks/warren-buffett-right-class-war-taxes-rich-bernie-sanders-2020-8-1029532804# (retrieved 19/09/20)
[210]https://www.focus.de/finanzen/boerse/studie-zeigt-amerikanische-milliardaere-werden-durch-corona-434-milliarden-dollar-reicher_id_12020383.html
 https://www.theguardian.com/technology/2020/apr/15/amazon-lockdown-bonanza-jeff-bezos-fortune-109bn-coronavirus (retrieved 19/09/20)

empathy, our intelligence, our skills, our creativity and our capacity for love.

What I realise is that all this is still possible in the here and now in 2020, despite everything that's going on, and hopefully for many years to come. And I invite others to develop with me the very real richness and wealth that lies within them too.

The 'Second Wave'

By the end of the Easter holidays it is becoming increasingly clear that the seasonal flu epidemic is coming to an end and that it is no longer possible to keep making a panic scenario out of it. Professor Bhakdi speaks once again with his usual clarity in an interview with an Austrian broadcaster. He points out all the scientific weaknesses inherent within the panic-based actions of the governments of Austria and Germany and their scientifically unconvincing mouthpieces.[211]

Bill Gates is also coming under increasing pressure. In the USA, more than 410,000 citizens have signed a petition against him for 'crimes against humanity', which, according to the American Constitution, means it must now be dealt with by the White House.[212]

However, Gates continues to get good airtime on American TV shows spreading his ideas about the pandemic and generating fears about new future pandemics. In an interview at the end of March, for example, he spoke of a Phase Two that could now possibly come in the form of a bioterrorist attack that would be unleashed on humanity in the form of a virus from a laboratory. Of course, this too is another conjured up nightmare scenario.[213]

On the subject of an exit strategy: The idea that 'We are doing this to protect the risk group of the very elderly' is also meeting with resistance from within their ranks.

"I don't care about Corona,' says Helga Witt-Kronshage (86), for example. She would rather die than be locked up without a single visitor being allowed to come and see her. She has no garden, no sun and has hardly left her room in the nursing home for five weeks. She is supposed to be protected from the corona virus - but nobody has asked if she really wants

---

[211] https://www.youtube.com/watch?v=LzRCHPLNlEM (retrieved 30/04/20) – This video has been taken down, but a subtitled alternative interview from around the same time can still be found at: https://www.youtube.com/watch?v=WbWJ4xIPAkA (retrieved 30/10/20)

[212] Here's an English language article from a couple of months later when the petition had reached even more signatures: https://justthenews.com/politics-policy/coronavirus/white-house-petition-investigate-bill-gates-foundation-gets-over-600000 (retrieved 30/10/20) SL

[213] https://m.youtube.com/watch?v=8uLlx1leiso (retrieved 01/05/20) – Video removed.

that. She wants to live and die in her own self-determined way.'[214]

At the same time, panic is being stirred up again. Children are now being said to be particularly infectious and could therefore infect the at-risk groups. Once again, Mr Drosten is the main alarmist.[215] On the other hand, the Heinsberg study by Professor Streek says that children in particular are hardly likely to be carriers of the infection at all.

It becomes downright grotesque when a video from Tanzania appears in which a scientist explains that test swabs were taken from goats, birds, papayas and motor oil, and these were sent to a laboratory but labelled with people's names. And lo and behold, even plants, animals and the motor oil tested positive for corona.[216]

Since the Global Impact Alliance has good relations with the Chinese leaders who are participating in all this, rumours of a new type of swine flu virus pop up. It has allegedly started in China and will start spreading across the world from the end of June. This time the young people are not immune either.[217] It benefits the Global Vaccine Alliance the longer this pandemic of terror continues.[218] I'm left asking myself, how low can intellectual standards in this discussion still sink?

In his questioning by an extra-parliamentary committee enquiry, Dr. Wodarg explained with precision and enormous detailed knowledge how the so-called swine flu pandemic of 2009/10 was a staged attempt to push through a global vaccination programme. Fortunately, it was finally stopped because of his initiative in the Council of Europe.[219] But the media have rapidly shunted this story

---

[214] https://www.rnd.de/gesundheit/corona-ist-mir-egal-warum-helga-witt-kronshage-86-lieber-sterben-will-als-eingesperrt-zu-sein-

3MEBDIOBEFA6BDULC4N5WGZJG4.html?utm_source=pocket-newtab (retrieved 01/05/20)

[215] https://www.watson.de/leben/coronavirus/167073333-virus-kann-sich-da-vermehren-ohne-ende-virologe-drosten-ueber-corona-und-kinder (retrieved 01/05/20)

[216]https://www.youtube.com/watch?v=wKRcPFk3v9k&feature=emb_title (retrieved 07/05/20) – video since taken down.

[217] https://www.oe24.at/video/welt/Neue-Schweinegrippe-Art-in-China-entdeckt/435895333 (retrieved 01/07/20)

[218] https://www.n-tv.de/wissen/Droht-jetzt-eine-Doppel-Pandemie-article21883363.html (retrieved 03/07/20)

[219] https://www.youtube.com/watch?v=cWdF7Q3266I (retrieved 14/07/20)

to the sidelines of the news agenda during the corona pandemic in 2020.

Nuclear-Weapons Capable Combat Aircraft

How credible can a government's interest in the health of its people really be when, in the midst of this corona pandemic, a lively dispute begins within the ruling parties over which 'nuclear-weapon-capable aircraft' should now be purchased. If you ask 'Does Germany have nuclear weapons?' The answer would come 'Of course not'. But if you ask a slightly different question, namely 'Could the Bundeswehr (the unified armed forces of Germany) use nuclear weapons in an emergency?' And then, the answer is 'Yes'. At an air force base near the village of Büchel in the Eifel region in West Germany, some twenty B-61 hydrogen bombs are stored, each several times more powerful than the Hiroshima bomb. In the event of war, German Tornado fighter jets could be equipped with them and German pilots would carry them to their targets.

However, the bombs belong to the USA, without whose consent they cannot be used. This is called 'nuclear sharing', and has existed in Germany since the 1950's. After the end of the Cold War, nuclear sharing was significantly reduced, but the USA still 'shares' its nuclear weapons with several NATO countries, including Turkey. Use is always subject to the two-key principle, i.e. both the USA and the recipient country must agree to the deployment…

In terms of which aircraft Germany should invest in, the most likely possibility would be the F-35, a so-called fifth generation multi-purpose combat aircraft manufactured by the US company Lockheed-Martin. This is incredibly expensive, but technically state-of-the-art. Most other NATO countries are also buying this model and it would be practical for the whole of NATO to use the same aircraft.

But in January, the German government categorically ruled out buying the F-35 jet. The decision was due in no small part to pressure from the French defence group Dassault and the Franco-German aircraft manufacturer Airbus. Although there is no European-made fifth generation fighter jet comparable to the F-35, Germany and France plan to develop their own sixth-generation model by 2040, which will eclipse the F-35. Spain, which is also involved in Airbus, is also participating in this project'.[220]

It took a matter of seconds for the two Japanese cities of Hiroshima and Nagasaki to be razed to the ground by two American nuclear bombs ('Little Boy' and 'Fat Man') on 6th and 9th August 1945. At least 200,000 people died as a result.[221] These two bombs were not decisive in ending the war against Japan. Rather, they were probably more used as a test of this type of weapon in a real war situation and a demonstration of power towards the USSR, the main enemy in the Third World War, which was effectively immediately started after the end of the Second World War and which continues to this day as a proxy war in various countries of the world (including Korea, Vietnam, Cuba, Nicaragua, Chile, Afghanistan, Ukraine, Syria).

So far I have not heard anything about the fact that this Third World War is being put on hold in order to protect the health of the world's population. On the contrary, China is now also taking part in this deadly power game. Why are people not being frightened in regards to the mountains of corpses that could result from nuclear bombs? Nuclear weapons would be much easier to destroy than SARS-CoV-2 and you don't have to search for them with a tracking app. There are apparently 20 of them near the German village of Büchel.

---

[220] https://jungle.world/artikel/2019/20/welcher-bomber-darfs-denn-sein (retrieved 20/04/20)

[221] https://en.wikipedia.org/wiki/Atomic_bombings_of_Hiroshima_and_Nagasaki (retrieved 01/10/20)

Infectious Diseases As A Business Model - A Conspiracy Against Humanity

Interview And Lecture – 25th May 2020

1. Infectious Diseases: once something is declared an 'infectious disease' it does not matter whether the infection has consequences for the person affected. The bottom line is Infection = disease = must be socially controlled = must be medically treated; Because: whoever is infected potentially could infect others.

2. The General Objective: having used a concrete example ('Coronavirus'), it is demonstrated that in future a viral infectious disease will be considered a pandemic case and that lock down, social distancing, surveillance measures and mass vaccinations will be habitually accepted as the solution to the problem. Therefore, the social and economic costs of this example pandemic cannot be too high.

3. The Business Model: governments are the buyers for the manufacturers of vaccines and antiviral drugs; the financial risk from damage caused by vaccines and antiviral drugs is also borne by the public purse; manufacturing companies have a monopoly and can dictate prices to governments; the customers are potentially every single person on this earth; business opportunities also exist for the IT industry (health and surveillance apps) and manufacturers of medical aids (masks, protective clothing)

4. Long-term Preparation: learning from the mistakes of the swine flu disaster of 2010; changing the WHO definition of a pandemic; preparing detailed pandemic plans and instituting them in different countries by law; putting key-players in political decision-making positions; infiltrating political decision-making bodies with key-players; engaging

scientists who participate and keeping them happy; establishing a press that is on side; shaping public opinion (Bill Gates in TED talks and at the Security Conference 2017); testing the Event 201 simulation game for real-world suitability.

5. On-going Image Building: uphold the WHO as a neutral institution committed to world health; present the Bill and Melinda Gates Foundation as a charity organisation; praise Bill Gates as a philanthropist.

6. Develop the Narrative for Mass Communication: 'novel' virus, highly infectious; causes agonising death by suffocation; operating with worst-case-scenarios; overburdening of health care systems; helpless caregivers, keyword 'triage'; no one is supposed to die; in principle, it can affect anyone; solidarity of the young and strong with the weak and especially vulnerable; focusing all social resources on defending ourselves against a supposed end of the world and there is no alternative; planning ahead in dealing with resistance, branding 'corona deniers' as irresponsible, selfish people lacking in solidarity.

7. Invention of a Corona Virus Disease = COVID-19: present a single virus type as novel and potentially lethal; make this corona virus visible, measurable and thereby countable by PCP testing; define this corona virus as an essentially invariant and specific pathogen (SARS-CoV-2 = Severe Acute Respiratory Syndrome Corona Virus 2).

8. Determine the Conventional Medical Treatment Plan in advance: intensive care units, respirators required due to the threat of suffocation; ignore all systemic causes and conditions in the usual manner of conventional medicine (air pollution, food and eating habits that cause illness, the nocebo effect of scaremongering, previous damage caused by medication or vaccinations, trauma biography of the people affected, etc.) and claim SARS-CoV-2 not only

as a trigger but as the ultimate cause of serious and fatal cases.

9. Initiate the Pandemic: declare the pandemic on the back of an expected wave of influenza; launch the pandemic through the WHO (originally it started in Brazil, then China - what role is Jack Ma, the Chinese billionaire and Gates admirer playing in all this?); call on governments to activate their national pandemic plans

10. Policy Implementation: coordinate leading politicians and encourage them to play along and issue tough pandemic regulations; 'until there is a vaccine, there can be no all-clear and no easing of restrictions without simultaneous conditions like obligatory face-coverings.' Bavarian Minister President Markus Söder would advocate a compulsory vaccination against the coronavirus in Germany'. (Focus, 23.4.2020); ridiculing and isolating politicians who continue to pursue their own agenda.

11. Continuous monitoring through scientific expertise: putting individuals and institutions in the position of being the chief experts, who keep the pandemic game going with their headstrong and unsympathetic arguments; imposing the view that the number of infections is the problem in itself, thereby hoping to cloud what if any symptoms the infections actually elicit; heartlessly ignoring the harmful effects of the lockdown; making the decline of the influenza wave a success of the pandemic measures; excluding scientists who disagree by ignoring them or not allowing them to explain their views.

12. Activation of pandemic-friendly mainstream media: media exploitation of influenza pandemic hotspots (Italy, Spain, USA); targeted distribution of horror images of corpses and mass graves; extrapolation of death figures allegedly caused by COVID 19; daily bombardment of the public with panic-stricken images, individual fates, statistics; epic depiction of

desperate, heroic ways people are dealing with all this and focus of problems coming from bureaucratic details, denouncing failure (too few masks ordered, toilet paper hoarded); at the same time scattering pharmaceutical and vaccination-friendly reports ('How close are we to getting a vaccine?')

13. Prevention of collective resistance: through isolation (home office work, closure of universities, short-time work in factories); combating resistance by the legislative power (amending infection protection laws, threatening administrative penalties; bans on demonstrations and the most restrictive conditions for them); by the executive power (police presence, arrests); by trying to bring the judicial power on its own side; bringing all political parties into line.

14. Hold out for the prospect of rescue: link the end of the pandemic to the availability of vaccines; spend public money on research into vaccines as quickly as possible; reduce vaccine testing requirements; develop immunity-detection tests; use information technology to monitor cases of infection; prepare immunity identification documents.

15. Keep the pandemic going: maintaining a sense of threat and stress despite the end of the flu epidemic (continued social distancing, compulsory masks, bans on travel and demonstration); rewarding the population with gradual relaxation of coercive measures; threat of withdrawal of relaxation in the event of increased numbers of infections; media staging of inevitable or deliberately provoked outbreaks of infection; 'Second Wave'; even if there were no more actual cases of infection, the use of the PCR test alone could keep the pandemic going with a rate of 1.4% false positive results.[222]

16. Dealing with growing resistance: pathologising (making opponents out to be allegedly heartless

[222] https://multipolar-magazin.de/artikel/warum-die-pandemie-nicht-endet (retrieved 25/05/20)

corona deniers, incorrigible anti-vaxxers, right-wing and left-wing radicals, conspiracy theorists, crackpots who are away with the fairies), criminalising them through police investigation; dismissing dissenters from their jobs; trying to bring alternative media under control; praising those involved as 'people of character'.

17. And this list can go on and an...

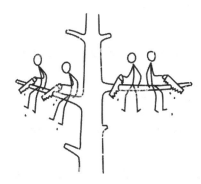

Figure 18: Why are so many people sawing through the branch they're sitting on?

On top of the delusion that there is a novel, highly infectious and potentially fatal virus called SARS-CoV-2, there is now the delusion about testing. Following the same logic of people who suffer from obsessive-compulsive washing, almost daily tests for the coronavirus are now being considered. Those who are tested 'negative', of course, have no guarantee that this will always be the case. They could have been infected with the virus right after the test. Even a school in Mecklenburg-Western Pomerania believes that it has to play a role as an example here and is offering all its students a free corona test twice a week[223]. In the end, all this only costs time, a

---

[223] https://www.web24.news/u/2020/05/back-to-school-a-pretty-unique-experiment-2.html (retrieved 25/5/20)

lot of money and keeps the fear of the supposed killer virus alive. [224]

Why?

What is propelling so many people to cut away at the branch of life that they themselves are sitting on? Even the tough unfeeling drivers of this corona pandemic, along with their ardent supporters, stubborn defenders and fearful followers, are themselves affected by all these inhuman and disease-causing measures. They too are no longer able to move around freely, they cannot simply pop out and meet friends for lunch or quickly nip out to a restaurant in the evening, they can't go jetting off on holiday anymore. Even their children are unable to go to school, they are to be vaccinated, their newborns may be born into a face-masked and plastic covered environment. Is this what they really want? Is this a future worth living? A future in which they are always suspected of being infectious and have to prove their immunity and constantly be having the next vaccination administered in time?

What Next?

Once this infectious disease business model, and the pandemic plans that come with it, are socially accepted, resourceful moneymakers could come up with the idea of bringing a new highly infectious substance into the world and at the same time claim to have the antidote. In our present day and age laboratories for biological warfare agents can easily provide the means for this in the form of something like inhalable anthrax.

We have long been familiar with this psychological dynamic: it's the fireman who starts the fire himself, only to be celebrated as a hero when he puts it out. But now we are seeing it in a much more dangerous form where

---

[224] https://www.heise.de/tp/features/Neue-Normalitaet-als-Geschaeft-und-scheinbare-Sicherheit-4765678.html (retrieved 25/5/20)

the people who plan these things are not lone perpetrators but financially powerful and well-connected organisations.[225]

[225] https://www.youtube.com/watch?v=vQKYegj6S-4&list=PLWoCxYI63N_6ws8U4USVOT (retrieved 30/05/20)

The Protests And Demonstrations Are Growing

The longer the lockdown measures are maintained despite all available evidence, and the more humiliating the regulations become (e.g. to wear nose and mouth protection for no medical benefit) the more apparent it also becomes how elementary human rights are being restricted by arbitrary imposed measures and the more resistance is stirring across all strata of society:

- More and more lawyers and specialists in constitutional law are waking up to the fact that what is being ordered 'from above' is arbitrary and unconstitutional.[226]
- Doctors are making impressive appeals, summarising all the arguments against maintaining measures and pleading for an immediate end to the pandemic.[227]
- Psychiatrists and psychotherapists give impassioned speeches of resistance.[228]
- Pastors deliver long sermons from their pulpits against the madness of this pandemic.[229]
- Professors of economics present their critical views in a cleverly structured way at large-scale demonstrations.[230]

Demonstrations, vigils and candle-lit processions now regularly take place in many cities, both large and small. Creative new forms of resistance are also popping up, such as meditations on the Grundgesetz (the Basic Constitutional Law of Germany). The authorities are still prohibiting and hindering these initiatives as much as they can and invoking the Infection Protection Act. For example in Munich, one demonstration that was organised to be on

---

[226] https://www.youtube.com/watch?v=j_55__DAR5Y (retrieved 15/05/20) – Video taken down. (Whilst translating this section I found many of the videos Franz quotes had since been taken down. Youtube are becoming more efficient at removing any videos that are critical of the official Corona narrative – SL)

[227] https://www.youtube.com/watch?v=__0fi7ugj6s (retrieved 15/05/20) – Video taken down.

[228] https://youtu.be/eScAxp3i2-o (retrieved 16/05/20)

[229] https://www.youtube.com/watch?v=adIENXkXU1I (retrieved 16/05/20) – Video taken down.

[230] https://www.youtube.com/watch?v=a7FOLdWUCzY&feature=em-uploademail (retrieved 16/05/20) – Video taken down.

the huge Oktoberfest meadow is crammed into a small area that only 1,000 demonstrators are allowed to enter. When more people turned up and were refused entry, they refused to accept this and this led to a scuffle with the police, complete with arrests and identity checks. The state power provokes violence so that it can say afterwards that troublemakers and right-wing extremists have gathered.

When I go for a bike ride along the Isar river in the beautiful spring weather on 16th May, I have the impression that the people of Munich are demonstrating in their own quiet way against the pandemic madness. The people are sitting close together on the banks of the Isar, not wearing face masks and even doing team sports with body contact. Even lovers can be seen who have probably only just got to know each other and are falling in love. Surely that's not really allowed in pandemic times!

Figure 19: The people of Munich demonstrate in their own way against the pandemic madness on 16.5.2020 (own photo)

My Message To All Those Protesting Against The Continuation Of The Corona Pandemic

29/05/20 – Speech Given At The Demonstration In Darmstadt On 30th May 2020

A very warm welcome to you all!

The corona pandemic is not a natural phenomenon, but a situation deliberately brought about by the World Health Organisation (WHO) and the national pandemic plans that have been implemented. The WHO defines a new form of disease, it deems it an infectious disease, and therefore all people, even all healthy people, are considered sick and infectious. The cure for everyone should be a vaccine.

Everything we are being told about this virus and how harmful it is is still speculation, even if people die because of it or merely with 'corona' in their system is a highly controversial topic of discussion in the scientific community. The only real thing that we can say for certain, it seems to me, is that there are massive negative consequences worldwide as a result of the Corona pandemic.

I therefore welcome all of you who are not now locking yourselves up at home in a state of fear, but who have the courage to take to the streets and publicly express your protest against this continuation of the Corona pandemic.

I welcome all you women who do not want to give birth to your babies whilst forced to wear face masks, but who wish to be able to show your newborn babies your face openly and lovingly.

I welcome all you mothers and fathers who wish that your children could play again without fear and could learn meaningful things at school that will help equip them for their lives without being subject to the terror of Corona.

I welcome all you children who do not want to be talked into feeling guilty that you are responsible for the illness or even the death of your parents or grandparents.

I welcome all you grandparents who do not want your grandchildren to be deprived of a future worth living out of a false concern for your life and health.

I welcome all you pupils who, with your critical minds, sense what is truth and what is propaganda.

I welcome all you teachers who want to pass on your knowledge and wisdom to your students and do not want to be taken advantage of and used as supervisors having to police senseless social-distancing rules.

I welcome all of you who are just completing their school-leaving certificate, vocational training or studies and do not want your future plans and hopes to be taken away by the lockdown.

I welcome all you restaurant owners, hoteliers and pub landlords who do not want to spoil your guests' appetite and a pleasant stay in your establishment with nonsensical facemasks and distancing rules.

I welcome all you freelancers who want to be using your qualifications and skills and who do not want to be condemned to inactivity by the ruin of your customers.

I welcome all you artists who need to be close to your audience and do not want to sink into depression at home in isolation.

I welcome all those of you who are deprived of your independent professional life by the pandemic and who are degraded to the status of alms recipients dependent on state subsidies.

I welcome all those of you who are suffering from illnesses and who expect real help from your doctors, not corona panic-mongering.

I welcome all you doctors and nurses who, because of your expertise and professional experience, know best how to prevent infection and what measures can help sick people recover.

I welcome all you nurses who work in old people's homes who feel that the elderly can only stay healthy through genuine human closeness and are made ill by being kept locked away alone and frightened.

I welcome all you students who critically question whether the corona pandemic really serves the public good.

I welcome all my colleagues in the academic community who are now using your scientific expertise to enlighten and seek truth and clarity instead of subordinating yourselves to lobbying interests.

I welcome all you scientists who are now exploring what is at stake in SARS-CoV-2 and who are engaged in open dialogue to counter the false number crunching, virus mythologies and panic-inducing predictions.

I welcome all you journalists who are honestly researching facts, providing the population with a variety of information and reporting on the masterminds and profiteers behind the corona pandemic.

I welcome all you newspaper readers and television viewers who, despite weeks of panic mongering and corona-minded terror, continue to still form your own opinions.

I welcome all those of you who think that the mania for Corona testing that is currently rampant is a senseless waste of money.

I welcome all of you who do not believe that viruses are the devil and vaccinations are God.

I welcome all of you who are still sceptical about whether 'the corona virus' is actually highly dangerous after all and need time to form your own opinion in open-ended discussions.

I welcome all of you who are here with another good intention that I have not yet mentioned.

I welcome all of you who want this haunting, distressing and traumatic corona pandemic situation to end immediately and unconditionally.

This corona pandemic is becoming increasingly delusional. The climate within our society is becoming more and more aggressive and intolerant. As a result, existing divisions are widening even further.

I would therefore like to ask the following questions. First off, I've got some general questions that I'd like to put to the politicians who are currently implementing this corona pandemic in 2020:

- Why are you giving us an additional problem – namely this virus - instead of getting round to solving the problems that already exist - such as environmental pollution, the threat of war, hunger, instability of the world economy, war and poverty migration?
- Do you want to go down in history as problem solvers or problem makers?
- Why are you so recklessly putting the entire public finances, and monetary stability itself, at risk for this idea of an infectious disease?
- What are you trying to look away from right now?
- What hidden anger, aggression and cruelty are you living out right now, which you then blame on a virus?
- What harm has been done to you, what violence did you suffer which you are now re-enacting and inflicting on others from your positions of power?

I have questions for all of our democratically elected representatives:

- Why are you participating in this? You are sawing through the branch of the very democracy that elected you into office.
- Why do you allow the government to listen to only one or two experts that none of us voters have elected to dominate our lives?

- Why don't you see through the fact that super-rich people are cunningly marketing their business model as apparent 'philanthropy'?
- What kind of illusions of being a saviour do you yourselves have, when you think you have to save society and the world, but in reality ruin it in the process?
- Why do you support this pandemic - which makes the rich even richer and the poor even poorer?
- Why are you allowing the population to be made physically and mentally ill all over the country in the name of health?

I have questions for the judges:

- Why do you stand idly by when laws for the common good are arbitrarily bent for the special interests of a vaccine industry?
- Why do you not stop the erosion of our fundamental rights?

I have questions for mainstream media journalists:

- Why are you belittling the honour of people who are now protesting because they are seriously concerned about freedom, democracy and their health?
- Why do you yourselves undermine the great good of freedom of expression, which is also the basis of your profession?

I have questions for the police officers:

- How do you feel when you take off your uniform and weapons after duty?
- How do you deal with the curtailment of your fundamental rights to a free life?

I have questions for the vaccine manufacturers:

- What is your real concern here – is it actually my health or is it your profits and the rise in your share prices?
- Do you yourselves actually seriously believe in a vaccine that will make 7 billion people immune to corona, whether they are newborns or 90 years old?
- How much do you personally trust your own immune system?
- Do you really feel your own happiness depends on the substances you are producing?

I have questions for everyone who is now participating and obedient:

- What are your repressed primal fears that you are now projecting onto the idea of a single highly dangerous virus?
- Is this the future you want to live in, in constant fear of being infected and infecting others?
- In a constant need to prove that you are immune?
- In a constant worry of getting all the supposedly saving vaccinations in time?
- Under total supervision and control by the ministries of a health dictatorship?

Personally, I see my future differently than shimmying from one vaccination to the next. I do not want my life to be only surviving in a state of fear. I want, to quote Albert Schweitzer: 'to be in the midst of a life that wants to live'. I also want to welcome my death when it is time to say goodbye to this earth and my fellow human beings.

I don't want any 'social distancing', but to live in solidarity with all those who also want to be alive. I don't want to live in a world where my mouth is covered, but to open my mouth to the world and raise my voice in a society that's worth standing up for.

As a trauma researcher, I know that no one is responsible for becoming a victim of trauma. But each of us does bear the responsibility if we become trauma victims of other people because of our own undealt with victimisation. As a child of two traumatised parents, I am particularly sensitive to the fact that people try to suppress the truth by looking away, or by aggression and violence.

I am certain that our deep need for truth, clarity, honesty, compassion and genuine solidarity will change this situation. Then, collectively, we will have the chance for a new and healthy normality.

My desire is for a free and happy life in good fellowship with all.

Keeping The Panic Going

By the end of May, although it is clear in Germany that this year's flu epidemic was much milder than in previous years, the corona pandemic is still not declared to be over.[231] Instead, politicians are demonstratively walking around with masks on their faces. Instead of coffins from Italy, pictures of mass graves in the Amazon region and allegedly hundreds of thousands of Covid-19 deaths in New York are now being disseminated to give the impression that the danger still exists.

Wolfgang Wodarg makes a serious accusation in an interview on 31st May 2020. He says that the malaria drug hydrochloroquine is being deliberately administered to dark-skinned people. Many of whom frequently suffer from an enzyme defect called G6PD deficiency (commonly called 'favism').[232] For human populations living in areas where the Anopheles mosquito is endemic, this defect offers some protection against malaria infections and is therefore evolutionarily beneficial. Giving hydrochloroquine to patients deficient in G6PD can however have fatal consequences. Wodarg states that this is happening so as to give the impression that Covid-19 was the cause of death. He describes the wearing of the masks as completely pointless and as a gesture of submission. He says how it's nonsense to talk of a second wave being expected because in reality there has not been a first wave.[233]

Are the loosening of the restrictive measures that began in early June a rearguard action by those responsible? Do they want to try and get out of the whole thing and save face? Or is it just an attempt to keep the corona pandemic going and then use a new wave of influenza or even a laboratory-bred pathogen to restart the freedom-robbing measures again in the future? In my view, as of today (03/06/20) I don't think this been decided upon yet. Therefore, critical education and protest on the part of the population is still needed. The creators of the WHO master plan and its local implementers will probably not give up without a fight, even if they seem to be on the verge of losing face at the moment. Which poisonous arrows do they still have in their quiver?

---

[231] https://swprs.org/facts-about-covid-19/ (retrieved 01/10/20)

[232] https://en.wikipedia.org/wiki/Glucose-6-phosphate_dehydrogenase_deficiency (retrieved 01/10/20)

[233] https://www.youtube.com/watch?v=Vaw_3F3Kq50 (retrieved 01/06/20)

The Corona Pandemic 2020 – A Test Case For The Infectious Diseases Business Model

Twenty-Fourth Article – 3rd June 2020
Published As KenFM Daily Dose And In The Rubikon

When the World Health Organisation (WHO) was founded in 1946, it had the following definition of health as part of its constitution:

'Health is a state of complete physical, mental and social well-being and not merely the absence of disease or infirmity. The enjoyment of the highest attainable standard of health is one of the fundamental rights of every human being without distinction of race, religion, political belief, economic or social condition'.

Since then, the WHO has increasingly become influenced by donations from industry and dubious foundations. It has become more and more of a lobbying organisation for those interested parties and the more money that comes in from them the more the WHO narrows its definition of illness and health to the same medical-biological model of infectious diseases that they are propagating. As a result, its focus has narrowed primarily now to pathogens that 'need' to be combated with vaccines and medicines. The self-healing activities of the body's own immune system, the psychological, social, economic, nutritional and environmental factors that decisively determine a person's state of health are in this way radically ignored. Large amounts from both public and private funds are now invested in the prevention of infections and the research and distribution of vaccines, as if the well-being and health of the whole of humanity was inextricably linked to this small handful of viruses. In 2019, the WHO presented a strategy paper to this effect:

'WHO today released a Global Influenza Strategy for 2019-2030 aimed at protecting people in all countries from the threat of influenza. The goal of the strategy is to prevent seasonal influenza, control the spread of influenza from animals to humans, and prepare for the next influenza pandemic.

"The threat of pandemic influenza is ever-present," said WHO Director-General Dr Tedros Adhanom Ghebreyesus. "The on-going risk of a new influenza virus transmitting from animals to humans and potentially causing a pandemic is real. The question is not if we will have another pandemic, but when. We must be vigilant and prepared – the cost of a major influenza outbreak will far outweigh the price of prevention."

Influenza remains one of the world's greatest public health challenges. Every year across the globe, there are an estimated 1 billion cases, of which 3 to 5 million are severe cases, resulting in 290 000 to 650 000 influenza-related respiratory deaths. WHO recommends annual influenza vaccination as the most effective way to prevent influenza. Vaccination is especially important for people at higher risk of serious influenza complications and for health care workers.

The new strategy is the most comprehensive and far-reaching that WHO has ever developed for influenza. It outlines a path to protect populations every year and helps prepare for a pandemic through strengthening routine programmes. It has two overarching goals:

Build stronger country capacities for disease surveillance and response, prevention and control, and preparedness. To achieve this, it calls for every country to have a tailored influenza programme that contributes to national and global preparedness and health security.

Develop better tools to prevent, detect, control and treat influenza, such as more effective vaccines, antivirals and treatments, with the goal of making these accessible for all countries'.[234]

For the WHO, it makes no difference whether the whole thing is called an *influenza* or a *corona* pandemic - the main thing is that its pandemic masterplan can be implemented worldwide. Despite the unproven hypothesis that a virus has spread from animals to humans, this 2020 attempt to make a credible case for a pandemic has given the virus the positive sounding name of 'Corona'. Unlike in the past, when there was talk of a swine, bird, cattle or camel flu, this time we were immediately given a memorable image of the red glowing Corona sphere with its spikes on the surface, so that everyone could easily imagine this supposed killer.

The assertion that viruses jump from animals to humans is important for the entire infection construct because it can then be claimed that the human immune system is not prepared for such a virus attack. This idea is even maintained when it is then established in practice that 95 percent of people infected with the alleged killer virus 'Corona' do not suffer any serious damage to their health.

How This Was All Implemented - Using Bavaria As An Example

Using an example that is local to me, we can trace how the WHO's masterplan strategy for the declaration and practical implementation of a pandemic was manifested in reality. Looking through the systematic and detailed 'Bavarian Framework Plan in the event of an Influenza Pandemic', we can see it contains all the keywords: 'novel virus', 'high mortality rates', 'overburdening of health

---

[234] https://www.who.int/news-room/detail/11-03-2019-who-launches-new-global-influenza-strategy (retrieved 02/06/20)

care systems' ... which will then be used later on, in 2020, in relation to a 'corona pandemic' to justify to the population the drastic measures of restrictions placed on their usual freedoms through mantra-like repetitions of these phrases. Because otherwise the Bavarians aren't going to keep quiet when they're denied their 'folk festivals'!

So looking at some extracts from this Bavarian framework plan we can see how this works out in practice:

'A pandemic is a worldwide epidemic. An influenza pandemic is caused by a new type of influenza virus. Since this new pathogen has not previously been present in the human population or has not been present for a very long time, the immune system is not prepared. The human population is therefore not protected. Pandemics can therefore lead to increased morbidity and mortality rates, which are many times higher than the rates caused by annual influenza waves. As a result, they could lead to extreme strains on the medical care system and the public health service and even pose a considerable threat to public order and the functioning of the entire national economy. [...]

General measures aim to curb the dynamics of infection by reducing social contacts in the general population or in specific groups of people. They may be used alone or in addition to individual measures to counter the spread of influenza by people who are still healthy or only slightly ill. By their very nature, they are accompanied by major restrictions on public life and sometimes have significant economic or organisational consequences. They may conflict with fundamental basic rights and are therefore reserved exclusively for situations where less restrictive measures are not sufficient. Events/major events are affected, for example cultural, sporting or political events, markets, fairs, festivals. They may be restricted, prohibited or subject to infection-reducing measures. The basic rights affected are freedom of opinion, artistic freedom, freedom of occupation; and in the case of political events - also freedom of assembly. The closure of public or private institutions where large numbers of people gather is also a possibility. [...]'

The Bavarian government is also in full agreement with the WHO with regard to the way this state of pandemic can be brought to an end:

'The ability to vaccinate the population in the event of a pandemic with a novel influenza virus is a key safeguard in any modern pandemic planning. Against the background of the technical framework conditions for the production of a pandemic vaccine, several months are to be expected between the WHO recommendation and the comprehensive delivery of the vaccine by the manufacturer... This must be taken into account in the conceptual planning for coping with a pandemic. The aim is to secure the vaccine supply as quickly as possible for those parts of the population for which vaccination is recommended'.[235]

The Corona Pandemic In Detail

Under the name of 'Corona', a pandemic like the one described above is currently being carried out with military precision. The following components make this possible:

- SARS-CoV-2, an allegedly highly infectious killer virus: From the start this corona virus is not given

---

[235] https://www.stmgp.bayern.de/wp-content/uploads/2020/02/influenza-bayern.pdf (retrieved 02/06/20)

the name of a viral RNA sequence like many other viruses, but is immediately associated - within its name itself - with a disease, that of 'Severe Acute Respiratory Syndrome Corona Virus 2'. The virus, which could in reality have all sorts of consequences such as no symptoms at all or a slight sore throat or a runny nose, should therefore be assumed as having the worst possible consequences - i.e. it will lead to severe acute respiratory problems and people will suffocate to death. This immediately, in the very talking about the disease, then arouses extreme existential fears.

- Covid 19, a disease that can be defined at will: since the virus itself already bears the name of a terrible disease, the disease that is supposed to be linked to it is then simply called Covid-19, i.e. a coronavirus disease from 2019. This has the further advantage that it can mean anything that they need to apply it to in order to stage this pandemic: they could say the virus can attack the brain, the heart, the kidneys, etc. The main thing is that people have the impression that it is an unpredictable villain that can strike anywhere and at any time. But in fact, according to experienced specialists, there are no specific symptoms that can solely be attributed to Covid-19.[236]

- A test that detects the virus and the infection at the same time: Professor Dr. Christian Drosten, who at the age of only 32 years, has already been highly decorated with awards from pharmaceutical-based foundations, pulled this trick out the bag very quickly in his Berlin institute (the Berlin Charité) without any major independent validation studies.[237] This test, which in reality at best just detects the

---

[236] https://www.youtube.com/watch?v=CEZ9q7pqOhM German Video (retrieved 14/06/20)

[237] https://www.rubikon.news/artikel/die-galionsfigur In German (retrieved 02/06/20)

presence of certain sections of the base sequence of a coronavirus, is thought of as a test that makes it possible to diagnose the possible infectious disease SARS-CoV-2 or Covid-19. The more tests that are carried out, the more supposed cases of disease are brought to light.

- An epidemic on which the case for a pandemic can be based: In Germany this was the seasonal flu epidemic. After the news from China came out, this was the wagon on which the pandemic was pinned so that the infectious disease could noticeably be seen to be spreading.

- A new way of looking at things and risk projections: An infection with a coronavirus is defined as a possible disease. Anyone who is infected is therefore either potentially at risk of becoming seriously ill, or is themselves at risk of being a source of infection for others who might potentially become seriously ill. Numbers games and extrapolations with worst-case scenarios help to fuel the fear in the population. By concentrating on this concept of infectiousness, all healthy people, whether they be young or old, are potentially ill and must be monitored and controlled preventively. And once the vaccine is available, it makes logical sense to vaccinate them all.

The manipulative nature at the heart of this construction of corona disease can also be seen in how easily all sorts of symptoms or even deaths can be blamed on this one virus and how dizzyingly high death figures can then be projected. From my time in occupational health and safety, I remember how fiercely it had to be fought over, in expert committees or in court, as to whether a worker's years of exposure to hazardous substances could result in, and should be recognised as, a disease caused by the work itself or whether the worker in question had not inflicted the damage themselves due to their lifestyle (smoking!) or previous illnesses.

This argument usually also plays out in regards to harm caused by vaccination. Hardly anyone succeeds in court in proving that their child has been harmed by a one-off vaccination. Here too, possible other causes are always cited and claims for compensation are usually rejected. However when it comes to the case of SARS-CoV-2 everything is suddenly turned on its head: it is the virus that has harmed and killed this person. He is definitely a 'Death by Corona'!

The Concept Of An Objectifiable 'Disease'

The thinking behind so-called orthodox medicine has, for a long time, been based on a narrow scientific viewpoint that has completely ignored any psychological influences on human health. The fact that a human being is a subject; that a person has an 'I', a want, a consciousness; that they have needs and emotions and that their entire life history has a great influence on their state of health; all this is deemed to be of secondary importance in this medical way of thinking (Ruppert and Banzhaf 2018). Instead, a person is measured in terms of objective quantifiable variables, for example blood pressure or insulin levels in the blood. These are then evaluated as tangible evidence of this person's 'illness' and provide the basis on which treatment is given. And, when it is given, this treatment is purely physical or chemical in nature. The person in question is called a 'patient', from the Latin 'patiens' (sufferer), even if he or she is not suffering at all from a specific symptom or is experiencing something completely different entirely.

The aim of orthodox medicine is not to improve a person's overall well-being and certainly not to support them in their personal development. Its sole focus is to change something but only within the parameters of the disease that has already been defined as existing within the person's body. Illness means 'having symptoms' and health is therefore equated, in essence, with being free from these symptoms, so all these symptoms must be physically quantifiable and measurable.

Such an approach, which completely ignores the whole person and their living environment, necessarily results in new problems arising through the suppression and elimination of certain symptoms. This does not, however, lead to any scepticism in orthodox medicine about it's own approach to treatment. Rather, it spurs on their ambition to find new drugs, operations, radiation therapies, and so on, in order to go on and then combat what are known as the 'side effects' of the conventional medical treatment they are already prescribing.

In psychiatry, for example, 'patients' are sometimes prescribed ten or more drugs at once to control the consequences of the effects of the other drugs. These people are then predictably rarely free of one symptom or another, and are more and more likely to be given the status of being 'chronically ill' the longer they are in psychiatric treatment. And so therefore, according to this mind-set, long-term medication is then definitely called for. The failure of orthodox medical efforts is not blamed on their misguided theory of disease or on the devastating consequences of their disease treatment, but on the supposed incurability of the diseases themselves, and therefore also on the supposed incurability of the patients. This is a 'perfect' example of how the perpetrator-victim-reversal works in traumatised societies (Ruppert 2019).

In monetary terms, however, this bottomless barrel of symptoms is a goldmine for those who play along with this 'disease system'. To be a patient once means to be a patient forever, and therefore a lifelong money-earning opportunity.

To avoid being accused here of questioning the honest efforts of the majority of doctors who are there to help those who are sick, I would like to say I know many doctors in my private and professional environment who I value very highly and consider to be highly competent. However, when they work in a conventional medical context, they all admit to me that they feel trapped in this system, which is not designed to do good for those who are sick, and that this is not where they as doctors want to be and it does not allow them the freedom to do what they actually want to do.

What Is New About This Particular Construct?

This new concept of an infectious disease that is now being applied in relation to Covid-19 is different from other models of disease as defined within conventional medicine. While for the treatment of 'cancer', 'diabetes', 'obesity', 'high blood pressure', 'schizophrenia' or 'depression' etc. people have to show symptoms, in other words they have to demonstrably display some form of physical or psychological abnormality, this circumstance is now completely eliminated with Covid-19. Here, the mere suggestion that there is a dangerous pathogen around is enough to ascribe to all people worldwide the characteristic of being potentially infectious and of therefore potentially infecting others, and if we're saying that everyone is infectious we're effectively diagnosing everyone as having this infectious disease. Everyone is therefore automatically a patient and must consequently be so-called 'treated' with vaccinations.

The logical trick of not seeing diseases as something purely constructed by orthodox medicine itself, but as something natural that lies within the patient himself, is also used by orthodox medicine in relation to other diseases. Instead of saying that a person has been diagnosed with a disease called 'cancer', 'diabetes', 'high blood pressure' or 'depression' when certain physical or psychological abnormalities are present, it is simply said that this person has 'cancer', 'diabetes', 'high blood pressure' or 'depression'. This then justifies 'medical treatment' and its billing via the health insurance companies within the set-up of state-run healthcare systems, which are dominated by conventional medicine almost everywhere in the world.

In this context, orthodox medicine has, in more recent times, increasingly used the trick of redefining 'diseases', independent of the subjective suffering that the 'patient' is undergoing. One way of doing this is by lowering limit values in regards to the quantifiable symptoms, by doing this you can suddenly increase the number of 'patients' to be treated, for example in the definition of hypertension. High blood pressure is now defined as readings of 130 mm Hg and higher for the systolic blood pressure measurement, or readings of 80 and higher for the diastolic measurement. That is a change from the old definition of 140/90. Through manipulating the statistics in this way, the turnover and profits of the medical industry can increase enormously.[238]

The Infectious Diseases Business Model

As a business model, 'Infectious Diseases' offer enormous advantages for the manufacturers of supposedly antiviral drugs and vaccines:

- Vaccine research is supported by government grants.
- The manufacturers of the pharmaceutical products can sell their products directly to the respective countries and governments at monopoly prices, because the governments themselves have to protect their populations.
- The richer countries, such as Germany, should also bear the costs for the poorer countries, for example the African states.
- The risks involved in compensating for vaccine damage must also be borne by the state coffers

---

[238] https://www.youtube.com/watch?v=0obDIkEDUtU (retrieved 26/05/20)– This video is now listed as 'Private'

because of the urgency of having such vaccines available as quickly as possible.

- An influenza or any other pandemic can be declared by the WHO at any time and makes vaccination as a preventive measure a viable long-term business.

There is no need to necessarily order compulsory vaccinations, which, at least in countries like Germany, could not be easily enforced if there was public resistance. What would be sufficient would be to implement restrictions on the public in terms of freedom of expression, artistic freedom, freedom of occupation and freedom of assembly as specified in the pandemic plan through an infection protection law meaning that without immunity these freedoms would be denied and there would be no way to prove immunity other than having the protective vaccination.

As a precautionary measure, it is already being said in terms of 'Corona' that proof of immunity is only valid for a few days. Even those who have already been tested for the alleged killer virus and showed no symptoms after 14 days of quarantine, or who now even have antibodies against SARS-CoV-2 in their blood, are not promised a guarantee of non-infectivity or immunity for life. We are told instead that this insidious virus could become even more dangerous over time and then kill more people in a second wave. For most people, agreeing to permanent vaccinations will then seem like an easier way than being constantly pressured to prove their immunity without an electronic vaccination record.

So the corona pandemic is now the test case for the brave new world order that will come afterwards. The costs and damage of the 2020 pandemic cannot be high enough to ensure that this policy will not be questioned in the years to come: what would you prefer? Another pandemic with a lockdown and all the agonising measures that the population has to go through, and this happening year after year, or would you rather just have a vaccination every winter, like the current influenza vaccination, for both young and old? Maybe we could all have gift vouchers for it nicely wrapped under the Christmas tree. That's how you turn healthy people into junkies addicted to the vaccination needle!

A Community United In Delusion

One of the biggest misconceptions continues to be that the coronavirus is a natural phenomenon transmitted to humans from a bat, to which politicians had to react urgently to in order to protect the population from millions of deaths. The more drastic the measures taken, the more plausible the high-risk nature of the virus is made out to be. And so as the pandemic planning continues with social distancing and compulsory masks, although in Germany, for example, there are no more serious cases of illness[239], this can then be interpreted as the natural reaction to an unpredictable virus that could strike again in a second wave.

Similarly, the absence of the predicted high mortality rates and the fact that intensive care units remain empty is not attributed to a population building up a natural immunity, as would be expected in the course of a flu epidemic, but to the drastic pandemic measures – it 'proves' that they are working. Even the failures of medical treatment with the over-reliance on ventilators, as a result of predefining the disease within its name ('acute respiratory syndrome'), or the administration of chloroquine tablets that made people sicker or led to their deaths, or the massive damage caused by the social lockdown to previously healthy elderly people, or to children or to those who are working; in all these cases the true causes are simply ignored and everything is stubbornly recorded as consequences of the virus. The same is true of the far-reaching economic damage and the danger of an immense national debt and a spiralling

---

[239] https://www.youtube.com/watch?v=Vaw_3F3Kq50 (retrieved 02/06/20)

inflation rate – this is not the fault of the lockdown and the pandemic measures – it is the fault of the virus.

In the language of psychotraumatology, I see this as a psychological separation from connection to reality. In this corona pandemic, both victims and perpetrators form an unshakeable, conspiratorial community which simply blocks out, or reinterprets in a delusional way, all realities which do not fit into its interpretation of the deadly virus. And in doing so they reciprocally spare each other from having to clearly name and acknowledge their own victimhood or perpetrator nature. Anyone who disturbs this illusory harmony, with critical questioning and references to the real causes and consequences of this mad project to bring the whole of society to its knees in one fell swoop, is then an evil conspiracy theorist who hinders the good people in their actions. To allow the insight that the entire population and the whole economy has long been in the hands of profiteers in the field of health and that the ruling politicians are currently helping to take this to the extreme by using the infectious disease model would be asking the question of the system: Is this domination of the people still legitimate? That is why many people, rather than seeing the reality of this domination, are now turning this insight around: Our government is faced with a new situation, yes, it makes mistakes and sometimes exaggerates, but basically it protects us.

Please Wake Up From The Delusion

Waking up from this delusion will be more painful for all of us the longer we stay in it. And therefore I ask everyone caught up in this to please wake up now!

Scientists Are People Who Love Questions

In this book I've tried to present my own personal process of becoming conscious and aware of what is going on. At the beginning a lot of information was still unavailable and I made some wrong assumptions. These could only gradually be corrected during my continued search for clarity and truth. There are some lines by Rainer Maria Rilke, from his 'Letters to a Young Poet' which echo these sentiments and I find them particularly touching:

'You have to give things
their own, quiet
undisturbed development.
This comes from deep inside,
It cannot be pushed,
It cannot be accelerated,
Everything must take its gestation - and
Only then can it give birth…

Things must ripen like the tree,
Who does not force his sap
But stands confidently in the storms of spring,
Unafraid
That beyond it, summer
May not come.

But it does come!

But it only comes to those who are patient,
Who stand there as if eternity
Lay before them,
So unconcerned, silent and vast…

You have to be patient

With all that is unresolved in your heart
And to try to love the questions themselves
Like locked rooms and like books that are written
For now in the most foreign of tongues.

The point is to live everything.
If you live the questions now
Perhaps then, someday far in the future,
You will gradually,
Without even noticing it,
Live your way into the answer

Rainer Maria Rilke (1875 - 1926)

Humanity In 2020: Cognitively Highly Intelligent But Emotionally Infantile

Twenty-Fifth Article – 8th June 2020
Published By KenFM

Studying Books Makes You Smart

Since I am neither a virologist, nor an epidemiologist, nor a doctor, I felt, like most people, that I was caught off-guard at the beginning of this corona pandemic by the arguments of the 'chief virologists' who told us this story of the highly infectious, novel SARS-CoV-2 over and over again and claimed that they could detect it by means of these new tests that could show the infections and infection chains and pathways. And I, like everyone else, had to believe their claims that this particular virus would be responsible for serious lung diseases and could kill so many people. A layman has to believe at first what experts tell him.

Now that I've started to doubt more and more what these experts are telling me, I have bought some books and tried to form my own opinions about virology. The book 'Viruses: More Friends than Foes' (2017), written by the virus and cancer researcher Karin Mölling, already in its title aims to stop this demonisation of viruses.[240] It clarifies that it cannot be the corona virus alone that causes a disease, but 'additional risk factors are involved, such as air pollution, family structures or health care, population density'. (Mölling 2020, p. 176 German e-book version).

The book by Torsten Engelbrecht and Claus Köhnlein 'Virus Mania' (2020) thoroughly dispels one of the central myths of virology that a virus is responsible for a disease.

---

[240] Mölling's 'Viruses: More Friends than Foes' is available in English – published in 2017 by World Scientific Publishing – Original German title: 'Supermacht des Lebens' The Superpower of Life

The book's subtitle is: 'How the medical industry constantly invents epidemics, making billion-dollar profits at our expense'. In the book, statements can be found which cast considerable doubt on the corona pandemic narrative. In China, for example, by no means all people who tested positive for corona had been in contact with the market in Wuhan, where the epidemic allegedly started. Also, not all family members in families investigated as corona cases became infected (p. 449 ff.). Those who died may not have died from SARS-Cov-2, but from the drugs they were given:

'On 15th February, a study was printed in the Lancet describing the cases of 41 Chinese people who suffered from severe pneumonia and had tested 'positive'. All of them were given antibiotics, some of which were administered intravenously, and almost all (93 percent) were given the antiviral drug oseltamivir. Nine of them (22 percent) were also given anti-inflammatory drugs (corticosteroids), which also have many side effects. Six of them died as a result'. (Engelbrecht and Köhnlein 2020, p. 470).

In this book, they also provide essential information about these PCR (Polymerase Chain Reaction) tests, which are supposed to clearly prove the existence of a virus. This only works, however, if these tests are sterile and provide complete particle purification, this is apparently a prerequisite so that other cell components, which are created, for example, by cell stress, are not detected by the test. The tests used to detect the corona virus apparently do not meet these requirements (p.456).

It is therefore more or less a matter of chance whether a so-called corona test actually detects the virus that is being searched for. In this way, people who have tested positive can also be tested negative afterwards, and then positive again later. This is unfortunately not used as an argument against the test, but this test chaos is attributed to the virus and its unpredictable nature.

The authors come to the following conclusion:

'So if there is no doubt that

a) there are 'no unmistakable specific symptoms' for COVID-19,

b) it is 'clinically impossible to differentiate between pathogens',

c) no one has evidence that SARS-CoV-2 is an exceptional hazard; and that

d) non-microbial factors such as industrial poisons and various drugs such as antipsychotics, opiod analgesics, anticholinergics or even antidepressants may be a cause of severe respiratory problems such as pneumonia, and thus also COVID-19,

Then it is impossible to conclude that only what is called SARS-CoV-2 can be considered as the cause of the symptoms in patients who have the 'COVID-19' label attached.' (Engelbrecht and Köhnlein 2020, p. 455 f.)

Worshipping At The Altar Of The God Of Money

It remains inconceivable to me how an enlightened world community, which has been trying to emancipate itself from superstition around dark forces, evil and the devil for over 200 years and instead claims to rely on rationality and science, will mentally revert back into the Dark Ages in regards to this corona pandemic. Suddenly, we are in the midst of a religious war with ardent followers fighting against the alleged heretics. Even in a region like Bavaria, where the ruling party has the word 'Christian' in its name (the CSU – Christian Social Union Party), its leadership believes more in salvation through vaccination than in God. It is not even deterred from its course of action by criticism from church representatives that their activities, especially church services, are also severely hampered by the requirement of social-distance.

In global terms, the worship of money, or the idea of abstract wealth, has taken the place of God. This is most clearly expressed in the media's admiration for the super-rich that gives them a good chance of even becoming president of a country.[241] It is the God of Money who rules the world in the 21st century and whom everyone worships either publicly or secretly. The whole thing should not, however, appear outwardly like a childish belief in the Redeemer and so it is cloaked in pseudo-rational arguments. We believe that because we have created the idea of money ourselves we have taken our fate into our own hands. In reality, however, we have only changed the focus for our dependence. Now it is the stock market, exchange rates and even scientists who decide the fate of all mankind.

Science – An Opportunity For Enlightenment And Emancipation

Science could indeed be a chance for us to emancipate ourselves from irrationality, like a belief in ghosts, and our childlike fear of existence. But to do so, it would have to be truly free and independent in its thinking and research. There should not be any prestige attached to which person is right and which is wrong and what is the right argument and so on. There should be no dogmas. Science should be a shared process of casting off our old mistakes and seeking out new insights.

Let's imagine something for a moment. What if there was a student who:

- submitted his doctoral thesis to a university entitled 'SARS-CoV-2 - a novel, highly infectious virus with a high mortality risk, causing Covid-19, which will

---

[241] https://www.br.de/nachrichten/deutschland-welt/bill-gates-und-sein-kampf-gegen-corona (retrieved 07/06/20)

overburden healthcare systems and necessitate a pandemic'
- and this student came up with a unreliable PCR test and in his studies assigned all sorts of things to this Covid-19
- and he claimed he could he could measure the spread of infectivity using a tautological reproduction formula R,

If this happened, I suspect this student would be met with utter scorn, or at the very least mild indulgent smiles, from his examiners. What is definitely true is he would certainly not succeed in defending his hypothesis and would therefore not get his doctorate.

If, however, the people who present this 'science' are civil servants, they have bestowed upon them professorships and doctorates like titles of nobility. When researchers have to make a career within a hierarchically ordered system, dependent on third-party funding, and confirm each other in their false paradigms purely within their own communities, science remains in its infancy. In order for it to grow up, it would be necessary for the scientists themselves to go through a personal maturation process. To do so, most of them, given the traumatising circumstances in which we all live, would then have to deal with their own early childhood trauma. They would not be able then to abuse science and use it to protect themselves, as they try to stop their traumatic feelings coming up by constantly staying in their heads and seeking refuge in the abstract spheres of supposed rationality.

It is known, for instance, that the Director-General of the WHO Dr. Tedros Adhanom Ghebreyesus lost a brother when he himself was seven years old. He has cited this as a motive for why he does the job he does:

'When he was seven years old, Tedros Adhanom Ghebreyesus witnessed the death of his brother who was two years younger than him. His brother had succumbed to a disease that could have been cured in a country with a functioning health system, he says. But that did not exist at that time in his home country of Ethiopia. Tedros has been telling this story ever since he applied for the post of Director-General of the World Health Organisation (WHO): The death of his brother, says the now 52-year-old, drives him to this day to fight for better health care. He does not want to accept that someone has to die 'just because he is poor', as his family was then'.[242]

My experience with trauma therapy tells me that it would be better for him to work through this personal trauma of loss first, in other words to allow his childhood pain to be truly felt to its fullest extent, before he involves the whole world in what is otherwise his loss trauma survival strategy. After all, what do vaccinations really have to do with the reduction of poverty?

There is an encroachment and control that underpins these strategies of the vaccination community in their plan to rescue the world. Disguised as scientists, they make out that their strategies are the 'smart' thing to do. And they spread them with a smile on their faces and a lot of rhetoric and argument around philanthropy. This allows them to strongly distinguish themselves from the warlike, uncouth, brute-force implementers of power such as the likes of Trump or Bolsonaro. Nevertheless, even these 'disguised' perpetrators, though well-trained in the art of communication, need the state and police authorities on their side when there is too much opposition and resistance to their plans. At first, biting journalistic chain dogs are unleashed against those who doubt the rationality of these arguments they have constructed. If this does not bear fruit, then new laws and regulations will have to be enacted; if necessary, these

[242] https://www.dw.com/de/dr-tedros-nur-im-ausland-ein-prophet/a-38974699 (retrieved 07/06/20)

will make the enforced happiness of humanity through drugs and vaccines a reality: [243]

- By definition, I am now a 'virus carrier', regardless of whether I have any symptoms of illness or not.[244] I am basically dirty and disgusting. Therefore others must be protected from me. I also have to continually disinfect my hands to kill this evil virus over and over again. It would be best if I could wash out this virus inside of me with soapy water.
- By definition, I am suddenly a person that others can infect, whether I am sick or not. I therefore need to be kept at a distance from them, at least one and a half meters (in Germany). Please don't let anyone come too close to me! I am so vulnerable and unprotected.
- The government must therefore protect me from myself in its holy war against viruses, the community at large must also be protected from me and I must be protected from the community.

So it's not a great leap of the imagination before we see children in their classrooms kneeling down to pray: "Dear Mr. Gates, dear Mrs. Merkel, dear Mr. Spahn and all the other enlightened ones, you who dwell in the heaven of all wisdom about our disgusting human nature, please redeem us from the stigma of our infectiousness by the grace of your vaccinations. So that we may become completely pure again until the next virus comes. Amen!"

The Head Is Strong, The Heart Remains Weak

For me, this corona pandemic mania in 2020 can be partly explained to the extent that, from a global perspective, we have trained and developed our cognitive

---

[243] https://www.sozialgesetzbuch-sgb.de/ifsg/1.html (retrieved 08/06/20)
[244] https://youtu.be/Ul0aCFVpYHg (retrieved 07/06/20)

intelligence through more and more schooling, but have remained emotionally infantile. On a global scale, we persist in doing everything we can to ensure that children are so severely traumatised by prenatal experiences, birth processes and, in the first years of their lives, by loveless neglect, outside care and crèche care that they lose full access to their needs and feelings and their healthy self-awareness. Like a car that was originally designed as a high-performance six-cylinder powerhouse, most of us then go through life on a stuttering emotional two-stroke engine. We have to suppress our real needs, we are frightened of our feelings and therefore we take refuge in our heads. We learn to turn our left brain hemisphere into a supercomputer, while our right brain hemisphere is mostly left unused. We abandon it to itself and by doing this it means it cannot then exchange information with the left brain hemisphere and therefore truly integrate and process reality.

If we are then, as is currently happening worldwide, put into states of anxiety and fear by targeted and continuous media panic-mongering, our psyche switches to this underdeveloped right brain hemisphere at lightning speed. We can then be easily manipulated by these specifically prepared terrifying images and exaggerated horror stories. Simple associative-correlation, false connections brimming with logical contradictions suddenly appear completely plausible, although they do not, for a second, stand up to scientific cause and effect analysis or critical examination.

So, for example, protective masks are worn, even if their meaning and purpose cannot be rationally substantiated or can only be argued for by overcoming all rationality:

'Tedros said that masks could not replace hand hygiene, observing social distance and tracking down patients and their social contacts. Masks alone could not protect against Covid-19.

Governments should encourage people to wear masks where the virus is widely spread and where it is difficult to keep distance from other people, such as on public transport, in shops or in crowded or confined areas. The WHO also noted that 'sewing masks enables people to do something about the virus and is a potential source of income".[245]

The *'tracking down patients along with their social contacts'* is a scary statement that reminds me of the witch-hunting days. Where is the she-devil herself, and who has she already bewitched?

In his statement, Mr. Tedros turns the wearing and sewing of masks into an illusionary survival and poverty reduction programme. My mask is my talisman, my comforter and helper in need. I am also familiar with such connections from psychotraumatology - I recommend my own trauma survival strategies to others as the wisdom of last resort.

Even highly educated people fall back into primitive reaction patterns once under the influence of fear. They react helplessly as if they were children, fearing death, separation and loss, and hope for rescue through strong parent figures and miracle cures such as drugs or vaccinations. This is the moment when all the profiteers and political leaders are able to take a stand and pretend to be our saviours. And we will have to pay dearly for our rescue. On the one hand financially, on the other hand through submission and obedience. Out of fear of death and abandonment we ultimately give up everything that, when we are in our right minds, is dear and precious to us.[246]

---

[245] https://www.rtl.de/cms/mundschutz-gegen-corona-who-aendert-empfehlung-zum-tragen-von-gesichtsmaske-4555763.html (retrieved 07/06/20)
[246] https://youtu.be/rhvTHvb6Qb8 (retrieved 07/06/20)

The Corona Pandemic As An Opportunity For Collective Maturation

Blindly taking part in everything laid down upon us from above, has its psychological roots in the fact that people primarily want to belong to the majority because then they believe that they will enjoy the best possible protection in life from being a part it. The fear of being an outsider is understandably great. In principle, they also have immense trust in the leaders within their group ('herd'). But when these leaders themselves are traumatised and emotionally underdeveloped, you may well end up like Mr. Palmström from Christian Morgenstern's poem:[247]

> Palmstroem, an aimless old rover,
> walking in the wrong direction
> at a busy intersection
> is run over.
>
> "How," he says, his life restoring
> and with pluck his death ignoring,
> "can an accident like this
> ever happen? What's amiss?
>
> "Did the state administration
> fail in motor transportation?
> Did police ignore the need
> for reducing driving speed?
>
> "Isn't there a prohibition,
> barring motorized transmission
> of the living to the dead?
> Was the driver right who sped . . . ?"
>
> Tightly swathed in dampened tissues
> he explores the legal issues,

[247] http://www.alb-neckar-schwarzwald.de/morgenstern/morgenstern_poems.html

and it soon is clear as air:
Cars were not permitted there!

And he comes to the conclusion:
His mishap was an illusion,
for, he reasons pointedly,
that which must not, can not be.
(Christian Morgenstern 1871-1914)
Translated by: Max E Knight (1909-1993)

This corona pandemic could be a tremendous opportunity for our personal and collective growth. We would then be able to recognise which of our social leaders (parents, teachers, bosses, journalists, doctors, scientists, judges, politicians) has grown into an emotionally mature person in the course of their lives and who has remained at an infantile level. Placing the fate of all of us in the hands of adults, who have remained infantile and who are controlled by these constructs that exist only in their heads, has often had fatal consequences, as German history, in particular, has shown.

Welcome To Absurdia

And as it all becomes more and more absurd, the Robert Koch Institute is not letting up, as we can see in this article in Die Welt Newspaper:

> 'The Robert Koch Institute (RKI) sees no reason to relax contact restrictions to any large extent despite the drop in the number of new infections. "We have achieved a lot in recent weeks," said the Vice-President of the Robert Koch Institute, Lars Schaade, on Tuesday in Berlin. "But the situation is still serious. There is no end of the epidemic in sight, the number of cases may rise again'. Schaade stressed that only a vaccine could help. Until then, everyone must continue to practice the rules of hygiene and conduct. And there is still no medicine that could help to heal an infection, he said [...].
>
> The Vice-President also said: 'Children are affected in a similar way to adults. However, many do not show symptoms'. Although there are no studies on the exact role they play in transmission, Schaade is sure that 'children play a certain role in transmission'.[248]

The following Facebook entry from someone in Thailand shows the horrible ideas that this heartless thinking leads to. Then the babies that are born will know immediately in which crazy plastic world they have landed:

---

[248] https://www.welt.de/politik/deutschland/article207394539/RKI-zu-Corona-Ohne-Impfstoff-keine-Rueckkehr-zur-Normalitaet.html (retrieved 22/04/20)

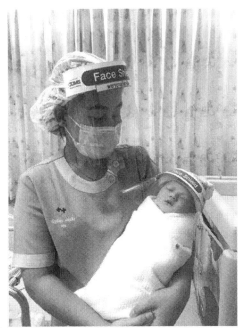

Figure 20: Welcome, little citizen of the earth, to the world of corona madness[249]

Surrogate motherhood, which is highly questionable anyway in terms of trauma even if it weren't for Corona, is becoming especially traumatising for new citizens of the earth as a result of the Corona pandemic:

'Earlier this week a video from Ukraine was broadcast in which several babies were seen in beds in a hotel in Ukraine waiting to be picked up by their 'parents that had ordered them' (who could not come and collect them because of travel restrictions that had been imposed). They were born by surrogate mothers who are not the babies' biological mothers.

---

[249] https://sea.mashable.com/culture/9915/these-cute-babies-from-thailand-got-mini-face-shields-to-protect-them-from-coronavirus?fbclid=IwAR0y18u8ztP4sq3UW0JyMKNR7B28-nHQiCfeNd4t7AH-aNgIfSgh8xorpKA (retrieved 19/05/20)

Couples from other countries have paid for Ukrainian women to carry their children.'[250]

In order to be able to supposedly return to normal life faster, a secondary school offers its pupils voluntary corona tests. Those who are not infected are marked with a green dot - and different rules apply to them than to pupils who do not get tested. Psychologist Thilo Hartmann criticises the procedure:

"The psychological risk clearly outweighs the practical benefit," he states. Even worse: the procedure like the one at Gymnasium Carolinum could fuel the fascistic behaviour and thinking patterns already present in the Corona crisis. "Everyone can see whether I follow the rules, whether I wear a mask, whether I get tested. This can lead to dangerous conformity behaviour, especially among pupils.

When he first heard about the strategy, it made Hartmann think of the teacher-led experiment 'The Third Wave' from 1967. To draw analogies to that time seems blatant. But the insight from more than 50 years ago is still valid today: if you divide people into subordinate groups, you are playing with fire.

In 1967 in Palo Alto, California, the American teacher Ron Jones initiated The Third-Wave experiment with a class from Cubberley High School. It was intended to demonstrate the spread of fascism … During the experiment, Jones showed how quickly and how lastingly a dictatorship like the one during the Nazi era can come into being.'[251]

On 7th June I receive the following e-mail from a psychologist colleague:

'I have a client - she is a teacher in a primary school. One of the girls in her class hurt herself and was crying, she ran to

---

[250] https://www.piqd.de/gesundheit/leihmutterschaft-in-der-pandemie-wie-geht-es-tragemuttern-und-babys-in-der-ukraine?utm_source=piq-Link&utm_medium=social&utm_campaign=user_sharing (retrieved 20/05/20)
[251] https://www.focus.de/familie/eltern/familie-heute/schule-kennzeichnet-nicht-infizierte-mit-gruenem-punkt-psychologe-schlaegt-alarm_id_12004568.html, (retrieved 19/05/20). Some background to the Third Wave experiment can be found here: https://en.wikipedia.org/wiki/The_Third_Wave_(experiment) (retrieved 10/10/20)

the teacher and said: 'Can you give me a hug? I can hold my breath while you do it.' Oh, it just made me cry. I could hardly stand it.'

Even people who previously had great trust in their politicians can no longer close their eyes to all these contradictions in the figures, statistics and arguments that are being put forward.

A video in the form of an open letter from a mother to the German Chancellor, Ms Merkel, has already received 474,000 hits on 26th April 2020. The mood of the people is starting to boil over. By 7th June there are already 690,667 hits.[252]

The psychosomatic doctor Dr. Hans Joachim Maaz knows the slogan 'without alternative' only too well from his life under the dictatorship of the Socialist Unity Party of Germany (the East German Communist Party). He urgently warns that the Corona pandemic is currently transforming democracy into a dictatorship of opinion and demonising those who think differently.[253]

It was a Thursday, 23rd April 2020, and I was working in my therapy practice, with a woman who grew up in the former socialist Czechoslovakia. Her parents were both alcoholics and they allowed an uncle and an aunt, who came to visit regularly, to sexually traumatise her. When they visited, they always brought smuggled-in alcohol and cigarettes as a gift to the parents. The thought came to my mind as to whether at present the Chancellor and the Federal President are not also selling their population to people from outside, such as Mr Gates and his entourage of vaccination maniacs, and leaving them open to these perpetrators for traumatisation.

The separation between the reality of the disease and the concept of infection is becoming absurd. The far-reaching consequences this has for human life can be seen in this report in the Münchner Merkur of 13th/14th June 2020:

'At an asparagus farm in the district of Aichach-Friedberg, 95 employees have now tested positive for the corona virus. This was announced by the local district administration office on Friday. After the first cases of corona had become known among the seasonal workers on the farm in Ichenhofen on

---

[252] https://www.youtube.com/watch?v=pgjA9E2HXWQ (retrieved 07/06/20)
[253] https://youtu.be/eY6nRA9oJkc (retrieved 20/05/20)

the Whitsun weekend, the health department carried out a test among the total of 525 employees of Lohner Agrar GmbH. Despite the positive test last week, the tested workers did not show any Covid-19 symptoms, according to the head of the health department, Friedrich Pürner. According to the District Office, all contact persons of the sick people are currently being identified.'

So people who do not show any symptoms of the disease are still deemed as being sick! They represent a danger to the world population, which is why the District Administrator's Office is immediately issuing a warning to citizens

'from the district of Aichach-Friedberg, who are planning a holiday trip, [...] to enquire whether regulations apply at their destination for people arriving from regions with an increased incidence of infection.'

Once one wrong assumption is made, everything else that follows can sound perfectly logical.

In many institutions, compliance with the Corona rules is now becoming more important than the actual work that they do, as this e-mail to me from 5th July shows:

'The majority of my colleagues are 'on the offensive', from small-scale whining to full-on masked-up inspectors and whistle-blowers. They follow the rules but they don't want to question them. The GDR is alive and well! The compulsory enforcement is for the sake of the company, otherwise the health department would close it down. To be against it or to inform? Please, where do I fit in?

As an employee of a large institution for the disabled, our approved 'Hygiene Plan' (the standard measures currently being implemented by the Sars-Covid-19 pandemic) has been in place since April and means obligatory masks and the 1.5m social distance for EVERYONE, in all rooms and corridors. Except for the period when we are at our own personal workplace. This is the reason people can temporarily remove their masks, while at the same time keeping the 1.5m distance between their work tables. Woe betide anyone who does not keep to it! I was threatened with 'breaking house rules', fines or possible dismissal, because of multiple 'complaints' about me.

Woe betide too any of our disabled people who gets up go up and into the toilet! There is only a maximum of 2 people allowed and they must be wearing a mask! As you queue for breakfast and lunch you must have a mask on, as you're served your food and go to your table – you must wear a mask. Once there it may be taken off - for the period of food intake. Or also at the outdoor smoking area ... there's no need to wear a mask there otherwise your lungs won't be able to breathe in the smoke properly!

Wherever you go – be it in the dormitories or the workshop –there are stickers, posters, barrier tapes, signs on the floor and hand-sanitiser dispensers and rubber gloves for personal use. Prior to this, all rooms had to be re-organised like a 'war hospital', in addition we are obligated to keep a 'ventilation log' for each room: four times during the working day for half an hour each time: and we must record in writing the date, who's doing it, when and for how long the ventilation is to be done.

Also, from 22nd June, it is obligatory that EVERY employee or participant presents a medical certificate from a doctor in order to be able to visit the workshop in its 'restricted normal operation'. This is required by the health authority and service provider. If there an application for emergency care (reason: it is no longer bearable at home). The doctor must confirm on the short form that the disabled person, despite his or her possible previous illnesses, will not experience a severe bout of Covid-19!

People with disabilities who need transport arrive early with their mask on or are driven home with it on, if more than one person is sitting in the 'passenger compartment' of the minibus.

I am really concerned and frightened by the enormously destructive energy with which the state is creating and enforcing insane laws and regulations on every operational, public-legal level and creating new institutions in order to manifest this 'Corona pandemic'! Basically all this just reinforces it by confirming the situation as they keep repeating it to be. That we are acting preventively against Corona regardless of any mental upheaval. What has happened to the power of facts? How can something so delusional ever be reversed? And who will be able to reverse it? Undoubtedly we are at a unique moment in the history of mankind. Where is the power to resist the 'mainstream' going to come from, when the 'virus pandemic instigators' themselves are so intent on seeing their goal achieved? The LAWS are formulated to serve their interests'.

The ultimate absurdity is that now one of the only scientists who has made an effort with his research team to shed light on the Corona story by means of empirical facts has had a criminal complaint filed against him.[254] This is then reported equally widely by the vaccine-alliance media.[255] Fortunately, the public prosecutor's office did not accept the charges, which is a ray of hope that this mafia-like behaviour can occasionally still be still met with resistance.

---

[254] https://www.uni-bonn.de/neues/111-2020 (retrieved 03/07/20). An English article is here: https://710keel.com/german-study-says-covid-19-may-not-be-as-deadly-as-previously-believed/ (retrieved 10/10/20)
[255] https://www.wa.de/nordrhein-westfalen/hendrik-streeck-heinsberg-studie-anzeige-betrug-nrw-virologe-coronavirus-zr-13819774.html (retrieved 03/07/20) An English language report is here: https://notrickszone.com/2020/07/03/criminal-complaint-against-lead-author-of-heinsberg-2020-covid-19-paper-dismissed-by-prosecutor/ (retrieved 10/10/2)

I Refuse To Play This Pandemic Game Any Longer

Twenty-Sixth Article - 12th June 2020

As soon as the last article I wrote has gone viral in the form of a 'Daily-Dose' on KenFM, [256] the swarm intelligence of the Internet community provides me with further information that sheds even more light on the Corona pandemic conspiracy:

- Dr. Tedros Adhanom Ghebreyesus turns out not to be the blank slate I thought he was. The human rights organisation Human Rights Watch [257] is making serious accusations against him from his time as Minister of Health in Ethiopia.[258] He is also alleged to have been involved in supporting Bill Gates' vaccination programmes in his country of origin.[259]
- 'Supporting the next level of German leadership in global health' - This is the title of a study from July 2019, by the Bill & Melinda Gates Foundation and the Charité Global Health, supported by the Boston Consulting Group, which develops the idea of increasing the share that the private sector and private foundations has in the health sector. The head of the Charité Global Health is Professor Dr. Christian Drosten'.[260]
- When it comes to the introduction of a digital identity certificate, it is again Bill Gates who, with

---

[256] https://www.youtube.com/watch?v=WtUP-colb1o&list=PLeJoe5WGh0K0Ly3rojKIwzXmg9XOIs-6B&index=2&t=0s (retrieved 08/06/20)
[257] https://www.youtube.com/watch?v=5yD3o6_QGJI (retrieved 09/06/20)
[258] https://www.ambapu.org/sites/default/files/2017-04/APU_opposes_candidacy_of_Dr_TAG.pdf (retrieved 09/06/2020)
[259] https://coronadatencheck.com/who-wer-ist-tedros-adhanum/ (retrieved 09/06/20)
[260] http://www.corodok.de/mehr-privatisierenstudie-von-charite-global-health-und-bill-melinda-gates-foundation/ (retrieved 09/06/20)

his foundation and his sheer immeasurable wealth, is forging alliances in this direction, apparently paying the best brains and corrupting them with money. For him, vaccination seems to be the best vehicle for making the introduction of a digital ID compulsory for all people, so that, among other things, it can be checked at any time who was vaccinated, when and how often.[261]

- 'The World Economic Forum, which is jointly run by the world's largest corporations, launched a global campaign on 3rd June entitled 'The Great Reset'. Apparently they want to use the Corona crisis for a fundamental transformation of the world in their own interest. The video statement by the head Klaus Schwab at the start of the campaign looks like a scene from a James Bond film, all he's missing is a white cat to stroke.[262]

- Even newborns are not exempt from this vaccination mania: 'In a GatesNotes post on April 30th 2020, Bill Gates even states that he 'suspect[s] the COVID-19 vaccine will become part of the routine newborn immunization schedule.'' In other words, a novel vaccine that alters your DNA and RNA - turning your body into an antigen-producing factory - will be given to newborns, if Gates has his way.[263]

- Bill Gates is confident of victory in an interview on 9th April 2020. The economic damage to justify his vaccination programme cannot be high enough for him. He talks about the biggest economic recession since 1929, or at least the biggest economic depression of his lifetime. Fear of losing his own wealth does not seem to bother him. He knows that he will be one of the winners if the world accepts his

[261] https://www.heise.de/tp/features/Ueber-Impfstoffe-zur-digitalen-Identitaet-4713041.html?seite=all (retrieved 10/06/20)

[262] https://www.youtube.com/watch?v=pfVdMWzKwjc&feature=youtu.be&t=4682 (retrieved 10/06/20)

[263] https://articles.mercola.com/sites/articles/archive/2020/06/09/newborns-and-coronavirus.aspx?cid_medium=etaf&cid=share (retrieved 10/06/20)

business model, curing infectious diseases through vaccination. He sounds defiant when he states: 'For the world at large, normalcy only returns when we've largely vaccinated the entire global population.[264]

- Politicians in Germany continue to link the end of the corona pandemic to the availability of a vaccine: 'The economic stimulus package adopted by the coalition committee of CDU/CSU and SPD on 3 June 2020 entitled 'Combating corona effects, securing prosperity, strengthening sustainability' contains a key sentence under point 53. It reads: 'The corona pandemic will end when a vaccine is available to the population'. This means two things: until that time, the restriction of basic rights will remain in place - in accordance with the decision of the Federal Chancellor and the Prime Ministers of the Länder of 15 April 2020: 'A vaccine is the key to a return to normal everyday life'. And the situation remains that, according to §20 of the Infection Protection Act (IfSG), paragraph 6, the Federal Minister of Health has the possibility to order compulsory vaccination, which is contrary to the right to physical integrity according to Basic Law Act 2, paragraph 2. Anyone who does not get vaccinated despite compulsory vaccination according to the IfSG may then make themselves liable to prosecution and, due to the assumed non-immunity, lose additional basic rights such as the freedom to travel according to the Basic Law, Article 11'.[265]

There is an article on the Swiss Policy Research website called simply 'Facts about Covid-19', it is fully referenced and brings together all the arguments which refute every detail about the Corona pandemic. One read of this

[264] https://www.ft.com/video/d6c22464-6dce-42eb-81d4-38e8b55d8c12 (retrieved 11/06/20)
[265] https://www.openpetition.de/petition/online/sofortige-aufhebung-aller-in-der-corona-krise-verfuegten-einschraenkungen-buergerlicher-freiheiten (retrieved 14/06/20)

should actually be enough to put an end to this unspeakable pandemic, if it were really only about the risk of infection by a virus.[266]

'Health' As A Front To Make Billions Of Euros In Profits

So is this corona pandemic really about human health? Are we to be protected from death by suffocation, whilst all the while not being able to breathe properly under these masks? Is it an expression of solidarity with the sick and the weak to be refused entry to shops, even with a certificate that states that that person cannot wear a mask? How on earth can this heartlessness, mask ugliness and ice-cold bureaucracy that is now spreading throughout societies still be considered an expression of philanthropy? The corona pandemic is certainly creating more suffering and disease than a highly infectious bacterium could ever do.

All the evidence suggests that 'health' is only the justification and front for making untold billions of dollars in business through billions of vaccinations and bringing humanity even further under digital control. Health or the fear of diseases of all kinds and the promise of salvation through drugs, vaccinations, operations etc. is to become even more of a field for huge investment than it already is. So that those who do not really know where to invest all their exponentially growing money wealth can make even more exorbitant profits. And this will be on the one hand, without any state supervision and legal restrictions, and on the other hand, of course, by plundering the state coffers and forcing them to accept the burden of the damage obviously caused by a pandemic.

Even conventional medicine, with its one-sided scientific approach, causes immense damage.[267] As a rule,

---

[266] https://swprs.org/facts-about-covid-19/ (retrieved 04/07/20)

however, the consent of the 'patient' is still obtained before medical interventions are made on his body. The monstrous thing about this new strategy of marketing the commodity of health is that the will of people is completely ignored and they are just considered to be mere objects for vaccination. This is still easy to do with children, because they cannot defend themselves against it. It isn't going to help them however much they baulk and cry when a doctor comes at them with a needle. Adults however are physically stronger than them. Adults still need convincing, unless you decide that a corona police force is to be used for vaccination. If we are now collectively forced by the logic of infectious disease to have vaccines injected into our bodies that affect us on a genetic level, then the physical and psychological consequences are incalculable. This whole vaccination mania project is in my view extremely culpable, abusive, sadistic and the highest violation of human rights.

Ways Out Of The Virus Mania

I wish that there were more and more doctors like this man who contacted me by e-mail. He wrote me the following words:

'In my studies and in my training as a doctor, it was important for me not to let myself be corrupted by the medical industry. So today, at the end of my professional career, I can still look at myself in the mirror and look into my own eyes'.

I wish that now all those who are fearful for their health and their lives were able to look at their own biography. And ask themselves, what situations have I been in where I was in extreme danger? Which traumas are still lying unprocessed in my body? In what ways do I ignore

---

[267] https://www.youtube.com/watch?v=jyemPnEstEw German Video (retrieved 14/06/20)

my healthy living needs? In what ways am I just functioning and participating in everything that's happening in the hope of being recognised and belonging? How can I change this?

Once again, my appeal goes out to all those who are currently involved in this Corona pandemic as trauma perpetrators: wake up, leave the path of your innumerable infantile concepts of the world and human beings, become more autonomous and more adult. Deal with your inner life. Return to your real needs. Endure the feelings of fear, anger and pain when your early childhood traumas come up. Leave other people alone. Do not try and pull them or force them deeper and deeper into the impenetrable web of your own self-created dependency structures. Discover the wealth within yourselves so that you do not have to chase the hollow money-wealth outside of you.

For our happiness and to experience true joy in life, we need closeness with fellow compassionate people who can think for themselves, we do not need your vaccinations.

Karina Reiss And Sucharit Bhakdi Have Done Extensive Research On All This

On 11th June 2020 I downloaded the new book by Karina Reiss and Sucharit Bhakdi onto my I-Pad. I read it in one go early in the morning. It reinforces the sources of information I have gathered over the last few months. The Corona pandemic is, objectively speaking, a complete false alarm. The damage it causes is much greater than the benefits it brings. The two authors also flatly reject the supposed salvation that will be delivered to us all through a corona vaccine:

'There is no point in trying to develop a vaccine to combat a virus that is not dangerous to the public, especially when partial immunity already exists in the general population. Moreover, if the virus or its 'strains' are constantly changing, the project is inherently foolish. In addition, vaccination can only strengthen the antibody response, but not the cellular defence, which is at least as important in corona viruses. In addition, older people often have a reduced immune response, so the corona vaccine would contain amplifiers, which always carry the risk of serious side effects. It is already safe to say that the damage from corona vaccination would be greater than any potential benefit'. (Reiss and Bhakdi 2020, pp. 171-173 e-book version).

Dr Reiss and Dr Bhakdi's book 'Corona, False Alarm? Facts and Figures' was released in an English language Version on 1st October 2020.

My Visit To A Beer Garden

At the entrance gate to my favourite beer garden, I have to fill in a form with my name and telephone number. As expected, the young person manning the gate does not know the answer to any questions I have about what will happen to my information in regards privacy. Once my details are recorded, I can then pass without a mask because I have a mask exemption certificate. The rule is to keep the mask on until you find a table. Then you may take it off. If you then go and get something to eat and drink, you have to put it on again. And you have to put it on again to leave.

I try and look as little as possible at all these faces around me disfigured by their masks. Visiting a beer garden is usually a pleasure for me, in part because I get to see so many beautiful women there. But with those monstrous rags on their faces, these young women look quite disturbing. So I prefer to look at the ducks, geese and swans that swim in the water and waddle over begging for food. In nature at least, everything still seems to be okay.

Then in the evening a cry for help comes in the form of an email from a woman who is almost at the end of her tether because of the compulsory mask-wearing:

'Dear Professor Ruppert, I am writing to you today out of desperation. You are my last hope. I am 60 years old and come from North Rhine Westphalia. When I was 14 years old, I almost suffocated as a result of severe pneumonia in both lungs. Since then I have been suffering from a suffocation trauma. As soon as I have anything in my mouth, nose or throat, I immediately find that my breathing is blocked and I start to panic that I will suffocate. It has not affected me all my life, because I have by and large been able to avoid situations that cause this panic. But since compulsory mask-wearing has become a thing, I suffer more and more from it. If I don't wear a mask, I am not allowed to enter a grocery shop and I am also denied access to doctors' surgeries. For three weeks I have had nothing to eat and only tap water to drink. I tried asking my neighbours to do some shopping for me but this has also failed. The people with whom I used to barbecue and celebrate street parties refuse to help me. They call me a mask refusenik and treat me as if I was the plague personified. I have tried to get a medical certificate, but they won't let me into any doctor's surgery to get one. Not even my high blood pressure is treated. Then today I've learned that Mrs Merkel has decided that masks should remain compulsory for the foreseeable future. For me this means that I have to starve to death. Please, would you be so kind as to issue me a medical certificate to release me from the obligation to wear a mask?'

I cannot give her a medical certificate myself, but I can refer her to a good doctor, which I do.

My Immune System Works Fantastically And It's Mine!

Twenty-Seventh Article – 21st June 2020

The Virus

There are two main factors involved when an infection occurs:

- An infectious germ (bacterium, fungus, virus etc.) - which is called a pathogen.
- A host body (the living - in this case human - organism) colonised by the potential pathogen.

The number of infections, diseases and deaths that result depends on the type of microbe and the host body's immune system, in other words, the interaction between the two.

In the corona pandemic we have a corona virus as a potential pathogen. Corona viruses have long been known in virology. Like all viruses, they mutate. Now, apparently at the end of 2019 and the beginning of 2020, there was a 'novel' corona virus, the novelty of which probably consisted in its having slightly modified grappling hooks ('spike molecules') with which it can gain access to the cells of a human host body. If it succeeds in establishing itself in a host body and multiplying there by invading many of the host body's cells and inducing them to replicate its genetic structure, the host body may also excrete these new viruses, especially in the form of moist exhaled air. This type of corona virus, like all related viruses of the same family, can pass from one host body to another.

The Host Body

If we look at the host body there are three possibilities as to what happens when it encounters the virus:

- It could lead to a superficial colonisation of the host body with this corona virus.
- There could be an intrusion of this virus into cells of the host body.
- There could be replication of this virus by the cells of the host body in large numbers.

Which one of these actually happens depends on the response of the host body's immune system:

- The corona virus only remains on the surface of the body because the B cells of the immune system produce sufficient numbers of antibodies to prevent the virus from penetrating the cells with its spikes.
- The virus manages to penetrate into body cells, but the cells are strengthened by the so-called helper cells of the immune system in such a way that they manage to keep the intruder at bay without dying themselves.
- The virus succeeds in boarding host cells in large numbers, forcing them to replicate so that they can no longer defend themselves against it. Then the T-killer cells of the host body's immune system come into play and kill these cells infected by the corona virus.
- If this infection of cells by the virus get out of hand and the T-killer cells can no longer keep up with the killing of the infected cells, a fourth stage of the immune defence comes into effect, the scavenger cells. These now destroy both the infected and healthy cells at the site of infection, e.g. in the throat or lungs. This is an 'ultima ratio' with the intention of saving the entire organism from its demise by locally destroying body tissue. This is often successful and the host body then needs time to recover from its wounds. Scars may also be left behind.

The Relationship Between Pathogens And Immune Response

So because it comes down to the relationship between a virus and a host body, it makes no sense to describe a virus per se as 'novel', 'highly infectious' or even 'deadly'. The corona virus that caused the pandemic was defined at the outset as the causative agent of a serious respiratory disease: SARS = 'Severe Acute Respiratory Syndrome'. This is misleading because it gives rise to the idea that this pathogen can and will always and everywhere cause serious respiratory diseases. However, this is only true if the immune system of a host body fails completely on all four levels of defence. So:

- If the B-Cells do not prevent the pathogen from entering the cells of the host body.
- If the helper cells are unable to give the body cells enough support,
- If the killer cells do not succeed in killing overwhelmed infected cells fast enough,
- If the phagocytes fail to contain local sources of infection and in their actions carry out large-scale destruction of cell tissue to prevent the rest of the organism from deteriorating.

So, when this corona virus causes a corona virus disease (corona virus disease = covid), this initially only shows that all necessary stages of a host body's immune defence are highly active. Only if all attempts by the immune system to contain the virus fail to stop it from spreading in the host cells can the host body fail completely. How often this happens depends on various conditions:

- General immune status of the host body, which may be compromised, particularly due to its advanced age.
- Other strains on the host body's immune system caused by other factors such as toxins in the air we

breathe, food, pre-existing illnesses, interpersonal conflicts, etc. in other words, everything that is known to weaken the human immune system and block its activities.

- Wrong medical treatments and psychological stress and trauma factors also play a major role in this.

Corona Patients And Deaths?

Whether there is a specific corona virus disease ('Covid-19') at all is questionable because the symptoms referred to here (inflammation of the mouth, throat and lungs) can also be caused by other factors (e.g. bacteria or influenza viruses). If something like a rapidly occurring oxygen deficiency can be attributed to this viral infection, this problem can probably be best remedied by administering blood-thinning agents and under no circumstances by emergency ventilation on a lung machine.[268]

Furthermore, the attribution of a death to this corona virus is arbitrary as long as no autopsy is actually carried out on the person who has died, which only happens in the rarest of cases. Even with the annual waves of influenza, the number of influenza victims is not proven by autopsies in individual cases, but is roughly estimated by a summary assessment of the so-called excess mortality.

Conversely, it is also not possible to determine how many people do not fall ill or are actually saved from death as a result of a voluntary flu vaccination. In this way, the death figures given in connection with 'Corona' are nothing more than wild speculation.

The Role Of Medicine

Medical treatments that hinder and weaken the immune system in its work are of fundamental concern. These include:

---

[268] https://healthcare-in-europe.com/de/news/thromboseprophylaxe-blutverduennung-muessen.html (retrieved 21/06/20) In German

- Lowering the fever, because the general increase in body temperature serves to increase the activity of the immune system according to the rule of thumb, 1 degree higher body temperature = 100% increase in the activity of the immune defence.
- Preventing the removal of infected and killed cells, e.g. by taking medication that suppresses coughing and mucus and stops the nose running.
- Generally immunosuppressive drugs which quickly remove 'inflammation'.
- In the specific case of corona, this also appears to apply to chloroquine when administered to people who cannot tolerate certain proteins because of their resistance to malaria.
- The expectation effect also plays a role: people who are told that they have received an effective drug will become healthy, even if there is no active ingredient in that drug. This is called the placebo effect. And conversely, people become hopeless and give up when a doctor tells them that they only have six months to live, for example, if they are diagnosed with cancer. This is called the nocebo effect.

So in order for an infectious disease not to become serious or even fatal, medicine has to find ways to strengthen the immune system and thus promote the host body's self-healing powers. It already makes a difference when I tell someone "You are seriously ill" or tell them "Your immune system is currently highly active to help you get well again". The former weakens, the latter strengthens the immune system. A hopeful message promotes the conscious and unconscious defence of a person against an infection.

The same applies, for example, to mental illness. People who have been diagnosed with schizophrenia, with the message that it is genetic and that long-term medication is necessary, are caught in a downward spiral for the rest of their lives. If, on the other hand, you work with them to find the life-history cause of their symptoms, they will regain hope and get well again.

Is All This Now Forgotten?

By chance, I get an e-mail exchange that refers me to an article on the T-Online website (t-online.de is Germany's biggest news portal, owned and published by digital multi-channel media company Ströer). The article dates originally from 27 November 2019 and is entitled 'What Is A Virus Infection And When Is One Contagious?' It is largely factually informative and includes the following:

Cold viruses 'are distributed in the air as aerosols when you cough or sneeze, and thus easily reach others. If you get viruses in your mouth, it is no problem because you swallow them with your saliva and the stomach acid destroys the pathogens. So it is not a problem to drink from the glass of someone else who has a cold, for example. Kissing is also safe in and of itself. However, it can happen that droplets of the person with a cold get into the other person's nose or eyes while they are talking - these are the actual entry points for viruses from the air.

When are you contagious?
The incubation period of a cold infection is usually between one and four days. This means that you are infected with rhinoviruses, for example, and 24 hours later the first symptoms like a cold, a scratchy throat or fatigue can appear. As soon as symptoms like a cold, sneezing and coughing start to appear, others are at risk of being infected. You should therefore keep your distance and avoid shaking hands. Do not sneeze or cough into your hand, but into the crook of your arm or a handkerchief. As soon as your nose stops running and the acute phase is over, there is no longer any

risk of infection. A virus-induced cold lasts for about seven days. As a rule, you are only contagious in the first few days.

Reproduction of viruses
Once the virus has found a host cell, it begins to implant itself. It first attaches itself to the cell surface. The virus envelope then fuses with the cell wall and the virus introduces its genetic information into the cell. The cell then produces new viruses, which are then released.

The immune system can prevent viruses from attaching to cells. To do this, the antibodies of the immune cells occupy the corresponding receptors of the viruses and block them. Host cells that have already been attacked release a messenger substance to the surrounding cells, which inhibits the reproduction of the virus there. In addition, immune cells are attracted, which destroy the infected cells.

In this way, the body gradually gets rid of the pathogen itself and the infection subsides. Flu is therefore usually over after about two weeks without any treatment being necessary. However, the body cannot fight off some pathogens on its own.

These include the Ebola virus, for example, which destroys cells so quickly that the immune system cannot keep up.'[269]

It is now known that this 'novel' corona virus does not have the risk potential of the Ebola virus. Nevertheless, on 20 June 2020, the day I read this article on t-online, next to the article of 27 November 2019, there are also reports such as: 'Risk Radar Proves Corona Cases Are

[269] https://www.t-online.de/gesundheit/krankheiten-symptome/id_59645936/virusinfekt-dauer-ansteckung-und-behandlung.html#arten_von_virusinfektionen (retrieved 20/06/20)

Rising Sharply In These Districts' or 'Corona Outbreak:
These Brands Contain Meat From The Tönnies Factory'.
Is this confusing strategy intended to destroy the last bit
of rational thinking from the readers of the t-online
website?

The Role Of Testing

Detection of the corona virus in the current pandemic
situation is done by a PCR test. This test can only tell
whether fragments of the RNA of this virus are present
with a certain probability or not. A 'Positive' result means
that fragments of the corona virus are present. However,
this test cannot distinguish between:

- A superficial colonisation of the virus in a host body
- An already existing infection of the host body
- The degree of infection of a host body
- Disease within a host body
- And an infection that has already been overcome.

This test cannot distinguish whether the RNA structure
of the virus is present because the host body has just been
colonised by this corona virus, or whether the RNA
fragments are still present as a result of a survived
infection of cells. It is therefore unable to differentiate
between corona viruses with the potential to reinfect and
those that have already been rendered harmless and
'dead' by the effects of the immune system. Virus
fragments still detectable in a person's faeces are not
infectious.

   In order to find out whether someone has already been
through a corona virus infection and has therefore also
produced antibodies against this virus, a special test is
needed which determines, by taking a blood sample,
whether antibodies against the corona virus are
detectable there. Even then it is not certain whether

there is immunity to this corona virus or to another virus from the corona family.[270]

In any case, it is a completely short-sighted argument to say that a positive PCR test is a clear indication of infection and a sign of illness of the person tested. Here again, the calculation is made completely without reference to the host, i.e. its immune system. Even very elderly people can be tested PCR-positive, but still be fit as a fiddle or 'pumperl-gsund', as they say here in Bavaria.

Measures That Cause Stress And Trauma

In the corona pandemic in 2020, the focus has been on measures to prevent human-to-human transmission of the virus, mainly through droplets in exhaled air. This means that there have been:

- Social Distancing rules,
- Coverings for the mouth and nose
- Prevention of interpersonal contacts
- Frequent disinfection of hands.

This may prevent the corona virus from spreading in some cases, but it is naive to think this will bring an end to it all if the virus is so highly infectious that it has spread across the globe so quickly.

This containment strategy would also never work in the long term if this virus remained as highly infectious, because new outbreaks of infection could then pop up in different places, which in theory could then spread again like wildfire.

The only true way to neutralise the disease potential of the virus at the heart of the corona pandemic, officially designated SARS-CoV-2, can be through the actions of

---

[270] https://www.youtube.com/watch?v=6fa-FE7sDt4 (retrieved 26/06/20)

the immune system. This is true both on an individual level, in terms of the immune system of each individual person, but also on a society-wide level with the immune system of the entire collective. Once this corona virus is recognised by the immune system, it can then specifically target its defences to respond to it and in doing so a person protects himself or herself from possible infection and disease. In this way he helps to prevent others from being infected. With this we have then achieved so-called 'herd immunity'. Since corona viruses are not really anything new for the human immune system, i.e. there is already a so-called cross-immunity, this is achieved in a population within weeks and therefore relatively quickly.

The current containment measures have the major disadvantage that they weaken the immune system of the people affected enormously. The human immune system reacts to both physical and psychological stress:

- Fear puts a person under stress. His nervous system is flooded by stress hormones and because of the excessive production of cortisol his immune system is hindered in its activity.
- Being locked up for weeks on end, preventing movement and sporting activities does nothing to help reduce stress.
- Isolation and loneliness also put people in a high state of inner stress.
- Arguments and conflicts make people aggressive and increase such stress.
- Negative thoughts, e.g. hopelessness with regard to their professional future, also weaken the immune system.

In my view, the corona pandemic measures create a traumatising situation in which people find themselves powerless and at the mercy of others. They feel increasingly hopeless and therefore find themselves in a state of high stress, which they can ultimately only cope with by separating themselves off from their true feelings. In this way a separation occurs in the connection between their body and their mind. The supreme authority that the body has, which can tell what is good for it and what is not, is lost. This can lead to, among other things, excessive eating, even less exercise, even faster irritation in interpersonal conflicts, even more alcohol, cigarettes or medication etc. Children in particular also suffer from the stress of adults.

In short: the longer the pandemic containment measures last and the less that there is a definite end in sight, the more damage is likely to occur to health in general, regardless of the corona virus. The measures prevent people from dealing properly with their otherwise existing problems, conflicts and diseases. They drive many into existential ruin and some even into suicide.

Moreover, those implementing this agenda that has been set by the WHO and its national pandemic plans are using their positions of political power to bring it into being. Meaning that:

- Any practical resistance to it is prevented, if necessary by police force.
- Intellectual resistance to it is stifled by a press that only spreads the ideology of the highly dangerous virus and suppresses the crucial role of the immune system.

And so for many people they feel that the situation is out of their control. They then either become aggressive and rebellious or slip into a depressive lethargy. The longer the pandemic state is maintained, the more the whole society is divided into:

- Those who still rebel against their disempowerment or
- Those who cease to think for themselves and submit and resign themselves to what is going on.

Why Do Only Vaccinations End The Pandemic?

What is extraordinary is that from the very beginning, back in March when the pandemic was launched by the WHO[271] the only way touted for the corona pandemic to end, by the WHO, the national pandemic plans and from many ruling politicians, is through the availability of a vaccine, the development of medicines and even the implementation of compulsory vaccination for the entire world population. Once again, the calculation was made without any reference to the host body and how it was affected by the virus. It is made out that the immune systems of everyone in the world, without exception, are unable to cope with this corona virus and later other influenza viruses which may spread across the globe every year. Which is obviously not true, because

- 95% of people colonised with this year's corona virus show no or only mild symptoms of infection,
- Only a few people experience infections with signs of disease, and
- Only a few die because of a combination of unfavourable other factors that are exacerbated in the presence of the corona virus infection.

This feeds the suspicion that this pandemic is nothing more than a way to lead to mass vaccination of all demonstrably healthy people. This of course promises billions in profits for those companies that are now in the race for the vaccine. The damage caused by this pandemic cannot be great enough for this purpose. For only such consistent ruthlessness that continually thwarts the needs of life and freedom of all will create sufficient

---

[271] https://www.youtube.com/watch?v=zv9J0fKlhA0 German video referencing Event 201(retrieved 21/06/20). Here's an English language video outlining the simulation plans of Event 201 https://www.youtube.com/watch?v=t5H308HeuWc (retrieved 01/10/20).

pressure in the population to accept the vaccination as the wisdom of the last resort - for this corona pandemic and for all further influenza epidemics which will sweep across the globe every year.

The Undermining Of My Immune System Through Vaccination?

Vaccinations can only affect the human immune system. Whether they do so in a way that actually supports this immune system in its work, or whether, on the contrary, they actually hinder its wonderful work, is a question people don't seem to want to look at. It used to be the case that the way vaccines would work would be that the immune system would be stimulated in its activity by the introduction of a dead pathogen. However nowadays the direction vaccine research seems to be heading is towards a genetic manipulation of the immune system and this is highly alarming. Wolfgang Wodarg warns:

'In some of the planned or already ongoing clinical trials, genetic processes of inter-cell communication are being interfered with so that our body cells produce new substances that have so far been supplied from outside via vaccination. Our cells are to be reprogrammed into bioreactors for internal vaccine production'.[272]

When discussing the development of these RNA-based vaccines, it is let slip that SARS-CoV-2 is not quite as 'novel' as is always claimed.

'Scientists from the Paul Ehrlich Institute (PEI) report in a recent publication that there are certain epitopes (the antigenic determinant – i.e. the part of an antigen that is recognised by the immune system) that are highly consistent between SARS-

---

[272] https://www.rubikon.news/artikel/unter-falscher-flagge-5 (retrieved 20/06/20)

CoV-1 and SARS-CoV-2. This could mean that vaccinations targeting such epitopes could have a cross-protective effect, i.e. provide protection against different corona viruses and emerging viral mutations'.[273]

Any cross-immunity that our immune system has because of its knowledge of defending itself against already existing corona viruses has so far been explicitly denied in order to emphasise the uniqueness of SARS-CoV-2 and to justify the pandemic proclamation!

At this point one could certainly draw a parallel with the development of genetically modified seeds. The justification for this is also that certain crops should become immune to pests and the use of herbicides. But farmers who use genetically modified seeds are becoming increasingly dependent on the seed producers. They can no longer use their own seeds in the future. They are in this way undermined in their core competence as farmers.

Is this also what is going to happen to our immune system in future? Is my immune system currently being abandoned by the state and given to the vaccine manufacturers and sellers to do business with in order to take it away from me? Should something that basically works wonderfully anyway, namely our human immune system, be manipulated like this? It could have consequences we cannot foresee but could make us dependent on more such vaccinations in the future? In this way are they going to secretly dispossess me of my own immune system?

The Immune System Deniers

The Corona Pandemic 2020 is based on a corona virus, which has been singled out as an extreme danger because

---

[273] https://www.aerzteblatt.de/archiv/214122/Genbasierte-Impfstoffe-Hoffnungstraeger-auch-zum-Schutz-vor-SARS-CoV-2 (retrieved 21/06/20)

the containment effect that our human immune system would have on it has been systematically negated. The self-protection that most people already have against such a virus and, as can be seen, is quickly built up, is consistently ignored. On the contrary, this self-protection is even being targeted and systematically negated by the pandemic measures. 'Herd immunity' is devalued as an antiquated idea. All people are then, because of this, portrayed as helpless and at the mercy of this corona virus. They are persuaded that they are ultimately dependent on vaccination to save their lives and health.

In my view, the initiators of the Corona Pandemic 2020, with their death rate inventors, alarmists and immune system deniers, are themselves like a disease. They have conspired, consciously and unconsciously, to systematically undermine and even weaken the human immune system. They want to sell us their 'modern' vaccines and plunder the state coffers on an unprecedented scale, and this has already begun. In order to implement this new business idea, they even tolerate the immense economic costs for the currently still relatively healthy economies. Whether this parasitic calculation will work out against the host body, in other words whether in the long term they are able to remain healthy states with healthy economies, is entirely unknown. Perhaps the host body will soon collapse under the gigantic burden of debt caused by the vaccine trafficker viruses, and then it will be bankrupt and lose its internal cohesion. Anyone who traumatises babies, toddlers, schoolchildren, young people, students, workers, employees, mothers and fathers, old and sick people so comprehensively traumatises a whole society.

Sleepwalking Into Delusion

If someone is waging a war against viruses, which by definition are not living organisms in their own right but can only survive once latched onto a host body, then this war is at heart always a campaign against living organisms, in other words, against humans themselves. In the witch hunt for these ominous viruses, people are killed in extreme cases. If society leaves the path of rational argumentation and follows such delusional ideas of a supposedly unpredictable killer virus, it leads to believers and non-believers starting to fight each other, first only with words but that could soon escalate and that is not a future worth living in. Here in Germany in particular we should have learned all this from our painful experiences with both fascism and communism.

Despite all this there do still exist the voices of some sensible scientists: 'So: Sars-Cov-2 isn't all that new, but merely a seasonal cold virus that mutated and disappears in summer, as all cold viruses do — which is what we're observing globally right now,' so says the well-respected Professor Dr. Beda M. Stadler, the former director of the Institute for Immunology at the University of Bern.[274] But still we listen to the handful of pseudo-experts, paid for and appointed by the pandemic makers, instead of serious virologists, infectiologists and immunologists, and if these pseudo-experts continue to be left in charge, then the lights will soon go out everywhere!

Why Are So Many Going Along With This Across The Globe?

That the arguments of the pandemic makers do not meet the normal scientific standards becomes more and more obvious after three months of apparent debate around 'Corona'. Anyone with any intelligence can see the manipulation of figures and statistics, the contradictions and inconsistencies in the tests, and the arbitrariness of the measures. But why do so many people still take part and put on these unspeakably ugly masks, whose efficiency is close to zero if not even counterproductive?

---

[274] https://medium.com/@vernunftundrichtigkeit/coronavirus-why-everyone-was-wrong-fce6db5ba809 This is a translation of the original article (retrieved 15/10/20)

Fines of up to €25,000 and threatened closures of businesses naturally have an effect here. But what works most of all is the constant drumbeat of panic mongering, with which the virus danger is talked up and rolled out wall-to-wall across all the mainstream media. The creation of panic has an effect even on those who were themselves not feeling afraid for their health and lives.

I experienced it myself early on. My intellectual distance did not help me to avoid being emotionally unsettled by the flood of panic messages. It was only when I discovered in a piece of therapeutic work this child part of me, who almost died of hunger and loneliness shortly after birth, that this panic-mongering could no longer affect me so much. In other people I have worked with in IoPT therapy, the corona virus has been representative of a rejecting mother or an abuser, for example, and this is why we can become so emotionally unsettled by it.

So here is my suggestion for a little awareness exercise: Take a chair that represents your 'I' and take another chair that represents 'Corona', 'SARS-CoV-2', 'Covid-19' or whatever name you associate with this pandemic. Intuitively place this second chair in relation to your first chair. Then start with one of the two chairs, sit on it and feel what comes up. If it was the I-chair first, then switch to the pandemic chair and feel what appears there. You can then change the chair positions and, if necessary, switch back and forth several times. Make sure that it is not too much for you and seek psychological support if necessary.

I suspect that because early childhood traumatisation is a worldwide pandemic, even people in countries where the government does not prescribe coercive measures are getting scared. They even voluntarily distance themselves from their partners and children and insist on rules of distance. Such self-imposed lockdowns also take place in companies, because colleagues no longer want to get too close to each other for fear of infection. I have recently been told about experiences of this kind by friends from Brazil and Portugal.

My Conclusion: I Love And Protect Myself!

Because, after everything that I've been through since the beginning of the year, I feel that now I have managed to get a handle on what is going on and I am no longer afraid of being excluded from mainstream opinion. There are enough people like me who are alarmed by this Corona pandemic and are starting to question it and think for themselves and trust their feelings that something is very wrong here. With them I know that I am in good company.

In the face of assault from this globally traumatising insanity, there can only be one response, which is that, in spite of everything you say and do, I still have my own immune system, which is doing me wonderful service in relation to this corona virus and will continue to do so. If I need medical or psychological help, I will contact you. And, no thanks, I certainly do not need this corona vaccination.

In the meantime, until this pandemic is over, in order not to further undermine my physical and psychological immune system, I'm taking it easy. I'm going to avert my eyes from the terrifying pictures in the mainstream media, I'm going to close my ears to the drumming of the panic-makers. I also know that there can be exaggerated scaremongering by some who are now in the resistance and that this does me no good either. I'm going to try to use my common sense by reading thoughtful non-fiction books according to Kant's motto of the Enlightenment. In 1783 Immanuel Kant wrote, in an article in the 'Berlin Monthly':

'It is not the lack of understanding but indecision and a lack of courage to use one's own mind without another's guidance. Dare to know! (Sapere aude.) 'Have the courage to use your own understanding,' is therefore the motto of the enlightenment.

Laziness and cowardice are the reasons why so many people gladly remain children all their lives, long after nature has freed them from needing external guidance. This is why it is so easy for others to set themselves up as guardians. It is so comfortable to be a minor. If I have a book that thinks for me, a pastor who acts as my conscience, a physician who prescribes my diet, and so on--then I have no need to exert myself. I have no need to think, if only I can pay; others will take care of that whole disagreeable business for me'.[275]

So from now on I will only do what is good for me and my immune system. I will find my own personal joy in life in by being in contact with the other living things that surround me. I will objectively clarify what I consider to be reality and what is delusion. I will take pleasure in entering into dialogue with others who want to listen and think for themselves. Real health and true human solidarity can only be found where there is a love of truth.

---

[275]https://en.wikipedia.org/wiki/Answering_the_Question:_What_Is_Enlightenment %3F (retrieved 25/10/20)

Always Keep Your Distance!

The pandemic game continues to play out here in Munich: on stairs, in corridors, at supermarket checkouts, people are now backing away from each other, eyeing each other suspiciously as to whether the other person is getting too close. It's as if suddenly from now on, the very human need for physical closeness is experienced as threatening. I cannot and will not believe it. If somebody had specifically planned to bring human community into total dissolution, this would have been the way to do it: make people scared to death to get too close to each other and to touch each other! I'm left asking myself, what will it be like at the end of all this - whenever that will be – for all these people who have been made frightened of other people?

When I cycle to my practice, I sometimes think the air is a little clearer and cleaner. But then it doesn't take long for one of the few vehicles that are out on the road to drive past me and blow its unfiltered diesel exhaust out into the air and this little moment of tranquillity is over again.

I try and remind myself that, after all, things here in Munich are not yet as bad as they are in Bombay, where the police pull people off their motorbikes and beat them up on the open road, making them kneel down as punishment and beg for mercy. But please remember, it's all for your own good and all in the name of health! A student's Bachelor's thesis on the cruel patriarchal conditions in India (Mühlbauer 2020) had at least mentally prepared me for the fact that such images are probably nothing exceptional in this heavily populated country, supposedly the largest democracy in the world.

While I was out cycling I came across the following picture. It breaks my heart to see what is now considered just normal advertising that beforehand would have scared everybody stiff.

Figure 21: This is what advertising looks like in times of a corona pandemic. It translates as: '2 metres is not enough for us. The Techem remote and wireless smoke detectors have an even greater range'.

The Vaccine Alliance In Power. Reality And Delusion In Times Of The Corona Pandemic

Twenty-Eighth Article – 30th June 2020 - Published By KenFM

The Master Plan

The Corona Pandemic 2020 has been in preparation for a long time.[276] The master plan that is being pursued is as straightforward as it is deceitful: people are being deprived of their old freedoms, allegedly because of a highly infectious virus. They will only get them back if they are vaccinated, genetically manipulated and put under comprehensive surveillance. Once this goal has been achieved once, the next time the new price for the old freedoms will probably be even higher.

All the arguments at the heart of the corona narrative - 'novel', 'highly infectious', 'lethal', 'specific disease outcomes', 'asymptomatic infection', 'overloading of health systems' - have now been refuted. They do not stand up to scientific scrutiny. [277] Even the WHO admits that infection by a person who shows no symptoms of disease is 'very rare'.[278] This would mean that the enforcement of all these measures such as 'social distancing' and compulsory masks are no longer necessary. Nevertheless, the master plan is unwaveringly adhered to: the pandemic should last until the vaccine is available. And so it comes as no surprise that the WHO's lapse into truth was immediately followed by a backpedal with the caveat that someone could also be 'pre-symptomatic' and infect

---

[276] https://www.strategic-culture.org/news/2020/06/28/2022-vaccination-passport-eu-keeps-quiet-over-suspicious-documents/ (retrieved 29/06/20)

[277] https://www.youtube.com/watch?v=Juugv0T7inc&fbclid=IwAR2gf1yvscci3HjgxEAwEiIRp4c9o_5kNJKpcAXe1SvXNRat8CODLcivqxU (retrieved 29/06/20)

[278] https://www.bbc.co.uk/news/health-52977940 (retrieved 09/06/20)

others during this time.[279] Of course, with the logic of possibility, as has been said several times in this book, everything can be justified. And whoever is in power can then impose his viewpoint by force.

Stress And Trauma In The Corona Society

On the basis of this fiction around a corona disease ('Covid-19'), the world population has now been put into a state of high stress since the middle of March 2020. Many people are even put into traumatising situations. While in stress situations there is still the possibility of fight or flight, a traumatic situation is defined by the presence of existentially threatening factors against which there are no longer sufficient personal resources to protect oneself physically or psychologically. This leads to the experience of emotional, psychological and practical overwhelm, confusion, feelings of helplessness, desperation, blind rage, resignation and an inability to act. In order to somehow survive physically and psychologically, people who are placed in a hopeless situation have to split internally because they cannot change the external situation on their own and are prevented from doing so by force. They lose contact with themselves, with their real needs and healthy feelings. They develop an exaggerated need for protection, which makes them more and more restricted in their own lives. They even wear their masks outdoors and when driving a car or bicycle, although this is not required of them. They become the henchmen of the pandemic instigators and attack others who do not comply by not wearing their masks.

The Man-Made Catastrophe

In psychotraumatology we distinguish between natural and man-made disasters. It is now clear that it is not this

---

[279] https://www.statnews.com/2020/06/09/who-comments-asymptomatic-spread-covid-19/ (retrieved 04/07/20)

corona virus that is now making humanity feel powerless. The immune system of at least 99% of all people on this earth has no problem whatsoever in rendering this virus harmless and immunising itself against it within days without suffering serious damage in the event of an infection. Those who really get serious problems are often additionally treated wrongly by orthodox medicine. It is the pandemic state with its false assumptions, panic mongering and arbitrary coercive measures, implemented with unrelenting bureaucratic inevitability by the WHO and most governments of the world, which creates the stress and trauma. The longer this pandemic condition lasts, the more people end up not only in stressful conditions that are harmful to their health, but also in traumatic conditions that make them helpless. In addition, many of them are being re-triggered into already existing old traumatic states, which they have up until now been able to successfully repress.

Stockholm Syndrome

In order to survive such situations of powerlessness, victims of trauma often identify with the views of the perpetrators that put them in this situation in the first place. In their heads, they twist the facts against their own interests and basic needs until they see their perpetrators as saviours and benefactors.

'Stockholm syndrome is a condition in which hostages develop a psychological alliance with their captors during captivity. Emotional bonds may be formed between captors and captives, during intimate time together, but these are generally considered irrational in light of the danger or risk endured by the victims'.[280]

---

[280] https://en.wikipedia.org/wiki/Stockholm_syndrome (retrieved 29/06/20)

In fact, the whole of humanity is currently being held hostage by the pandemic makers, from which they will not be released until everyone is vaccinated. People who are put under such pressurised fear, which is built up on a daily basis across the media, are increasingly giving up on their own needs and their own thinking. In the end they harm themselves through their own actions. They subject themselves to senseless restrictions seemingly voluntarily, but basically only out of their programmed will to survive.

The Child's Innate Love Is Exploited

In traumatising societies, perpetrators and victims form a conspiratorial community that fiercely resists the uncovering of truths because those truths would lead to a sense of shame for both the protagonists and the participants. As a counter strategy illusions of common goals are created. In this corona pandemic, the arbitrary curtailment of basic freedoms of perfectly healthy people is reinterpreted as an act of solidarity in a shared effort to combat an unpredictable virus.

To this end, the unconditional love of children towards their parents and grandparents is also being shamelessly exploited. The natural solidarity that children have for others is exploited and they are made to feel guilty that they could infect the old, weak and sick. Instead of protecting children and young people from sacrificing their vitality and their future for the panic and survival strategies of the traumatised previous generations, they are indoctrinated with the corona narrative in kindergartens and schools. The German public children's television channel KiKa even vaccinates children against conspiracy theories, which their parents could possibly infect them with. They should not believe these under any circumstances.[281] Normally this kind of thing only exists in totalitarian regimes. The Federal Government is

---

[281] https://www.kika.de/timster/videos/video82638.html (retrieved 29/06/20)

paying millions of euros for public relations campaigns to bring the fear of Covid-19 to the masses.[282]

Divided People

Traumatisation leads to splits forming within a person's identity. Fortunately, there are still healthy structures that can be used and activated. At the same time, however, within this person, the traumatised structures are also stored and they are kept in check by a third part, the survival part. The essence of the survival parts is that

- they are trapped in a state of chronic stress,
- they are endlessly working on symptoms and thereby
- they are always creating new problems instead of solving the old ones.

For traumatised people, the very meaning of their lives then becomes bound up with the denial of the reality that is too painful for them to recognise. Therefore, in their survival strategies, they can no longer distinguish between delusion and reality. From blindly keeping busy to meticulousness and obsession, survival strategies like these are manifested. In society at large this can be seen in the attempts that are currently being made to enforce distance rules in kindergartens, schools or companies, although it depends only on an external political decision as to whether and how long the pandemic state will be maintained.

Trauma Victims And Trauma Perpetrators

Children become victims of trauma because they are not wanted, not loved and not protected from violence by their mother and/or father. By being forced to give up on

---

[282] https://www.weser-kurier.de/deutschland-welt/deutschland-welt-politik_artikel,-bund-zahlt-100000-euro-gagen-fuer-websiteauftritte-von-stars-_arid,1831292.html (retrieved 29/06/20)

themselves and trying to adapt to their parents in any way possible, they hope, if they make enough effort, to finally be wanted and loved after all. It is a culmination of this self-abandonment that leads to victims of childhood trauma becoming trauma perpetrators themselves.

Since all trauma perpetrators completely repress the fact that they were victims in their own childhood, they do not recognise and feel when they turn others into trauma victims. They are then firmly convinced that they are entitled to make these assaults on other people. They convince themselves that they are doing good for their victims with their verbal and practical acts of violence. In the name of supposedly higher values (in the corona pandemic it is in the name of 'health') the greatest callousness can be justified. When trauma survival strategies are at work, the result is always the opposite of the stated goal. In the case of the corona pandemic, this means more physically and psychologically ill people, more deaths and even more perpetrator-victim spirals that will divide society. The lockdown measures are the disaster, not the virus.[283]

The Trap Of Power And Powerlessness

There can only be powerful people when there are also powerless people. If the powerless were in their own power and were not hoping for rescue by the powerful, then all rulers would be superfluous.

Those who strive to get power have experienced feeling powerlessness themselves, usually back in their early childhood at the hands of their own mothers and fathers. However, with all the power that they manage to acquire in the course of their lives, they can never undo and heal their own feelings of powerlessness from their childhood. They can only make others powerless. The greater the pain they experienced from their own powerlessness, the

---

[283] https://www.rubikon.news/artikel/der-lockdown-irrsinn (retrieved 27/06/20)

greater the need in them to make others equally powerless and helpless and to watch them suffer. Their acts of aggression are therefore not an expression of strength and greatness, but a clear sign of a lack of reference to their own 'I' and their own inner support and strength. Those who are with themselves do not need to rule over others.

If someone enters into this power game, they are at the mercy of its rules which are based on trauma logic. There is always the threat of someone who is even more powerful than you. You may work as part of a power elite against the powerless, but at the same time you are always on the lookout to outdo the partner you are working with, to build-up dossiers detailing his weaknesses, in order, when the time is right, to overthrow him in this race to power. The supposed friend of today is already the enemy of tomorrow. The ideal is sole dominion over all mankind. The higher someone rises in the hierarchy of power, the more they live in a world of permanent mistrust and hold increasingly delusional fantasies of omnipotence. They become more and more separated from the real world. The more powerful someone acts on the outside, the weaker and emptier they are inside. They become only a faceless mask of power. In the same way, all other people blur into an anonymous mass of human beings, which can be disposed of at will. Vaccinating billions of people like factory farmed pigs, putting them under constant surveillance and monitoring their state of health, then seems natural and logical.[284]

The way out for someone who is caught in this power trap can only be reached when they really look at their own experiences of powerlessness. That takes a lot of courage. But that would be true human strength.

---

[284] https://frankfurt5gfrei.home.blog/2020/06/25/internet-of-bionanothings/ (retrieved 27/06/20)

The Corona Pandemic 2020 In My Therapeutic Practice

The logic of powerlessness at the heart of the Corona Pandemic plays a major role in my psychotherapeutic practice at the moment. I work with a therapy method, which I call the 'Self-Encounter through the Intention Method'. For this, a person formulates an Intention and chooses a maximum of three elements from it for the piece of work that constitutes their process. She asks other people in a group to resonate with these elements.

In this way, non-verbal information channels, intuitive perception skills and bond-related dynamics are used to change things for this person, step by step, through this therapy. I will give three recent examples below.

'I Billy Gates'

A woman formulated this intention: 'I Bill(y) Gates'. It was comprised of two elements: 'I' & 'Bill(y) Gates'. She said she felt compelled to take a closer look at this issue right now, because she was feeling this murderous hatred towards Bill Gates as a contributor to the 'pandemic' and the dictatorial measures being imposed.

As became clear later on in her self-encounter process, she was confusing 'Bill(y) Gates' with her father, of whom she was still internally very afraid because he had sexually traumatised her as a small child. Rejected by her mother, she had for a long time admired her father because he was a musician and had impressed her intellectually. She had sacrificed herself to look after her mother, his wife, who was in need of care, together with him for three years up until his death.

Through the good contact she had with the traumatised child part of her, represented by her 'I' in this self-encounter process, she gradually came to feel the pain of the psychological, verbal, physical and sexual violence that she had suffered in her family. By doing this, she internally became more and more calm and self-confident. The childhood fear of her father completely disappeared in the course of the process. The violent trembling she had relaxed in her body, so that in the end the only thing that was important to her was her good emotional connection to her 'I'.

After the process, the person resonating with 'Billy Gates' wrote to me:

'I felt the need to sum up my experiences and feelings that came up for me during the self-encounter when I was resonating with 'Bill(y) Gates', as these 'insights' were very powerful and revealing. The following impressions, perceptions and perspectives from the Resonating Role are exclusively mine and do not claim to be fully or partially identical with the actual person of Bill Gates.

When resonating with 'Bill Gates', internally I found myself feeling very unsure that I was sufficiently mature enough when it came to the mammoth task that I had to successfully take on in public.

I felt called to 'higher things' and felt a real need to achieve 'great things' in the world. I didn't consider myself as a common or garden member of the wider human race, but saw myself as something separate and special, as part of an elite caste of rulers whose members live for generations mostly in the background and play a decisive role in turning the big wheels of the world.

My whole endeavour was directed towards taking an equal place in the ranks to my ancestors and mentors by proving that I was equally as great in the world as they were. My aim was to keep humanity permanently small, whilst also maintaining and expanding the global influence of the self-proclaimed elites and their great lords, that is all happening behind the scenes.

But I had a personal dilemma when it came to this task. On the one hand, I didn't feel that I had any special abilities or outstanding talents. My feeling was: I am not really very good at anything. But I had enough financial means and plenty of support from my backers. Even my computer software was always developed by others for me!

The other thing was, I had no inner reference of my own that could tell me how 'successful' I needed to be in order to get the recognition from my supporters that would allow me to feel equal to them. This recognition and equality, I considered to be vital for my survival and I was prepared to do anything to get it.

I felt a disapproving and disparaging attitude towards the wider human race. To me people were nothing but inferior playthings.

I had to eavesdrop on (monitor) humanity in order to always know where they are up to as regards their level of knowledge. Are they going to wake up? Are people going to recognise that they are being manipulated and suppressed?

When people are busy most of the time - just making a living, experiencing hardship and misery, getting entangled with each other, warring with each other and hardly able to see a way out of their psychological suffering, then these are the best conditions for me to successfully manipulate humanity.

When they are like this, they are receptive to my technological or medical offers of help as a supposed solution or way out of their misery (corona apps, vaccinations etc.). This doesn't in truth reduce the problems of mankind, actually in reality my offers of help make these problems bigger. But nobody should see through this or that in truth it's all only serving my own goal, to get the recognition I so long for from my elite caste.

When, in the course of the piece of work, the woman whose self-encounter this was and her 'I' (who both represented for me the wider human race) reached a moment of shared calm and connectedness and healing insight, I immediately felt an inner restlessness. For me these two represented the human race in general and the panic I felt was that if humanity felt this togetherness then that could dramatically worsen the global common base-line state that I needed humanity to be in in order to do my work. In other words, I was justifiably afraid that my hopes would be dashed and that humanity in this unified state would no longer be receptive to my manipulative intentions. In other words, social and above all personal contacts - face to face contact with touching/hugging etc. are the most dangerous 'opponents' when it comes to achieving my goals.

I immediately wanted to try to stop this close social communication. I wanted the people to get involved with something outside of themselves again, such as software updates, new operating systems, etc., so that any 'self-reflection' and therefore this human sense of community would cease to exist. Because it felt very dangerous for me.

On this subject, there was one really interesting insight that came to me when in this role, namely that the communication of only two people, analogue and face-to-face with physical contact, is many times richer in information on so many different communication levels such as on the biological cell level, cognitive, emotional, body language level and therefore has a much stronger effect on the human swarm intelligence than any digital communication via so-called social networks even though that may reach thousands of recipients at the same time.

When my mother (i.e. Bill Gates' mom) was finally included in the constellation, I felt like a 5-10 year old Bill Gates, who became afraid of his mother coming towards him and I spontaneously decided to seek refuge from her under a large rug. I shouted to her from my hiding place under the rug: "You were never there for me as a mother, and if you were, it was dangerous and hurtful for me". My mother agreed to this assessment without hesitation.

My mother also made it very clear that she needed me, her son, only for herself. In place of a true relationship, she lavished me with luxuries, so that later on, as a mother, she would have reason to be proud of me. I hesitantly accepted this offer, according to the motto: Better a mother with her own agenda than no mother at all.

These impressions may be passed on anonymously to interested parties. Best regards J.'

A week later I received another email from J. about the penultimate paragraph of his experiences as 'Billy Gates':

'I looked into this and you will not believe what I found. In the New York Times archive of 1994 there was the following article: 'Mary Gates, 64; Helped Her Son Start Microsoft'.

"Mary Gates, a prominent Seattle businesswoman who helped her son, William H. Gates 36, get the contract that led to a lucrative relationship with I.B.M. for his fledgling Microsoft Corporation ... She is widely viewed as one of the strongest people in this community for getting things done... Mrs. Gates was a director of several companies, including First Interstate Bancorp, U S West Inc. and KIRO-TV of Seattle.'

'I Want To Stand By My Need For Distance And Closeness'

In another practical case study, a woman was struggling with a contradiction that she felt that so far she had been unable to resolve within herself. On the one hand, she wanted distance and on the other she wanted closeness. The original need of every human being is the desire for closeness and physical contact, which every child has towards its mother. In her case, however, the mother could not be reached because of her own traumatisation. In her search for closeness out of her unquenched childlike need, her father and grandfather, both of whom were severely traumatised by their experiences in the Second World War, subsequently violated further boundaries.

At the beginning of her self-encounter, the 'I' of this woman was frozen in a state of shock. Her 'want' was extremely weak and panicky and had to back away and just felt a need for distance. During the process I myself was able to remind her that as a small child she had an original need for closeness and contact. This woke her 'I' up from its state of shock. Even her 'want' was able to give up its basic insistence on keeping a distance.

This piece of work also gave a possible answer for me to the question as to why many German women, who had previously protested against Muslim women being forced to wear headscarves and veils, are now suddenly wearing these ugly masks over their own faces. How many of them must have experienced sexual assaults as children? Are these face masks, like the headscarf and veil, now the expression of their own desire for distance to protect themselves from male assault?

'I Feel Great Anger About The Corona Restrictions'

In the third process I'm going to describe here, the current corona restrictions were the trigger for early childhood experiences of being left alone by the person's mother and being drawn into an ongoing struggle between her mother and grandmother. Her childhood was like a life in prison without any room to develop her own feelings and needs. For this 50-year-old woman, the Corona pandemic repeated the impression of being made an object once again, where her whole life just seemed to consist of being patronised and imprisoned. It was important for her in her self-encounter to see that, unlike then, she is now no longer a child and that she can maintain her own living space despite the massive 'Corona' restrictions on the outside and even expand it, and give herself more room in her life, by coming to terms with her traumatising childhood history.

A Field Report From A Friend

'This was the first time I'd been on the underground during the pandemic. I had an appointment with the doctor. I got on the train with the intention of consciously observing the other people there. What effect would this protective mask have on me and my fellow passengers? The underground was about a quarter full. There was silence, nobody was talking. Only the noise of the train. People were staring out of the windows or into their smartphones. There was no possibility of making any contact at all. Four months ago, the last time I took the underground, it was twice as packed and full of noise and emotions.

While I was on there I saw a father with a cap pulled right down to his eyes and a dark blue mask, characteristic for the current insanity of 'social distancing'. He was getting onto the underground with his son who was about two and a half years old. He had his son in a pushchair. The father took a seat with the pushchair parked next to him. The child was sitting up in his buggy with his feet stretched out resting on his dad's thigh.

He asked his dad why everyone here had these masks on. Unfortunately the father didn't try to give the child a plausible answer. My feeling was that he was overwhelmed by the situation. He just sat there, slumped down in his seat. The boy looked into his father's face, in which the only thing he could make out was father's eyes, apart from that he couldn't see any of his father's facial expressions.

How was daddy? How could I be myself? The child looked around, only empty faces or bits of faces. The boy seemed to be really confused. But then the child discovered his tablet. And from this point on, he just stared into the screen. What a welcome distraction not to have to feel the loneliness of this non-contact!

It touched me deeply to feel the inner loneliness of this child. I could feel it all the way across in my seat. I tried to really tune myself into the little guy – what must it be like for him? I felt confusion, where was I actually, where was anyone I could recognise? I was glad that I could put my feet on daddy's legs, that gave me a little bit of security. Actually I was afraid, but I wasn't allowed to show that. My father couldn't handle it either. I kept looking at the tablet to calm myself down, but somehow it doesn't work as well as I need it to. I'm still hungry, mumbling something about bananas, my dad doesn't really understand me, he says yes. Then I lower my gaze back onto the tablet. I suck on my dummy. 'What a peaceful, quiet child,' thinks my dad 'He's so well-behaved, he doesn't bother me!'

I wonder what this generation will be like in 15 or 20 years, or 30 years. How will this nightmare affect them in their lives? When I think about what can be seen in many biographies of my clients, how many traumas! And now on top of all that, this social distancing. Which traumatisations have these children of today already suffered in their short lives? Which possibilities of relationships can they have in later life? Are these children even going to be capable of having relationships? Will it only be a distanced relationship, as they have learned from the beginning? Perhaps the subject of 'healthy identity development' should be introduced at school. But teachers and politicians would first have to face their own biographies. So there is probably still a very long way to go before that happens.

Best regards H.'[285]

Observations From The Day-To-Day Life Of A Psychotherapist Colleague

'A client of mine is pregnant. And because she suffers from various illnesses, she had to take medication and is now afraid of having a handicapped child. When I asked her what she meant by 'handicapped', she said that she could bear to have a Down's Syndrome child. When I asked her why this particular feature was causing her stress, she told me that children with Down's Syndrome could not keep a distance. She said she had seen that a child in an institution in

---

[285] https://gesundcoach.tv/?p=12057 (retrieved 29/06/20)

Hamburg was put into a glass box 'to learn how to keep distance'.

Another client has a niece in southern Germany who is in 3rd grade. The niece had a homework assignment, which asked: 'Imagine that there are not enough vaccinations against corona in Germany! Who would you want to vaccinate first?' The little girl wrote: 'Mum, Dad, Grandma, Grandpa...'

I've got another client who has started, a couple of weeks ago, to take her 2-year-old son back to the day-care centre again. The children, who are already able to walk, have to walk alone over the threshold into the day-care centre and keep their distance from the teacher. They are not allowed to be welcomed or walked in on their parent's arm. The children who are not yet able to walk are placed in a buggy and pushed over the threshold. The centre only runs up until lunchtime so the children do not sit together at the table too often. The parents pack breakfast and snacks for the children. The little ones then all sit separate, far away from each other in the room, and eat. I can imagine that the children are left with this permanent feeling of having done something bad and feeling that they are being punished.

It is all these moments like this, that my clients tell me about, that bring tears to my eyes.'

Ed Tronik's 'Still-Face' experiments show very impressively how quickly children get scared when their mother puts on a poker face. The researchers then quickly stopped these experiments so as not to cause permanent harm to the children involved.[286]

But now, in a ruthless field experiment, children all over the world are currently being terrified of 'the virus' and brainwashed to a degree that they cannot defend themselves against. In this way, they themselves become watchdogs monitoring whether others wear these nonsensical masks and keep the supposed safety distance. "Mummy, the virus doesn't like this" or "Daddy, people without masks are talking!" are the words spoken by small children in Germany today.

[286] https://psychhelp.com.au/what-does-the-still-face-experiment-teach-us-about-connection/ (retrieved 27/06/20)

Using Every Trick In The Book To Keep The Pandemic Going

Although there is no longer any danger from the coronavirus SARS-CoV-2, the pandemic state in Germany is to be maintained by every means possible until a vaccine is available. For this reason, PCR tests artificially create hotspots of corona infections so that they can say that the risk has not yet been eliminated. Although PCR tests do not tell us whether a positive test indicates an active virus or a virus already rendered harmless by the immune system, they pretend that virus colonisations are the same as an infectious disease. This lack of compassion continues to drive many people to despair.

An acquaintance of mine from Gütersloh in Westphalia recently published the following letter:

'Dear people in the district of Gütersloh and Warendorf, I am one of your fellow citizens.

Those people who make decisions about the way we live our lives and about our health have been treating our lives with such a lack of respect and dignity for weeks now, destroying many, many economic livelihoods. They keep us in a state of fear and terror with the virus called SARS-CoV-2, which is supposedly so life-threatening for mankind. Every day it is repeated again and again.

These decision makers frighten me. Their inhumanity, which they disguise as care and protection. This too is repeated again and again. On some days everything seems so hopeless: they are managing to make us cause each other immense suffering and we consider it appropriate and necessary. I too am still dependent on this system for my existence and this experience is terrible.

No, I cannot and will not live in such a world. 'Real health and true solidarity can only exist where there is also a love of truth'. (Quote: Prof. Dr. Franz Ruppert).

I need people, not only through digital contact, but in my real everyday life. People who want to live and shape a society that affirms life in all its diversity, who want to separate themselves from this system that is so destructive to life.

M. E.'

Another person emailed me from Saxony, echoing these sentiments and telling me:

> 'A teacher tested positive after seeing her doctor. As a result, 3 of the 7 classes that had just been laboriously returned to school were sent back into quarantine and they were all tested too. Of these 50 pupils, about 16 were positive. This was the beginning of absolute chaos. Further tests followed, the whole school was closed, all public facilities and day care centres were tested, etc. The whole community was in alarm mode. But there was one thing missing: any sign of actual illness from even one of these many students who had been tested'.

Meanwhile, in the pandemic press, celebrities are speaking out, supporting the need for vaccinations and proof of immunity:

> 'Only those who present their second passport - the vaccination card - should be able to visit a stadium! Especially when I look at the ticket situation in football, theatre or other events, I can't see another way. I'll go even further: all activities, be it sports, culture or travel, should in future only be possible with this second passport. That's how I'd like to see it in the future'.

This is what Paul Breitner, the great German footballer (who played in the World cup when Germany won in 1974) said in the Münchner Merkur newspaper on 26th June 2020. Presumably he's been busy carefully weighing up all the arguments from virologists, epidemiology, infectiology, immunology, pulmonology and psychotraumatology before coming to the profound conclusion that there is no alternative to this personalised vaccination card in the future.

The Pandemic As An Opportunity For Me

This corona pandemic is also proving to be a good opportunity for me to break away from old habits that are not good for me. I am therefore removing Paul Breitner from my gallery of people I admire. In the meantime I have also cancelled my subscription to my daily newspaper, because it makes me sick to read all the one-sidedness and disinformation that otherwise makes its way to my breakfast table every day and invades my own house. I haven't watched the 'Heute' TV programmes or the 'Tagesschau' for weeks, which I used to do regularly. Talk shows have not been on my daily routine now for some time. That gives me a lot more time every day to do things that I consider to be more worthwhile. I also cancelled my membership to my professional association when I found out that they were supporting the pandemic game by offering psychological advice to its organisers. I concentrate even more on what gives me joy in life. Whilst researching on the internet I come across a quotation from Rosa Luxemburg. It reads: 'as Lassalle said, the most revolutionary act is and forever remains to "say loudly what is".[287]

Already in my book 'Who am I in a Traumatised and Traumatising Society?' I wrote in the preface that:

> 'None of us can 'save the world', and perhaps we should be particularly cautious of those who try. Every one of us has only a short snapshot of life within an unimaginable dimension of time and space, and we should, therefore protect this personal precious life from harm. We can even enjoy it in every given moment, as far as the respective international situation and our own life resources allow. We can protect ourselves from the insanity of other people as far as possible. However, in order to be able to do this we have to learn something important by working on our own traumatised psyche, so that we do not allow ourselves to be constantly pulled into the vortex of perpetrator-victim dynamics of others that can so easily be established within ourselves.' (Ruppert 2019, p.xiii)

I am glad about every person who now can stay in their healthy parts, because with these people a constructive relationship is possible. I am happy for everyone who uses the current crisis to wake up from their illusions and their trauma survival strategies and to recognise what is really going on.

I have now given my Psychotherapy Practise an additional name. I'm calling it 'A Space for Health, Truth and Joy in Life'.

---

[287] https://www.rosalux.de/en/publication/id/39794/show-us-the-wonder-where-is-your-wonder-1/ (retrieved 10/10/20)

The Impact Of The Corona Pandemic On People's Mental Health

Notes From A Lecture Given At The Extra-Parliamentary Corona Inquiry Committee - 12th July 2010

There Are Massive Restrictions On The Enjoyment Of Life

Singing, dancing, doing sports, celebrating festivals, visiting cultural events, travelling and much more, is prevented, hindered and punished by the lock-down.

Our Basic Needs For Physical And Social Interaction Are Frustrated

Elementary human needs for closeness, physical contact, love, social connectedness are frustrated, hindered or even completely suppressed by 'social distancing'. Purely virtual contacts cannot replace closeness that is experienced directly and in person. Compulsory masks create additional distance, fear, insecurity and subliminal as well as open interpersonal hostility. Old and sick people become even more lonely in hospitals, nursing and old people's homes.

Our Need For Autonomy And Freedom Is Also Frustrated

Prohibitions on going out, contact, work and travel frustrate basic needs for self-responsibility and autonomy. They create feelings of being patronised, subject to paternalism and this elicits fear, insecurity and anger. They impede the planning of one's private and professional life. They undermine the individual and collective feeling of security. Adults are put back into a dependent position, degraded to relying on alms, treated like dependent children.

Confusion Instead Of Mental Clarity

The coercive measures are purported to be scientifically justified but there is a widespread lack of empirical, scientific research. Instead things are based on arbitrary theoretical models and assumptions. Truth is not worked out as a result of dialogue, but is rather unilaterally determined. Features that are supposed to guide us are in themselves confusing:

- What does, for example, a PCR test actually tell us: that there is colonisation of the host body by the virus? That there is infection? That there is actual disease?
- What is the actual ratio between illness and death: are people dying because of corona or just with it? Is corona making people ill or is it killing them?
- What does the reproduction number 'R' actually tell us?
- There is the arbitrary prediction and threat of a 'second wave'.
- People become psychologically insecure and confused.
- Irrationality and the development of pure one-sided beliefs are encouraged.
- Delusions are created on a society-wide scale.

Generating Chronic Psychological Stress

Frustration of our social needs as well as our needs for personal autonomy, alongside this lack of mental clarity creates high and lasting inner stress. Stress is also caused by the loss of work and income opportunities, unemployment, the threat of losing one's home and so on. This stress is further exacerbated by targeted panic-mongering and psychological warfare in the public and social media.

Creating A Psychologically Traumatising Situation

Coercive measures with threats of fines and police action, a general sense of defencelessness because of the absence of political opposition and imperceptible legal protection, all combine to create feelings of powerlessness and helplessness. In the long term, this victimisation can only be sustained by splitting off from oneself and one's own needs. People then switch into a survival mode. The victims identify with their perpetrators and submit to them ('Stockholm syndrome'). Perpetrators are then experienced as saviours. Illusory solutions offered by perpetrators (vaccinations, medication) are accepted or longed for without contradiction.

Traumatisation Of Children

People are giving birth wearing masks. Parents wearing masks leads to an interruption of the contact between parent and child and this leads to contact-related disorders. Crèches, kindergartens and schools are forced to take senseless protective measures. Scaremongering, blackmailing and indoctrination of children. The children feel guilt towards their parents and grandparents. The pandemic measures reinforce existing social inequalities.

Stress And Trauma Situations

Situations of stress and trauma are also created for pupils, trainees and students who lose school years and semesters and are robbed of their future prospects. 'According to the study, 71 percent of the children and young people interviewed felt emotional stress in the course of the pandemic. Two thirds of those surveyed consider their quality of life to be low - before the crisis, according to the UKE, it was only one third'.[288]

---

[288] https://www.zeit.de/amp/news/2020-07/10/mehr-psychische-probleme-bei-kindern-in-der-corona-krise (retrieved 11/07/20). Other surveys across the globe about the health of Young People during the pandemic have found similar results. Here are the results of a UK survey from the charity Young Minds:

Collapse Of Social Cohesion
Pretending to create a false harmony between political leadership and the population, by citing high approval rates. The coercive measures lead to the formation of extreme social camps. Those who take part will be stirred up against those who resist. Images of the enemy are created: right-wing and left-wing radicals, opponents of vaccination, conspiracy theorists, pathologising and psychiatrising those who are protesting: 'esoteric nutcases', 'psychopaths', 'lunatics'. And on the other side, those who are so excluded from the mainstream often feel hatred towards those who are still accepted.

Conclusion In Terms Of Psychological Stress
The corona pandemic is creating the opposite of what it is supposed to do:

- It does not promote the health and well-being of the population, it undermines it.
- It generates a high amount of chronic psychological stress, instability and irrationality.
- It generates material, social and spiritual impoverishment, self-damaging behaviour, susceptibility to illness, disease, death and suicidal tendencies.

The corona pandemic is not an expression of philanthropy, it tortures people both physically and psychologically the longer it is sustained.

Conclusion In Terms Of Psychological Traumatisation
The orthodox medical system, with all its offshoots (government departments, agencies, universities, doctors,

---

https://youngminds.org.uk/about-us/reports/coronavirus-impact-on-young-people-with-mental-health-needs/ (retrieved 21/10/20) medical industry etc.), which is based on purely scientific, biological and technology-centred assumptions, is like a traumatised mother or a traumatised father who forces their trauma survival strategies – in other words their false and one-sided ideas of illness and health - on their children and makes them the objects of their survival strategy measures. This system traumatises people.

Conclusion In Terms Of The Psychological Effect On Personality
The orthodox medical system does not promote personal growth and emotional or spiritual growth in people. Instead of promoting self-responsibility for one's own immune system, vaccinations offer a false security. They do not help the world population as a whole to better health and a better life.

Conclusion From An Anthropological Perspective
We blame nature ('viruses') for what we as humans do to each other in terms of violence. We thereby continue to traumatise our bodies and our psyche and our environment. We have the illusion that we can repair our broken and traumatised humanity through technological innovations ('genetically modified vaccines').

As A Member Of The World Population I Have The Choice Between
Masks, panic, lies, vaccination mania, elite dictatorship or
A healthy 'I', love, truth and genuine community.

What If The Worst Case Scenario Is True?

Twenty-Ninth Article – 14th July 2020

Covid 19?

From the vast network of people closely watching what is happening in this Corona pandemic, I get forwarded a video. The person who sends it to me says, 'I don't know yet what to make of this - Fake or truth?'

In this video message[289], an American doctor, who has been universally recognised and loved by his patients, is first surprised that his health authorities ask him to give false information about the causes of death and, where possible, always mention 'Corona' as the cause of death on death certificates. The health authorities later accuse him of spreading false information about Covid-19. The video then cuts to a man from Nigeria reading out a text (allegedly from the Rockefeller Foundation's Lockstep 2010 plan) describing everything that has happened so far in the pandemic and what might be planned next. He says that this corona virus was first developed in a biological weapons laboratory in America, then via a laboratory in Canada, and finally ended up in Wuhan where it was released. They then waited for the virus to spread all over the world before the WHO declared the pandemic. This man from Nigeria is increasingly outraged by the plans to maintain the pandemic and the possible use of even more dangerous ('weaponised') viruses to keep people compliant with the lockdown and genetically modified vaccines. He therefore calls the pandemic a 'plandemic'.[290]

Of course there are immediately people who put their own video messages on the net refuting assumptions that the Corona pandemic is planned and dismissing it as fake

---

[289] https://www.youtube.com/watch?v=fiecPHpBTcI (retrieved 13/07/20)
[290] Excerpt from Thomas Williams THI Special Exposé Part 2:
https://www.youtube.com/watch?v=vEM6NLzg8Rw(retrieved 13/07/20)

news. They obviously want to continue to believe in the good that their governments are doing and protect them from such serious accusations.[291]

I realise how difficult it is for me to really believe that these whole worst-case scenarios could possibly be true, even though I do believe that the corona pandemic is being staged to help the vaccination business model achieve a global breakthrough. Could the people who might be behind all this, who plan and implement such things, really be so cruel that they are playing this diabolical game with the life and health of the entire world population?

Other Worst-Case Scenarios

It makes me think of all the other previously unimaginable things that I have already been confronted with in my 63 years of life here on this planet:

- 9/11 and Terrorism: Like most people, I assumed on 11th September 2001 that two planes had brought down the two towers of the World Trade Centre. That it was Islamist terrorists who hijacked these planes and then steered them into the towers. The possibility that the whole thing could have been anything other than this seemed unbelievable at first, but there are countless indications that the official narrative of the American government does not add up. The Internet is full of them and anyone who wants to can research this information for themselves.
- Anthrax: In addition, I am now confronted with information that the anthrax attacks in September 2001[292] may also have been staged by American secret services and the military to justify the war against Saddam Hussein, who was framed for the

---

[291] https://www.youtube.com/watch?v=TWpjc1QZg84 (retrieved 13/07/20)
[292] https://en.wikipedia.org/wiki/2001_anthrax_attacks (retrieved 13/07/20)

attack.[293] In plain language, this would mean that those who wage wars against 'terrorists' are terrorists themselves and do not shy away from terrorising even their own people.

- Nuclear Weapons: Although such weapons can turn the entire earth into a lifeless desert, they were still built and their effectiveness was tested at the end of the Second World War by the destruction of the cities of Hiroshima and Nagasaki. [294] These kind of weapons are still being developed and further 'modernised.' Their possible further deployment is not ruled out. Radioactive ammunition is being used in the wars that are taking place now. All this under the name of 'peacekeeping'!

- Nuclear Power Plants: Although they produce radioactive waste that will pose a radiation hazard for an infinite period of time, they are still being built. And even accidents at nuclear reactors such as Three Mile Island, Chernobyl or Fukushima do not lead to the discontinuation of this high-risk programme. Radioactive waste, for which there is no real safe storage, continues to be produced every day across the world.

- Deforestation of the Rainforest: Although all climatologists point out how important this forest area is for the stability of the climate, to ensure that our world is habitable, it is being further reduced: to sell tropical wood, to gain pasture for livestock that will be devastated within a short time, and to currently grow soya for the global market, which will then be used mainly for fattening livestock for slaughter.[295]

- Child Prostitution: As a psychotherapist, people have come to me who were sold as children by their

---

[293] https://kenfm.de/heiko-schoening/ (retrieved 13/07/20)
[294] https://www.youtube.com/watch?v=nsMrl4Rye-Q (retrieved 13/07/20)
[295] https://www.wwf.org.uk/sites/default/files/2019-10/WWF-UK_Retailers_Soy_Policies_October2019.pdf (retrieved 13/07/20)

parents to sects that worship evil and even torture babies in the most disgusting and cruel ways. After a while, I realised I personally could only work therapeutically with one or two of these people at any one time, it was too unbearable for me otherwise.

- Capitalism: During my student days, when I started to understand our economic system better, I realised that in the end it was all about the multiplication of capital. In other words, what someone owns in terms of property, goods or money is supposed to become even more property, more material possessions and even more money. I then understood that this only works if, on the other hand, there are people who are deprived of their living space, who own almost nothing and who work for a pittance to produce the goods that are sold in this economic system. This leads to the development of a world economy in which there are large corporations, agricultural, pharmaceutical, food, health cartels etc. and the mega-rich people who exploit the rest of humanity across the board and mercilessly manipulate and control it for their own purposes.

A View Of The World Left Over From The Dark Ages

The 'new normal', as repeatedly conjured up by the WHO, Bill Gates, the vaccine industry and their political players, is a relapse into the mentality of the dark ages. Although they are working with state-of-the-art IT and genetic engineering, their basic assumptions around 'virus' and 'disease' are based on primitive, monocausal thinking. 'Out there' is the devil, an evil viral enemy who wants to destroy mankind. We can only survive if God, or Bill Gates and his host of good archangels, saves mankind from this by using vaccines to recreate mankind by changing his genome.

In this way 'Covid-19' has nothing to do with science, which discusses basic assumptions, empirically tests hypotheses, rejects false assumptions and promotes a pluralism of theories. Instead, belief in this particularly dangerous corona virus has become a dogma that separates the crowd of believers from the unbelievers. Even the thousandth scientific refutation is sovereignly ignored by the believers. They wear their masks as their sign of recognition, wash their hands umpteen times a day, keep their distance from each other – these have become like religious rituals by which they can tell who belongs to their clan of believers and who does not. For their delusion that the virus is always and everywhere, the followers of this doctrine are prepared to sacrifice all personal freedoms and let their religious leader tell them what to do.

The was an old rivalry in science between Louis Pasteur (1822-1895) and Pierre Jacques Antoine Béchamp (1816-1908). Whilst Pasteur advocated his 'germ theory' of disease (killing germs would prevent disease), Béchamp argued a 'cellular theory' of disease – essentially saying that germs were everywhere and that 'when the tissue of the host became damaged or compromised that these germs began to manifest as a prevailing symptom (not cause) of disease'. He stated that the best way to prevent illness was not the elimination of germs but the cultivation of health. This old argument has now been simply decided in Pasteur's favour solely on the basis of which virologists have the most power and money behind them, in the form of the Bill and Melinda Gates Foundation. But even Pasteur on his deathbed admitted: 'The microbe is nothing, the terrain is everything'.[296]

[296] http://maronewellness.com/pasteur-vs-bechamp-an-alternative-view-of-infectious-disease/ (retrieved 21/10/20)

My Own Personal Worst-Case Scenario

It is above all in the 'terrain' of a traumatised child's psyche that the fear of 'evil' becomes most deeply rooted. Children take refuge in their survival strategies because they cannot bear to admit to themselves that in reality the greatest danger comes from their own parents. They also firmly believe that it is their own fault that they are not wanted, not loved and not protected by their parents and that they would have to change themselves in order to find favour in their parents' eyes again.

Up until the age of 50 I had believed I was a planned child. I was the son and heir of my parents. I'd been given my father's first name and therefore should continue the 'Ruppert' family line. But I didn't have any children, and this made me feel bad. One thing that mitigated it slightly and calmed me down a bit was that three of my siblings soon had children of their own and so the family tree could be continued. But then gradually as I came to understand what my physical symptoms, that I was being plagued with, were trying to tell me, it led me more and more to comprehend the way it really was for me as a child. My mother did not want to get pregnant in the first place. She tried to get rid of me during the pregnancy. And then during the birth process and afterwards as a mother she was totally unavailable to me - I couldn't establish any emotional contact with her. She only breastfed me for a short time and I almost died from a diet of powdered-milk substitute. I was left alone a lot. My whole childhood was a time of massive anxiety. My father was also not interested in me, but only in his sheep and then later his chickens and his house building project and he showed perhaps a little more interest in my siblings who came after me.

I eventually became a psychologist and a psychotherapist. This was more an unconscious act than any conscious decision. And so basically today, I find myself working with people who are also focussed on accepting their own personal worst-case scenario as the truth: they were not wanted or loved by their own parents, they were not protected by them from emotional neglect, physical violence or even sexual assault. I myself know very well what people can do in order not to have to accept this worst-case scenario. They may, for example:

- have some form of diminished sensory perception (I became very short-sighted, for example),
- become emotionally numb,
- hold a steadfast refusal to believe it all,
- have a belief that it is their own fault - if their parents don't like them, then they must try harder, to be good, to perform well, to do everything perfect,
- distract themselves with work, sport, politics,
- occasionally rebel against their parents, be angry with them but then have a guilty conscience about being an ungrateful child, who after all was given life by his parents,
- always believe in the good in people and in the world and work for a better world,
- want to prevent others from believing in worst-case scenarios, and on no account make them feel despondent and hopeless.

What If All This Is True?

But what if all these worst-case scenarios were indeed true? Suppose it was true that it is the same situation you find yourself in with the government you elected as it was with you and your parents:

- You are not wanted. You are actually seen as something useless or superfluous - an unemployed person, a welfare recipient, an asylum seeker etc.
- You do not receive any personal attention, let alone love, but you are still supposed to be there for the trauma survival programmes of those who are in power. You are allowed to vote in elections every four

years, and now you are supposed to behave and wear a mask and not question what it is all for. In extreme cases this translates as 'Your state is everything, you are nothing!'

• You are not protected from violence, but on the contrary, you are defencelessly exposed to it at the hands of those who hold the reins of power and who put a lot of effort into planning further scenarios of violence.

Why do parents enact these worst-case scenarios on their children? The answer is quite simple: because the same thing was done to them when they were children. They were not wanted; they were not loved; they were not protected from emotional, physical and sexual violence. And so, in this way, the old trauma victims of one generation become the new trauma perpetrators of the next. Because the trauma perpetrators do not want to admit the unbearable pain of their own victimhood, they idealise their parents and try to suppress the powerlessness they felt as children by trying to become powerful themselves. The very action of running away from their own feelings of trauma mobilises enormous energies in many people, and they inevitably end up in leading positions within a society: in politics, the economy, the financial system, the education system, the health system, the military and the secret services. There they take up the fight against supposed 'evil', a fight which, in their view, justifies everything: Caesarean section births, crèches, schools that are fixed on competition, nuclear, chemical and biological weapons, sophisticated control and monitoring systems. Deeply hurt and divided from themselves, these people then follow their misguided ideas with great tenacity. In order to escape their own inner chaos, they fight for a just world order as they understand it to be, in which neither diversity nor liveliness prevails, but rather a cemetery-like peace, in which the illusion can persist that everything should go smoothly and without resistance. The immense possibilities that information technology offers promotes this idea of creating a perfect world in which everything functions according to one's own ideas and everyone is supposed to believe that this is for their own personal good.

However, this will never happen, because these supposedly order-giving projects end up creating even more chaos. The inner chaos of those who indulge in such power fantasies will not be healed either, but will become worse and worse. In addition to the traumatic feelings they carry within themselves from being victims, they now also accumulate all the feelings of guilt and shame that inevitably arise from being a perpetrator. The healthy part of their psyche, which is still present in them, knows how much human life they already have on their conscience to bring such projects into reality.

So even if all seven billion people on this earth are vaccinated, digitally monitored and obediently undergo all other 'necessary' vaccinations that come along, humanity will not be better, but rather the world will only sink ever more into chaos. For me, the question then also arises as to what rulers and the rich really have to gain by ruling over a traumatised population?

A Virus As The Worst Case Scenario

The current corona pandemic is based on the assumption that we humans are dealing with a new unpredictable killer virus that can strike at any time and cause severe damage and harm to people. That this is obviously not true has now been sufficiently proven. So I think there must be a deeper psychological dynamic going on behind it, because it's as if everything that's possibly bad is still being attributed to this virus. It is basically our own human destructiveness, which is within ourselves, that we are then projecting onto a natural phenomenon. Especially our early traumas and the violent experiences that countless people have undergone, all these create a huge potential of suppressed fear around death, immense feelings of shame and pent-up anger, which must not be directed against the original perpetrators, i.e. one's own mother and father.

These undigested fears, feelings of shame and rage are then unloaded against perceivable external enemies – 'the Russians', 'the Americans', 'the terrorists', 'the infidels' etc. - and now, the latest in the list, against SARS-CoV-2, an enemy that is not even visible to the naked eye. The invisibility of the virus may in fact make it even more suitable for unloading our undigested fears onto because we can project all kinds of traumatic feelings that cannot find expression in normal everyday life.

The 'war against the virus' is immediately a war against the people who carry this virus within themselves and who can or could spread it further. So now all the inner undigested horrors of childhood can be directed towards the fantasy of a killer virus, whereby the virus basically only symbolises the perpetrators who almost killed you as a child. In the same way, the pent-up hatred and suppressed anger can be directed at those people who are not taking this threat of a virus seriously enough and thereby put everyone else at risk. This can then apparently justify governmental measures of violence on an almost unlimited scale.

Facing The Worst-Case Scenario

It has helped me a lot to look my own personal worst-case scenario in the eye, to stop suppressing my fears, to stop suppressing my anger, to let my tears flow and to feel the real pain of being the unwanted, unloved and unprotected child that I was. In this way I can also see the worst-case scenario in my fellow human beings and accompany them through the painful processes as they realise it bit by bit.

I can now also recognise as truth all these worst-case scenarios created by those who close their eyes to their own traumatisation, run away from it and drag other people down with them. The trauma perpetrators come and go, I have seen many in my 60+ years, both nationally and internationally. There are countless numbers of them. When one of them leaves the stage, the next one has already taken his place in the spotlight. So it doesn't help to fight against individual perpetrators. They are produced en masse by traumatised and traumatising societies.

Facing up to my own worst-case scenario means that I have stopped blindly following such trauma perpetrators, as I did in my childhood and youth. I no longer place my trust in them to make my life better. I prefer to turn to people who can look truth in the eye. I no longer need illusions to avoid becoming depressed and despairing. I know that there is a great need in every human being to belong to a community where he is loved and valued and in which he can express his love. I know that the fight against 'evil' will not produce 'good'. It is the acceptance of personal truth that heals. It is the expression of our own feelings, especially the acceptance of our own suppressed pain,

- which opens the way to true community,
- which makes battling on an intellectual level with other people's entrenched opinions unimportant,
- which causes the trauma perpetrators to let go of us and
- may even lead them to find their own way back to their own pain and to their real basic needs.

My future does not lie in becoming a better person or being perfect. I am perfectly fine as I am. I do not have to prove this to anyone. My goal is not to create a better world, but to find my way back to my own self-love and to connect with the people in this world who want to do the same.

What Good Things Have Come Out Of This Pandemic For Me?

Diary Entries:

I am writing these lines (22.4.2020) just as I have finished an online IoPT session with a client, who is a teacher. She is 60 years old and at the moment can only contact her students from her office at home. She is desperate because she is not familiar with the technology and does not know how to send documents or hold online meetings on her new computer. This situation catapults her back to the situation after her birth. She was all alone, desperate and so tightly wrapped up that she couldn't move and could only barely breathe. At the end of her therapy session she feels as if she has been liberated. She gets in touch with her own internal sources of strength and feels competent to master the technical problems that arise. She now also sees the advantages of online pedagogy in these Corona times. She is no longer responsible for disciplining her students or making them work. Learning is now more voluntary, driven by interest. She feels relieved of a burden that had previously made her chest tight.

I also see many advantages in online lectures and seminars. I don't have to be annoyed when students play with their mobile phones, I don't have to spend ages trying to persuade the projector to work, I don't have to bother with the different sorts of PCs at the university, the technology in my home office is all in my own hands. I don't have to get up an hour earlier in the morning to get to the campus.

In the meantime (15.5.2020), I even realised that holding our international IoPT conference in October 2020 online now has its advantages. We are not dependent on whether such a major international event is approved or whether the so-called second wave will be staged this autumn. Therefore our association, which organises this event, has made the decision to run the conference live online and we are planning accordingly.

Pandemic Makers Stick To Their Programme

Because of the shutdown of the whole economic sector, the following fear starts to grow in me: what if in all the speculation around financial capital, my pension now also gets gambled away. It is something which, up until now, I have just relied on being there without a second thought. On 16th May an article appears in the

Münchner Merkur newspaper with this headline across the front page: *Corona Empties The Pension Fund. Contributions Likely To Rise Soon - Billion-Euro Burden For The Federal Government Foreseeable*

Nota bene: It is not a virus that empties state coffers, but the actions of those who are staging the pandemic. They are cheerfully sawing off one branch after the other, branches on which not only they, but also their entire population are sitting. Without thinking about the colossal damage they are causing, they are mercilessly continuing with their programme:

'The European Commission has concluded exploratory talks with a pharmaceutical company to purchase a potential vaccine against COVID-19. The envisaged contract with Sanofi-GSK would provide for an option for all EU Member States to purchase the vaccine. It is envisaged that, once a vaccine has proven to be safe and effective against COVID-19, the Commission would have a contractual framework in place for the purchase of 300 million doses, on behalf of all EU Member States. The Commission continues intensive discussions with other vaccine manufacturers.

President von der Leyen said: "The European Commission is doing everything in its power to ensure that Europeans have rapid access to a vaccine that is safe and protects them from coronavirus. Today's step forward with Sanofi-GSK is a first important cornerstone of a much broader European Vaccines Strategy. More will follow soon. We are in advanced discussions with several other companies. While we do not know today which vaccine will work best in the end, Europe is investing in a diversified portfolio of promising vaccines, based on various types of technologies. This increases our chances to obtain rapidly an effective remedy against the virus. A vaccine would be a truly global good. We are committed to help secure access also for more vulnerable countries to find their way out of this crisis."

Stella Kyriakides, Commissioner for Health and Food Safety, said: "A safe and effective COVID-19 vaccine is the surest exit strategy from the crisis. For that reason, we have been negotiating a united EU approach to secure doses of promising vaccine candidates in recent weeks. Today's announcement of the conclusion of exploratory talks with Sanofi-GSK is the first important step in this direction, to provide equal access to the vaccine for our citizens.'[297]

At the same time, the objections against any corona vaccination at all are becoming more and more scientifically substantiated. Professor Sucharit Bhakdi urgently warns against this vaccination, because he says it would basically be pointless. There would be no need for an antibody against SARS-CoV-2 because cross-immunity already exists. This means that the immune system with its helper and killer cells can kill all cells infected with SARS-CoV-2. That is why 80-90% of all infected persons show no symptoms of the disease or if so, then only very mildly. The risks, especially of an RNA-based vaccination, are obvious. If such mass vaccinations were to be carried out, thousands of people would suffer lifelong vaccination damage, as has already happened in the course of the swine flu vaccination campaign.[298]

Fortunately, There Is Still Healing And Health Around Me

All the while I spend a lot of time in my beautiful garden and as spring turns into summer I have the opportunity to marvel at how everything in turn blossoms, withers and makes room for new things: crocuses, daffodils, forsythia, daisies, dandelions, tulips, irises, lilacs, vines, rhododendrons, lilies of the valley, poppies, roses, peonies, oleanders. In amongst all this, our two wonderful cats roam through the grass, looking for the most beautiful places to lie, sometimes in the sun and sometimes in the shade. And there seem to be more birds this year than in previous years. It is obviously good for the rest of nature when people put themselves in chains. Luckily we even have a swimming pool in our little garden, so that I hardly need to be drawn out into the world of the masked people at all. I hardly ever ride on the underground anymore and I more and more

---

[297] https://ec.europa.eu/commission/presscorner/detail/en/ip_20_1439 (retrieved 04/08/20)
[298] https://www.youtube.com/watch?v=0n8sqeWK_RI ;
https://www.youtube.com/watch?v=2wJQrkwlptA&t=195s; https://www.youtube.com/watch?v=LR6Ao-7UqlI -All in German (retrieved 04/08/20). A later English-language interview with Professor Bhakdi can be found here:
https://youtu.be/ZnpnBYgGARE (retrieved 12/11/20)

appreciate the relatively effortless freedom of movement that my beautiful e-bike gives me.

When I finished the manuscript for the first edition of this book at the beginning of July, I received an e-mail from an acquaintance who was delighted to receive it. She told me that a group of people all over 64 years of age, who allegedly belong to the at-risk group for this ominous corona virus, have written a petition in which they protest against being misused as a supposed object of protection in the corona pandemic.[299] Although I am only 63, I add my name to it.

---

[299] http://chng.it/b5jJDpwKCh (retrieved 04/07/20)

My Conclusion

The narrative with which this corona pandemic began in March 2020 has now been refuted in all its points:

- Novel Virus: This virus cannot be so fundamentally novel as has been made out, otherwise you would not have a situation where 90 percent of the people infected according to the test, suffer from only a mild course of the disease; a considerable proportion of them are even completely symptom-free.
- Highly Infectious: it has been shown that people who live together in close proximity do not automatically infect each other. Even in those countries that were extensively reported by the mainstream media to be hotspots of the pandemic, it was only certain regions and never the whole country. And now even the WHO admits this: "From the data we have, it still seems to be rare that an asymptomatic person actually transmits onward to a secondary individual,' Dr. Maria Van Kerkhove, head of WHO's emerging diseases and zoonosis unit, said at a news briefing from the United Nations agency's Geneva headquarters. 'It's very rare."[300] The argument that someone who is infected can infect others even though they themselves do not yet show any symptoms was one of the main reasons for the lockdown, social distancing and compulsory mask-wearing. If this argument fails, then there is no longer any reason for the freedom-limiting measures.
- Highly Dangerous/Fatal: in most people, this corona virus causes at most a slight sore throat or temporary loss of taste or smell. The mortality rate for the disease 'caused' by this virus is in the range of 0.01-0.3 depending on how it is counted. The vast majority of people who have died have many other symptoms of disease at the same time, and almost everyone is beyond the average life expectancy. 'A male child born in Germany today will live an average of 78.7 years. German women live on average 4.7 years longer, reaching an age of 83.4. Incidentally, the global average is considerably lower, at 70.4 years for men and 74.9 years for women. Within the European Union the figures are 78.3 and 83.8 years

---

[300] https://www.cnbc.com/2020/06/08/asymptomatic-coronavirus-patients-arent-spreading-new-infections-who-says.html (retrieved 11/06/20)

respectively.'[301] 'The average age of those who have died from the virus in Germany is about 80, and 87% of the deceased patients were older than 70' [302]

- Overburdened Health Systems: The 'health care system' in Germany was never overloaded at any time during this pandemic. On the contrary, many clinics, specially prepared for corona patients, stood empty and doctors were put on short-time working contracts. Patients from France and Italy were even admitted because of the excess space. In countries such as Italy or Spain, where there was a short-term overload, i.e. for one or two weeks, this was, in a large part, due to the overall ailing health care systems in those countries, as a result of austerity or disinterest by the respective governments. In 2020, for example, the USA plans to spend almost $738 billion on its armaments. [303] In order to maintain health services, most Americans will have to dig deep into their own pockets.[304]

- Second Wave: There has not even been a first wave. So why should there be a second wave? Experience shows that corona viruses do not become more dangerous, but more harmless as they mutate. Even Christian Drosten now admits this: "Perhaps we will escape a second lockdown," he said in an interview with Spiegel magazine.[305]

In reality it could all be so simple: people who are not seriously ill with the corona virus cannot infect others. Only if the viral load is high enough is there then the possibility that a sick person can infect someone who is healthy. That is why doctors and nurses have to protect themselves against infections. Whether someone who has to deal with a person with corona disease actually gets sick depends on many factors, which I have already discussed in several places in this book. In any case, this is not an automatic process. As long as the Vaccine Alliance does not want this old school wisdom to apply to this allegedly 'new' virus, then all this madness will continue to be

---

[301] https://www.laenderdaten.info/lebenserwartung.php (retrieved 11/06/20)

[302] https://www.voanews.com/covid-19-pandemic/germany-staggers-world-low-covid-19-death-rate (retrieved 01/11/20)

[303] https://www.theguardian.com/us-news/2019/dec/11/house-approves-space-force-military-bill (retrieved 01/11/20)

[304] https://www.zaster-magazin.de/gesundheitsausgabe-usa (retrieved 11/06/20)

[305] https://www.spiegel.de/wissenschaft/medizin/virologe-christian-drosten-vielleicht-entgehen-wir-einem-zweiten-shutdown-a-71724496-a9b5-4a26-aa1d-ecdf866c7f4e (retrieved 11/06/20)

organised with lockdowns, social distancing, distanced learning and wearing masks until ultimately vaccinations can be presented as an apparent release from the evil.

This pandemic has made it crystal clear: the orthodox medical system with all its offshoots (government bodies, research establishments, universities, doctors, the wider medical industry etc.) is like a traumatised mother who imposes her trauma survival strategies, in other words her misconceptions of illness and health, on her children and makes them the objects of her measures.

There is no justifiable reason to continue this corona pandemic. Therefore I want my freedoms back:

- My freedom to breathe freely wherever I go - without a mask over my mouth and nose.
- My freedom to exercise my profession as a university lecturer and psychotherapist as I see fit.
- My freedom to travel wherever I want, whether for seminars and lectures or for my holidays.
- My freedom to decide for myself whether I want to take any medical measures and what I consider useful.
- My freedom to meet with others and to express my opinion publicly.

Anyone who wants to remain voluntarily in pandemic mode can do so. Those who think they need a Covid 19 vaccination can have one. If you want to keep yourself in a state of fear, you can do so, but you are certainly not going to become healthy because of it.

I myself don't want to have anything more to do with it and I want to be left alone by all those who want to force their twisted view of things on me; who try to abuse me as an object of their misconceptions about health and illness and therefore try to use me for their ideas of domination and business; who always live in this mode of struggle and war because they cannot be with themselves; who enslave others because they themselves are enslaved.

I want a world where everyone can be a subject, where everyone has his or her own value and retains his or her dignity and has the chance to be at peace with himself or herself.

If Bill Gates were to donate me a few million for my Identity Oriented Psychotrauma Therapy (IoPT) and my Association for the Promotion of Healthy Autonomy Development, I would gratefully accept the money. If he did this, he really would be a philanthropist in my eyes. With that money, my colleagues and I could offer many destitute people a form of therapy that would bring them into deep contact with themselves. This work would be very healing, both physically and psychologically, and would actually be beneficial to health.

I am sure that there are still many people worldwide who do a lot for the genuine health of other people. Bill Gates could also give them all the money he doesn't need and still have enough for a good life for himself and his family.

Social Division Through Deception, Lies And Violence
Thirtieth Article – 6th September 2020

I started this article at the end of my holidays and finished it at home in Munich.

What Was My Experience In Greece?

Two more days here in Greece, in what I think is one of the most beautiful places on earth. Picturesque olive groves, blue sea, a beautiful house, dogs and cats wandering free, fresh spring water from the mountains, wonderful food, good wine in the company of dear friends - what more could my heart want?

Alongside all this, unfortunately, there's sometimes the noise of hammering and general construction work going on. New houses are still being built in this beautiful landscape. Although there are already many magnificent houses here, there are now also the numerous half-built skeletons of buildings that disfigure the landscape. Often no one lives in any of them or they just stand there empty waiting for rich people to come and stay for just a few weeks each year. They come especially for this purpose from Athens or England, Germany or Scandinavia. In terms of practical value, building a house and a home here therefore makes little sense. But when someone can earn money from it or speculate on turning a humble olive grove into a lucrative building plot, then it's all systems go. For people for whom money-making is the guiding principle of life, it is simply irresistible to sacrifice natural beauty when there is a temptation to make money.

Greece, the 'cradle of democracy' is taking a hard dictatorial course of action in these Corona times. In the shops everyone has to wear masks. As soon as we get to the supermarket, a security guard stands at the entrance and controls the wearing of 'face-coverings'. At an open-air market, policemen walk around and ensure that all the stall-vendors are wearing masks. In the restaurants and even in the beach cafés the waitresses have to hide their smiles behind face-coverings despite the sweltering heat and completely dry air. They always look scary to me among the unmasked guests, like people who are being punished and made to do hard work for little pay.

The already weak Greek economy is also suffering from the Corona pandemic. Tourism has undergone considerable losses this year. This means that many people, even with a few additional state hand-outs, are barely able to keep afloat.

Antisocial Distancing

But anyone who publicly doubts the corona narrative in Greece is punished as a 'corona denier' and a danger to public safety.[306] This policy has an impact on people's behaviour. They seem rather subdued, frightened and insecure. As the sun is setting one evening, I choose a nice spot on the sandy beach, but this causes the lady behind me to run to the small café nearby to complain that I am not keeping the legally required distance.

So as not to always be left standing outside the front of shops, I have a mask with me but I've written 'muzzle' on it. I like the idea of using this enforced and, from an infectiological point of view, completely useless mask as a means of demonstrating in my everyday life and so have been writing my own slogans on them: 'I'm completely healthy', '1984' or 'Corona vaccination - no thanks'. There's no limit to the fun and creativity you can have. After all, the Bavarian Minister President Markus Söder has his blue and white mask to demonstrate his political stance, so why shouldn't I? Speaking of Bavaria, I have just heard that first graders are now being given free school bags from the Bavarian state and each school bag

---

[306] https://greekcitytimes.com/2020/08/21/greece-announces-up-to-life-in-prison-for-violating-coronavirus-quarantine-rules/ (retrieved 28/10/20)

contains a mask. What was that story about the Trojan horse again? Timeo danaos et dona ferentes – Beware of Greeks bearing gifts.

Figure 24: An everyday demonstration – The word 'Maulkorb' translates as 'muzzle'.

The Old Wars Between Nations Continue As Normal

In the background to all this, the age-old conflict between Greece and Turkey continues to smoulder. The President of Turkey, Recip Tayyip Erdogan, is currently provoking the situation by drilling exploratory wells for natural gas in the seabed near the Greek islands, which Greece is claiming is its property. The Greek state is forming a strategic alliance with other Mediterranean countries such as Egypt, Israel and even the Palestinians. Threats of war are looming and sometimes we see fighter jets race through the blue sky above us. Under the conditions of competition between states and capital accumulation, discovering and exploiting mineral resources is still not a blessing for the respective populations, but rather a reason to feel afraid. The Greek military is mobilising and acquiring new military equipment, even though the state is already heavily indebted.

Contrary to Bill Gates' wishful thinking, national egoism continues to be the driving force for countries across the globe and not his idea of a common fight against the new enemy SARS-CoV-2.

The Demonstrations In Berlin

I follow the anti-corona measures demonstration that takes place on the 29th August in Berlin via email messages from the Rubikon and through various live streams. It's a day of ups and downs. To start with I was very disappointed that demonstrations by right-wing groups looked like they were going to be allowed, whereas demonstration by the Querdenken group was to be banned. (The Stuttgart based anti-lockdown movement 'Querdenken' literally translates as 'Lateral Thinking'). I'm relieved when lawyers for the Querdenken Movement manage to ensure that their demonstration is allowed to take place after all. But on the day of the demonstration, again the frustration mounts as the police refuse to allow the march to start, crowding people together and then claiming that social-distancing is not being kept and that the demonstration must be stopped. This is followed by relief that the people will not let themselves be provoked by the police and that the demonstration is not escalating into violence. Finally, there are the peaceful pictures of the Victory Column and the many impressive speeches, including one by Robert F. Kennedy Jr., who clearly points out the background and masterminds behind this corona pandemic.[307]

Unfortunately, the next morning, pictures emerged of heavily masked police, officers acting under orders from the Berlin Administrative Court, trying to break up a tented camp of demonstrators. Also a shocking video is posted of a 60 year old woman lying on the ground,

---

[307] https://www.youtube.com/watch?v=-u3H3PvebBU (retrieved 05/10/20)

surrounded by at least six martial looking policemen, one of whom hits her in the back twice with his fist before she is then handcuffed.[308] Will there now be spontaneous demonstrations with the slogan 'White Women's Health Matters'?

The Perpetrator-Victim Dynamic Is Escalating

After the demonstration, the mainstream media play their usual game. The number of demonstrators is reduced by at least a factor of ten to 38,000. No details are reported about their substantive arguments and justified concerns. Instead, the reporting focuses on the storming of the stairs of the Reichstag Parliament building[309] - possibly even co-staged by the secret services themselves.[310] This is seen as particularly embarrassing and shameful, especially in Germany, where in 1938 a gentleman by the name of Adolf Hitler and his SA-staff used the burning down of the Reichstag as a pretext for the abolition of civil liberties and the locking away of unwelcome opponents of the Nazi regime. There is considerable debate as to what hand the Nazi powers themselves played in setting fire to the Reichstag.[311] This well-known game is called a 'false flag', where you blame your political opponent for a crime you commit yourself.[312] As with so many things in this pandemic, the whole incident should urgently be investigated and

---

[308] https://www.blick.ch/news/ausland/berliner-polizei-wird-nach-corona-demo-mit-falschen-vorwuerfen-bombardiert-wir-haben-am-wochenende-keine-frau-umgebracht-id16071636.html (retrieved 21/10/20)

[309] https://www.youtube.com/watch?v=ABqWZBLVvj0 (retrieved 21/10/20)

[310] https://www.heise.de/forum/Telepolis/Kommentare/Was-ist-eigentlich-am-Samstag-am-Reichstag-passiert/Die-Geheimdienstaktion-vor-dem-Reichstag-ist-nicht-zu-kaschieren/posting-37329294/show/ A German forum post questioning the involvement of German Secret Service in the protests (retrieved 05/09/2)

[311] https://www.smithsonianmag.com/history/true-story-reichstag-fire-and-nazis-rise-power-180962240/ (retrieved 29/10/20)

[312] https://www.history.co.uk/article/the-truth-about-false-flags-from-nazi-germany-to-the-vietnam-war (retrieved 29/10/20)

clarified by an independent body.[313] But where in this system, which is so highly infected by money and power interests, are there independent people who can think freely and are allowed to do so?

The Trauma Of Being A Perpetrator

The statement of the Federal Government by the government spokesman on the Monday after the event is unfortunately a document par excellence on how people who traumatise others (i.e. the trauma perpetrators) exalt themselves as victims. The Head of the Social Democrats also sung from the same hymn sheet and spoke of enemies of democracy.[314] She said that the violence came from the opposite side and that we must therefore fight against it with all our might. The talk was of the police officers that were injured and not a word about the violence they committed. The social divide is therefore being deepened and this is coming from above. We, the government, are the good guys, the protestors are the bad guys, the enemies, who then only understand the language of violence.[315]

Shouldn't it be the task of a democratic head of state to bridge old rifts in a society instead of creating new ones? But this is how the perpetrator-victim dynamic works, as I have described before in my book 'Who am I in a Traumatised and Traumatising Society?' Trauma perpetrators not only traumatise their victims, but also their own psyche. They then have to constantly calm their guilty conscience and fight off the perfectly natural shame that they should be feeling about their actions. They have to appease their fear of being caught and then need more and more perpetrator attitudes in order to

---

[313] https://www.youtube.com/watch?v=TK72HH0eHuE German Video calling for investigation into the Reichstag incident at the Corona protests – (retrieved 04/09/20)
[314] https://www.theguardian.com/world/2020/aug/03/berlin-protests-against-coronavirus-rules-divide-german-leaders (retrieved 29/10/20)
[315] https://www.bloomberg.com/news/articles/2020-08-31/merkel-government-decries-reichstag-protest-as-shameful (retrieved 29/10/20)

survive psychologically. Unfortunately, there is then a tendency for them, in their increasing isolation and loneliness, to resort to more and more radical means in order to avoid being socially ostracised and excluded themselves. They must try harder and harder to disguise themselves as benefactors, even if what they actually do in practical terms proves the opposite. Being in the orbit of perpetrators means never being sure whom I can still trust and whom I cannot.

Basic Law Of The Land Versus Arbitrary State Measures

Fortunately, there does seem to be some good contact between the demonstrators and police. Due to their basic democratic training (they are 'citizens in uniform'), many policemen and policewomen in Germany are apparently finding themselves faced with a great conflict of conscience when it comes to acting against fundamental rights and exercising violence in the name of these senseless corona measures, which also of course have an effect on themselves. Several police officers have already made this known at Corona demonstrations and invoked the German civil law of 'remonstration'[316], whereby an official who has doubts as to the legality of an order given is obliged to raise these concerns. This is enshrined in law in Germany to ensure there is not the blind following of orders, which has had such historically disastrous consequences. Whilst there is not such a framework in English law, the Police Code of Ethics 2014 still states that a police officer 'will...give and carry out lawful orders only, and will abide by Police Regulations...There may be instances when failure to follow an order or instruction does not amount to misconduct. For example, where a police officer reasonably believes that an order is

---

[316] https://www.youtube.com/watch?v=vFs2Q-010Bg (retrieved 06/09/20) – Video taken down. https://de.wikipedia.org/wiki/Remonstration (retrieved 14/11/20)

unlawful or has good and sufficient reason not to comply.'[317]

To make it legally clear: due to the catastrophic experiences with the Nazi dictatorship, the Basic Law of the Federal Republic of Germany contains, with good reason, many paragraphs that protect citizens from the arbitrariness of the state. It has deliberately been set out to prevent third-party laws, such as the Infection Protection Act, overriding these fundamental rights. Therefore, we see once again the dangerous situation where power equals being right. Those who sit at the levers of power can easily create all the legal foundations to legitimise their interests. And by doing this they make themselves out to be morally justified.

The Road To The Corona Dictatorship Continues

In Melbourne, Australia, the government violence is escalating on an unprecedented scale, despite hardly any significant numbers of infections. The lockdown in the Philippines is leading to famine amongst its population.

The extent to which the Corona pandemic has already turned what was a democratic constitutional state like Germany into a dictatorship can be seen by the fact that there is no longer a public discourse in which dissenting opinions can be represented and different points of view can be discussed. The assertion that there is a dangerous situation of national importance, and therefore something like a state of war, is decreed from above and then attempts are made to justify it with scientifically meaningless statistics and non-validated test procedures. Hardly anybody in Germany or in other countries falls ill with what is called SARS-CoV-2 or Covid-19. Hardly anybody who is marked as 'corona-positive' by the mass

---

[317] https://www.college.police.uk/What-we-do/Ethics/Documents/Code_of_Ethics.pdf (retrieved 14/11/20)

application of PCR tests shows even more than mild symptoms of the disease.

Even a publication like the New York Times points out that this PCR test, on which this whole pandemic is essentially based, is actually just nonsense. [318] Mr Drosten, the originator of this test, might as well be reading the tea-leaves trying to make sense of the masses of test data collected, as he makes the confusing suggestion of reducing the quarantine from two weeks to five days to prevent a further lock-down in the autumn.[319]

Denial Of The Immune System By Using Confusing Language And Primitive Models

Vast numbers of scientific and medical experts do not see SARS-CoV-2 as a serious threat to the world population.[320] If you want to hear someone who is well versed in infections and the immune system, this speech on a talk show by Angela Spelsberg is warmly recommended.[321] Basically, an infection is something that only exists in relationship. And the pathogen must work hard to establish that relationship with the host body so it can create an infection – it must ensure first of all that

[318] https://www.nytimes.com/2020/08/29/health/coronavirus-testing.html (retrieved 04/09/20)

[319] https://www.dw.com/en/coronavirus-quarantine-germany/a-54811004 (retrieved 05/09/20)

[320] https://www.youtube.com/watch?v=pvJXm3Q891s&feature=youtu.be (retrieved 05/09/20) – Video now unavailable. But the number of scientific voices questioning the threat of Covid and the lockdown measures can be witnessed more and more with examples like the Great Barrington Declaration https://gbdeclaration.org/ (retrieved 01/12/20)

[321] https://www.youtube.com/watch?v=jtZkl5SAjOk (retrieved 05/09/20) On this talk show (in German) Angela Spelsberg talks about how in reality of the severity of the disease of Covid 19 is far less than the projections were making out early on and does not justify the lockdown measures because our immune systems already have the infection under control. In the UK Dr Mike Yeadon, former chief scientific advisor at Pfizer, has been making similar points: https://youtu.be/4FQUmw5QljM (retrieved 01/12/20) & https://www.bitchute.com/video/J0JWur5LNePt/ (retrieved 01/12/20)

it is not dissolved by UV rays and then has to overcome all the many barrier mechanisms of the body's immune defence (fatty acid mantle of the skin, mucous membranes in the mouth and nose, stomach acid, antibodies, helper cells, killer cells, macrophages etc.[322]). Then, and only then, can an infection, i.e. the multiplication of viruses in the organism itself, finally occur. So reducing the definition of an infection to mean purely the presence of a potential pathogen alone is unscientific in the extreme.[323] We can't be basing the actions we take that have such far-reaching consequences on such a crude model (Figure 25).

Corona Model

• Pathogen (P) = Infection (I) = Illness (Covid-19)

$$P \longrightarrow I = Covid\ 19$$

• The Pathogen must be controlled or contained

• The human organism is helplessly exposed to the pathogen without vaccination

• Individuals must be saved by virological experts and the government

Figure 25: The primitive model of the corona pandemic

This would be like me saying, as a psycho-traumatologist, that every death is a trauma for everyone, in and of itself, regardless of whom the death affects or what relationship someone has to the person who has died. If I said that people would object. Even when I do say that the vast majority of people are traumatised, people often counter me with the argument that there is a natural 'resilience' within us. Yes, that's true - age, social support, our own skills and ways of

---

[322] https://geekymedics.com/immune-response/ (retrieved 29/10/20)
[323] https://www.globalresearch.ca/what-is-covid-19-sars-2-how-is-it-tested-how-is-it-measured-the-fear-campaign-has-no-scientific-basis/5722566 (retrieved 04/09/20)

handling things are important factors when it comes to whether a person is traumatised by an external event or not. This is why most of the deep traumatisation that happens to us takes place when we are still very young and small and have hardly any resources to protect ourselves against the dangers and, above all, rejection and violence that comes from outside.

Political Action Is Shaped By Ideology Not Science

Mental confusion often begins with words. Basically, it makes no sense to speak of a 'new' virus. It always depends for whom a virus is new. In everyday life we think the same way: for one person something may be completely new, but for another it can already be old hat. Even 'highly infectious' is not a property of the virus itself, though the misleading name given to it of 'Severe Acute Respiratory Syndrome Corona Virus 2' suggests otherwise. The virus itself is incorrectly attributed to the reaction of the infected organism. But this virus does not appear to be highly infectious to bats, at least according to those who claim that the virus has spread from such animals to humans.

Science can only come to true knowledge if it is free of external interests and is only interested in researching facts. That is the difference between science and ideology, which is concerned with making the facts fit its own interests. Science enlightens, ideology indoctrinates.

The Pandemic Plays Out Against All The Facts To The Contrary

The health care system in Germany, Austria and Switzerland has never been overburdened by Covid-19.[324] Scientific analyses show that the lockdown and the

---

[324] https://www.thelancet.com/journals/lanres/article/PIIS2213-2600(20)30316-7/fulltext (retrieved 05/09/20)

compulsory wearing of masks did not change anything in the course of the Covid-19 epidemic - if it existed at all in isolation separate from a seasonal flu.[325] Meanwhile, the numbers of those who get seriously ill and die have to be constantly revised downwards. [326] [327] There are now completely different explanations for the supposedly horrendous death figures in the USA than the raging of the virus. Hospitals and doctors were apparently won over with large sums of money to write Covid-19 as the cause of death on the death certificates whenever possible.

'Drs. Dan Erickson and Artin Massihi of the Accelerated Urgent Care Hospital say: 'Hospital administrators might well want to see COVID-19 attached to a discharge summary or a death certificate. Why? Because if it's a straightforward, garden-variety pneumonia that a person is admitted to the hospital for—if they're Medicare— typically, the diagnosis-related group lump sum payment would be $5,000," said Jensen, whose claim was fact-checked by USA Today. "But if it's COVID-19 pneumonia, then it's $13,000, and if that COVID-19 pneumonia patient ends up on a ventilator, it goes up to $39,000'.'[328]

Even though artificial respiration in this way has been now shown to increase the risk of death.

[325] https://www.aier.org/article/lockdowns-and-mask-mandates-do-not-lead-to-reduced-covid-transmission-rates-or-deaths-new-study-suggests/ (retrieved 04/09/20)
[326] https://scilogs.spektrum.de/fischblog/warum-covid-19-weniger-toedlich/?utm_source=pocket-newtab-global-de-DE (retrieved 05/09/20)
[327] https://www.spiegel.de/wissenschaft/corona-stagnierende-todeszahlen-trotz-steigender-infektionen-das-deutsche-paradox-a-1c86a930-45c1-4b8e-b9f2-08716b57f630?utm_source=pocket-newtab-global-de-DE (retrieved 04/09/20) Here's a UK based example of figures being revised: https://www.bbc.co.uk/news/health-53722711 (retrieved 21/10/20)
[328] https://fee.org/articles/physicians-say-hospitals-are-pressuring-er-docs-to-list-covid-19-on-death-certificates-here-s-why/ (retrieved 05/09/20)

It is painful for me to observe how the public arena is now made up almost entirely of confused claims, frauds, lies and threats of violence:

- In Switzerland, for example, it is now claimed that a PCR test is a proof of infection, even though we knew this was not really the case from as early as May this year.
- A semblance of scientific accuracy is conveyed despite using completely unclear infection figures.
- Suggestive images are used to try to turn people who test positive into sick people, making out that they all immediately end up in intensive care.
- Scientists get paid for creating vaccination propaganda in the form of false claims and falsified statistics.

There are no evidence-based grounds for these drastic governmental measures. [329] From a scientific point of view, everyday masks are completely unsuitable to prevent air-borne infections and, on the contrary, even promote the possibility of infection. [330]

- Nevertheless, the Berlin Senate now wants to make masks mandatory for all demonstrations. [331]
- Nevertheless, compulsory tests are still being carried out.
- Nevertheless, masks are still to be worn whilst on the train, although the risk of infection is almost zero. [332]

---

[329] https://www.ckb-anwaelte.de/corona-update-17-august-2020/ (retrieved 05/09/20)

[330] https://www.deutsche-apotheker-zeitung.de/daz-az/2020/daz-33-2020/hauptsache-maske (retrieved 05/09/20)

https://www.independent.co.uk/news/health/coronavirus-news-face-masks-increase-risk-infection-doctor-jenny-harries-a9396811.html (retrieved 01/11/20)

[331]

https://www.rbb24.de/content/rbb/r24/politik/thema/2020/coronavirus/beitraege_neu/2020/09/berliner-senat-will-maskenpflicht-fuer-demonstrationen.html (retrieved 04/09/20)

- Nevertheless, children are to wear masks at school, even though a large study in Saxony proves that children have nothing to do with the infection and suffer enormously from school closures.[333]
- Nevertheless, universities are not being released to start up regular teaching again.
- Nevertheless, people who do not wear masks are being fined.[334]

The fact that left-wing politicians are also involved in the restriction of freedom and ideological indoctrination of children is still hard to get my head around.[335] The idea that we are being threatened by an ominous virus obviously has to be maintained by hook or by crook until the population can finally be offered corona vaccination as the supposed only solution.

Panic And Aggression - Rift And Domination

This arbitrariness of the state's measures and the daily panic mongering that is being propagated is driving people psychologically and emotionally insane. On the one hand, they hear the message that masks basically do not help that much - because they have to be prepared for the fact that only vaccination can really end the pandemic - but on the other hand, face-coverings have to be worn, because it helps maintain the appearance of a dangerous situation in which we are all at risk. People are called upon to act in solidarity and at the same time they are told that the number of infections continues to rise

---

[332] https://www.infosperber.ch/Artikel/Gesundheit/Pro-12000-Zugfahrten-steckt-sich-hochstens-eine-Person-an (retrieved 05/09/20)

[333] https://www.youtube.com/watch?v=oXuFN7WpuT4 (retrieved 05/09/20)

[334] https://www.bz-berlin.de/deutschland/beschlossen-mindestbussgeld-von-50-euro-fuer-maskenverweigerer (retrieved 05/09/20)

[335] https://www.freiepresse.de/vogtland/plauen/linke-schutz-verstaerken-artikel11040231 (retrieved 05/09/20)

dramatically and that they are still powerless against the virus.

People are left feeling so insecure but without anywhere to channel their frustration. So they turn their aggressions against their fellow citizens who, in their eyes, are not going along with everything without questioning like they are. It is not possible for them to direct their frustration against those who are actually responsible for the whole chaos, so long as they believe that all the restrictions are being organised for their own protection. This is why anger and verbal abuse is hurled at those who are on the streets demonstrating or why fights have broken out on the underground when someone is spotted not wearing a mask. Or when a customer is manhandled out of a shop or verbally abused or threatened because he refuses to go along with the obligation to wear a mask.[336]

Even scientists, such as this neurologist from Bremen, unfortunately do not refrain from preaching violence against those who will supposedly not listen to reason. He says that the only thing that will have any affect on these people who do not agree with the lockdown measures and will not listen to 'facts' is to lock them up and threaten them with 'state power and police action'.[337] It is in ways like this that the principle of arbitrary rule starts to bear fruit: divide and rule. Let your victims smash each other's heads in so you don't have to.

Against this background of division, it is like a small ray of hope for me when economics professor Christian Kreiß sends me his new book on 'Bought Science'. In it, he argues that the study of truth is in everyone's best interest. And that science that depends on donations from large commercial enterprises cannot be committed to the general good, because it must always be thinking of how

---

[336] https://www.youtube.com/watch?v=Y_O1MQ5h8HM (retrieved 06/09/20)
[337] https://www.rnd.de/gesundheit/corona-regeln-nicht-beachtet-bei-manchen-helfen-nur-drohungen-angst-und-schrecken-3NKFQP3ATLPEF7JILNM3SUDGCM.html (retrieved 21/10/20)

any research will benefit the donors who have funded it. These donors then pay very close attention to who takes what position where and this exerts a massive influence on the whole industry.[338]

At present, it is easy to see where private universities that rely solely on donations are heading. The Johns Hopkins University in Baltimore, the most cited scientific source during the Corona pandemic and frequently held up as one of the leading centres for scientific study in the world, has its three main sources of funding from Rockefeller, Bloomberg and the Gates Foundation. [339] Even the WHO is basically now just a private organisation, kept alive by those who give it their donations, for as long as it still protects their interests.

It is therefore like a ray of sunshine breaking through the clouds when I am forwarded a research paper showing me that some scientists are still taking a critical look at the current corona media coverage. In the paper the authors analyse

'two coronavirus-related programmes broadcast on public German television (ARD Extra and ZDF Spezial) from the perspective of media and cultural semiotics. The authors see these TV programmes as closed models of the world containing implicit norms, values, and ideologies, and focus on the crisis as a specific narrative model with negotiated social ideologies, cultural self-images, as well as images of others and the visibility or invisibility of social actors and groups'.[340]

---

[338] https://menschengerechtewirtschaft.de/wp-content/uploads/2020/08/Buch-Gekaufte-Wissenschaft-pdf.pdf (retrieved 05/09/20)

[339] https://www.isw-muenchen.de/2020/05/pandemien-korrumpierte-wissenschaft-johns-hopkins-university-und-ihr-global-health-security-index/ (retrieved 06/09/20)

[340] https://www.researchgate.net/publication/343736403_Die_Verengung_der_Welt_Zur_medialen_Konstruktion_Deutschlands_unter_Covid-19_anhand_der_Formate_ARD_Extra_-Die_Coronalage_und_ZDF_Spezial (retrieved 05/09/2o)

Bought Journalists And Free Journalists

Paul Schreyer has provided a detailed description of how the Corona topic has increasingly become the main focus of all media coverage.[341] This persistent pandemic state would no longer exist if the leading media in all countries did not join in and all sing from the same hymn sheet, systematically stirring up panic about the virus, suppressing important counter-arguments, failing to research essential background information, spreading false reports, refraining from giving alternative views, intimidating and defaming critics who openly threaten to destroy the existence of the virus. Should the interviewee inadvertently not fit into the concept of the official corona narrative, it becomes almost comical, as this excerpt from a Spanish television programme shows, where the newsreaders interview a doctor who does not tow the line when it comes to fuelling the corona narrative.[342] [343]

'He who pays the piper calls the tune' is certainly the wisdom that applies to the vast majority of journalism at the moment. It is known that the Bill and Melinda Gates Foundation has paid 250 million dollars to the world-famous media houses in the last few years. And also to the so-called fact-checkers, who are then also essentially bribed.

'A Columbia Journalism Review exposé reveals that, to control global journalism, Bill Gates has steered over $250 million to the BBC, NPR, NBC, Al Jazeera, ProPublica, National Journal, The Guardian, The New York Times, Univision, Medium, the Financial Times, The Atlantic, the Texas Tribune, Gannett, Washington Monthly, Le Monde, Center for Investigative Reporting, Pulitzer

---

[341] https://multipolar-magazin.de/artikel/wurde-die-corona-krise-geplant (retrieved 17/09/20)

[342] With English subtitles at: https://www.youtube.com/watch?v=endX6Cz4ZDA / (retrieved 01/11/20)

[343] https://www.rubikon.news/artikel/der-kontrollverlust (retrieved 06/09/20)

Center, National Press Foundation, International Center for Journalists, and a host of other groups. To conceal his influence, Gates also funnelled unknown sums via subgrants for contracts to other press outlets. His press bribes have paid off. During the pandemic, bought & brain-dead news outlets have treated Bill Gates as a public health expert— despite his lack of medical training or regulatory experience'.[344]

This is also reminiscent of the familiar intelligence methods of confusing and manipulating the public. This was rehearsed on a global scale during the assassination of John F. Kennedy in 1962. A CIA letter was sent to all editorial offices stating that all those who did not believe in the official narrative of the lone perpetrator should be portrayed as 'conspiracy theorists' and completely unbelievable. There should only be this one official opinion! This threatening behaviour was accompanied by the request to destroy this letter after reading it. Which of course not everyone did, so that it still exists today. An Austrian freelance journalist has researched this thoroughly.[345]

Free journalism is necessary for a free society.[346] In recent months, I have been in contact with a number of women journalists who used to work in the mainstream media, but left for reasons of conscience, because they were no longer able to support the manipulation of journalists by the public broadcasters.

'There is a crack, a crack in everything, that's how the light gets in', as Leonard Cohen puts it in one of his

[344] https://bretigne.typepad.com/on_the_banks/2020/08/shock-report-fact-checkers-remove-article-detailing-bill-gates-funding-of-fact-checkers.html (retrieved 05/09/20)

[345] https://youtu.be/l0eQEWJjz6s (retrieved 05/09/20). A document from the CIA attempting to quell any deviation from the official line taken by the Warren Commission can be found here: http://www.jfklancer.com/CIA.html (retrieved 29/10/20)

[346] https://www.rubikon.news/artikel/wir-machen-journalismus-2 (retrieved 05/09/20)

songs. This also applies to the mainstream press. An interview on ORF 1 with Prof. Martin Haditsch, a top-class expert who is very committed to education around this corona pandemic, is one of these light-filled exceptions. [347] An article with the following thought-provoking title appeared in the Neue Züricher Zeitung recently: 'What If The 'Covidiots' Were Right?' Yes, what would happen if the whole delusional entity of this pandemic collapsed and nothing but the naked truth came out. As Wolfgang Wodarg has been saying since the beginning: The emperor isn't wearing any clothes!

The Conspiracies Happening Behind The Scenes

There is still much speculation as to quite how and for whose political and financial plans this corona pandemic is beneficial. But it is becoming increasingly clear who has an interest in this pandemic. As so often, the old maxim 'follow the money' is the right instinct here. An American Youtuber, who calls herself Amazing Polly and has over 360,000 subscribers, succinctly uncovers how the American Center for Disease Control, the WHO, the Bill and Melinda Gates Foundation, the World Bank, the World Economic Forum and many other institutions mutually build on and commission each other to put the world in a chaotic state, by means of these threatening scenarios, in order to be able to save it through vaccinations and even more far-reaching ideas of social control and surveillance. [348] [349] [350]   Governments are put

---

[347] https://oe1.orf.at/programm/20200904/611366/Martin-Haditsch-Mikrobiologe-Facharzt-fuer-Hygiene-und-Mikrobiologie-Infektiologie-und-Tropenmedizin (retrieved 05/09/20) Here's a video in English (with subtitles) of Martin Haditsch criticising the global pandemic measures:
https://www.youtube.com/watch?v=lzdLruKMo5M (retrievd 29/10/20)
[348] https://www.youtube.com/watch?v=1Z5VYqJqrtI&feature=youtu.be (retrieved 04/09/20) – Amazing Polly's Youtube account has subsequently been closed. All her videos are now on the Bitchute site (described by Wikipedia as 'a video hosting service known for accommodating far-right individuals and conspiracy theorists, and for hosting hateful material' but where a lot of lockdown-sceptical videos are being posted

under pressure or financially rewarded for such lofty global projects.[351] All civil liberties of ordinary citizens must be abolished as completely as possible. Because the people themselves are becoming increasingly impoverished, the coffers of those countries are being plundered where there is still something to be gained. The European Union is playing along, ordering millions of vaccine doses in advance and pledging €400 million to Mr Gates to pay for vaccinations in the poorer countries of the world.[352] Now, giving 400 million euros directly to the poor people – that would be something worth celebrating!

Meanwhile, at an EU level, the legal arrangements are also being advanced for compulsory Covid 19 vaccinations.[353] Any damage caused by the vaccination will also have to be paid out of national budgets, as has already been contractually agreed. Any scepticism that vaccinations are not a magic bullet is met with a condescending paternalistic attitude on the part of the states.[354] It seems the perfect business idea were it not for a pesky little thing called reality that, as is well known, always scuppers the perfect crime.

The World Is Run By Narcissists

It is not only Mr Gates who wants to be celebrated in a narcissistic way as the great saviour of mankind. The

---

because they have been taken down or banned from more mainstream sites like Youtube, Twitter and Facebook). Here is the video Franz references:
https://www.bitchute.com/video/avIpEV7p7oo/ (retrieved 29/10/20)

[349] https://reliefweb.int/sites/reliefweb.int/files/resources/GPMB_annualreport_2019.pdf (retrieved 05/09/20)

[350] https://marialourdesblog.com/we-are-in-a-live-exercise-corona-ist-ein-perfider-plan-der-hochfinanz/ (retrieved 05/09/20)

[351] https://www.anderweltonline.com/klartext/klartext-20202/corona-die-gekaufte-pandemie/ (retrieved 05/09/20)

[352] https://deutsche-wirtschafts-nachrichten.de/506067/EU-unterstuetzt-Impf-Allianz-von-Gates-und-WHO-mit-400-Millionen-Euro (retrieved 04/09/20)

[353] https://www.watergate.tv/eu-erlaesst-ausnahmeregelung-fuer-covid-19-impfstoff/ (retrieved 05/09/20)

[354] https://www.rubikon.news/artikel/der-impfkrieg (retrieved 05/09/20)

Russian President Vladimir Putin was the first to launch a vaccine that neither BIG-Pharma nor the shareholders of companies owned by the super-rich in the West have anything to gain from. Of course, it is then immediately said that 'Sputnik V' could not possibly be a first-class vaccine and that they, the West, would have to continue research on their own vaccine.

The American president Donald Trump would also like to be re-elected and is working with all the forces at his disposal to be able to present a vaccine to the American people as his great saving act before the elections in November. And as always, the richest of the rich will benefit the most in this gold-rush for the new vaccine, while populations around the world continue to be driven further and further into poverty.[355] [356]

Collapse Of The Financial System?

Heiko Schöning says: 'It is not only the vaccination business that is at stake. It is not even at the core of medicine, pharmaceuticals, medical technology or tracing/monitoring; these are merely welcome side businesses for the mafia. In essence, it is about the monetary system. More precisely: it is about the restart of the mafia-like monetary system - THE GREAT RESET. This is the long established title of the World Economic Forum in Davos in January 2021'.[357] Financial expert Wolff Ernst also believes that the financial system is unsalvageable and he sees that 'Corona' offers a good opportunity for it to collapse in a way that nobody can be blamed for.[358] Some super-rich people are already making provisions for themselves, selling their shares and going

---

[355] https://www.infosperber.ch/Artikel/Gesellschaft/Trump-lasst-Milliardare-Profit-schlagen-aus-der-Coronapandemie (retrieved 05/09/20)
[356] https://www.querschuesse.de/author/querschuss/ (retrieved 05/09/20)
[357] https://www.youtube.com/watch?v=Sfm1oXpvkTA (retrieved 05/09/20)
[358] https://www.youtube.com/watch?v=SOiTYOEWW8o (retrieved 05/09/20)

'into gold'.[359] Others even bet on the collapse and hope to make their extra profits that way.

Based on completely insane and inhuman assumptions, these plans to let the whole world sink into chaos in order to take advantage of it, are still having a lot of meticulous planning put into them.

Why Do So Many Still Go Along With The Madness?

Since most people are not aware of what is going on behind the scenes and are probably afraid to venture deep into this frightening abyss of money and domination, a certain mental block prevents the full extent of the threatening financial, social and personal catastrophes getting in. Many people's psyches would be overwhelmed by the information and therefore switch to survival mode. They prefer to continue to believe in the official corona narrative of a natural disaster that has befallen mankind (see Figure 26) and try to reassure themselves that: *It will not be so bad. The pandemic will soon be over. Then we can all get vaccinated.*

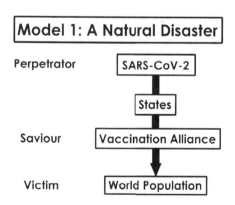

[359] https://deutsche-wirtschafts-nachrichten.de/505872/Warren-Buffett-trennt-sich-von-Bank-Aktien-und-setzt-auf-Gold (retrieved 05/09/20)

Figure 26: Corona pandemic presented as a natural disaster

If someone points out this survival strategy and says that we are dealing with a man-made catastrophe (see Figure 27), in which there are perpetrators and victims and that the perpetrators are being celebrated as saviours, that person is likely to be shunned because it is easier than hearing the monstrous truth of what they are saying.

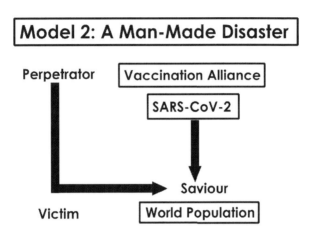

Figure 27: The corona pandemic as a man-made disaster

What then happens if Covid-19 is 'defeated'? Do we all fall into each other's arms again and dance around with joy? Or will we be told that the next virus is already on its way and we better still keep our distance from each other?

Standing Up Bravely In The Quest For Truth And Human Love

But we can see that, across the world, people are waking up. There are now enough well-educated, highly qualified self-aware people who are using their skills to understand the situation and develop counter-strategies. Designated experts and warm-hearted people like Professor Sucharit Bhakdi, for example, are doing their utmost to explain the dangers of RNA vaccinations and saying that they are completely superfluous, since the population already has immunity to this ominous SARS-CoV-2.[360] [361] It is actions like these that are helping prevent even more damage being done to human health.

It so good to see that there are more and more people out there in the world who are prepared to think for themselves and want to search for truth and clarity. People whose hearts have not yet turned to stone, who care about humanity, genuine solidarity and the common good. I've just come across, for example this 'International Alert Message From Health Professionals', which summarises the basic arguments against this corona pandemic mania. [362] The German-language website 'Corona Transition Switzerland' is also worth reading and is very informative, with many reports on the current situation.[363] A colleague of mine has just published an article putting the whole corona pandemic in a nutshell, looking specifically at the trauma aspects of it all.[364] Even the taxi driver who drives us back home from Munich airport seems to have a good grasp of what is really going on in the pandemic mania and tells me a lot of what I suspect and know. He has had to cash-in his insurance policies that he had put by for his old-age, in order to make ends meet over the last few months.

---

[360] https://www.youtube.com/watch?v=u0cIaQwAw2A (retrieved 05/06/20) VIDEO REMOVED. An English language interview with Professor Bhakdi can be found here: https://youtu.be/ZnpnBYgGARE (11/11/20)
[361] https://www.cicero.de/innenpolitik/covid-epidemiologen-virus-bhakdi-mansmann-masken-streitgespraech (retrieved 05/09/20)
[362] https://covidinfos.net/wp-content/uploads/2020/08/EN-international-alert-message.pdf (retrieved 05/09/2)
[363] https://corona-transition.org/?mot=13 (retrieved 05/09/20)
[364] https://www.rubikon.news/artikel/die-corona-traumatisierung (retrieved 05/09/20)

What Do I Want: To Really Live My Life Or Just To Survive?

Back in Germany the mood is subdued and depressed. Gross national product has apparently already shrunk by 10% in the second quarter of 2020. In view of the uncertainties and the difficulty of continuing to plan for the future, even I sometimes find myself lacking in confidence and joy in life.

I am glad that I have a lot to do on that first day back - at home and in our garden. And it's good weather so I can mow the lawn, trim the hedge, clean the pergola. And I'm still lucky that I'm able to write informative articles. Someone said this ingenious sentence the other day: 'I don't want a new world order, but a world that is in order'. I also find this passage at the end of an article by Johannes Mosmann remarkable:

'Covid-19 isn't going to be the last virus that threatens human life. There will come a future in which every real encounter carries a risk. Then we will have to decide: do we want to prolong the life expectancy of our human bodies at the price of no more people actually getting to live in these bodies, or do we want to preserve the human being and accept disease and death as a fact of life? In other words: what is the true point of human community?'[365]

The title of our next international IoPT conference that's due to take place (now online) in October therefore seems more topical than ever: 'What Do I Want: To Live Or Just To Survive? The real happiness we can find when we meet ourselves.'

---

[365] https://anthroposophie.ch/de/wirtschaft-gesellschaft/news/artikel/corona-virus-menschheit-am-scheideweg.html (retrieved 05/09/20)

A Pandemic Of Inhumanity – A Plea For A Humanity With A Healthy 'I'

Thirty-First Article – 27th September 2020

To Be A Subject Or An Object?

Living beings are subjects. They behave towards their environment according to their needs. A living being that is hungry reacts differently to offers of food from one that is full. A living being that fears for its life acts differently than one that feels safe. This applies to the plant and animal kingdom as well as to human beings.

Stones cannot be turned into a state of joyful excitement with the offer of tasty food. Nor can you manipulate them by scaring them into thinking that millions of stones will soon die. Stones are objects. They do not therefore have to resist being treated like objects because they lack the need to be treated as anything different.

Mobile phones and computers also remain objects, even if they give us the illusion of a life of their own, because they are still active even when we do not directly input commands into them. However, they are controlled in the background by other machines, which are ultimately the product of humans and therefore their needs.

As living organisms, we humans are particularly suited to being subjects. We not only have numerous needs, we can even say 'I'. We are also not only driven by unconscious forces, we have a will – a want of our own. We can say: I want this and I don't want that. Even so-called 'transhumanism'[366] is only the result of human needs and the question always arises: what are these needs? Are they humane, characterised by love and compassion? Or inhumane, motivated by fear and anger?

---

[366] https://www.corbettreport.com/transhumanism-and-you/ (retrieved 29/06/20)

Attacks On Our Basic Human Needs

The Corona pandemic is an attempt to turn us human beings into a herd of apparently 'I'-less and 'will'-less creatures. We are degraded to the state of objects, we are treated like chickens or pigs in animal production. We are allowed the bare minimum of our basic needs by the supposed Corona protection measures.

Not even breathing freely is possible under these restrictions. Coughing and sneezing, actions that help the body rid itself of something harmful, are now considered antisocial and should be suppressed as much as possible. Anyone who has ever sneezed or coughed into a mask knows what I am talking about. Masks cause oxygen deficiency and poisoning of the brain. Unfortunately, the more the brain damage progresses, the less you notice this. What a crime it is to incite people to such self-damaging behaviour![367] [368]

Our need for human contact, for eye contact, to touch each other's bodies and skin is suddenly made out to be highly dangerous. Our needs to communicate are considerably reduced or completely suppressed by these unspeakably ugly masks. We sit silently in buses and trains and lose ourselves ever more in virtual worlds. We are no longer supposed to stand together and have animated conversations. We should no longer sing and dance and hug each other with joy when our favourite club has scored a goal.

Our needs for self-determination are also denied us. People are not even allowed to move out of their homes when they are sent into 'quarantine' or protective custody. They are even supposed to stay locked away within their family, in their own separate room like in a prison cell. Food should be passed to them from outside or simply placed in front of their cell door. And the same denial of self-determination applies to freedom of movement and travel: if a country or a city is defined as a

---

[367] https://www.youtube.com/watch?v=n-_mdIQqFBo (retrieved 27/09/20)
[368] https://youtu.be/K5SX3ak7A2Q (retrieved 27/09/20)

'risk area', it is better not to travel there, so that you are not threatened with protective custody.

People are now only allowed to see their relatives that are stuck in care homes under exceptional circumstances and, even then, have to hide behind plexiglass walls, as if visiting their partners, children and grandchildren were a visit to a prison and these relatives of theirs were in involuntary 'protective custody'. In addition, many of the residents of care homes are no longer even allowed to go outside, even if they are mobile enough to do so. They are expected to just put up and suffer with this 'social death', even though it will almost certainly accelerate their biological death.

Mothers are supposed to give birth wearing masks and their newborns are immediately given a nasal swab if there is any suspicion of corona. I would not be surprised if babies have probably already died as a result.[369]

What Or Who Should I Actually Be Afraid Of?

In this way we are all treated like objects, with the supposed justification that we are being protected from a deadly danger. Yet this deadly danger does not exist in the way they are claiming. Only the last remnants of coronaviruses are being detected, but the millions of tests that are being carried out are able to produce a high enough sounding number to make a pandemic threat seem plausible. Even though those who test positive are not definitely infected. And those who are infected are far from being sick, because they have their immune system at their disposal, which is generally enough to protect them. And even if these people were ill, they do not automatically infect other people. To do so, they have to have a high enough 'viral load'. The myth of the 'superspreader' is one of many myths used to stage this pandemic. As if every sore throat, every cough and sniffle

---

[369] https://www.impfkritik.de/pressespiegel/2020082302.html (retrieved 27/09/20)

was already an unmistakable sign of 'Covid 19'. It could not be more unscientific, prejudiced and ideological.

This constant panic-mongering is actually damaging to the brain. For example, when I am full of fear and stress, I often forget people's names. Fear can make you stupid. Behind the current, politically intended and media-supported, staging of a second wave, there is still, as at the beginning of the pandemic, the intention to put us all into such a state of fear and terror that we long for the corona vaccination to come and save us. 'This pandemic will not end until a vaccine is available.' This is what was claimed back in March and is still being claimed now. But RNA vaccines, have never been approved for human use; they are still completely untested on such a scale and are likely to be far from safe. They are a human experiment that will wreak predictably irreparable damage on the many people who are vaccinated. As has been seen before it is not SARS-CoV-2 that 'kills', but the supposed protective measures that are taken to counteract it, and this pattern looks set to continue.[370] So it is not a virus I need to be afraid of. What I should be afraid of is those who are using this virus to pursue their power and business interests on a world scale. This supposed virus pandemic is a war of the power and money elites against the entire world population.

Do We Have To Participate?

If I, as a human being, remain a subject then this diabolical game is easy to see through. If, on the other hand, I allow myself to become an object, I am trapped. But nobody can force me to read the newspapers that fuel the Covid panic by their constant lying, tricking and cheating. No one can tell me to listen to these ghastly talk shows in which the same people spread the same untruths. Nobody can make me go to the doctor when I feel the beginnings of a slight sore throat or now, as

---

[370] https://www.youtube.com/watch?v=vthCRDgxFCo (retrieved 27/09/20)

autumn comes round again, my nose starts to run. No doctor can be induced to immediately do this nonsensical, meaningless PCR test and test all his clients 'for corona'.

It is enough to make you weep when a nursery teacher describes the current situation in the day-care centres with such clear words as these:

'Pedagogy is an action based on philosophical, sociological, psychological and, more recently, neurobiological findings. Pedagogy as a theoretical discipline in its own right has always been questionable and has now obviously failed. Corona has shown: it is not worth a damn.

Good teachers have known this for a long time: if you don't have a heart for children, you should steer clear of these professions. Corona immediately made visible what some had guessed: the majority of educators and teachers care nothing for children. They are trapped in their own fears. They are easily manipulated, compliant and unwilling to look at themselves. They have no opinion of their own, hardly any empathy and hunt frantically and in anticipatory obedience from one measure to the next.'[371]

Already severely traumatised societies are now defining themselves, in relation to SARS-CoV-2, as completely ill: everyone is potentially infectious and everyone can potentially infect others. Everybody is helplessly at the mercy of this supposed killer virus, a person's immune system won't help at all and he therefore needs rescue from outside in the form of the vaccine! All healthy people are sick because they might infect others even if they are showing no symptoms. The already reductionist understanding of illness in orthodox medicine is being taken even further to the extreme. It is an objective ideology and it follows this logic: Once the object is

---

[371] https://www.rubikon.news/artikel/die-kita-als-kaserne (retrieved 27/09/20)

created (in this case the disease Covid-19) it demands objective medical treatment which leads to all healthy people without any signs of illness becoming objects of such measures. Human subjects are degraded to the status of mere bodies, into which one can pump profitable doses of vaccine at will.

It cannot be more clearly seen than in an article in the Frankfurter Allgemeine Zeitung where Bill Gates himself states that the mass vaccination of all people on this globe is at stake: we want to vaccinate all of you, only then will this pandemic be over.

> 'The World Is On The Brink Of A Scientific Masterpiece: Early next year a safe and effective vaccine against COVID-19 will be available, probably even several. This will finally give us the chance to put an end to the threat of the pandemic - and to return to normality. If there is a vaccine against the virus, governments can lift the measures to distance themselves from it. We will no longer need to wear masks. The world economy will be back to full speed. But this development is not inevitable. To get there, the world first needs three things: the capacity to produce billions of doses of vaccine, the financial means to pay for them and systems that can spread them.'[372]

'He who has a hammer, searches the world for nails!' Many people unconsciously fall into this psychological trap. They apply their thought patterns and methods to everything they come across. They can also knowingly misuse this attitude for their own interests: I have here my vaccination method - so where are the people I can vaccinate and therefore become even richer?

---

[372] https://www.faz.net/aktuell/gesellschaft/gesundheit/coronavirus/gastbeitrag-bill-gates-drei-bedingungen-um-die-pandemie-zu-stoppen-16977815.html?GEPC=s5 (retrieved 01/10/20)

To stay with that image: Hunting for this corona virus is in fact like trying to swat a fly with a hammer. You don't kill the fly, but you demolish your whole house.

Is The System There For Us Or Are We There For The System?

To ask us to put our health and livelihood at risk so that the health system should not be overburdened is a heartless ideology of domination that turns everything upside down. It is saying essentially that people should be there for the system, not that the system should be there for the people. This comes down to the most fundamental question of humanity: are the political and economic systems there for us humans, or do we humans have to be available to the domination and profit interests of such systems, now even by putting our healthy bodies at their disposal?

What happens is that those who expose and criticise such ideologies are then insulted and smeared, and this shows up another basic psychological law. The attributions we put on others are what we should be applying to ourselves. Whoever calls others a 'covidiot', a 'right-wing radical' or a 'conspiracy theorist' is all of these things himself. Whoever's Wikipedia entry is altered and amended with such devaluating terms, whoever's YouTube video has been censored and deleted, can be sure that he has spoken the truths that the ruling power and money elites would like to suppress.[373] Where the truth can no longer be told, a society sinks into madness and barbarism.

Humanity's Self-Healing Powers

From my psychotherapy, on the other hand, I know for sure that people become and remain healthy when their physical and psychological self-healing powers are active.

---

[373] https://www.youtube.com/watch?v=5VIKwcupOKo (retrieved 29/09/20)

477

Real healing comes from within, when we can experience ourselves as a subject who wants to live and grow. We doctors and psychotherapists can only give the space, time and our goodwill to allow these self-healing powers to unfold. Whoever degrades people to objects, ignores and blocks what is essential in them (their will to live, their life energies and their joy of life) is in the end not promoting this person's life but their death.

Being a subject means taking responsibility for our own lives. Being a subject also means seeing other people as subjects and appreciating them. What need should I have as a subject to degrade others to the status of an object? Something like this only occurs when a person does not experience himself as the subject of his own life, but is driven by inner impulses to which he feels powerlessly exposed. According to my therapeutic experience this has a lot to do with early childhood traumatisation. Only those who have been hurt and ignored in their primal childhood needs so early on, will not notice as adults when they humiliate their own children, or other children in their supposed care, and treat them as objects.

Look At Yourself

I therefore hope that all those who are now staging this pandemic and consider it a good thing, and all those who are now participating in it, will eventually turn their attention to themselves and their early childhood. To look at their life in their mother's womb, to look at their birth and the three years after. If they do, I am sure they will look into an abyss of fear, anger, shame and pain. Unfortunately, however, most people, instead of looking at themselves, try to distract themselves:

- By looking outside of themselves and at others.
- By thinking they have to solve the problems of others who do not even have them.

- By holding on to seemingly objective facts that do not exist.

The pain of not having been noticed and loved by our own mother when we were a child is so deep in many people that they would rather give up their own needs or even die unconscious of all of this, rather than be a burden to their mother. On top of this, there is an enormous amount of anger that cannot be expressed towards one's own mother and father (who is usually also traumatised), and this anger is then misdirected against one's own needs and the needs of other people. In this misanthropic attitude people then begrudge others their happiness in life too. You should not be any better off than I am! Other people should have to wear these masks tight over their mouths and noses, just like I have to! They shouldn't be spared this vaccination either!

Therefore I say it here in quite a deliberately personal way: I am not affected by Corona and do not need this supposed help and protection! I am not going to be talked into there being a problem either! I can see for myself if something is dangerous for me or if I am a danger for other people. The survival strategies of traumatised people, who interfere in my life with their unimaginable ruthlessness, are the greatest danger for me.

Is This Humanitarianism Really 'Philanthropy'?

So if school administrators and teachers, judges and police officers, people who work for the health authorities, shop owners and their employees, restaurant owners and their waiters now check other subjects (i.e. children and young people, customers and guests) to see if they are wearing their masks properly, are they then responsible fellow human beings who respect the subjectivity of other people? Or are they just the henchmen of a power and money cartel, which is acting in secret with the aim of making all people on this earth the object of vaccinations and total control? What kind of inner attitude must these creators and designers of such inhuman systems have towards themselves when they invoke these 'restrictions' on others and hide their personal interest behind the law? They want others to go along with it as if it were the natural and right thing to do.

Making people into objects is inhuman. To take part in this dehumanisation, whether as a political officer, journalist or simple citizen, is irresponsible towards humanity. Therefore, unfortunately, the absurdity currently arises that human subjects rob themselves of their own human dignity by imagining an alleged killer virus. Dehumanising themselves and degrading themselves to the status of objects. And this is all happening in the name of health protection, and in the name of 'philanthropy'- pretending to be 'a friend to all men'!

Half a year ago I would not have dared to think how deep humanity could still sink in its ignorance of itself and its resistance to deal with its own traumatisation. By the way, in this staged pandemic we also learn that there are state-funded laboratories (e.g. the one in Wuhan) where research is being done to design viruses and bacteria into lethal weapons. For example, attempts are being made to combine anthrax bacteria with corona viruses to make them even more destructive.[374] It has become utterly absurd to still believe that those who have the power and the money are concerned about the health of their populations! They are entangled in dozens of perpetrator-victim dynamics and are trying by any means possible to find the best way to kill their fellow human beings, whom they define in their minds as enemies, be that with nuclear, chemical or biological means. That this would include their own collective destruction seems to be something they don't care about. They have split off any

---

[374] https://ef-magazin.de/2020/09/13/17512-wahrer-ursprung-von-covid-19-neue-kuenstlich-erzeugte-coronaviren-befinden-sich-in-entwicklung (retrieved 26/09/20)

compassion for themselves, are physically and emotionally frozen. So why should they have compassion for their fellow human beings?

Humanity With Enough Healthy 'I'

As long as I can, I will resist and raise my voice to avoid being dragged into this abyss of blindness, stupidity and cynicism, that is masquerading in the name of the common good. I know how I want to live and that I want to meet other people in love and compassion. I do not want to frighten anyone. Even if I get angry when others disregard my needs and violate my boundaries, I do not hate anyone and am always open to constructive problem solving. If I don't like something and therefore don't want it, I don't do it and conversely I don't want to talk myself out of doing something because the system currently says it's not permitted. Together with my ethically responsible colleagues, I will continue to look at my own traumatising past and to free my 'I' and my will so that I can live in the present in a self-determined, healthy and loving way. And if we all do this, there will be a future worth living for everyone.

A Good Or A Bad Life

We lead a good life

- when we can breathe freely,
- when we have pleasant physical contact,
- when we feel safe being in proximity to others,
- when we perceive, feel, think, decide and act for ourselves.
- when we have the financial means to afford good food, spacious housing, social, cultural, educational and health activities,
- when we live in real solidarity and true community with fellow free people,

- when the countries where we live do not wage military or economic wars against each other.

Our lives go badly

- when our basic physical and psychological needs are limited,
- when we have to wear masks that make us sick,
- when we have to practice 'social distancing',
- when our education is limited to 'distanced learning',
- when our freedom of movement, travel and occupation is denied us,
- when we are threatened with compulsory tests and vaccinations,
- when we become impoverished,
- when we live in an enforced pseudo-community,
- when we are drawn into interstate wars.

Social Leaders
Leaders in a society, whether they be politicians, managers, doctors, teachers, scientists, journalists, etc. can promote us living a good life

- when they are committed to the framework conditions that make up a good life (listed above),
- when they tell the truth to the best of their knowledge and belief,
- when they produce proper arguments and justify their actions with scientific evidence and compassion,
- when they resolve existing old conflicts instead of creating new ones,
- when they care more about the general interest of everyone rather than the special interests of lobbyists,
- when they don't misuse the power granted to them for their own personal, conscious and unconscious interests.

Leaders in a community, however, create the conditions for a bad life

- when they are bribed or corrupt,
- when they lie, deceive and cheat
- when they blackmail us,
- when they scare us,
- when, through their words and actions, they make it impossible for us to live a good life,
- when they use force instead of convincing arguments,
- when they secretly conspire against the common good,
- when, through the power they have been given, they are basically only using that authority to combat and cover up their own powerlessness, which stems from their own childhood trauma.

The corona pandemic clearly shows us which leaders are there for us, supporting us to live a good life and which are not. Criminals and panic-makers, cowards and hypochondriacs, people with entrenched violent perpetrator structures are unsuitable to be leaders and cannot create good living conditions for all. Leaders who enforce the current conditions for a bad life worldwide with psychological pressure and tangible violence no longer deserve our trust. We should quickly replace them across all our communities with those who are honestly serving the common good and respecting our needs for true solidarity, community and freedom. We should no longer chase after those who, either out of a lack of self-reflection or from greed, are leading us into a collective abyss. This means we have to learn more and more what is really going on and take the lead ourselves when it comes to living our own good life.

The Reverse Principle

There is a psychological rule of thumb that says that a lot of what I say about other people are basically statements I should be making about myself. The founder of psychoanalysis, Sigmund Freud, speaks here of projection rather than perception. I do not perceive another person for what he or she really is, but rather I interpret in him or her the ideas and intentions that are present in me. Therefore:

- anyone who accuses people who are committed to a good life of being 'corona deniers' should ask themselves the question as to how far they are not themselves corona inventors and immune system deniers.
- anyone who says that others are unscientific 'tin-foil hat wearers' should take a self-critical look at the scientific evidence on which they base their opinions.
- anyone who believes that the people who are now protesting are anti-social and against the 'common good' should look themselves in the mirror and realise how much their claims are currently dividing society and driving the community they live into the abyss.
- anyone who accuses people who want to live well of being right-wing extremists should answer the question of how radical their own arguments are and consider what radical right-wingers would do differently if they had the political say: Would they create a parliament without opposition? Impose a state of emergency? Ensure the press offers no opposition? Increase the dependence of the judiciary? Abuse the police and military for their own ideological purposes? Silence trade unions? Create images of the enemy that will terrify people? After this reflection, they could apply the result of their reflection to the current situation now created by the ruling and opposition democratic parties.

484

- anyone who berates people who want a good life and calls them conspiracy theorists should ask themselves to what extent they are practically involved in the current conspiracy against the common good and are working in favour of the data collection and vaccine industry?

The Imaginary Pandemic

Our human psyche consists of different levels of information processing: perceptions, emotions, imagination and thoughts. This Covid 19 pandemic basically exists only in the imagination:

- SARS-COV-2 as a 'killer virus' is a purely hypothetical horror scenario.
- The assertion that our human immune system cannot cope with this corona virus and needs a vaccination to help is pure fantasy, as at least 99% of all people can cope well with such corona viruses.
- The fear of exponential spread was and remains a mere model calculation.
- Fortunately, the idea that 'the virus' would lead to mass mortality is not coming true.
- The horror scenario that the intensive care units in hospitals would be hopelessly overloaded has not come true either.
- The idea that the corona PCR test would indicate who is infected and who is contagious is either a deliberately false claim or an untrue one based on lack of understanding.
- The idea that the corona measures are effective is mere wishful thinking on the part of their supporters.
- A 'second wave' is a mental construct that has nothing to do with the reality of infection with this ominous virus.

What is real, however, is, amongst many other things

- The damage caused by incorrect medical treatment in this corona pandemic (e.g. by excessively fast forced lung ventilation or high doses of hydroxychloroquine).
- The damage caused by masks that impede our freedom to breathe.
- The psychological damage caused by keeping distance in interpersonal contact and the loneliness that is the result.
- The damage caused by the destruction of people's professional lives.
- The damage caused by the poisoning of the social climate.
- The damage to democracy.
- The profound psychological damage caused to people of all ages, who are no longer able to distinguish reliably between reality and fiction in the face of the constant barrage from the media.
- The damage of having been cheated of one's zest for life for almost a whole year now and being put under constant stress.

As if people did not have enough trouble under the normal social conditions

- to earn their living,
- living in cramped housing conditions,
- reconciling parental responsibilities and professional obligations
- or dealing with their own real health problems.

This fiction of a pandemic is now being imposed on people with such psychological pressure and real tangible violence, that in the end they believe that by obediently keeping their distance and wearing masks they can prevent the next lockdown, which in the end will be decided at the discretion of the pandemic makers themselves anyway. This participation, by shouting the ugly word 'mask' at people on the subway or in shops who dare show themselves with open faces, feels disgusting to me.

As Within So Without

My human psyche is a means to make the outside world (i.e the world itself) a world in which I can live well. Through this I can recognise, among other things, whether this world is dangerous or safe for me. This works well as long as my psyche is not traumatised. It is traumatised mainly by experiences of violence, early childhood neglect, lack of love and the feeling of not being welcomed into this world, especially by my own mother and father.

A traumatised psyche can no longer clearly distinguish well between the outer and inner world because it has been forced to give up the point of reference within itself and, in a state of fear, then looks outside of itself to protect itself from further injury. It tries to gain control over this outer world by orienting itself towards the perpetrators who hurt it and trying to anticipate their actions. By doing this, we suppress our own needs for a good life and fight desperately against our own feelings of fear, anger, pain and love. This makes us insensitive to the violence and disappointment that come our way, but we also no longer feel real love and joy. Our need for protection becomes independent to us, something that we cannot control, and this suffocates our vitality. We then no longer recognise who and what is really dangerous for us. So it can happen that we experience a virus as dangerous, although it is our early childhood fears of death and abandonment that really plague us.

In these psychological ways, children who suffer from the traumas of their parents become tyrants themselves, oppressing both themselves and others. This dynamic then continues outside the traumatic family environment, in kindergarten, school, work, sport, culture and politics. The entire society then becomes a collection of traumatised and mutually traumatising people. Traumatised people without their own healthy 'I' and free, un-entangled 'want' are easily manipulated. They readily sell themselves for money and (supposed) power, they quickly surrender to those with the strongest perpetrator structures.

I wonder whether those who, because of a model of health and illness that is unsurpassed in its primitiveness, are now spreading this panic about Covid-19, have any idea how much anger and hatred they are generating at the same time. Frustration always goes in two directions: aggression and depression. It never stays with the fear alone. So this corona pandemic, which has been going on for far too long, will cause more and more outbreaks of violence and will also drive more and more people into depression and suicide.

Conclusion

I want to live well. I want to live in good company and have the freedom to make my own decisions. I am working on the wounds that were inflicted on me in my childhood and am taking good care of my own health. Because then my fellow human beings will be safe too from any danger I might inflict because of my unresolved trauma. I don't want to harm them, but wish them a good life as well.

I do not want to be lied to, cheated, blackmailed or threatened by my fellow human beings. I don't want them to interfere in my private and professional life in such a completely excessive way. I want to have leaders in society that I can trust. Those who are blind to themselves are a danger to themselves and to others. I therefore also expect those who excel as social leaders to deal with their own biography and dissolve their own blind spots. Those who do not know themselves do not recognise their fellow human beings. Those who shy away from looking inside themselves are also blind to the outside, and therefore imagine dangers that do not exist.

Those who do not feel good about themselves do not lead a good life and create bad living conditions for other people. Fortunately, there are more and more therapeutic possibilities to change this. Make use of them!

If each one of us dares to face up to his or her split-off fears, and the feelings of anger and pain that come with that, we no longer need to pretend that those things exist outside of us. We no longer need to create images of an enemy ('witches', 'Jews', 'communists', 'capitalists', 'killer viruses' and so on), against which we must fight unconsciously until all our material and psychological resources are exhausted. If we each dare to look at ourselves, we can finally begin to work together to create the conditions for a good life, with compassion and respect for each other. Then we will be able to create a vision for a future worth living, both in our heads and hearts and also in reality.

The Fear-Dependency Trap And How We Can Escape From It

Thirty-Second Article - 18th October 2020

Fear As Part Of The Human Condition For Homo Sapiens

An essential characteristic of Homo Sapiens is his upright walk. This requires a pelvic girdle that connects the feet to the upper body in a stable manner. Among other things, this means stretching the human abdomen, which in women not only contains the gut but also the womb. When a woman is pregnant, the baby presses down into her pelvis and must be held back here until the birth. The heavier the child becomes, the more problematic this is. At birth, a woman's pelvis must open wide enough so that the baby can come out of its mother's womb.

The upright position means that the gestation period is kept as short as possible at 266 days. This is why we humans are still very much unfinished when we are born. Instead of the 18 or 21 months it would take for a child to be able to stand on its own legs and run after its mother within minutes of birth, similar to a horse foal, we humans have only just under 9 months of relative security and care in the mother's womb. In this sense, we humans are all premature babies who need intensive support in order to avoid dying of thirst, starvation and freezing to death after birth. Birth is only the transition from intra-uterine development to a growth and maturation process outside, but we still need to be in close contact with our mother's body.

Leaving his mother's body brings with it an enormous risk for a newborn baby. After all, what if his mother does not stay with him and abandons him? A new-born child, which, because of its high degree of vulnerability, quickly gets into mortal fears anyway, now has the additional problem of experiencing abysmal abandonment fears because of his utter dependence on his mother. He also experiences his biological fixation on his mother as a fundamental psychological dependence on her too. People therefore easily panic when they experience themselves alone and without contact.

From a psychological point of view, it is the mother's basic task to take away her child's existential fears of death and abandonment. She can only do this if she herself has overcome the fears from her own childhood and has become a psychologically mature adult. Unfortunately, this is often not the case. In societies in which people traumatise each other in many different ways (from partner relationships to the world of economics and politics) the mother-child relationship is also very often permeated by unkindness, neglect and violence. Children cannot feel safe with their mothers.

Traumatised mothers who do not want their children, do not love them and cannot offer them protection from danger represent a high risk potential for these children. But despite all this, children cannot simply turn their backs on their mother and focus their basic and existential needs on someone else, even if such a person existed. They therefore try with all their physical and psychological strength to establish and maintain contact with their mother. In order to do so, they may reduce their own needs and stop expressing their feelings of fear, anger, sadness and pain.

The older the child gets, the more he or she consciously tries not to be a burden on their mother, who is, on a real level or at least an emotional one, absent. The child may even try to comfort their mother if she is anxious or calm her if she is angry. Often this can becomes a person's life's work. Mothers and children very often become trapped in a fear dependency pattern for the rest of their lives. It is true that during puberty and adolescence there are various attempts to break out of this dependency trap. But these are at the expense of psychological consistency. The parts that now think they are independent simply abandon their own child parts, which are still in great need. In their remoteness from reality, they then easily enter into new relationships in which they unconsciously restage the misery of their early childhood. In the process, their own fears and their feelings of anger and sadness are also denied. This is not something 'one' talks about, and in traumatised societies it is taboo to speak openly about one's feelings.

Fear Reduces The Alternatives For Action

When a person experiences fear, the stress mechanism in his or her whole organism is set in motion. Their brain reacts in such a way that the entire body is flooded with stress hormones that prepare them for flight or fight reactions. According to the thinking that it is 'better to be too afraid than not enough, because that could be fatal', a bio-psychic anxiety system that is ready and alert at all times means that people can very quickly become restless and panicky and find it hard to calm down again. This stress reaction has negative effects on our digestive system, our immune system and our sexual drive. Chronic stress causes many physical symptoms and can even lead to death.

Therefore, the question is how can we get out of such stressful situations. On the one hand, it is by recognising that the danger we are frightened of does not exist or is already over. On the other hand, security and protection measures can help to calm the situation down. For all of us human beings, it is an essential calming factor that we feel safe and protected within a community. It is not only mothers but fathers and men in general that can also contribute a great deal to this, if they have reached a sufficient level of psychological maturity.

Ideally, once we are adults we should be able to recognise dangers, assess them correctly and take appropriate steps to protect ourselves. However, since the inner alarm state narrows our perception, not all people are able to do this. Many people quickly fall back into the state of their childhood fear-dependency trap. There is then a danger that they will again seek protection from people who are themselves caught in their own fear-dependency trap, because this is what they did as children. As in our postnatal period, we might then hope for rescue from an adult person who is themselves full of fear.

Collectives In The Fear-Dependency Trap

In most major societies across the world, the risk of falling into a fear dependency trap with our own mother is very high. Therefore, such societies as a whole are then caught in all kinds of fear-dependency traps. They are afraid of all sorts of things: of disease, social exclusion, unemployment, the collapse of the monetary system, war - most of which has been created by Homo Sapiens himself in the hope of coming out of existential dependency. There are then countless promises of salvation and many individuals who behave as if they could be saviours for all of us. With their supposed recipes for success, they make the situation even worse. Above all, people seek security in external systems (money, weapons, criminal justice and prisons, control and surveillance, medication, operations, radiation therapy etc.) and ignore their own inner world or try to manipulate it with morals and punishment.

Because all these institutional and ideological systems do not adequately resolve the original fear-dependency trap from childhood, which most people are not even aware of, all social attempts to provide protection and security are built on sand and sooner or later will wash away with the next tide. In Germany, for example, the promise of creating a 1,000-year-long Nazi empire petered out after only twelve years. Neither science, nor economics, nor politics, which are all only concerned with appearances, are able to calm people's fundamental fears.

Instead, these institutions continue to fuel people's fears through their actions.

Fear And Corona

'Corona' is a good example of how once fears are aroused, they are not so easy to calm down. Keeping your distance, wearing a mask, lockdown, talking about rising infection rates are like fanning the fire of the human biopsychic fear system. Even the vaccination, which is supposed to be a legitimised salvation from Covid-19, will not actually give anyone a real sense of security, but will instead promote additional fears about the possible risks of such a vaccination. Similar to the traumatising mother-child situation, it is the supposed adults in leading positions who are themselves full of fear and even deliberately spread panic. Now, the terrified population should not only mobilise its psychological forces to protect its own parents from the alleged threat of a Covid 19 death, but should even help those in political leadership positions by denying themselves their own needs, their own selves, so that these people in charge do not go completely crazy and stage the second and third wave of corona.

How Do We Get Out Of This?

Fortunately, it is now sufficiently clear that this SARS-CoV-2 is not a killer virus, that the PCR test cannot measure infections and that there is therefore no acute risk of disease for the vast majority of people. One can therefore confidently join a large number of competent people who have regained their mental clarity after an initial shock situation.

However, it is important that those who now realise what Covid-19 is all about do not just spread more fear and panic and create further uncertainty in those who are still unclear. What those people need is to be welcomed into a community of people who are emotionally stable and full of the joys of life. That is much more inviting than the accusation that it is high time for them to wake up from their twilight sleep. It is being a role model that has the most impact, regardless of whether that is attractive to everyone or not.

It is helpful to ask yourself whether your personal fear of a killer virus is not based on the fear-dependency trap of your own childhood. If, for example, you can break out of the fear-dependency relationship with an anxious mother, then this is a good way of removing yourself from other such dependency relationships where another person is still stuck in their own early childhood fears. It is not worth pursuing these people who are stuck in a permanent panic and are close to their own inner abyss. What it is worth doing is to counter these panic-mongers and prophets of doom with a healthy dose of distrust. You don't even have to listen to them - you can just turn off the TV or radio and stop reading the alarmist newspapers.

Real leaders are not at the mercy of their own trauma survival strategies. Whether they be parents, teachers, managers or politicians, they do not spread fear, but remain calm and clear when danger arises. That is their job.

2020 – Taking Stock Of The Year
Final Thoughts – 28th December 2020

It is now December and the second national lockdown, that has come into force in Germany, means that I will mostly be at home for Christmas 2020. This gives me the opportunity to do some more research, read some new books and take stock of the year. As I review the past few months, I start by looking at the situation in the wider world (on the outside, as it were) and then turn my attention to my own inner development, which has received an important boost towards clarity in the last couple of months.

The Situation On The Outside

What was already clearly being stated way back in March 2020, that the pandemic would not be over until a vaccine was available, is now coming to pass. Since then, tremendous nationwide effort has been mobilised to make the scale of this emergency seem irreversible, as those leading the pandemic have struggled to get through the Corona-poor summer by deploying mass testing, producing arbitrary infection figures and constant warnings of a second wave. Therefore, at the beginning of the winter holiday, there were again enough PCR-test positive cases to 'justify' another lockdown and the comprehensive obligation to wear masks. To this end, the Infection Protection Act in Germany was amended once again to lay the foundations for mass vaccination campaigns not only by ordinance, but by law.

In November, the WHO also followed suit, by reformulating its definition of herd immunity:

> 'On 9th June 2020, the WHO stated: 'Herd immunity is a form of indirect protection from infectious disease that occurs when a sufficient percentage of a population has become immune to an infection … through vaccination or immunity developed through previous infections.'
>
> As of 13th November 2020, the definition is: "Herd immunity', also known as 'population immunity', is a concept used for vaccination in which a population can be protected from a certain virus if a threshold of vaccination is reached.

Herd immunity is achieved by protecting people from a virus, not by exposing them to it."[375]

So basically, nothing short of vaccination is supposed to even be considered as a means of protecting a population from infectious diseases. In line with this way of thinking, in England, in America and now also in Germany, these new types of Corona vaccines are being legitimised by means of emergency fast-tracked approval. Mass vaccinations are being rolled out, which are essentially human trials, because there are no adequate long-term studies on possible effects and side effects.

In order to increase the willingness to vaccinate among the general population, pro-vaccination propaganda has been enormously increased. The vaccines are advertised by their manufacturers as extremely effective and without any side effects worth mentioning. The old advertising trick of 'here's something very special, make sure you get it first!' is being used to distract from the questionable content of the whole thing. Vaccination education on the Internet[376] and on social media is suppressed and censored even more. [377] The 'lateral thinkers' (the Querdenken protest movement) were first hosed with water cannons when they did assemble and then later their demonstrations were banned outright.

Individuals who are sceptical about the whole Corona measures and vaccinations and actively resist them are slandered ever more and find themselves put under both professional and private pressure. This is what happened, for example, to Dr. Bodo Schiffmann, a very active and therefore prominent Corona educator in Germany.[378]

Many people who are highly suspicious of this Corona pandemic are placing great hope in the legal team around Dr. Rainer Fuellmich and his 'Crimes Against Humanity' initiative. In Germany, a lawsuit

---

[375] https://2020news.de/who-aendert-definition-der-herdenimmunitaet/ (retrieved 25/12/20). In English at: https://www.aier.org/article/who-deletes-naturally-acquired-immunity-from-its-website/
https://twitter.com/simondolan/status/1341306917076021248?s=20 (retrieved 27/12/20)

[376] https://youtu.be/iAJd5owgHbQ abgerufen am 25.12.2020

[377] www.kla.tv/17757 abgerufen am 25.12.2020

[378] https://m.youtube.com/watch?v=8qq7QSw5tiI (retrieved 25/12/20) In German

has been filed against Christian Drosten and a so-called class action in Canada, America and Australia is in preparation. [379]

An important film that provides good information about vaccinations, especially for parents, was made by a couple here in Germany entirely at their own expense. It opened my eyes once again about this extremely dubious vaccine research. There is basically no public control of those who produce and distribute the vaccines. [380] Moreover, the follow-up costs for vaccine damage are always borne by the public purse.

Even in these first few days of the vaccination roll-out, the extent of the considerable damage that vaccination may cause is becoming clearer. An English study shows that it could be as high as 3% of people who are vaccinated receive serious 'side-effects'. [381] So, for example, on 18th December, out of 112,807 doses administered in the UK, 3,150 suffered from 'Health Impact Events' meaning they were 'unable to perform normal daily activities, unable to work, or required care from a doctor or health care professional.' There were also widely reported cases of anaphylaxis.[382] And there was the very public example of Tiffany Dover, a thirty-year-old nurse in America who was demonstratively vaccinated on camera in America on 21st December and then fainted whilst being interviewed afterwards.[383] A week later and there is still much debate about whether she is ok. [384]

---

[379] https://cormandrostenreview.com/cease-and-desist-order-fuellmich-drosten/ (retrieved 28/12/20)
Here is a video of Dr Fuellmich speaking in English
https://www.youtube.com/watch?v=KF3zO5evS4U and here is the original reference Franz quotes in German:
https://m.youtube.com/watch?v=Wz5GMxtGTBM (retrieved 25/12/20)
[380] https://www.youtube.com/watch?v=DgEWRHaxrM4 Part 1 &
https://www.youtube.com/watch?v=D_q-ok06zH8 Part 2 – Both in German (retrieved 25/12/20)
[381] https://www.youtube.com/watch?v=YzW5gG7aNdI&feature=youtu.be (retrieved 27/12/2020) in German. Here is an English video detailing the same report:
https://www.bitchute.com/video/0uRhpFUdKwkE/ (retrieved 05/01/20). And here is the original data they are drawing on:
https://www.cdc.gov/vaccines/acip/meetings/downloads/slides-2020-12/slides-12-19/05-COVID-CLARK.pdf
[382] https://www.bbc.co.uk/news/health-55244122 (retrieved 30/12/20)
[383] https://www.youtube.com/watch?v=p9agUz5cQCk (retrieved 28/12/20)
[384] https://www.youtube.com/watch?v=8MBk39-G3Dw abgerufen am 28.12.2020

The Situation Inside Of Me

One of the most persistent symptoms I suffer from is a whistling in both ears ('tinnitus'). I have had this since I took up my professorship at the University of Applied Sciences in Munich, almost 30 years ago now. My appointment as a professor was, for me, the fulfilment of my dream when it came to my professional life. I was overjoyed. This joy was abruptly dampened when, on my first day at work at the university, I found flyers complaining that yet another man had been appointed to the department of psychology and not a woman. Objectively, I could understand this argument, since the proportion of women students at this university is more than 90% and there were already three full-time male psychology professors. But personally, it was an enormous grievance for me and it became a heavy psychological burden. This situation put me under considerable stress to try and justify my appointment, and I tried to compensate with special achievements, which of course led to even more stress.

Today I realise that this was just a reflection of the situation I found myself in when I came into being. I came into existence full of joie de vivre and life-force and, almost straight away, I experienced my mother's 'no' to me from the outside. She did not want to be pregnant and become a mother. As a result of this 'no', I went into a state of shock and spent nine months in my mother's womb without any emotional connection to her. Even after my birth, I found myself confronted with a mother who could not regulate herself emotionally, and who would either offer me no physical closeness at all or smother me. She was emotionally needy, like a toddler herself, or angry and disappointed when I didn't live up to her expectations. She didn't breastfeed me for long enough because she could not handle the feelings that came from breast contact.

I was able to feel all this very clearly again a few days ago in an IoPT self-encounter process. I was also able, in the last few weeks, to further clarify my relationship with my father through another of my own self-encounters, this time in the men's group that I facilitate. It was painful to realise that now, in his old age, just as in my childhood, he has no psychological capacity available to show an interest in me as a person and to really see me. In our conversations, he continues to be stuck only in his own imaginary world. There is no emotional bridge between us and nothing in common that connects us. Incidentally, my father wants to be vaccinated, as he said in a conversation with me on 27th December, because he only gets his information from the mainstream media. He does not make an enlightened decision. He is doing what he has done all his life: adapting to what is expected of him by the 'powers-that-be'.

At the beginning of 2020 I felt that I was at the peak of my personal and professional development. My books and insights were steadily spreading all around the world. There was even a Persian version of 'Who Am I In A Traumatised Society?' being published. I was planning the dates for both my German and English-language trainings way ahead into the year 2023. I was getting great feedback about the personal progress that people were making with 'Identity-Oriented Psychotrauma Therapy' from all across the world and this really pleased me. All the flights for my activities abroad were already booked. Then, in March, 'Corona' was declared and suddenly physical person-to-person contact, which is of enormous importance for my therapeutic work, was declared to be something forbidden and dangerous.

At least, thanks to ZOOM, I was still able to hold many of my seminars, that had been scheduled to take place in Germany and abroad, live online instead. It took me by surprise that it is still possible to initiate highly emotional self-encounters with the Intention method via video and to still bring about profound psychological changes in people in this way. We were also able to organise the 5th International Conference on IoPT as a live-online event, which I consider was a great success under the given circumstances.

Since all people who speak critically about the Corona measures are defamed on Wikipedia, by the end of 2020 my entry too is now also peppered with vicious hostility, despite whoever wrote it never having had any dealings with me personally. Such intimidation from outside, leads me at times to feeling more extreme feelings of threat, as was the reality at the beginning of my life. However I am able to counteract these feelings thanks to the therapeutic work I continue to do on myself. The feelings of fear calm down most sustainably when I experience how many other sincere and honest people from all walks of life there are who have woken up in the course of this year and do not simply put up with the deprivation of their freedoms and the continued attack on their physical and mental health. At least I now clearly feel that I am no longer threatened by my parents and can therefore better assess the real dangers outside.

My wish is still to live in a community of people I don't have to be afraid of and with whom I feel safe, because they are authentic and with themselves. I notice how this feeling of safety then has an effect on my tinnitus - whether the whistling in my ears intensifies or whether it fades to a barely audible hum depends upon how safe I feel. This 'symptom' will probably continue to be my indicator of how at peace I am with myself and my fellow human beings for a while at least. I also now know, from a resonance experience in a self-encounter, something else that I find very reassuring and comforting. Namely, that once I am dead, I will no longer have any needs. This means that I don't have to worry about those who are dead either. They are at peace. It is the living who have to express their pain so that they can let the dead rest.

The Major Lines Of Development

In my view, three major lines of development are converging when it comes to the Corona Pandemic 2020:

1. Following the collapse of Soviet-style communism, the military-industrial machine has continued to search for a new enemy image to justify its own raison d'être. Since then, it has managed to place 'terrorism' in this role as the main enemy of society. Currently, it is also using the idea of biological warfare as the number one enemy, and has been running simulation planning games on how a release of viruses would be handled. These include the task of gaining absolute control over news coverage including the internet and social media, keeping the population in their homes by police and military control, setting social life to zero as far as possible, getting people used to protective masks and getting them ready for rapid vaccination. [385]
2. The pharmaceutical industry is also continuing to hatch its plans to make vaccination compulsory for everyone of all ages. It believes that with the new RNA/DNA vaccines it can appease the counter-arguments of the vaccination critics and that it has an extremely flexible and time-saving method of vaccine production at its disposal. [386]

---

[385] https://www.youtube.com/watch?v=SSnJhHOU_28 in German (retrieved 26/12/20)

[386] https://blog.nomorefakenews.com/2020/12/15/the-covid-vaccine-and-the-commercial-conquest-of-the-planet-the-plan/ (retrieved 26/12/20)

3. The capitalist financial system is finding itself facing an increasingly uncertain future since 2019 and is looking for new ways to transfer the wealth of the money and power elites into new forms of currency. [387] The great mass of humanity is to remain poor and dispossessed even in the event of a system reset.[388]

All these ideas of omnipotence and keeping the perpetual stream of money to the already super-rich flowing will not work in the long run, in my opinion, because these are all thought constructs that fundamentally go against the biological as well as the inner nature of our humanity. And where, for example, is the money for military spending and mass vaccinations to be found amongst the state budgets, when even those countries that are still considered rich are driving their economies to the wall through lockdowns and rising mass unemployment?

It is very possible that the large-scale attempts to make mass vaccinations the norm for the entire world population will bring about the very opposite. The damage caused by these vaccinations will probably become so obvious that vaccination itself will lose the good reputation it still has amongst large parts of the population.[389]

And perhaps then the fact will also penetrate the consciousness of those in the hitherto still rich countries who are afraid of dying of a corona infection at the age of 83 that millions of people are dying of poverty, poor hygiene and hunger as a result of lockdowns in the developing countries. Whatever the case, vaccinations alone will not feed all the children in the poor parts of the world.

In my first public contribution on the corona pandemic, I already emphasised the delusional nature of it. However, what looks like delusion and madness on the outside often has a hidden meaning. There are essential facts that are concealed and are not meant to be recognised by the majority because that would be too embarrassing and shameful for the whole system, be it a family or a larger community. Such facts would break the cohesion of the community.

---

[387] https://www.youtube.com/watch?v=_DKQTDFCH8Q in German (retrieved 26/12/20). Here is an English language summary: http://www.tlaxcala-int.org/article.asp?reference=28704 (retrieved 07/01/20)

[388] https://www.weforum.org/agenda/2020/06/now-is-the-time-for-a-great-reset/ (retrieved 26/12/20)

[389] https://www.youtube.com/watch?v=iiTrttV7Q8A in German (retrieved 27/12/20)

The leaders of such communities would thereby lose their legitimacy. Therefore, only when these facts come to light does it become possible to see what lies behind the madness (in families this may be, for example, murdered children, or incest and sexual assaults on children or children brought up not knowing their parents are someone other than who they believe them to be because of some shameful secret as to their true parentage). As in families, we already see the expected reactions on a societal level when there are secrets: those who point out that something is wrong in the system are portrayed (by those who defend the system they feel they belong to) as the crazy ones who should best be committed to a psychiatric ward. The perpetrators can always trust that the majority of their victims, who feel dependent on them, will protect them.

Presumably, only with greater distance will historical research bring to light what really happened behind the scenes in 2020 and who the main protagonists were. In these times of a free Internet, I hope that this can even more quickly become the case.

Coincidentally, I took a book off my shelf the other day about the Spanish Catholic Monarchs Ferdinand and Isabella (Melveena McKendrick 1969). It shows how this royal couple united the Iberian Peninsula into one large empire in the years between 1469 and 1516. To this end, they waged countless minor and major wars, drove the Muslim dynasties out of Spain once and for all, brought the Inquisition into the country and laid the foundations for their grandson Emperor Charlemagne's further world conquests. Both, however, were unhappy and depressed at the end of their seemingly successful lives. Whatever our outward success, our personal tragedy will always come to the surface if we are not with ourselves and are not able to live our lives according to our own needs and what we really want. Rulers, like Ferdinand and Isabella, do not live their lives according to what they truly want but define their existence primarily in terms of family, ethnic and religious affiliations. Therefore, they are also not free people either, but are subject to ever-changing group pressures and expectations. Driven by their own ideologies, they have to fight compulsively on the outside because they cannot find inner peace and have no reference point within themselves. They are not left in peace by their fellow human beings because they also identify themselves through their affiliations and only act on the outside. And as always, it is the subordinate peoples of such ruling figures who have to work hard for it and pay the blood price for the crazy ideas of their elites and their incessant striving for even more power and gold. Through skilful propaganda, this slave service is sold to the people as something that is to their own advantage. Enemy images are skilfully created and fuelled, envy and ill-will are promoted among the people in order to divide them and therefore make them able to be ruled over with almost no effort at all.

It would be too good to be true if, for the first time in human history, what was going on now was really about the well-being and health of the world's population, and not just another new variant of the greed for power and money on the part of those who believe themselves to be the spiritual elites of humanity.

If we want a more humane future, it will depend upon how much we are willing to face up to our truth, both individually and collectively. Because all these survival strategies, from epochs of humanity caught up in the madness of power and money, will only lead this earth further into chaos and into the erosion of any existence worth living. As has often been the case in human history, an empire that has become overpowering will then collapse because of the ignorance and decadence of its elites. In the long run, truth can never be replaced by propaganda, justice can never be superseded by the arbitrary use of force, and true humanity cannot by replaced by cynicism and hypocrisy.

In the long run, humanity will only get out of the chaos that it has been creating for itself since the beginning of history if it deals with its own inner life and its development. This is actually not so difficult and in truth it is much easier than all the elaborate efforts we make to close ourselves off from our own psychological injuries by every conceivable means. This repression and dissociation causes us to get into stress even at the smallest conflicts and to fight as if it were a matter of life and death. It creates this feeling in us that there is always too little and never enough. It creates a fundamental distrust of other people and therefore prevents true solidarity.

It is actually much easier to live in true humanitarianism with ourselves and each other than it is to live in an idealistic spiritualism or a meaningless materialism that thinks it can defeat death with computers and nanotechnology. Whatever the future for humanity, I will continue to walk the path of self-knowledge and welcome anyone who wants to walk it together with me.

Select English Bibliography

Bhakdi, S. & Reiss, K. (2020) Corona False Alarm? Facts and Figures. Chelsea Green Publishing

Ganser, D. (2004) NATO's Secret Armies. Routledge

McKendrick , M. (1969) Ferdinand and Isabella, Cassell, London

Moelling, K. (2020) Viruses: More Friends than Foes (Revised Edition) World Scientific Publishing

Orwell, G. (2004) Nineteen Eighty Four. Penguin Modern Classics Edition – Originally published 1949 by Secker & Warburg

Rogers, C. (2003) Client Centred Therapy. Constable

Rosenberg, M. (2015) Nonviolent Communication – A Language of Life. Puddle Dancer Press

Ruppert, F. (2008) Trauma, Bonding and Family Constellations. Green Balloon Publishing

Ruppert, F. (2011) Splits in the Soul. Green Balloon Publishing

Ruppert, F. (2012) Symbiosis and Autonomy. Green Balloon Publishing

Ruppert, F. (2014) Trauma, Fear & Love. Green Balloon Publishing

Ruppert, F. (2016) Early Trauma. Green Balloon Publishing

Ruppert, F. (2019) Who Am I in A Traumatised and Traumatising Society. Green Balloon Publishing

Ruppert, F. (2020) Love, Lust & Trauma. Green Balloon Publishing

Ruppert, F. & Banzhaf, H. (eds) (2018) My Body, My Trauma, My I. Green Balloon Publishing

Watzlawick, P. (1980) The Invented Reality. W.M. Norton & Company

Watzlawick, P. (1983) The Situation Is Hopeless But Not Serious. W.M. Norton & Company

Original German Bibliography

Bachinger, E. (2015). Kind auf Bestellung. Ein Plädoyer für klare Grenzen. Wien: Deuticke Verlag.

Bhakdi, S. & Reiss, K. (2016). Schreckgespenst Infektionen. Berlin: Goldegg Verlag.

Bauer, J. (2015). Selbststeuerung. Die Wiederentdeckung des freien Willens. München: Karl Blessing Verlag.

Bode, S. (2004). Die vergessene Generation. Die Kriegskinder brechen ihr Schweigen. Stuttgart: Klett-Cotta Verlag.

Bode, S. (2009). Kriegsenkel. Die Erben der vergessenen Generation. Stuttgart: Klett-Cotta Verlag-

Dilling, H., Mombour, W. & Schmidt, M.H. (Hrsg.) (1993). Weltgesundheitsorganisation - Internationale Klassifikation psychischer Störungen. ICD-10 Kapitel V (F), Klinisch-diagnostische Leitlinien. Bern: Huber.

Engelbrecht, T. & Köhnlein, C. (2020). Virus-Wahn. Lahnstein: emu-Verlags- und Betriebs-GmbH.

Fischer, G. & Riedesser, P. (1998). Lehrbuch der Psychotraumatologie. München: UTB Verlag.

Ganser, D. (2016). Illegale Kriege. Wie die Nato-Länder die UNO sabotieren. Eine Chronik von Kuba bis Syrien. Zürich: Orell Füssli Verlag.

Gresens, R. (2016). Intuitives Stillen. Dem eigenen Gefühl vertrauen. München: Kösel Verlag.

Haas, W. (2009). Das Hellinger-Virus. Kröning: Asanger Verlag.

Hellinger, B. (1994). Ordnungen der Liebe. Heidelberg: Carl-Auer-Systeme Verlag.

Hühler, L. (2018). Die ungelösten (physikalischen) Rätsel des 11. September 2001. Ist es höchste Zeit für eine neue Untersuchung? Martin Luther Gymnasium Hatha.

Maaz, H.-J. (2017). Das falsche Leben. Ursachen und Folgen unserer normopathischen Gesellschaft. München: Beck Verlag.

Maaz, H.-J. (2020). Das gespaltene Land. München: C.H.Beck.

Moeller, M. L. (1988). Die Wahrheit beginnt zu zweit. Reinbek: Rowohlt Verlag.

Mölling, K. (2020). Viren: Supermacht des Lebens. München: Beck Verlag.

Mühlbauer, J. (2020). Frauenfeindlichkeit in Indien - transgenerationale Traumata aus der Perspektive der IoPT. KSH München.

Münzing-Ruf, I. (1991). So stärken Sie Ihr Immunsystem. München: Heyne Verlag.

Orwell, G. (2008). Nineteen Eighty-Four. London: Penguin Books.

Reiss, K. & Bhakdi, S. (2020). Corona Fehlalarm. Zahlen, Daten und Hintergründe. Berlin: Goldegg Verlag.

Rogers, C. (1994). Die klientenzentrierte Gesprächspsychotherapie. Frankfurt/M.: Fischer.

Rosenberg, M. (2010). Gewaltfreie Kommunikation. Eine Sprache des Lebens. Paderborn: Junfermann.

Ruppert, F. (2001). Berufliche Beziehungswelten. Heidelberg: Carl Auer Systeme Verlag.

Ruppert, F. (2002). Verwirrte Seelen. München: Kösel Verlag.

Ruppert, F. (2005). Trauma, Bindung und Familienstellen. Seelische Verletzungen verstehen und heilen. Stuttgart: Klett-Cotta.

Ruppert, F. (2007). Seelische Spaltung und Innere Heilung. Traumatische Erfahrungen integrieren. Stuttgart: Klett-Cotta.

Ruppert, F. (2010). Symbiose und Autonomie. Symbiosetrauma und Liebe jenseits von Verstrickungen. Stuttgart. Klett-Cotta.

Ruppert, F. (2012). Trauma, Angst und Liebe. Unterwegs zu gesunder Eigenständigkeit. München: Kösel Verlag.

Ruppert, F. (Hg.) (2014). Frühes Trauma. Schwangerschaft, Geburt und erste Lebensjahre. Stuttgart: Klett-Cotta Verlag.

Ruppert, F. & Banzhaf, H. (Hg.) (2017). Mein Körper, mein Trauma, mein Ich. Anliegen aufstellen, aus der Traumabiografie aussteigen. München: Kösel Verlag.

Ruppert, F. (2018). Wer bin Ich in einer traumatisierten Gesellschaft? Wie Täter-Opfer-Dynamiken unser Leben bestimmen und wie wir daraus aussteigen. Stuttgart: Klett-Cotta Verlag.

Ruppert, F. (2019). Liebe, Lust & Trauma. Auf dem Weg zur gesunden sexueller Identität. München: Kösel-Verlag.

Ruppert, F. (2020). Hallo Mama, hallo Papa, wo seid Ihr hinter Euren Masken? Mein Erkenntnisprozess während der Corona-Pandemie 2020. München: Eigenverlag.

Schulz von Thun, F. (1992). Miteinander reden. Störungen und Klärungen. Hamburg: Rowohlt Verlag.

Vester, F. (1991). Phänomen Stress. München: dtv-Verlag.

Watzlawick, P. (2018). Wie wirklich ist die Wirklichkeit? Wahn, Täuschung, Verstehen. München: Piper Verlag.

Watzlawick, P. (2019). Anleitungen zum Unglücklich sein. München: Piper Verlag.

Weber, G. (Hg.) (1995). Zweierlei Glück. Die systemische Psychotherapie Bert Hellingers. Heidelberg: Carl-Auer-Systeme Verlag.

Wernicke, J. (Hg.) (2017). Lügen die Medien? Propaganda, Rudeljournalismus und der Kampf um die öffentliche Meinung. Frankfurt/M.: Westend Verlag.

Wodarg, W. (2015). Falscher Alarm: Die Schweinegrippe-Pandemie. In Borch-Jacobsen, M. (Hg.) (2015). BIG PHARMA, S. 310-325. München: Piper Verlag.

About This Book

A pandemic is not a natural phenomenon, but an action plan that has been translated into a reality. The corona pandemic has been prepared for a long time and is a test case for the implementation of further pandemics.

Instead of looking at those who are healthy, under pandemic conditions a society caught up in the infection mania focuses only on those who could possibly become ill or die. And then, above everything else, mass vaccinations are supposed to promote the salvation of all humanity. For this delusional project, the gentle approaches of an open society are abandoned and destroyed.

The Global Impact Alliance consists of its makers and its participants. Besides the visible mastermind Bill Gates and other super-rich people, the movers and shakers are many leading politicians and their advisors, usually lobbyists from vaccination and IT companies. It is also those in the judiciary who tolerate the state of lawlessness; it is the people in the civil services who blindly carry out all orders from above. It is the many journalists who panic and try to squash any resistance that speaks out against this madness. It is also all those who eagerly try to meticulously implement the coercive measures in crèches, kindergartens, schools, universities, companies, authorities, doctors' surgeries, hospitals, nursing homes. And it is all those who obediently wear masks and keep their distance without questioning the sense of such measures.

The globalised vaccination mania is not a path to a golden future for mankind, but a further step towards the collective abyss. When I experience all this so close at hand I get angry and my heart bleeds. I can take good care of my own health. I use all my freedoms to do so: my freedom of movement, my freedom of feeling, thinking and speaking, my freedom of occupation, my freedom of assembly. I therefore want to take back all my freedoms and live my life together with people who are honest, cooperative, peaceful and compassionate. To all those people who want to lie, cheat, manipulate, exploit other people, make them ill and vaccinate and monitor them for the interests of profit – I say to you, please keep your distance from me! This situation is a chance for each of us to take off our masks and ask ourselves: who am I and what do I really want in my life? It is an opportunity for all men and women, for all mothers and fathers to wake up from their trauma trance and finally become adults instead of risking their children's future for the sake of their own trauma survival strategies.

Franz Ruppert

Franz Ruppert is Professor of Psychology at the University of Applied Sciences in Munich, a post he has held since 1992. He gained his PhD in Work and Organisational Psychology at the Technical University of Munich in 1985.

Since 1995 he has focused on psychotherapeutic work, specifically on the causes of psychosis, schizophrenia and other forms of severe mental illness. He has combined this with his interest in bonding and attachment theories and modern trauma work in order to understand the effect of traumatic events better, not just for those who suffer the event, but on whole bonding systems and the wider society. He has developed his theory and methodology of Identity-oriented Psychotrauma Therapy (IoPT) to work with clients and understand the subtle and hidden dynamics of trauma in systems.

He teaches trauma theory at the University of Applied Sciences, works with individuals and facilitates workshops in Germany and across the world, including the UK. He also teaches his theory and method at his own institute in Munich.

www.franz-ruppert.de

For information about Franz's work and a list of IoPT practitioners in the UK please visit www.healthy-autonomy.co.uk

Printed in Great Britain
by Amazon

55512930R00307